Ancient Indo-European Languages between Linguistics and Philology

Brill's Studies in Historical Linguistics

Series Editor

Jóhanna Barðdal
(Ghent University)

Consulting Editor

Spike Gildea
(University of Oregon)

Editorial Board

Joan Bybee (*University of New Mexico*) – Lyle Campbell (*University of Hawai'i Mānoa*) – Nicholas Evans (*The Australian National University*)
Bjarke Frellesvig (*University of Oxford*) – Mirjam Fried (*Czech Academy of Sciences*) – Russel Gray (*University of Auckland*) – Tom Güldemann (*Humboldt-Universität zu Berlin*) – Alice Harris (*University of Massachusetts*)
Brian D. Joseph (*The Ohio State University*) – Ritsuko Kikusawa (*National Museum of Ethnology*) – Silvia Luraghi (*Università di Pavia*)
Joseph Salmons (*University of Wisconsin*) – Søren Wichmann (*MPI/EVA*)

VOLUME 18

The titles published in this series are listed at *brill.com/bshl*

Ancient Indo-European Languages between Linguistics and Philology

Contact, Variation, and Reconstruction

Edited by

Michele Bianconi
Marta Capano
Domenica Romagno
Francesco Rovai

BRILL

LEIDEN | BOSTON

Library of Congress Cataloging-in-Publication Data

Names: Bianconi, Michele, 1991- editor.
Title: Ancient Indo-European languages between linguistics and philology :
 contact, variation, and reconstruction / edited by Michele Bianconi [and 3
 others].
Description: Leiden ; Boston : Brill, [2022] | Series: Brill's studies in historical
 linguistics, 2211-4904 ; volume 18 | Includes bibliographical references and
 index.
Identifiers: LCCN 2022006178 (print) | LCCN 2022006179 (ebook) |
 ISBN 9789004508811 (hardback ; acid-free paper) | ISBN 9789004508828
 (ebook)
Subjects: LCSH: Indo-European languages. | Languages in contact. | Language
 variation. | Reconstruction (Linguistics) | Extinct languages. | LCGFT: Essays.
Classification: LCC P901 .A48 2022 (print) | LCC P901 (ebook) |
 DDC 417/.7–dc23/eng/20220210
LC record available at https://lccn.loc.gov/2022006178
LC ebook record available at https://lccn.loc.gov/2022006179

Typeface for the Latin, Greek, and Cyrillic scripts: "Brill". See and download: brill.com/brill-typeface.

ISSN 2211-4904
ISBN 978-90-04-50881-1 (hardback)
ISBN 978-90-04-50882-8 (e-book)

Copyright 2022 by Michele Bianconi and Marta Capano. Published by Koninklijke Brill NV, Leiden,
The Netherlands.
Koninklijke Brill NV incorporates the imprints Brill, Brill Nijhoff, Brill Hotei, Brill Schöningh, Brill Fink,
Brill mentis, Vandenhoeck & Ruprecht, Böhlau and V&R unipress.
Koninklijke Brill NV reserves the right to protect this publication against unauthorized use. Requests for
re-use and/or translations must be addressed to Koninklijke Brill NV via brill.com or copyright.com.

This book is printed on acid-free paper and produced in a sustainable manner.

Al nostro Maestro Romano Lazzeroni
(*1930–2020*)

ἡ ἀλήθεια ἐλευθερώσει ὑμᾶς
John, 8:32

Contents

Foreword   IX
  Alexandra Y. Aikhenvald
Acknowledgements   XII
List of Figures and Tables   XIII
Notes on Contributors   XV

Introduction   1
  Michele Bianconi and Marta Capano

1   Divine Witnesses in Greece and Anatolia: *Iliad* 3.276–280 between
    Contact, Variation, and Reconstruction   11
      Michele Bianconi

2   Achaemenid Elamite and Old Persian Indefinites: A Comparative
    View   48
      Juan E. Briceño Villalobos

3   Phenomena of Spirantization and Language Contact in Greek Sicilian
    Inscriptions. The case of ΤΡΙΑΙΝΤΑ   88
      Marta Capano

4   Egyptian Greek: A Contact Variety   115
      Sonja Dahlgren

5   Substrate Matters   153
      Franco Fanciullo

6   Natural Language Use and Bilingual Interference: Verbal
    Complementation Patterns in Post-Classical Greek   166
      Victoria Fendel

7   Where Does Dionysus Ὕης Come From?   196
      Laura Massetti

8   Alignment Change and Changing Alignments: Armenian Syntax and the
    First 'Death' of Parthian   211
      Robin Meyer

VIII

9 Rewriting the Law: Diachronic Variation and Register in Greek and Hittite Legal Language 234
   Katharine Shields

10 Lexical Variation in Young Avestan: The Problem of the 'Ahuric' and 'Daevic' Vocabularies Revisited 254
   Elizabeth Tucker

11 Greek ἄγυρις 'Gathering' between Dialectology and Indo-European Reconstruction 276
   Roberto Batisti

12 Here's to a Long Life! Albanian Reflections of Proto-Indo-European Semantics 301
   Brian D. Joseph

Index 313

Foreword

Alexandra Y. Aikhenvald

Throughout centuries of linguistic research, the Indo-European language family has been the paragon for historical and comparative linguistics. Indo-European linguistics has set the golden standard for the field—from the family tree model to the strict division between synchrony and diachrony. Any educated student of historical linguistics will be trained on the laws of Indo-European (explicitly summarised by N.E. Collinge in his 1985 compendium). Similar developments will then be discovered in the comparative studies for many other families, reaching into the previously undescribed languages of South America, Australia, and New Guinea, and giving them an extra glow of respectability. Studies of Indo-European languages have, in many senses, been laying down the law of the land for historical linguistics, hand-in-hand with painstaking philological studies of older sources of languages whose documentation goes back thousands of years—Hittite, Luvian, Ancient Greek, to name a few. New models of historical expansion and reconstruction of origins and ancestral homelands use the Indo-European family as a testing ground (for better or for worse, and oftentimes with dubious results). As the discipline of linguistics evolves and expands over time, so do studies of Indo-European languages.

Calvert Watkins, a classic of the field, remarked in 2001: 'far less familiar than the value of Indo-European for the traditional comparative method is the value of Indo-European as a laboratory for language contact and areal studies'. Now, more than twenty years on, this is no longer so. Indo-European linguistics—and more precisely, the study of Ancient Indo-European languages which have survived only in written sources—has progressed to embrace language contact, areal diffusion, and sociolinguistic variation. This volume is a testimony to this true progress in linguistics.

Back in the old days, language contact studies may have been considered a hand-maid of historical reconstruction. Chapters in this volume show, *inter alia*, how painstaking investigations of contact-induced change and the smatterings of sociolinguistic variation—gleaned from the ancient tablets and lore—can help improve and refine our reconstruction and fine-tune our knowledge of the proto-language. Using the metaphor by Brian Joseph (in this volume), the echoes of Indo-European heritage reverberate across semantic patterns in the daughter languages and those which come in contact with them. The Proto-Indo-European concept of 'long life' is a case in point.

As the discipline of linguistics evolves and we learn more and more about how languages work and what to look for, new phenomena come to light. We now know that many Ancient Indo-European languages, Hittite among them, had serial verbs, a phenomenon first identified for West African languages back in the later nineteenth century. A careful reconstruction of sociolinguistic situations—gleaned from the attested documents—sheds new light on the diffusion of grammatical categories and the emergence of typologically uncommon patterns. The periphrastic perfect in Classical Armenian was developed under the influence of Parthian, an Iranian language (in Meyer's chapter in this volume). The uncommon feature of this newly developed perfect was, for a period of time, 'tripartite marking'—with A (transitive subject), O (transitive object), and S (intransitive subject), each expressed in a distinct way—comes from the reanalysis of the Parthian ergative structure. The Old Persian indefinite pronouns bear an indelible impact of the contemporary Elamite, a neighbouring isolate (Briceño-Villalobos, this volume). Elamite must have been learnt as a second language of administration by Iranian-speaking scribes. The development of indefinite meanings in interrogative pronouns is hardly unusual. It is the context of this contact-induced change in the ancient world that makes it curious.

New ways of looking at ancient languages—in comparison with modern language situations—yield new results. We now know that Greek spoken from 1st century CE onward in Egypt bears a strong impact of Coptic, and appears to have all the trimmings of a contact language, not dissimilar to Finland Swedish, or Indian English (as shown in Dahlgren's chapter). And what was taken for granted no longer has to be. A passage of the *Iliad* that had been unquestionably taken to be of Near-Eastern origin, can in fact be traced back to Indo-European patterns of Anatolia (as shown by Bianconi). Different registers of a language—or, as Shields puts it, each 'situationally-defined variety'—would have their special, linguistic features. Differences in syntactic techniques employed in Ancient Greek legal inscriptions and in the Hittite Laws (many of which bear a strong impact of contemporary Akkadian laws) highlight their different functions in the two societies, and the differences in language material at hand, evolved over centuries. Many conclusions are tentative, and so they have to be: acknowledging the limits of what one knows is a mark of true scholarship.

For centuries, studies of Indo-European languages have led the way, in linguistics and philology. To be an Indo-Europeanist, one needs to be a polymath: the knowledge of languages, sources, history, often epigraphy, and many other associated disciplines are *de rigueur*. No place for short-lived rules and formal theories—none of which will ever outlive the languages they purportedly apply to. This volume is a compendium of polymaths, with each chapter a gem, and an impressive repository of knowledge and analytic depth. Studies like this one will lead the way to further glory for Indo-European scholarship. Here is to its long life—in the words of the title of Brian Joseph's chapter! Or—using an Albanian expression with a long Proto-Indo-European pedigree—*për (në) jetë të jetëve* 'for eternity', literally, 'for (a) lifetime of lifetimes'!

References

COLLINGE, NEVILLE E. 1985, *The laws of Indo-European*, Amsterdam: John Benjamins.

WATKINS, CALVERT 2001, *An Indo-European linguistic area and its characteristics: Ancient Anatolia. Areal diffusion as a challenge to the comparative method?*, in A.Y. Aikhenvald—R.M.W. Dixon (eds.), *Areal diffusion and genetic inheritance. Problems in comparative linguistics*, Oxford: Oxford University Press: 44–63.

Acknowledgements

This volume contains a selection of papers presented at a two-leg conference which took place in Pisa (April 2018) and Oxford (May 2018). We would like to thank the institutions that supported our project (the Ertegun Scholarship Programme in the Humanities, St Hilda's College, and the Faculty of Linguistics, Philology and Phonetics at the University of Oxford; the Dipartimento di Filologia, Letteratura e Linguistica at the University of Pisa) and the people who made it possible. Two independent volumes arose from this conference. In the making of this book, the only one we are uniquely responsible for, we have tried to give an inclusive and faithful representation of current researchers and research directions. We greatly profited from discussion with and help from both colleagues our age and more experienced scholars. Their advice has profoundly and positively impacted our work, although—as per the usual disclaimer—any infelicities are solely our responsibility. Most importantly, each article underwent a very rigorous peer-review process, which is the backbone of good academic practice. We would like to take this chance to thank our reviewers, whose work we deeply appreciated and respected, and Brill, which facilitated the entire process. Finally, we would like to thank our Authors, who entrusted us with their work, and followed us through the project with patience and generosity. We hope to have offered their contributions the volume that they deserve. This book is part of the PRIN project "Ancient languages and writing systems in contact: a touchstone for language change", funded by the Italian Ministry of education, University, and Research. During the long and often trying years of this project, we found support and inspiration from one another and from many friends, family members, both in and out of academia, and our respective life partners. They followed our work with love, encouragement and understanding, and to them we would like to express our deepest gratitude.

Michele Bianconi & Marta Capano

Figures and Tables

Figures

2.1	Old Persian, Middle Persian, and Achaemenid Elamite indefinites and their functions 79
3.1	The inscription of Antoninos 106
4.1	Map of Egypt 120
4.2	OGN I: 72, The Cairo Egyptian Museum 129
8.1	Incidence and trend of perfects with copula in fifth-century texts 222
8.2	Incidence of non-standard alignment patterns in fifth-century texts 223

Tables

1.1	Synoptic table of deities in Hittite treaties 36
2.1	The typology of indefinite pronouns 51
2.2	Words and phrases of (5) and (6) arranged according to their equivalent in each language 60
2.3	OP *kašci* and AE *akkar* 61
2.4	OP *cišci* and AE *aški* 63
2.5	The formula "whoever you are" in DB 69
2.6	OP *kā haya* and AE *akka(ya)* 71
2.7	OP *taya* and AE *appa* "whatever" 73
2.8	OP *aiva* and AE *kir* 76
2.9	AE *kaš* 78
4.1	The inflection of Egyptian names in Greek 127
4.2	Nouns ending in -*is* 132
4.3	Inflectional endings for Greek nouns ending in -*is* as perceived by a L2 learner 133
4.4	Comparing 'alternative' *kharis* to the inflection of Egyptian names ending in a vowel 134
4.5	Comparing alternative *polis* to the inflection of Egyptian names ending in a consonant 134
4.6	Comparing the inflection of Egyptian names ending in -*ês* to the inflection of *Periklês* 135
4.7	Comparing the inflectional endings of Egyptian names to the third declension nouns 136
4.8	Coptic integration of the Greek loanverb 144

XIV   FIGURES AND TABLES

6.1   Table head   175
6.2   Xenophon, historiography, 5th / 4th centuries BC, TLG, lemma γράφω (searches:
       June 2020)—98 passages in total   178
6.3   Plutarch, historiography, 1st / 2nd centuries AD, TLG, lemma γράφω (searches:
       June 2020)—36 passages in total   178
6.4   DDbDP, s.v. LEX γράφω, language: Ancient Greek, provenance: known,
       AD 250–700 (searches: June 2020)—256 passages in total   179
6.5   Private letters belonging to bilingual papyrus archives, 4th to mid-7th centuries
       AD, language: Ancient Greek (searches: June 2020)—61 passages in total   179
8.1   Summary of the Classical Armenian alignment pattern   216

Notes on Contributors

Roberto Batisti
is Teaching Assistant and collaborator of the Department of Classical Philology and Italian Studies at the Alma Mater Studiorum—Università di Bologna.

Michele Bianconi
is Diebold Researcher in Comparative Philology at the University of Oxford, Lecturer in Classics at St Hilda's College, and Fellow of the Harvard Center for Hellenic Studies.

Juan Briceño-Villalobos
is Postdoctoral Research Scholar at the Pontificia Universidad Católica de Chile. Fondecyt de Postdoctorado 2021 (ANID), Proyecto N° 3210689.

Marta Capano
is Post-Doctoral researcher at the Universiteit Gent and will be a Fellow of the Harvard Center for Hellenic Studies for the 2022–2023 academic year.

Sonja Dahlgren
is Post-Doctoral researcher at the University of Helsinki.

Franco Fanciullo
now retired, was formerly Professor of Historical Linguistics and Dialectology at the Università di Pisa.

Victoria Fendel
is Leverhulme Early Career Fellow at the University of Oxford.

Brian D. Joseph
is Distinguished University Professor of Linguistics and Kenneth E. Naylor Professor of South Slavic Linguistics at the Ohio State University.

Laura Massetti
is Carlsberg Foundation Visiting Fellow at the University of Oxford and Fellow of the Harvard Center for Hellenic Studies.

Robin Meyer
is Assistant Professor of Historical Linguistics at the Université de Lausanne.

Katharine Shields
is completing her PhD at University College London.

Elizabeth Tucker
is Emerita Jill Hart Research Fellow in Indo-Iranian Philology in the Faculty of Oriental Studies and the Faculty of Linguistics, Philology and Phonetics, University of Oxford.

Introduction

Michele Bianconi and Marta Capano

This book sets out to offer new insights on language contact, variation, and reconstruction, with a focus on the ancient languages belonging to the Indo-European family and with a method that straddles the divide between two disciplines which are nowadays very broad: Linguistics and Philology.

It is well known that studying the Indo-European (IE) languages means having a privileged viewpoint on diachronic language change. Because of the relative wealth of documentation of these languages, which spans over more than 3 millennia with almost no interruption, and because of the cultural position that they have enjoyed in human history,[1] the IE family has been the prime object of study of most branches of modern linguistic science. Whan it comes to the ancient IE languages, the scholarly focus has traditionally been on languages such as Greek, Latin, and Sanskrit, whose large corpora provide solid grounds for comparison. Languages which are more fragmentarily attested have consequanetly had a lesser inpact on the study of language change and reconstruction. Recent years have seen a shift, in that we now have an improved understanding of many of these *Trümmersprachen*, thanks to new discoveries and to a growing number of theoretical reflections on contact and variation in the ancient world. This has led to renewed attempts at integrating them in the reconstruction of Proto-Indo-European. Furthermore, over the past thirty years, scholars have brought new attention to previously understudied branches like Albanian (see Joseph's contribution in this volume) and Tocharian, which, in addition to the already lively interest in the Anatolian languages, have finally allowed a more balanced reconstruction of the protolanguage, which was predominantly reconstructed on the basis of Greek and Sanskrit until the half of the last century.[2]

Contact, variation and reconstruction have been thoroughly studied in the linguistic literature, but a volume which includes several under-studied Indo-European branches and takes into account the most recent findings in both linguistic theory and the philologies of the individual languages is still a *desideratum*. Here, we endeavour to offer a new and up-to date selection of case studies, most of which are looked at through inter-disciplinary and intra-disciplin-

---

1   One could just think of the importance of Latin in Medieval Europe or of Classical Sanskrit in Pre-Modern India.

2   E.g. MELCHERT *forthc.*; KÜMMEL 2007; JASANOFF 2017.

© MICHELE BIANCONI AND MARTA CAPANO, 2022 | DOI:10.1163/9789004508828_002

ary lenses. These contributions reveal at the same time the multiplicity and the unity of our discipline(s), both by showing what kind of results the adoption of modern theories on "old" material can yield, and by underlining the centrality and complexity of the text in any research related to ancient languages.

Two of the poles around which the current volume revolves can allow scholars to gain new insights on the third pole. Traditionally, in the history of Indo-European linguistics variation and contact have been used as tools for a better understanding of reconstruction; today we know that reconstruction itself—especially when carried out through a rigorous handling of the data—has the potential to shed light on previously-undetected phenomena of contact and variation. Several contributions in this volume will touch upon these issues in different ways. The study of living languages (to give a notorious example: the Romance dialects) shows that a monolithic view of spoken languages is a pure abstraction which is far from historical reality, as languages display sociolinguistic and geographic variation and interference with neighbouring languages at most (if not all) levels. The adoption of these two parameters in the study of corpus languages has the potential (*mutatis mutandis*) to influence the reconstruction methods and practices when it comes to proto-languages. An exemplary case of this type of research is Franco Fanciullo's work in this volume, where a variationistic approach is applied to the evaluation of the substrate of pre-Roman languages to Romance varieties.

As pointed out by several scholars, and as our late teacher Romano Lazzeroni used to say, language change happens on a three-dimensional level, which encompasses space, time, and society. The first parameter is superficially understood by any speaker, who might experience that their language varies in pronunciation and sometimes lexicon just in a matter of kilometres; the second one has been traditionally driving all studies of historical linguistics; the third parameter, however, has been overlooked in the studies of historical linguistics at least until the second half of the 19th century.[3] Of course, philologists and classicists from the past century, whose work focussed on literary texts with a strong diastratic component (such as, for instance, CAMPANILE 1957 on Petronius, or VINEIS 1974 on the language of the Latin Bible), noticed and analysed those texts on what we would now call a sociolinguistic level—but it was not until much later that a comprehensive theoretical model was available.

One of the most impressive changes in recent theoretical paradigms in historical linguistics is an improved understanding of language contact, which is

---

3 As is well known, a theoretical framework that fully addresses the social component of variation and change has been brought to the fore in historical linguistics by scholars who worked on modern languages, such as Labov (see e.g. LABOV 1972).

INTRODUCTION

possible the first of the three directories of this volume. Language contact studies have recently entered a 'golden era': the publication in the past two decades of several handbooks and companions on language contact and related topics[4] is only one of many hints thereof. Nonetheless, comparatively few works focus specifically on contact and variation in the ancient IE languages, and none—to our knowledge—does so on such a scale. For instance, recent books on language contact in the ancient world focus either on one or two individual languages,[5] or provide case studies whose *fil rouge* may be difficult to detect.[6] This book will have some predecessors, which however were published at a time in which some significant advances in our disciplines had not yet been made,[7] or mainly focussed on a specific area or on a specific part of language.[8]

The recent progress in language contact studies and historical sociolinguistics,[9] along with an ever-increasing capacity of handling sparsely—and often scarcely—attested data (cf. e.g. JENSET—MCGILLIVRAY 2017) and the application of new theoretical paradigms on diachronic data,[10] allows us to provide a fresh look on more- and less-studied topics. This volume combines the presence of the parameters of contact, variation, and reconstruction with their application to a wide range of ancient Indo-European languages in light of recent theoretical developments. However, dealing with ancient languages, especially those fragmentarily attested, poses some additional challenges in the interpretation of the material. All the contributions in this volume show how a thorough consideration of the philological (and sometimes even material) aspects of a texts can help untangle phenomena of contact and variation in closed-corpus languages, and effectively reconstruct both synchronic and diachronic aspects of such languages.

As one can infer from its prominent position within the title, the stand of this volume "between Linguistics and Philology" reflects an indissoluble bond which risks to be threatened by rather recent divisions between disciplines

---

4   THOMASON 2001, MYERS-SCOTTON 2002 and 2006, WINFORD 2003, HEINE—KUTEVA 2005, MATRAS 2020, HASPELMATH—TADMOR 2009, HICKEY 2010, 2017, and BAKKER—MATRAS 2013 just to cite a few.

5   These often happened to be Greek and Latin (e.g. ADAMS—JANSE—SWAIN 2002; ADAMS 2003); but recently also on Oscan and Greek: MCDONALD 2015; Luwian and Hittite: YAKUBOVICH 2010.

6   A recent example is MEISER—HACKSTEIN 2005.

7   E.g. CAMPANILE—CARDONA—LAZZERONI 1988.

8   E.g. BRIQUEL-CHATONNET 1996 on the Ancient Near-East; BLANC—CHRISTOL 1999 and GARNIER 2020 on lexical material.

9   Cf. ROMAINE 1982, LABOV 1994, CONDE SILVESTRE 2007, HERNÁNDEZ CAMPOY—CONDE SILVESTRE 2012, MAROTTA—ROVAI 2015, MOLINELLI—PUTZU 2015.

10   On the case of diachronic Construction Grammar, cf. recently BARÐDAL 2015.

(and departments). Philology and linguistics should in fact be treated as two sides of the same coin, especially if one is working with ancient languages only attested in a small corpus. Not only is the knowledge of linguistic phenomena fundamental to understand (and eventually emend) a text, and is a sound knowledge of the text (and all ancillary disciplines) fundamental in order to have reliable data on which to base linguistic analyses—but the two disciplines are tied as an even more fundamental level. A brief detour in the history of the discipline will exemplify it.

The first systematic attempt at drawing the relationships between the languages of the (then) newly discovered Indo-European family comes from August Schleicher (1821–1868), who was influenced by Hegel and by the contemporary models of the natural sciences. Schleicher conceived each language as an organism undergoing a life cycle, and proposed a genealogical model for the representation of languages and their relationships: the *Stammbaum*, or family tree. The theoretical premises behind the family-tree model are remarkably similar to those of the stemmatic method adopted in textual criticism, which was also developed in the 19th century and owed much to evolutionary theory. Manuscripts of a given text are evaluated according to their transcription errors (= innovations), which can be 'conjunctive' when they tell us that two or more manuscripts must come from a common source, or 'separative' when they indicate that a given manuscript (or group thereof) must be separated from another manuscript (or group thereof). The task of the editor is to find significant conjunctive errors, and therefore exclude all those trivial (= typologically common) innovations which may have occurred by chance. All manuscripts are then grouped in a family tree (*stemma codicum*) and collated (= compared) in order to reconstruct the original text or, more realistically the so-called *archetype*, the text originating the textual tradition. As is well known, the first and foremost reaction to the *Stammbaum* model was the so-called *Wellentheorie* ('wave model'), developed by Johannes Schmidt (1843–1901). In a way, the *Wellentheorie* could find a parallel in the very common situation of 'horizontal contamination' that one finds in those manuscripts which do not have a single source.

It is perhaps worth noting that both methods developed in a period in which sciences of nature and sciences of culture were more in contact than they are today. It is generally thought that Darwin and Schleicher did not read each other's works, but the fact that phylogenetic models were developed at the same time in different disciplines leads to the intrinsically *a posteriori* consideration that "the time was ripe" for such an advance in scientific methodology. The basic difference between the two fields does not lie in the method, but in the shape of the object of enquiry: texts can be definitely fixed, natural lan-

INTRODUCTION

guages cannot. In order to reconstruct the relationship between languages, or manuscripts, one needs to look at eventual innovations of one or more of them. Now, whereas in textual criticism these innovations often take the shape of *errors* (including lacunae, contaminations, etc.), in languages there is no such thing as an "error", and actual contact is intrinsically more pervasive.[11] This of course does not impinge on the validity of the method; it only shows some of its heuristic limits.[12]

Therefore, one can only admire the words of Giorgio Pasquali, who famously wrote that "the historical linguist—like the classical philologist—does not know disciplines; (s)he knows problems, and tackles them from all sides with every possible means". This volume sets out to represent this very approach, investigating language phenomena under the lens of the philologist and the linguist at the same time, in the conviction than any means should be utilised if they can ensure a better understanding to ancient languages.

This volume features contributions dealing with several branches of the Indo-European family (Anatolian, Indo-Iranian, Greek, Armenian, Italic, Albanian), as well as non-Indo-European languages (such as Elamite and Egyptian), and explores mechanisms of language change from multiple perspectives and through different heuristic paradigms. It also gives importance to some of the traditionally less studied areas, such as Albanian, Luwian, post-classical Greek, and the Middle-Iranian languages. In what follows, we offer a synthetic overview of the book chapters.

In his contribution, Michele Bianconi studies a much-debated passage from the third book of the *Iliad* through the lenses of contact, variation, and reconstruction. After a focus on the theme of lists of divine witnesses in oaths in various Near-Eastern languages (Hittite, Akkadian, Aramaic), he looks at the variation of such a theme in the Hittite material, and evaluates what can and cannot be reconstructed at an Indo-European level. He then adds

---

11   Contact is also more likely between two *lects* than it is in the transmission of written texts, or between—say—two specific manuscripts. Therefore, one needs to look at innovations *lato sensu*, and this is not always simple, because an innovation is such in opposition to an archaism, and linguistic archaisms are not as easy to detect as the original *lectiones* of a text.

12   One case in point. In languages, inheritance and contact do not necessarily exclude each other, as one may envisage *preservation* because of contact. This is a relatively understudied part in language phylogenetics and contact studies, because—as we saw above—it is *innovations* that establish relationships. However difficult to detect it might be, contact *may* help preserve archaisms, but this is often not directly inferable from the evidence.

a new piece to the puzzle, arguing that a newly-deciphered Luwian inscription shows a parallel with the aforementioned Iliadic passage, and seems to suggest a possible transmission route of the theme of divine witnesses in oath-swearing.

Juan Briceño-Villalobos compares Old Persian and Elamite indefinites in the Achaemenid Royal Inscriptions, the pre-Achaemenid Elamite Royal Inscriptions, and the Persepolis administrative tablets. Through an analysis of those elements whose syntactic distribution and semantic context may help us understand the expression of indefiniteness, he argues that the Elamite indefinite forms might explain the syntactic distribution of indefinites in later stages of the Persian language, and at the same time that the promotion of certain Elamite morphological elements was due to contact with Old Persian.

In her chapter, Marta Capano looks the issue of spirantisation of stops in Sicilian Greek through the lens of contact with Latin, of the comparative analysis of other areas of the Greek-speaking world, and of typological evidence. She then focusses on a specific case from a Sicilian inscription, arguing that a form, which was hitherto regarded as the result of an error of the engraver, is in fact an authentic product of the spoken language. The chapter offers a new piece of evidence for a case of language contact between Greek and Latin in the Roman period and outlines a periodisation of spirantisation of voiced velar stops in Sicilian Greek.

Sonja Dahlgren studies phenomena of language contact in the Narmouthis Greek ostraka, in which the many phonetic-based spellings show interference between Greek and Egyptian at the phonological level, both in segmental and suprasegmental features. By showing that transfer from L1 mostly takes place at the phonological level, Dahlgren argues that in the case of Egyptian Greek one can envisage a contact situation in which speakers of a prestige language who are still strongly attached to the original culture interact with speakers shifting from their original language to a L2.

Franco Fanciullo offers new methodological insights on the debate over the influence of pre-Latin substrate languages on regional Latin. After reviewing Ascoli's "proofs" for substrate and distinguishing between "substrate" as a specific subfield of contact linguistics and "substrate" as a specific theory of language change developed in the second half of the 19th century and popular until at least the first half of the 20th century, he argues that the debate between "substrate-maniac" and "substrate-phobic" scholars could have been less hot if one had considered the modern interaction between Italian dialects and Standard Italian. On these grounds, Fanciullo reconsiders a well-known case study (the assimilation of -nd- > nn and -mb- > -mm-), and puts it under a new light.

INTRODUCTION

Victoria Fendel endeavours to explain the form-function pairing in two instances of the verb γράφω ὅτι + deontic verb in an early 4th-century CE letter from the Oasis Magna in Egypt. Through a study of the verb profile of γράφω in classical and post-classical literary and documentary Greek sources, she suggests that this construction is a result of a combination of bilingual interference (with an L1 model), chunking of frequently recurring pieces of language, and the availability of insubordination in Greek.

Laura Massetti's paper endeavours to explain the origin of the Greek myth of Dionysus *Hyes*, 'Dionysus of the rain' through the establishment a new Anatolian parallel within the context of Greek-Anatolian religious contact. The figure of Dionysus *Hyes* is portrayed in different versions in the Greek sources, but the common point is that the god manages to escape persecution from an enemy (Lycurgus or Perseus) plunging into the see and receiving help from a female deity. Massetti investigates Dionysus *Hyes* both from a mythological and ritual perspective, with the reference to the *Agrionia* festivals, often connected with stories about Dionysus's persecution. This chapter shows how the narrative concerning young Dionysus has an Anatolian parallel, both on a ritual and mythological ground, in the "Sacrifice and Prayer to the Storm-god of Nerik" (*CTH* 671), a New Hittite text. Massetti argues that the similarities between the two myths are not of Indo-European origin, but rather a case of mythological/ritual borrowing from the Ancient Near East to Greece through the mediation of Hittite.

Robin Meyer argues in his paper that the construction of the Classical Armenian perfect, which consists of a participle in *-eal* (< PIE *-lo-*) and an (optional) form of the copula, is most accurately described as tripartite morphosyntactic alignment in which intransitive and transitive passive verbs construe with a nominative subject and subject agreement of the copula, and transitive active verbs take genitive agents, accusative objects, and the copula is a petrified third person singular. This alignment pattern can be explained as a case of pattern replication and pivot matching of a Middle Iranian, specifically Parthian, ergative-absolutive model in pre-literary times and subsequent adaptation to Armenian requirements. More generally, the existence of Iranian syntactic patterns in Armenian is due not only to language contact, but indeed to language shift of the Parthian ruling class to Armenian.

The chapter by Katherine Shields deals with two features associated with the revision and replication of Greek and Hittite legal texts: constituent order in conditional clauses containing the conjunctions *takku* and *mān* in the Hittite laws, and asyndeton in Greek legal inscriptions dating before 400 BCE. She aims to examine the diachronic development of the register of 'legal language': using a methodology informed by both sociolinguistic studies of register and construction grammar-based approaches, she considers what evidence these texts, which were frequently modified and rewritten, can provide for register development in a type of language often considered hyper-conservative and lacking in variation.

Elizabeth Tucker provides new insights on lexical variation in Young Avestan by studying the distribution of 'ahuric' and 'daēvic' vocabulary, i.e. those sets of lexical terms that apply to good versus evil animate beings. Her contribution focuses on how different Younger Avestan texts employ ahuric and daēvic vocabulary, and the variations that can be observed from text to text. She argues that that a philological analysis of the Avestan texts points to a developing literary convention which resulted in different composers selecting in various ways from the synonyms in their language to highlight the contrast between good and evil.

Through a study of the lexical family of ἄγυρις 'gathering', 'assembly', Roberto Batisti discusses one of the most problematic exceptions to the regular Greek sound change */o/ > /u/ in some specific (labial or palatal) environments—generally known as "Cowgill's Law". Against previous explanations according to which these irregularities are due to unconstrained variation or to improvable contact between different dialects, Batisti assumes that forms such as ἄγυρις are phonetically regular, and argues for a morphological explanation by way of a different derivational history involving an old u-stem.

Brian Joseph's conclusive chapter focusses on reconstruction by looking at diachronic lexical semantics, which has long been one of the less systematic enterprises in historical linguistics. He draws the attention to the cultural and pragmatic milieu, which can also reveal instances of semantic persistence, sometimes over long stretches of time. As an example such persistence, he discusses an example from Albanian, whereby details of usage for various present-day Albanian words and phrases reveal aspects of what can plausibly be reconstructed as Proto-Indo-European cultural semantics having to do with an interest in longevity. These echoes reflect a linguistic continuity lasting for more than six millennia.

References

ADAMS, JAMES N. 2003, *Bilingualism and the Latin Language*, Cambridge: Cambridge University Press.

ADAMS, JAMES N.—JANSE, MARK—SWAIN, SIMON (eds.) 2002, *Bilingualism in Ancient Society: Language Contact and the Written Text*, Oxford: Oxford University Press.

BAKKER, PETER—MATRAS, YARON 2013, *Contact Languages. A Comprehensive Guide*, Boston/Berlin: de Gruyter.

BARÐDAL, JÓHANNA—SMIRNOVA, ELENA—SOMMERER, LOTTE—GILDEA, SPIKE (eds.) 2015, *Diachronic Construction Grammar*, Constructional Approaches to Language, vol. 18, Amsterdam: John Benjamins.

BLANC, ALAIN—CHRISTOL, ALAIN (eds.) 1999, *Langues en contact dans l'antiquité. Aspects lexicaux*, Nancy: A.D.R.A.

BRIQUEL-CHATONNET, FRANÇOISE (ed.) 1996, *Mosaïque de langues, mosaïque culturelle: Le Bilinguisme dans le Proche-Orient ancien*, Paris: Jean Maisonneuve.

CAMPANILE, E. 1957, *Osservazioni sulla lingua di Petronio*, "ASNSP" Serie II 26: 54–69.

CAMPANILE, ENRICO—CARDONA, GIORGIO R.—LAZZERONI, ROMANO (edd.) 1988, *Bilinguismo e biculturalismo nel mondo antico: atti del colloquio interdisciplinare tenuto a Pisa il 28 e 29 settembre 1987*, Pisa: Giardini.

CONDE SILVESTRE, JUAN CAMILO 2007, *Sociolingüística histórica*, Madrid: Gredos.

HASPELMATH, MARTIN—TADMOR, URI 2009, *Loanwords In The World's Languages: A Comparative Handbook*, Berlin: de Gruyter Mouton.

HEINE, BERNDT—KUTEVA, TANIA 2005, *Language Contact and Grammatical Change*, New York: Cambridge University Press.

HERNÁNDEZ CAMPOY, JUAN MANUEL—CONDE SILVESTRE, JUAN CAMILO 2012, (edd.), *The Handbook of Historical Sociolinguistics*, Oxford: Oxford University Press.

HICKEY, RAYMOND 2010, *The Handbook of Language Contact*, Chichester/Malden (MA): Wiley-Blackwell.

HICKEY, RAYMOND 2017, *The Cambridge Handbook of Areal Linguistics*, Cambridge: Cambridge University Press.

JASANOFF, JAY 2017, *The impact of Hittite and Tocharian: Rethinking Indo-European in the 20th century and beyond*, in J. Klein—B. Joseph—M. Fritz (edd.), *Handbook of Comparative and Historical Indo-European Linguistics, Volume 1*, Berlin, Boston: De Gruyter Mouton: 220–238.

JENSET, GARD B.—MCGILLIVRAY, BARBARA 2017, *Quantitative Historical Linguistics: A Corpus Framework*, Oxford: Oxford University Press.

KÜMMEL, MARTIN J. 2007, *Konsonantenwandel. Bausteine zu einer Typologie des Lautwandels und ihre Konsequenzen für die vergleichende Rekonstruktion*, Wiesbaden: Reichert.

LABOV, WILLIAM 1972, *Sociolinguistics Patterns*, Philadelphia: University of Pennsylvania Press.

LABOV, WILLIAM 1994, *Principles of Linguistic Change. Vol. 1: Internal Factors*, Cambridge (MA)/Oxford: Blackwell.

MAROTTA, GIOVANNA—ROVAI, FRANCESCO (eds.) 2015, *Ancient Languages between Variation and Norm*, "Studi e Saggi Linguistici" 53/2.

MATRAS, YARON 2020^2, *Language Contact*, Cambridge: Cambridge University Press.

McDonald, Katherine 2015, *Oscan in Southern Italy and Sicily*, Cambridge: Cambridge University Press.

Melchert, H. Craig (forthc.), *The Position of Anatolian*, in A. Garrett—M. Weiss (edd.), *Handbook of Indo-European Studies*, Oxford: Oxford University Press.

Meiser, Gerhard—Hackstein, Olav (eds.) 2005, *Sprachkontakt und Sprachwandel. Akten der XI. Fachtagung der Indogermanischen Gesellschaft, 17.–23. September 2000, Halle an der Saale*, Wiesbaden: Reichert.

Molinelli, Piera—Putzu, Ignazio (eds.) 2015, *Modelli epistemologici, metodologie della ricerca e qualità del dato. Dalla linguistica storica alla sociolinguistica storica*, Milano: Franco Angeli.

Myers-Scotton, Carol 2002, *Contact Linguistics. Bilingual Encounters and Grammatical Outcomes*, Oxford: Oxford University Press.

Myers-Scotton, Carol 2006, *Multiple Voices. An Introduction to Bilingualism*, Malden (MA): Blackwell Publishing.

Radulescu, Mircea-Mihai 1994, *The Indo-European Position of Messapic*, "Journal of Indo-European Studies" 22: 329–344.

Romaine, Suzanne 1982, *Socio-Historical Linguistics. Its Status and Methodology*, Cambridge: Cambridge University Press.

Thomason, Sarah G. 2001, *Language Contact. An Introduction*, Edinburgh/Washington DC: Edinburgh University Press/Georgetown University Press.

Vineis, Edoardo 1974, *Studi sulla lingua dell'Itala*, Pisa: Pacini.

Weiss, Michael 2009, *Outline of the Historical and Comparative Grammar of Latin*, Ann Arbor: Beech Stave.

Winford, Donald 2003, *An Introduction to Contact Linguistics*, Malden, MA/Oxford: Blackwell Publishing.

Yakubovich, Ilya 2010, *Sociolinguistics of the Luvian Language*, Leiden/Boston: Brill.

CHAPTER 1

Divine Witnesses in Greece and Anatolia: *Iliad* 3.276–280 between Contact, Variation, and Reconstruction

Michele Bianconi

1 Introduction: Graeco-Anatolian Studies between Philology and Linguistics*

The renewed popularity of Graeco-Anatolian studies is affirmed by a relevant number of recent contributions,[1] in which scholars have looked at possible contact phenomena both at the linguistic and at the cultural level. This is a field that makes the intersection between linguistics and philology its *raison d'être*, and despite the absence of a comprehensive synthesis, it provides a generous array of case studies that may be looked at from different angles. The goal of this paper is to show how profitable it can be to look at specific case studies through the lenses of contact, variation and (Indo-European) reconstruction. This is a well-trodden path in traditional historical linguistics, but here I argue that such a method can also be of great help when it comes to cultural reconstruction. By looking at possible foreign models for a passage in the third book of the *Iliad*, I endeavour to demonstrate that the field of Graeco-Anatolian studies both lends itself to more fine-grained analyses on the basis of known material, and—thanks to the dramatic advances in Anatolian philology—provides "new wine for old bottles", allowing us to add fresh new data to ongoing discussions. Specifically, I am going to add a new piece of evidence, a Luwian inscription from Tell Ahmar (ca. 900 BCE), which shows a non-trivial parallel with the Homeric text: our Iliadic passage lists heavenly gods, rivers, earth, and underworld gods, and the Tell Ahmar text contains a set of specific gods (some of which also

---

* I wish to express my gratitude to José Luis García Ramón, Craig Melchert, Emily Kearns, Philomen Probert, and two anonymous reviewers for useful feedback on this paper; heartfelt thanks go to Emily Reith for improving its style. The usual disclaimer applies.

1 See e.g. BACHVAROVA 2016, BIANCONI 2015, 2020; COTTICELLI-KURRAS—GIUSFREDI 2018; DARDANO 2013; GARCÍA RAMÓN 2011, 2012; GASBARRA—POZZA 2012, 2019; HAJNAL 2014, 2018, HAWKINS 2010, MELCHERT 2014a, 2014b; METCALF 2015; RUTHERFORD 2020. A more complete list, together with a history of the studies in the field, may be found in BIANCONI 2021.

© MICHELE BIANCONI, 2022 | DOI:10.1163/9789004508828_003

appear in *Il*. 3.276–280), which includes heaven and earth, mountains and river-lands. We shall evaluate this parallel taking into account the evidence from other (IE and non-IE) traditions and look at the issue from the three points of views that characterise this volume: contact, variation, and reconstruction.

It is widely known that similarities in language may occur because of inheritance from a common ancestor, contact, or chance (the latter may include typological frequency). A very similar approach is adopted in the study of textual transmission, where the study of similarities in errors allows the scholar to establish the relationships between manuscripts.[2] In principle, the Comparative Method can be used with profit not only when looking at phonology and morphology, but also in when it comes to formulae, phraseology, and possibly even literary *topoi*—but one does need an even greater degree of care each time that cultural reconstruction is the goal (cf. some methodological remarks in LAZZERONI 1987, 1998 and CAMPANILE 1979). In order to successfully reconstruct (parts of) an unattested language, we usually look for systematic correspondences at the formal level, and try to establish which attested forms are archaisms and which are innovations. However, when there is no direct correspondence between form and function—e.g. whenever one aims at reconstructing a *system of values*, not an individual lexeme[3]—it might be more difficult to establish what is an innovation (in particular a non-trivial one) and to exclude parallel independent developments, which would prominently bring the element of 'chance' to the fore.

Contact complicates the picture even more. When a case of contact is hypothesised at the lexical level, one may look at the phonetics, at the morphology, or at the semantics.[4] However, when contact is combined with reconstruction, as in the case that we are about to analyse, an extremely careful approach and

---

2 A very similar approach is adopted in the study of textual transmission, where the study of similarities in errors allows the scholar to establish the relationships between manuscripts. Cf. the remarks in the *Introduction* to this volume.

3 "Cognate formulas, like cognate cultural institutions, may but need not be accompanied by cognate linguistic expressions. Lexical substitution and cultural change in the course of millennia may leave only the semantic features of the original expression present. But this must not mask the fundamental fact of the preservation of an inherited unitary formulaic and thematic "deep structure"" (WATKINS 1995: 49). Cf. also CAMPANILE 1979: 237.

4 For instance, while a lexeme inherited by two languages should show the respective regular sound changes, loanwords generally show some sound changes of the source language, and eventually some later sound changes of the target language, and should be integrated in a compatible morphological class (e.g. Latin second-declension nouns are generally adapted in Greek as *o*-stems). Or, when the meaning of a lexeme attested at a later stage of a given language resembles that of a similar lexeme in another language with which it came into contact, then it is possible to postulate that contact was responsible for the shift. These two

a solid methodology are essential to obtain a picture as clear as possible of the relationships between the given *comparata*. One must indeed keep in mind that cultural contact and language contact may overlap, but are not mutually interdependent. In other words, language contact may be a consequence of cultural contact, but cultural contact is not a necessary *and* sufficient condition for language contact to take place. Finally, typology plays a crucial role in this type of analysis, in that it helps us to weigh the different possibilities for the direction of language change. It is not always possible to *prove* something in the strictest sense when it comes to cultural reconstruction (not least because of the scarcity of the material and the gaps in our knowledge), but all of the above may allow us to make some informed guesses on what might be more probable.

Some historical areas and periods, such as the Aegean and the Near-Eastern world between the Late Bronze Age and the Early Iron Age, represent an excellent field to put these methodologies to the test. Not only do we observe a wide range of instances of cultural and linguistic contact throughout regions and centuries, but we are also progressively able to use an ever-increasing treasure trove of primary sources that allow us to identify varied and diverse examples of linguistic and cultural reconstruction. This is why, I argue, only a method that takes onto account both philology and linguistics, i.e. both the nature and context of our evidence and the mechanisms of language change, can produce real progress in this field.

In the specific case of contacts between Greek and the cultures of the Ancient Near East, opinions differ,[5] but—by and large—there are two schools of thought amongst those who do believe that a certain amount of contact has taken place. Some have argued for direct transfer of motifs directly from Mesopotamia and the Levant into Early Greek culture, while others believe that Anatolia was an important route of transmission for Near Eastern motifs to Greek epic literature.[6] In what follows, we shall take an opposite eastward route, and look at our case-study starting from the Greek text and moving to its

---

examples do not exhaust the typology of language contact at the lexical level; for an up-to-date bibliography on language contact studies, cf. the *Introduction* to this volume.

5   Cf. BIANCONI 2021 for an overview of previous studies and further references.

6   The first is represented by the studies of Walter Burkert (1991, 1992, 2004, 2005) and Martin West (1997). Burkert in particular envisaged a transmission from the East to the West through either wandering poets, or bilingual scribes who introduced Akkadian models into early Greek literature (cf. also BRYCE 1999, who hypothesised the presence of Anatolian scribes in Mycenaean Greece). More recently, Mary Bachvarova challenged these ideas by stressing the importance of long-distance élite interactions, and of a deep interconnection between Greek and Anatolian courts in the Late Bronze Age (BACHVAROVA 2016).

possible Near-Eastern sources. We will then focus on the variation of this motif in Anatolian sources and on the reconstruction of a possible Indo-European motif, and finally consider a recently deciphered Luwian passage that will shed some further light on the issue.

2 A Famed Iliadic Passage

The third book of the *Iliad* famously features the duel between Menelaus and Paris, which was supposed to resolve the war in favour of one of the opposing sides. At the very core of the book,[7] right before the duel, a ritual that accompanies the oath-swearing is performed. First, wine and water are mixed in a crater (ll. 269–270), the commanders' hands are washed (l. 270), and hair is cut from the heads of the sacrificial lambs and distributed to the Trojan and Achaean leaders (ll. 271–274). Then, Agamemnon invokes a series of divine figures (Zeus, Helios, the Sun-God, the rivers, the earth, and the two gods of the Underworld, Hades and Persephone), openly calling them μάρτυρες 'witnesses' and asking them to protect the ὅρκια πιστά, the 'trustworthy oaths':

(1) Γ 276–280

> Ζεῦ πάτερ Ἴδηθεν μεδέων κύδιστε μέγιστε,
> Ἠέλιός θ', ὃς πάντ' ἐφορᾷς καὶ πάντ' ἐπακούεις,
> καὶ ποταμοὶ καὶ γαῖα, καὶ οἳ ὑπένερθε καμόντας
> ἀνθρώπους τίνυσθον ὅτις κ' ἐπίορκον ὀμόσσῃ,
> ὑμεῖς μάρτυροι ἔστε, φυλάσσετε δ' ὅρκια πιστά

> Father Zeus, ruling from Ida, most lordly, greatest,
> and Helios, you who look upon everything, who listen to everything,
> and rivers, and earth, and you (two) who under the earth
> punish suffering men, whoever has sworn false oaths,
> you (pl.), be witnesses! (and) protect the trustworthy oaths

The ritual continues with Agamemnon spelling out of the conditions of the oath (ll. 281–291). Then the lambs are killed (ll. 292–294) and the wine is poured

---

7 Cf. Bowie 2019: 1–4 for a subdivision of the book into thematic sections. It appears that the remaining episodes are built around the oath-swearing, which takes 69 lines in the central part of Book 3.

DIVINE WITNESSES IN GREECE AND ANATOLIA   15

(ll. 295–296), before another prayer is said by some among the Acheans and the Trojans (296–301). The scene ends with Priam withdrawing from the battlefield and bringing the dead lambs with him (ll. 303–313).

Several scholars have pointed out the dependence of this Iliadic passage from Near-Eastern models, especially in the framework of shared ritual culture (one may find the latest and most comprehensive analysis in DARDANO 2021).[8] Here we shall focus on the list of divine figures invoked, which has received comparatively less attention in the existing literature.

The latest commentary on Book 3 of the *Iliad* reads as follows: "Zeus the highest god and Helios who sees and hears everything, the rivers and the Earth, and the gods of the underworld are all invoked as representatives of all parts of the universe: the division of the universe into three parts is a common feature of Greek and Near-Eastern cosmologies. This relatively short list of deities corresponds to the sometimes extremely lengthy ones in near-eastern oaths" (BOWIE 2019: 37–38).

This is certainly true,[9] but I contend that a more fine-grained analysis is possible. What is the specific model of the Greek passage? Where and when could the transmission have happened? In order to try and answer these questions, we shall first look at similar formulae in some Near-Eastern cultures, before moving to a closer scrutiny of variation in such formulae in the Anatolian context and of possible parallels in other Indo-European traditions.

3   Contact: Near-Eastern Parallels of an Invocation

That this ritual, which includes the invocation to the deities in *Iliad* 3.276–280, reflects Near-Eastern practices has become a mainstream idea in Homeric studies.[10] This is probably due to the influence of such a work as *The East Face of Helicon* (WEST 1997) on studies on early Greek literature. But the first (and

---

8   Here, the practices of sacrifices and ὅρκια πιστά are exhaustively and extensively treated, and the reader may find further references. See, among others, also the 'classic' WEST 1997: 20–23 with further references.

9   Though, for the threefold division of the universe as a PIE concept, cf. 4. *infra*.

10   Just to give the most recent example, Angus Bowie opens the preface to his commentary to *Iliad* 3 by saying that "a significant trend in current studies of Ancient Greek literature is an interest in the relationships between Greek culture and the cultures of the Ancient Near East" (BOWIE 2019: ix). He then introduces the section we are interested in (p. 37) stating that "in the oath-swearing [...] we can see something of the influence that Anatolian culture had on Greek customs". Cf. also ROLLINGER 2004a: 383–416 and 2004b, PUHVEL 1991: 9 and FARAONE 1993: 72–76.

16 BIANCONI

often forgotten) scholar who noticed that there were Near-Eastern parallels to this Homeric passage was Giovanni Nenci: in a very short article published in 1961, he compared the structure of divine witness lists in Hittite texts and in the Homeric epics, by mentioning the treaties between Šuppiluliuma and Mattiwaza (*sic*!) of Mitanni, Šuppiluliuma and Tette, and Muršili and Talmi-Šarma (NENCI 1961: 381 fn. 3). Martin West (1997: 20–22) lists not only the aforementioned Hittite treaties, but also some later Semitic and Greek parallels (cf. *infra*). One may find some further parallels in more recent literature (e.g. the treaty between Šuppiluliuma I and the king of Hayasa cited by BOWIE 2019: 38), but a comprehensive survey is still unavailable. The present section and the next one endeavour to start to fill this gap by giving a representative collection of examples (both in the original languages and in translation).

One of the most extensive examples of the Hittite typology, for which there is abundant evidence,[11] is the treaty between the Hittite king Muwattalli II and Alakšandu of Wiluša:

(2) *KUB* 21.1 rev. iv 1–30 (*CTH* 76)[12]

1   [ᵈUTU (*ŠA-ME-E* LUGAL KUR.KURᴹᴱˢ ᴸᵁSIP)]A UDU *ŠA* DUMU.LÚ.U₁₉.LU
    ᵈUTU ᵁᴿᵁ*A-ri-in-na*
    [MUNUS.LUGAL KU(R.KURᴹᴱˢ ᵈ10 *pí-ḫa-aš-*)]*ša-aš-ši-iš ŠA* ⌈SAG⌉.DU
    ᵈUTU-*ŠI* ᵈ10 NIR.GÁL
    [...ᵈ10 ᵁᴿᵁ*Ḫa-a*]*t-ti* LUGAL KUR.KURᴹᴱˢ ᵈ10 ḪI.ḪI ᵈ10 ᵁᴿᵁ*Zi-*⌈*ip*⌉*-pa-la-a*[*n-da*]
    [...]⌈ᵈ10⌉ KARAŠ ᵈ10 ᵁᴿᵁ*Ḫa-la-ap* ᵈ10 KI.LAM
5   [(ᵈ) ... *-t*]*i*? *Ù* ᵁᴿᵁ*A-ri-in-na* ᵈ10 ᵁᴿᵁ*Ḫe-eš-ša-aš-ḫa-*⌈*pa*⌉
    [(ᵈ10 ᵁᴿᵁ*Ku*)*m-ma-an-ni*] ᵈ10 ᵁᴿᵁ*Ša-mu-u-ḫa* ᵈ10 ᵁᴿᵁ*Ḫur-ma* ᵈ10 ᵁᴿᵁ*Ša-re-e*[*š-(ša)*]
    [...ᵈ10 ᵁᴿᵁ*L*]*i-i*[*ḫ-z*]*i-na* ᵈ10 ᵁᴿᵁ*U-da* ᵈ10 ᵁᴿᵁ*Šaḫ-pí-na* ᵈ10 ᵁᴿᵁÁ.TAḪ

---

11 For a more thorough analysis, cf. the next section. On the Hittite pantheon, cf. also YOSHIDA 1996, SINGER 1994, and SCHWEMER 2006.

12 The reference edition is still FRIEDRICH 1930: 42–102, but in recent years new translations have been published (BECKMAN 1999: 87–93, Starke *apud* LATACZ 2004: 105–110, DEVECCHI 2015: 151–159, DEL MONTE 2003: 65–67) which include some of the new fragments that have emerged (see DEVECCHI 2015: 152 for an overview). However, despite KITCHEN—LAWRENCE 2012, DEL MONTE 2003 and CHRISTIANSEN 2012 (they either offer an edition and translation based on Friedrich's manuscripts, or re-edit only parts of the text), a new complete edition with translation and commentary would perhaps be desirable. Here I am following, with minor changes, the edition of the passage given by Birgit Christiansen (CHRISTIANSEN 2012: 255–256).

DIVINE WITNESSES IN GREECE AND ANATOLIA

$[(^{\text{GÚ}_4}\check{S}e)]$-⌈$er$⌉-$ri$-$i\check{s}$ $^{\text{GÚ}_4}Hu$-u-ur-ru-$i\check{s}$ $^{\text{d}}Nan_x$-ni $^{\text{d}}Ha$-az-zi
⌈^{d}⌉$Hé$-$pát$ MUNUS.LUGAL $\check{S}A$-ME-E

10   ^{d}LAMMA ^{d}LAMMA $^{\text{URU}}Ha$-at-ti $^{\text{d}}Kar$-zi-$i\check{s}$ $^{\text{d}}Ha$-pa-an-⌈ta⌉-li-⌈ya⌉-$a\check{s}$
     ^{d}LAMMA $^{\text{URU}}Ga$-ra-ah-na ^{d}LAMMA $^{\text{KUŠ}}kur$-$\check{s}a$-$a\check{s}$ $^{\text{d}}AL$-⌈LA⌉-TU_4 $^{\text{d}}A.A$-$a\check{s}$ $^{\text{d}}Te$-
     $li[(-p)í$-nu-$u\check{s}]$
     ^{d}30! EN $NÉ$-$E\check{S}$ DINGIR-LIM $^{\text{d}}I\check{S}TAR$ $^{\text{d}}I\check{S}TAR$ $LÍL$ $^{\text{d}}I\check{S}TAR$ $^{\text{URU}}Ne$-nu-wa (ras.)
     ⌈$^{\text{d}}I\check{S}TAR$⌉ $^{\text{URU}}Ha$-at-ta-ri-na $^{\text{d}}Ni$-na-at-ta-$a\check{s}$ $^{\text{d}}Ku$-li-it-ta-$a\check{s}$
     $^{\text{d}}I\check{s}$-ha-ra MUNUS.LUGAL $NÉ$-$E\check{S}$ DINGIR-LIM $^{\text{d}}ZA$-BA_4-BA_4 $^{\text{d}}ZA$-BA_4-BA_4
     $^{\text{URU}}Ha$-at-ti

15    $^{\text{d}}ZA$-BA_4-BA_4 $^{\text{URU!}}Il!$-la-ya $^{\text{d}}ZA$-BA_4-BA_4 $^{\text{URU}}Ar$-zi-ya
     $^{\text{d}}Ya$-ri-$i\check{s}$ $^{\text{d}}Za$-ap-na-$a\check{s}$
     $^{\text{URU}}\check{S}a$-mu-ha-$a\check{s}$ $^{\text{d}}A$-ba-ra-$a\check{s}$ $^{\text{URU}}Hur$-ma-$a\check{s}$ $^{\text{d!}}Ha$-an-ti-da-$a\check{s}$-$\check{s}u$-$u\check{s}$
     $^{\text{URU}}A$-an-ku-wa-$a\check{s}$ $^{\text{d!}}Ka$-tah-ha-$a\check{s}$ $^{\text{URU}}Ga$-a-ta-pa-a-$a\check{s}$ MUNUS.LUGAL-$a\check{s}$
     $^{\text{URU}}Ta$-hur-pa-$a\check{s}$ $^{\text{d}}Ma$-am-ma-$a\check{s}$ $^{\text{URU}}Du$-un-na-$a\check{s}$ <^{d}>Hal-la-ra-$a\check{s}$

20    $^{\text{URU}}Hu$-u-$pé$-$e\check{s}$-na-$a\check{s}$ ^{d}GAZ.BA.A.A DINGIR^{MEŠ} lu-la-hi DINGIR$^{!\text{MEŠ}}$ ha-
     $\langle bi$-$\rangle ri$-ya-$[a\check{s}]$
     DINGIR^{MEŠ} LÚ^{MEŠ} DINGIR^{MEŠ} MUNUS^{MEŠ} hu-u-ma-an-te-$e\check{s}_{17}$ $^{\text{d}}Na$-a-ra-$a\check{s}$
     $^{\text{d}}Na$-$a[p$-$\check{s}a$-ra-$a\check{s}]$
     $^{\text{d}}Am$-mu-un-ki-$i\check{s}$ $^{\text{d}}Tu$-⌈hu-$\check{s}i$-$i\check{s}$⌉ ⌈^{d}⌉A-mi-iz-za-du-$u\check{s}$
     $^{\text{d}}Ku$-mar-bi-$i\check{s}$ «^{d}» ^{d}EN.LÍL-$a\check{s}$ ⌈^{d}NIN.LÍL⌉
     $^{\text{HUR.SAG}}Hu$-u-ul-la-$a\check{s}$ $^{\text{HUR.SAG}}Za$-al-li-ya-$[nu$-$u\check{s} ...]$

25   HUR.SAG$^{\text{HI.A}}$ I$_7$$^{\text{HI.A}}$ PÚ$^{\text{!MEŠ}}$ $\check{S}A$ KUR $^{\text{URU}}Ha$-$a[t$-$ti ...]$ x
     ne-⌈$pí$-$i\check{s}$⌉ te-$kán$-na IM^{MEŠ}-$u\check{s}$ al-$[pu$-$u\check{s} ... hu$-u-$m]a$-an-te-$e[\check{s}_{17}]$
     $\check{S}A$ KUR $^{\text{URU}}Ú$-lu-$\check{s}a$ ^{d}10 ⌈KARAŠ⌉ $^{\text{d}}[...]$x$(-)ap$-pa-li-u-na-$a\check{s}$
     DINGIR^{MEŠ} LÚ^{MEŠ} DINGIR^{MEŠ} MUNUS^{MEŠ} $[$x x x$]$ x x $[$x x x$]$x ^{d}KASKAL.KUR
     $\check{S}A$ KUR $^{\text{URU}}Ú$-i-$[lu$-$\check{s}a ... N]A$-RA-AM ^{d}10

30    $^{\text{URU}}Pí$-ha-$a\check{s}$-$\check{s}a$-$a\check{s}$-$\check{s}[i ... -a]n$-ni hal-zi-ih-hu-un

[The Sun-god] of Heaven, King of the Lands, Shepherd of Humankind,
the Sun-goddess of Arinna, [Queen] of the Lands, the personal Storm-god
of Lightning of My Majesty, the Powerful Storm God, [King of the Lands,
the Storm-god of Hatti], King of the Land, the Storm-god of Lightning, the
Storm-god of Zippalanda, [Storm-god of Nerik], the Storm-god of Aleppo,
the Storm-god of the Market (?), the [Storm-god of ...], the Storm-god
of Arinna, the Storm-god of Hisashapa, the Storm-god of [Sapinuwa],
the Storm-god of Samuha, the Storm-god of Hurma, the Storm-god of
Sarissa, the Storm-god of Lihzina, the Storm-god of Uda, the Storm-god
of Sahpina, the Storm-god of Help, Sheri, Hurri, Mount Nanni, Mount
Hazzi, Hebat, Queen of Heaven, the Tutelary Deity, the Tutelary Deity
of Hatti, Karzi, Hapantaliya, the Tutelary Deity of Karahna, the Tutelary

Deity of the Hunting Bag, Allatu, the Moon-god, Lord of the Oath, Ishtar, Ishtar of the Countryside, Ishtar of Nineveh, Ishtar of Hattarina, Ninatta, Kulitta, Ishhara, Queen of the Oath, the War-God, the War-God of Hatti, the War-god of Illaya, the War-god of Arziya, Yarri, Zappana, Abara of Samuha, Hantitassu of Hurma, Katahha of Ankuwa, the Queen of Katapa, Ammamma of Tahurpa, Hallara of Dunna, Huwassanna of Hupisna, the mountain-dweller gods, the mercenary gods, all the male and female deities, ⟨all the primeval deities⟩—Nara, Namsara, Ammunki, Tuhusi, Minki, Ammizzaddu, Alalu, Kumarbi, Enlil, Ninlil—Mount Hulla, Mount Zaliyanu, Mount Taha, the mountains, the rivers, and the springs of Hatti, the great Sea, heaven and earth, the winds, the clouds, all [the deities] of the land of Wilusa: the Storm-god of the Army, [...]appaliuna, the male deities, the female deities, the mountains, [the rivers, the springs], and the underground watercourse (?) of the land of Wilusa. I, My Majesty, [Great] King, Beloved of the Storm-god of Lightning, have summoned them to assembly in witness.

transl. Beckman

This passage is interesting for a number of reasons,[13] and it is worth noting that this is as close as one can get to the setting of the *Iliad*, even if just in merely geographical terms. In this text, various sun-gods and sky-gods join heaven, earth, and other natural elements in being called upon to witness the oath between the Wilusan (= Trojan) Alakšandu (generally interpreted as the Anatolian adaptation of Gk. Ἀλέξανδρος)[14] and the Hittite king.

One may find gods witnessing (and consequently protecting) treaties in several first-millennium texts from Semitic cultures. See, for instance, the following Neo-Assyrian treaty, dated 754 BCE:

---

13 For instance, the presence of the epithet ᴸᵘSIP DUMU.LÚ.U₁₉.LU 'shepherd of Humankind', which is reminiscent of the Greek ποιμένα λαῶν (said of Agamemnon in the *Iliad*); the mention of Mount Hazzi (cf. Mt. Kasios, connected with the eponymous cult of Zeus in later times); the mention of *Appaliuna* (cf. WATKINS 1986); the possible mention of an underground watercourse, which was identified by Korfmann in the Trojan archaeological site. Each one of these topics would require an individual discussion, but this goes beyond the aims and limits of this article.

14 KRETSCHMER 1924 is generally credited with the identification of this personal name, but it is worth noting that the discovery pre-dated the decipherment of Hittite. The first contribution in which we find the connection was LUCKENBILL 1911.

DIVINE WITNESSES IN GREECE AND ANATOLIA

(3) Ashur-nērārī V's Treaty with the Aramean king Mati'-ilu of Arpad (SAA 2.2: vi 6–26)

^{d}*aš-šur* MAN AN KI *tum$_3$-ma-tu$_2$-nu*
^{d}*a-nu-um an-tu$_4$* KI.MIN ^{d}BAD ^{d}NIN.LIL$_2$ KI.MIN
^{d}DIŠ ^{d}*dam-ki-na* KI.MIN ^{d}30 ^{d}NIN.GAL KI.MIN
^{d}UTU ^{d}*a-a* KI.MIN ^{d}IŠKUR ^{d}*ša-la* KI.MIN

10   ^{d}AMAR.UTU ^{d}*zar-pa-ni-tu$_4$* KI.MIN ^{d}AG ^{d}LAL$_2$ KI.MIN
^{d}MAŠ ^{d}ME KI.MIN ^{d}*uraš* ^{d}NIN.E$_2$.GAL KI.MIN
^{d}*za-ba$_4$-ba$_4$* ^{d}*ba*.U$_2$ KI.MIN ^{d}U.GUR ^{d}*la-aṣ* KI.MIN
^{d}DI.KUD ^{d}NIN.GIR$_2$.SU KI.MIN
^{d}*ḫum-ḫum-mu* ^{d}*i-šum* KI.MIN

15   ^{d}GIŠ.BAR ^{d}PA.TUG$_2$ KI.MIN ^{d}15 NIN ^{uru}*ni-na-a* KI.MIN
^{d}INNIN NIN ^{uru}*arba-il$_3$* KI.MIN
^{d}IŠKUR *ša$_2$* ^{uru}*kur-ba-il$_3$* KI.MIN
^{d}IŠKUR *ša$_2$* ^{uru}*ḫal-la-ba* KI.MIN
^{d}IGI.DU *a-lik maḫ-ri* KI.MIN

20   ^{d}7.BI *qar-du-ti* KI.MIN
^{d}[*d*]*a*-⌜*gan*⌝ ^{d}[*m*]*u?-ṣur-u-na* KI.MIN
^{d}[*mi-il-qar-tu* ^{d}*ia-s*]*u'-mu-na* KI.MIN
^{d}⌜*ku$_2$*⌝!-*b*[*a-ba* ^{d}*kar*]-*ḫu-ḫa* KI.MIN
^{d}IŠKUR ^{d}[x] ⌜x ^{d}!*ra'-ma'-nu*'⌝

25   *ša* ^{ur}[^{u} *di-maš-qa* KI.MIN]
^{d}*za-*[x x x x x x x x]

By Assur, king of heaven and Earth, you have sworn; by Anu and Antu, ditto;[15] by Enlil and Mullissu, ditto; by Ea and Damkina, ditto; by Sîn and Ningal, ditto; by Šamaš and Aya, ditto; by Adad and Šala, ditto; by Marduk and Zarpānītu, ditto; by Nabû and Tašmētu, ditto; by Ninurta and Gula, ditto; by Uraš and Bēlet-ekalli, ditto; by Zababa and Bau, ditto; by Nergal and Laṣ, ditto; by Madānu and Ningirsu, ditto; by Ḫumḫummu and Išum, ditto; by Erra and Nusku, ditto; by Ištar Lady-of-Nineveh, ditto; by Ištar Lady-of-Arbela, ditto; by Adad-of-Kurbail, ditto; by Hadad-of-Aleppo, ditto; by Palil, who marches in front, ditto; by the heroic Sebittu, ditto; by Dagan [and M]uṣuruna, ditto; by M[elqart and Eš]mun, ditto; by Kub[aba and Kar]ḫuḫa, ditto; by Hadad, [...], and Ramman-of-[Damascus, ditto;] by Za...

---

15   "The scribe's use of KI.MIN indicates how the scribe thought the gods were to be paired. Rather than appearing at the end of each line following a collection of divine names, KI.MIN typically appears after each pair of deities, who are often a divine couple" (ALLEN 2015: 119).

20 BIANCONI

In first-millennium Mesopotamian treaties, gods are generally paired, and lists are divided into three parts (BARRÉ 1983: 22): first, one finds the supreme god of the pantheon, Marduk in Babylon and Assur in Assyria; then comes a list of high gods that usually has the Sebetti as its last member; finally, foreign gods are mentioned, and a summary phrase ("all the gods of the land X and all the gods of the land Y") usually concludes the whole list.

In an 8th-century treaty from Sefire (near Aleppo, in Syria), this time in Aramaic, a list of gods is followed by natural powers, and once more they are grouped in pairs:

(4)   Treaty between Barga'yah of KTK and Mati'-ilu of Arpad (*KAI* 222: A 7–13)

> [qdm 'sr]
> wmlš wqdm mrdk wzrpnt wqdm nb' wt[šmt wqdm 'r wnš]
> k wqdm nrgl wlṣ wqdm šmš wnr wqdm s[n wnkl wq]
>
> (10) dm nkr wkd'h wqdm kl 'lhy rḥbh w'dm[h wqdm hdd zy ḥ]
> lb wqdm sbt wqdm 'l w'lyn wqdm šmy[m w'rq wqdm mṣ]
> lh wm'ynn wqdm ywm wlylh šhdn kl '[lhy ktk w'lhy 'r]
> pd(?)]

> "[before Assur]
> and Mullissu and before Marduk and Zarpānītu and before Nabû and
>   Ta[šmētu and before Erra and Nus]-
> ku and before Nergal and Laṣ and before Šamaš and Nur and before Sîn
>   [and Ningal] and [be]-
> fore NKR and KD'H and before the Gods of the open country and of the
>   [cultivated] ground and [before Hadad, that of A]-
> leppo and before the Sebittu and before El and Elyon and before
>   Heav[en and Earth and before Ab]-
> yss] and Springs and before Day and Night. Witnesses (be) all (you)
>   g[ods of KTK and gods of Ar-
> pad?]"

Divine lists are by no means confined to treaties. An incantation plaque from Arslan Tash in Upper Syria (7th c. BCE; cf. WEST 1997: 21) reads "Aššur has made an eternal pact with us [...] and all the sons of gods and the numerous generation of all the Holy Ones, with oaths by the Heavens and Earth, the eternal witnesses".

If later texts are valid proxies for earlier customs, one may draw two further parallels. One is generally thought to be the Greek translation of a Punic treaty,

DIVINE WITNESSES IN GREECE AND ANATOLIA

and features Hannibal swearing an oath and invoking a list of gods and of cosmic powers. Here is the entire passage, as reported by Polybius:

(5) Pol. *Hist.* VII, 9, 1–2:

> ὅρκος, ὃν ἔθετο Ἀννίβας ὁ στρατηγός, Μάγωνος, Μύρκανος, Βαρμόκαρος, καὶ πάντες γερουσιασταὶ Καρχηδονίων οἱ μετ' αὐτοῦ καὶ πάντες Καρχηδόνιοι στρατευόμενοι μετ' αὐτοῦ πρὸς Ξενοφάνη Κλεομάχου Ἀθηναῖον πρεσβευτήν, ὃν ἀπέστειλε πρὸς ἡμᾶς Φίλιππος ὁ βασιλεὺς Δημητρίου ὑπὲρ αὐτοῦ καὶ Μακεδόνων καὶ τῶν συμμάχων, ἐναντίον Διὸς καὶ Ἥρας καὶ Ἀπόλλωνος, ἐναντίον δαίμονος Καρχηδονίων καὶ Ἡρακλέους καὶ Ἰολάου, ἐναντίον Ἄρεως, Τρίτωνος, Ποσειδῶνος, ἐναντίον θεῶν τῶν συστρατευομένων καὶ Ἡλίου καὶ Σελήνης καὶ Γῆς, ἐναντίον ποταμῶν καὶ λιμνῶν καὶ ὑδάτων, ἐναντίον πάντων θεῶν ὅσοι κατέχουσι Καρχηδόνα, ἐναντίον θεῶν πάντων ὅσοι Μακεδονίαν καὶ τὴν ἄλλην Ἑλλάδα κατέχουσιν, ἐναντίον θεῶν πάντων τῶν κατὰ στρατείαν, ὅσοι τινὲς ἐφεστήκασιν ἐπὶ τοῦδε τοῦ ὅρκου.

(This is) the oath that the general Hannibal, Mago, Myrcan, Barmocar, and all Carthaginian senators present with him, and all Carthaginians serving under him, swore in front of the Athenian Xenophanes son of Cleomachus, the envoy whom King Philip, son of Demetrius, sent to us on behalf of himself, of the Macedonians and of the allies. In the presence of Zeus, Hera, and Apollo, in the presence of the deity of Carthage, of Heracles, and Iolaus; in the presence of Ares, Triton, (and) Poseidon; in the presence of the gods who battle with us and of the Sun, Moon, and Earth; in the presence of Rivers, Lakes, and Waters; in the presence of all the gods who possess Carthage; in the presence of all the gods who possess Macedonia and the rest of Greece: in the presence of all the gods of the army who preside over this oath

West just points out that Hannibal and his army "swore by a list that included Sun, Moon and Earth, Rivers, Lakes (?), and waters" (WEST 1997: 21), but one can go even further: the mention of the tutelary deities of both parts (ἐναντίον πάντων θεῶν ὅσοι κατέχουσι Καρχηδόνα, ἐναντίον θεῶν πάντων ὅσοι Μακεδονίαν καὶ τὴν ἄλλην Ἑλλάδα κατέχουσιν) is an even less trivial parallel with the Hittite texts under examination (for further examples, cf. 3. *infra*).[16]

---

16   BARRÉ 1983 offers a thorough analysis of this text, with special reference to Near-Eastern material. Interestingly enough, he does not seem to mention the Homeric passage we are interested in.

An even later possible parallel may be found in a passage from the Gospel of Matthew (5:34–35): in this part of the so-called "Sermon on the Mount", Jesus talks about oaths, and tells his followers: ἐγὼ δὲ λέγω ὑμῖν μὴ ὀμόσαι ὅλως· μήτε ἐν τῷ οὐρανῷ, ὅτι θρόνος ἐστὶν τοῦ Θεοῦ, μήτε ἐν τῇ γῇ, ὅτι ὑποπόδιόν ἐστιν τῶν ποδῶν αὐτοῦ "but I tell you, don't swear at all: neither by heaven, for it is the throne of God; nor by the earth, for it is the footstool of his feet". This is echoed by James 5:12: Πρὸ πάντων δέ, ἀδελφοί μου, μὴ ὀμνύετε, μήτε τὸν οὐρανὸν μήτε τὴν γῆν μήτε ἄλλον τινὰ ὅρκον "But above all things, my brethren, swear not, neither by heaven, neither by the earth, neither by any other oath". Both passages indirectly point to a custom that was present in Roman Palestine, and that might well date back a few centuries.

One may go on with the examples, but it should already be quite clear that listing divine figures in treaties was a prominent element of Near-Eastern cultures, and therefore the possibility of Γ 276–280 reflecting "foreign" practices is real. Given the diversity of the available evidence, establishing the specific relationships between each instance and pinpointing on a map the diffusion paths of such a phenomenon might prove a difficult task, one that would require an amount of space and knowledge that goes beyond the limits of this paper and of its author. However, it is in my view possible to argue, on the basis of the diachronic and diatopic extension, the variation, and the sheer amount of the Hittite material, that Anatolia represented a vector, if not even a model, for the diffusion of divine lists, both towards the East and towards the West.

In the next section we will take a closer look at instances of god lists in our Hittite corpus, with particular reference to their presence in the oath section of diplomatic texts.

4 Variation: Divine Witness Lists in Anatolia

The increased availability of Hittite texts allows us to take a fresh look at the theme of divine witnesses, and to focus on variation in our texts. Here we shall consider a specific genre, that of treaties between the Hittite king and the leader (or leaders) of a separate political entity. This sort of text has a fairly regular structure: most treaties feature a preamble, a historical introduction, a section with provisions, followed by a statement about the deposition of the tablet, and an oath featuring a list of divine figures and a series of curses and blessings.[17] In this type of documents, gods are explicitly called to witness and be protectors of the treaty.

---

17   For further details, see DEVECCHI 2015: 31–52 and BECKMAN 1999: 2–3 with references.

DIVINE WITNESSES IN GREECE AND ANATOLIA   23

As we have mentioned above, divine lists (either partial or complete) are a
standard feature of Hittite treaties. I counted 24 occurrences in our extant corpus (see *Appendix*).[18] These lists can be fairly lengthy (cf. (1.) *supra*), but despite
the fact that the precise sequence of deities is not the same throughout, we
notice several structural similarities, as certain members of the lists occur in
a fixed order.[19] The Sun-god of Heaven and the Sun-goddess of Arinna tend
to open the list, and they are immediately followed by a list of Storm-gods
(^{d}10) of different places (Hatti and Arinna are recurrent ones) and tutelary
deities (denoted by the sumerogram ^{d}LAMMA). Then generally come a group
of Babylonian deities (Allatu, queen of the Underworld, Ea, the god of water,
knowledge and creation),[20] either preceded or followed by Hebat or Telipinu (respectively the mother goddess of the Hurrians and the Hattic god of
fertility). Both may be mentioned multiple times, in association with their
cult places. Next is the goddess of love Ištar, often mentioned together with
her attendants Ninatta and Kulitta. She either precedes or follows the Moon
God and the goddess Išḫara, both qualified as protectors of the oath (EN
NÉ-EŠ and MUNUS.LUGAL *NÉ-EŠ*), and the War-gods (again, from different
places), which often come with Yarri, Zappana, and Hasammili.[21] Nikkal, the
Ugaritic/Canaanean goddess of orchards, sometimes appears in this section.
There follows a group of local deities: amongst them, one may find Hantitassu
of Hurma, Abara of Šamuha, Katahha of Ankuwa, Ammamma of Tahurpa,
Huwassanna of Hupišna, Hallara of Dunna, the Lady of Landa (possibly the
Hurrian Allani), Kuniyawanni of Landa, and Nin-šenšen of Kinza. The *lulaḫḫi*
and *ḫapiru* gods, protectors of foreign mercenaries (according to GURNEY 1977:
5 and LIVERANI 1967), come right after, but they are sometimes preceded by
Mount Lebanon, Mount Šariyana or Šariššiya, and Mount Pišaiša. The list goes
on with the deities of the Underworld,[22] starting (and sometimes ending) with

---

18   KESTEMONT 1976 has a useful collection of data, but a fresh new assessment proved to be
      necessary, as new data are now available, and Kestemont's subdivision is rather idiosyn-
      cratic and unsatisfactory in many respects (see criticism in BARRÉ 1983: 30–31).

19   The present account is based on an autonomous examination of the texts; the reader may
      find a similar (though not identical) analysis in GURNEY 1977: 4–6; cf. also BARRÉ 1983:
      30–37 and KESTEMONT 1976.

20   Marduk, the patron deity of Babylon, is only mentioned in *CTH* 42 (*KBo* 5.3 i 53).

21   Hasammili is only mentioned in *CTH* 51 (*KBo* 1.1 rev. 48) and perhaps in *CTH* 52.1 (*KBo* 1.3
      rev. 3), though the reading here is very uncertain.

22   In two cases, (*CTH* 106.A.I and *CTH* 106.B.II) Lelwani, a Hattian goddess of the Underworld,
      is mentioned at this point; in *CTH* 51 and 52, she is named right before Ea, while in *CTH*
      138.1 one may find her before Ištar.

the Sumerian Ereshkigal, sometimes called "Sun-goddess of the Earth",[23] and usually continuing with the so-called 'primeval deities', which are sometimes named: Nara, Namšara, Minki, Tuhuši, Ammunki, Ammizzadu, Alalu, Antu, Anu, Apantu, Enlil, Ninlil, and Bēlet-ekalli.[24] The list is generally closed by the mountain-dweller gods, the mercenary gods, the male deities, and the female deities, followed by mountains, rivers, springs, the Euphrates (only in *CTH* 51), the (great) sea, heaven and earth, the winds, and the clouds.

Despite close similarities and a fixed structure, we have no example of two identical lists: not only are local and supra-regional deities mentioned in some treaties and omitted in others, but also the natural elements that close the list are not always the same. An instructive comparison in this respect is that between *CTH* 106.B.II (treaty between Hattusili III and Ulmi-Tessub of Tarhuntašša) and *CTH* 106.A.I (treaty between Tudhaliya IV of Hatti and Kuruntya of Tarhuntašša).[25] The precise relationship between the two documents is still debated, as is the identity of the king of Tarhuntašša,[26] but here we are interested in the fact that these two treaties come from the same *milieu*, and they are therefore expected to show minimal variation. The two lists are however not identical, as the later document contains a few more deities:[27]

(6)   Treaty between Hattusili III of Hatti and Ulmi-Teššub of Tarhuntašša (*CTH* 106.B.II)

> In this matter the Storm-god of Lightning, the Sun-goddess of Arinna, the Storm god of Hatti, the Storm-god of Nerik, Ishtar of Samuha, Ishtar of Lawazantiya, and the Thousand Gods of Hatti shall be witnesses. And in regard to the fact that I have made this treaty tablet for you, the Thousand Gods are now summoned to assembly. They shall observe and listen and be witnesses: The Sun-god of Heaven, the Sun-goddess of Arinna, the

---

23   In *CTH* 53, 66 and 69 she coexists with Allatu, mentioned a few lines before. It does not seem to matter that they are essentially the same goddess.

24   Bēlet-ekalli is Ninurta's wife, and became assimilated into the Hurrian pantheon as Pentikalli (GURNEY 1977: 5). Her name only occurs in *CTH* 51 (*KBo* 1.1 rev. 53).

25   A comparison between the two treaties with Ugarit (*CTH* 46 and 66) would be as useful, but unfortunately the divine list in the treaty between Šuppiluliuma I of Hatti and Niqmaddu II of Ugarit is badly damaged, and one can only read a few divine names.

26   Cf. DEVECCHI 2015: 160–161 and BECKMAN 1999: 102–103 for discussion and further references. The two treaties are similar also because they both feature human witnesses.

27   In the following translations, taken from BECKMAN 1999, I have used boldface for those deities which are not present in the other text and italicised those deities which appear in a different position.

Storm-god of Heaven, the Storm-god of Hatti, the Storm-god of the Army, the Storm-god of Hisashapa, the Storm-god of Zippalanda, the Storm-god of Nerik, the Storm-god of Aleppo, the Storm-god of Uda, the Storm-god of Sapinuwa, the Powerful Storm-god, **the pihaimmi Storm-god**, the Storm-god of Lightning, Lulutassi, the Tutelary Deity, the Tutelary Deity of Hatti, Ayala, Karzi, Hapantaliya, *Sharrumma, Zithariya*, Hebat, Queen of Heaven, **Ishtar**, Ishtar of Nineveh, Ishtar of Hattarina, Ninatta, Kulitta, *Nikkal*, [Ishhara], *the Moon-god, Lord of the Oaths*, the Deity of Arusna, the War-god, the War-god of Hatti, the War-god of Illaya, the War-god of Arziya, Yarri, Zappana, *Abara of Samuha, Hantitassu of Hurma*, Katahha of Ankuwa, **the Queen of Katapa**, Ammamma of Tahurpa, *Hallara of Dunna, Huwassanna of Hupisna*, Lelwani, the mountain-dweller gods, the mercenary gods, the male deities, the female deities, the great sea, the mountains, rivers, and springs of Hatti and of the land of Tarhuntassa

transl. Beckman

(7)   Treaty between Tudhaliya IV of Hatti and Kuruntya of Tarhuntašša (*CTH* 106.A.I)

And in regard to the fact that I have made this treaty for you, the Thousand Gods are now summoned to assembly in this matter. They shall observe and listen and be witnesses; The Sun-god of Heaven, the Sun-goddess of Arinna, the Storm-god of Heaven, the Storm-god of Hatti, the Storm-god of the Army, the Storm-god of Hisashapa, the Storm-god of Zippalanda, the Storm-god of Nerik, the Storm-god of Aleppo, the Storm-god of Uda, **the Storm-god of Kizzuwatna, the Storm-god of Samuha**, the Storm-god of Sapinuwa, the Powerful Storm-god, the Storm-god of Lightning, Lulutassi, the Tutelary Deity, the Tutelary Deity of Hatti, Ayala, Karzi, Hapantaliya, **the Tutelary Deity of the Countryside, the Tutelary Deity of the Hunting Bag**, *Zithariya, Sharrumma*, **Hebat of Uda, Hebat of Kizzuwatna, Ishtar of Samuha, Ishtar of the Countryside, Ishtar of Lawazan- tiya**, Ishtar of Nineveh, Ishtar of Hattarina, Ninatta, Kulitta, *the Moon-god, King of the Oaths, Nikkal*, **Queen of the Oaths, Ishhara**, the Deity of Arusna, the War-god, the War-god of Hatti, the War-god of Illaya, the War-god of Arziya, Yarri, Zappana, *Hantitassu of Hurma, Abara of Samuha*, Katahha of Ankuwa, Ammamma of Tahurpa, *Huwassanna of Hupisna, Hallara of Dunna*, Lelwani, the mountain-dweller gods, the mercenary gods, the male deities, the female deities, **heaven, earth**, the great sea, the mountains, rivers, and springs of Hatti and of the land of Tarhuntassa

transl. Beckman

Most additions have to do with Storm-gods, Tutelary deities, Hebats and Ištars, i.e. deities that are identified with multiple cult centres, but it is interesting to note that *CTH* 106.B.II lacks heaven and earth, which are otherwise almost always present.

Even though the greatest majority of treaties contain similar lists to the ones seen in (2.) (6.) and (7.) above, we are able to isolate a second type, whose best-preserved example is the treaty between a Hittite king (possibly Arnuwanda I) and the Kaška people:

(8)   *KBo* 8.35, ii 8–13 (*CTH* 139.1; ed. GERÇEK 2012: 235)

> *nu ka-a-ša li-in-ga-i[n]* ⌜*i*⌝-*ya-u-en nu* DINGIR.MEŠ-*mu-uš ḫu-u-ma-an-du-uš*
> *tu-li-ya da-i-*⌜*ú*⌝-*en* ᵈUTU-*un* ᵈIM-*an* ᵈZA.BA₄.BA₄ ᵈLAMMA-*aš* ᵈE[N.ZU]
> 10   ᵈIŠTAR-*in* ᵈ*Iš-ḫa-ra-aš li-in-ki-aš iš-ḫa-a-aš ne-e-pí-i-ša-aš* DINGIR.MEŠ-*e[š]*
> *ták-na-a-aš* DINGIR.MEŠ *ka-ru-ú-i-[l]i-aš* DINGIR.MEŠ *ŠA* KUR ᵁᴿᵁ*Ḫa-at-ti* DINGIR.MEŠ-*eš*
> *ŠA* KUR ᵁᴿᵁ*Ka-aš-ka* DINGIR.MEŠ *ne-e-pí-is te-e-kán* ḪUR.SAG-*eš* ÍD.ḪI.A-*eš*
> *na-at ki-e-da-ni li-in-ki-ya ku-ut-ru-ú-e-ni-iš a-sa-an-du*

> We hereby made an oath. We placed all the gods in assembly: the Sun-God, the Storm-God, the War-god, the Tutelary Deity, the Moon God, Ištar, Išḫara, the Lady of the Oath, the deities of the heaven(s), the deities of the earth, the primeval deities, the deities of the Land of Ḫatti, the deities of the Land of Kaška, the sky, the earth, the mountains, the rivers. Let them be witnesses to this oath!

This text belongs to a type which is peculiar under many respects (cf. GERÇEK 2012: 115–118): *ZABABA*, the War god, appears at the beginning of the list, along with the chief deities, the Sun God, the Storm God, and the Tutelary Deity, and therefore has an otherwise unattested prominent position. The list is placed towards the middle of the text, and it coincides with the end of a section of the agreement. In *CTH* 138.1.A and *CTH* 139 (Middle Hittite), divine witness lists appear near the beginning. Another peculiarity is that in the former Hittite and Kaška gods are invoked and listed separately, though this also happens in the treaties between Šuppiluliuma I and Šattiwaza of Mitanni (*CTH* 51 and 52). This shorter typology of lists is common to a handful of texts connected with the Kaška people (*CTH* 138.1.A, *CTH* 138.1.B, *CTH* 139.1.A, and *CTH* 139.1.B), and schol-

DIVINE WITNESSES IN GREECE AND ANATOLIA

arship is divided as to whether this is an abridged version of the longer type or whether it is its forerunner.[28] In either case, it is notable that heavenly and chthonic gods are mentioned along with cosmic powers, which are never omitted.

The treaty between Tudhaliya I of Hatti with Šunaššura of Kizzuwatna, most of which has come to us in an Akkadian version, also contains a shorter list, but this is in a slightly different format, as the mention of the gods forms an integral part of the curse:

(9) *KBo* 28.110, 80–84 (*CTH* 41.1.1; Akkadian; ed. WILHELM 2011)

> [– – – – *a*]-*wa-at tup-pí an-ni-im e-et-ti-iq*
> [ᵈUTU ᵁᴿᵁ*A-ri-i*]*n-na* ᵈIŠKUR ᵁᴿᵁ*Ḫa-at-ti* ⌜ᵈLAMMA⌝ ᵁᴿᵁ*Ḫa-at-ti*
> [ᵈIŠKUR ᵁᴿᵁ*Ḫa-la*]-*ab* ᵈḪé-bat ᵈENXZU ᵈ⌜*IŠTAR*⌝ ᵈ*ZA-BA₄-BA₄*
> [– – –]x DINGIRᴹᴱˢ *ša* KUR ᵁᴿᵁ*Ḫa-at-ti ù* DINGIRᴹᴱˢ
> [*ša* KUR ᵁᴿᵁ*K*]*i-iz-zu-wa-at-ni ša-mu-ú er-ṣe-tu*[*m*]
> [...]x ḪUR.SAGᴰᴵᴰᴸᴵ.ᴴᴵ.ᴬ *ù* ÍDᴴᴵ.ᴬ NUMUN-*šu šum-šu li-ḫal-li-qú*

> [Whoever] transgresses the words of this tablet, [the sun goddess of Ari]nna, the weather god of Ḫatti, the tutelary deity of Ḫatti, [the Storm-god of Ḫal]ab, Ḫebat, the moon god, Ištar, the God of war, [...] the gods of Ḫatti and the gods of Kizzuwatna, heaven and earth, [...], the mountains and rivers will destroy his seed and his name.

It should be noted that in Hittite texts divine lists are not confined to oaths, but are also found in annals and prayers: famous examples are the gods 'running before' (= helping) Muršili II in battle (*CTH* 61) and the invocation which makes up most of Muwattalli's prayer (*CTH* 381). In the former, the list is much shorter (it only features the Sun-Goddess of Arinna, the Storm-god, Mezzulla—who incidentally never appears in treaties—and all the gods); the latter, instead, seems to reflect the shorter version of lists in treaties, and features, among other deities, mountains and rivers.

These texts reveal that the practice of listing divine witnesses was most diffused among the Hittites. The differences between lists are very likely due to regional variation and local deities, but the structure of divine lists is fixed at least from the times of Šuppiluliuma I. At a later stage, the pantheon was

---

28   Cf. LAROCHE 1974 and GURNEY 1977: 7 fn. 1 respectively. The latter is followed by BARRÉ 1983: 34 ff.

more articulated as new deities were included: this is thought to have happened not through assimilation (as is generally the case in ancient civilisations), but through a process of "agglutination" (as defined by Beckman),[29] which is very peculiar to the Hittites. The intense diplomatic activity of the Hittites, together with their military endeavours, might have helped the diffusion of such a cultural trait in the Near-East, and the impact of treaty-making might have determined its eventual survival in first-millennium languages, both related and unrelated (cf. 1 *supra* and 4 *infra* respectively).

Through a wide range of comparisons, we have seen that our Iliadic passage has a few traits in common with near-Eastern divine lists. At least three common features are present: 1) the Sun is represented as all-seeing; 2) Heaven and Earth are present, and sometimes even coupled; 3) celestial and underworld gods are invoked, along with natural elements, to be witnesses of human oaths. We have also seen that, despite some regional variation, Hittite deity lists in treaties remain rather similar over the centuries, and that they are expanded through an agglutination of new deities instead of being modified by substitution; we might be able to isolate two typologies of lists, a longer one and a shorter one, and the deities that are common to both are interestingly very similar to those mentioned in Γ 276–280.

All of this being said, we also know that similarity does not *per se* point to contact; it will now be a question of establishing whether or not we are able to postulate a common ancestor for these themes. In other words, a search in other Indo-European branches will allow us to determine to what extent this trait might have been inherited from PIE.

5 Reconstruction: A Possible Indo-European Motif?

The fact that sky deities, in particular the Sun, are all-seeing is a well-known PIE motif.[30] In the *Ṛg Veda*, the Sun (which is represented as both Surya and Savitṛ) is said to gaze on the entire world, and is defined as the eye of celestial deities (such as Mitra and Varuṇa).[31] It is defined as *viśvácakṣas-* 'all-gazing' (RV I, 50, 2;

---

29 BECKMAN 2002–2005: 308; cf. also SINGER 1994: 86–87, HUNDLEY 2014: 180, and ALLEN 2015: 72.

30 Cf. WEST 2007 (with references) and DURANTE 1976: 92.

31 RV I, 164, 44c *víśvam éko abhí caṣṭe śácībhir* "gazes upon everything with his powers"; VIII, 25, 16ab *ayám éka itthá purūrú caṣṭe ví viśpátiḥ* "This (Sun) here, as clanlord, gazes widely—the one (gazing) over the many"; VII, 63, 1ac *údveti subhágo viśvácakṣāḥ sádhāraṇaḥ súryo mánuṣāṇām cákṣur mitrásya váruṇasya deváś* "Upward he rises, bringing good fortune and

DIVINE WITNESSES IN GREECE AND ANATOLIA

VII, 63, 1), *vicakṣaṇá-* 'wide-gazing' (*RV* I, 50, 8) and *urucákṣas-* 'having a broad gaze' (*RV* VII, 35, 8; VII, 63, 4) The Indo-European association of the sun with an eye is not only evident from the Vedic evidence (cf. the famous myth of Puruṣa, *RV* X, 90, 13: "From his eye the sun was born"), but also from the etymology of Old Irish *súil-* 'eye', which is generally thought to go back to the 'sun'-word.

The idea of the Sun as the all-seeing god protector of oaths is certainly not residual in Greek culture: in the *Hymn to Demeter*, the eponym goddess goes to Helios (called θεῶν σκοπὸν ἠδὲ καὶ ἀνδρῶν) in order to find out the whereabouts of her daughter Persephone (*HD* 62 ff.); in a later oath in the *Iliad*, Agamemnon swears by Zeus, the Earth, Helios, and the Erinyes (T 258–259); the episode of the cattle of the sun[32] in the *Odyssey* (μ 260 ff.) is an excellent mythical *paradeigma* to show what happens to the transgressors of oaths.

This idea is also found in the non-IE Ancient Near-Eastern world. One example should suffice. In the Sumerian myth of Etana (attested in three different versions—Old Babylonian, Middle Assyrian and "Standard", cf. DALLEY 2008: 189), the eagle and the serpent swear an oath of friendship, calling Shamash, the sun god, as their witness:[33]

(10) Myth of Etana (transl. DALLEY 2008: 191–192)

> (But) come, let us stand up and [make a pledge (?)]
> **Let us swear an oath on [the net of Shamash (?)]**
> **In the presence of Shamash the warrior they swore an oath,**
> Whoever oversteps the limit set by Shamash,
> Shamash shall deliver into the hands of the Smiter for harm
> Whoever oversteps the limit set by Shamash,
> May the mountain keep its pass far away from him,

---

with his gaze on everything, the common support of the sons of Manu—the Sun, the eye of Mitra and Varuṇa"; VI, 51, 1 *údu tyáccakṣurmáhi mitráyoráṁ éti priyáṃ váruṇayorádabdham* "Up goes this great eye of Mitra and of Varuṇa—dear and undeceivable". On the role of Mitra as god of treaties or agreements, cf. ANTHONY 2007, with references.

32   This is a motif shared with Hittite, cf. the explicit mention of the Sun-god's sheep in the Telipinu Myth (*CTH* 324, in particular *KUB* 17.10, iii 3–4); this passage has been given various interpretations (see ARCHI 1993 with reff.), but the presence of the Sun-god's sheep is certain. Parallels of this myth from other cultures are given in PAGE 1972: 82–83 who however does not mention Hittite.

33   In a recent contribution, Hartmut Scharfe argues that the motif of the sun as an overseer comes into Indo-Iranian culture from Mesopotamia (SCHARFE 2016; I wish to thank an anonymous reviewer for pointing this out to me). This hypothesis is certainly fascinating, but it should be weighed against the typological evidence that we are going to see in what follows.

May the prowling weapon make straight for him,
May the snares (on which) the oath to Shamash (is sworn) overturn him
and ensnare him!
When they had sworn the oath on [the net of Shamash (?)]
They stood up (?) and went up the mountain.

One may even go one step further: some of the aforementioned motifs are found in cultures that are unlikely to have derived them from Indo-European models. For instance, as Raffaele Pettazzoni showed, omniscience is an attribute of a wide range of deities across different cultures. In the ancient world, beyond the aforementioned Indo-European and Semitic cultures, one should mention the figure of Ra in Egypt. There are several native American cultures in which the sun is an all-seeing deity: the Pomo people in Northern California, the Meskwaki in the region of the great lakes, the Siksikaitsitapi and Arapaho people, the Lenape people, and the Dakota people (here, the Sun both saw and heard everything). Again, the sun is the eye of Ra for the Egyptians, of the sky-god Ngai for the Masai in Kenya, and of Waqa, whom the Cushitic peoples revere as their supreme god, who also oversees oaths. The Sun is conceived as an eye by the Nuxalk people from British Columbia and by the Matsés (or Mayoruna) people between Peru and Brasil (PETTAZZONI 1955 *passim*). One could go on and find further parallels for other celestial deities who are conceived as omniscient; however, this should be enough to show that the omniscience of the Sun is such a common trait that its presence in two different cultures does not *per se* point to inheritance or contact. Obviously, the co-occurrence of other non-trivial particulars (such as the association with another deity or the presence in a certain context) suggests that the reason for the similarity must be sought in something different from chance.

As for heaven and earth, they are reconstructed for PIE,[34] but at the same time they are a natural couple in many cultures. Vedic provides a parallel to our Greek and Anatolian passages, in that the *ṚgVeda* features them acting as witnesses: (*RV* X, 12, 1ab) *dyā́vā ha kṣā́mā prathamé ṛténa | abhiśrā́vé bhavataḥ satyavā́cā* "Heaven and Earth, who speak what is real, become the first to hear

---

34   For instance, in the *ṚgVeda*, there are six hymns dedicated to *dyā́vapṛthivī́*. They are sometimes referred to as the primordial couple: (*RV* I, 164, 33ab) *dyaúr me pitā́ janitā́ nā́bhir átra bándhur me mātā́ pṛthivī́ mahyám* "Dyaus, my father, my parent, here (is) the relation; this great earth, my mother (is) the relation"; cf. also VII, 53, 2 and X, 65, 8. On Sky, Earth, and related matters see the synthesis (with further literature) of WEST 2007: 166–193; cf. also, most recently, GINEVRA 2019.

DIVINE WITNESSES IN GREECE AND ANATOLIA

in accordance with truth"; (*RV* I, 105, 4e) *vittám me asyá rodasī* "Take heed of this (speech) of mine, you two world-halves".

The call of celestial and underworld deities together with natural elements to be witnesses of human oaths, on the other hand, does not seem to be a universal, or something that can be reconstructed for the proto-culture of Indo-European peoples. Oaths sworn by the sun and other natural elements were certainly not restricted to Greece and Anatolia, but we find no unambiguous correspondences in other branches. One may perhaps cite an overlooked Celtic parallel: we do not know much about oaths in medieval Ireland besides the famous formula *tongu do día toinges mo thúath* "I swear by the gods my people swear by", but it is thought that the pagan inhabitants of Ireland "swore on solemn occasions by the sun, moon, wind, and other elements, the dew, the crops, and the countenances of men" (GINNELL 1917: 129). This *may* point to a primitive concept that was preserved in different branches, but a vague reference to natural elements in oaths is by no way comparable to the highly standardised structures presented above.

Up to this point, we have seen the extent to which our understanding may profit from a more fine-grained analysis of the evidence, even though much of it was already known to scholars interested in the field. It is now time to look at an entirely new piece of evidence, which to my knowledge has never been used in this context. We have said above that the fast-paced progress in Anatolian philology allows us to gain further insights into old issues: this is, in my opinion, a striking example thereof.

6   A Luwian Contribution

A Hieroglyphic Luwian inscription from Tell Ahmar contains a divine list of the type we are used to by now. However, this was not fully understood until very recently because of the unknown phonetic reading of two signs, 𒀭 (*128) and 𒈗 (*30):

(11) TELL AHMAR 6 §2 (late 10th–early 9th c. BCE; ed. HAWKINS 2006: 12 ff.)

> CAELUM (DEUS)TONITRUS-*sa* (DEUS)*ia*-[...] (DEUS)BONUS (DEUS)LUNA
> -*sa* |*á-ta-na* |(PES₂)*tara/i-za-mi-i-sa* (DEUS)SOL-*sa* (DEUS)CERVUS-*sa* ||
> (DEUS)*kar-hu-ha-sa* (DEUS)*ku*+AVIS (DEUS)*hi-pu-da-sa* |EXERCITUS-*la*/
> *i/u-na- si-ha* (DEUS)*sà-us-ka-sa* [(DEUS)]FORTIS-*sa* (DEUS)*SARMA-sa* |
> "CAELUM"-*ti-sa* |"TERRA"-REL+*ra/i-ti-sa-ha* (DEUS)AVIS-*ti-zi* (DEUS)*30-
> *da-ti-zi a-tá* |*ta-sa²-mi-zi* DEUS-*ní-zi* |(LITUUS)*á-za-ta*

... Celestial Tarhunt, [...], the Moongod, the benevolently inclined Sun-God, Runtiya, Karhuha, Kubaba, Hipuda (= Hebat) and Šauska of the Army, Teššub, Šarruma, Heaven and Earth, the divine AVIS-*ti-zi*, the divine *30-*da-ti-zi*, the ... gods loved (me, the first-born child)

In a recent article, Petra Goedegebuure convincingly argued that the two signs should be phonetically read as follows: 𝕏 (*128 = AVIS) = /wa/ and 𝕀𝕛 (*30) = /hapa/ (GOEDEGEBUURE 2019). Not only do the new readings of these signs add two divine names to the list, that is (DEUS)AVIS-*ti-zi* = (DEUS)wa_x-*ti-zi* /wat-tinzi/ 'mountains' and *30-*da-ti-zi* = /hapada^{n}ti^{n}zi/ "riverlands",[35] but they also provide another strikingly similar parallel with the Hittite and Greek passages analysed above ("[...] Heaven and Earth, *the divine mountains, the divine river-lands*").

It must be admitted that this is not an oath, but a celebratory text. However, the similarity with the Hittite materials we have seen does not require much comment, as we have noted how, in Anatolia, divine lists are not exclusively confined to treaties. So, this further parallel corroborates the hypothesis of a cultural motif shared on both sides of the Aegean. But there is more: the implications of this document are important for our understanding of the possible models of our Homeric passage, for both chronological and geographical reasons. Not only did Luwic-speaking populations very likely share this motif in certain types of texts (and this is significant, given the fact that Luwic populations might have been in proximity with the Greeks since the second millennium),[36] but this piece of evidence also gives us the first example of a divine list in a first-millennium Anatolian language. If such a motif survived in Luwic-speaking areas in the first millennium, the possibilities of Greek acquiring this trait are not confined to contact with second-millennium Hittites. It is true that Luwian very probably derived this feature from Hittite culture, though a contemporary influence by West-Semitic languages cannot be discarded *a priori*.

One can go one step further, as there is an additional piece of evidence that, in my opinion, links our Homeric passage to a Luwian *milieu*. As Giorgieri (2001: 441) suggested, that of slaughtering an animal in connection to an oath-swearing is a specifically Luwian practice:[37] this seems to be confirmed by

---

35   According to Goedegebuure, this form is a personifying -*ant*- derivation of (FLUMEN. REGIO)*hapada/i*- (c.) 'riverland', 'valley'.

36   This is the *communis opinio*, but cf. YAKUBOVICH 2010 and 2013 for a different analysis of the linguistic landscape of Western Anatolia; on the possibility of a Greek presence in Cilicia in the Early Iron Age, cf. YAKUBOVICH 2015.

37   An anonymous reviewer reminds me that the practice of sacrificing animals in oath cere-

DIVINE WITNESSES IN GREECE AND ANATOLIA

the Treaty between Arnuwanda I of Hatti and Huhazalma of Arzawa (*CTH* 28; cf. DEVECCHI 2015), which is the only Hittite treaty that attests to the throat-cutting of a sacrificial sheep,[38] and by the Zarpiya ritual (*CTH* 757), where an oath is again associated to animal sacrifice. The explicit mention of a sacrificial victim makes these examples well comparable to Agamemnon's oath, and this further parallel may help us establish more precise co-ordinates for where contact between these cultures could have taken place, especially in light of the western location of Arzawa. The possibility that a Near-eastern trait, which was particularly prominent by the Hittites, reached Greece also thanks to Luwian mediation, becomes more than an idle thought.

7 Conclusions

In this paper, I endeavoured to demonstrate that a well-known passage of the *Iliad* (Γ 276–280) whose Near-Eastern ascendancy is generally agreed upon, is to be specifically traced back to an Indo-European Anatolian *milieu*. This was argued with the support of internal and comparative evidence, and by using a methodology that took into account both the potential of typology, and the limits of cultural reconstruction.

The wealth of near-Eastern parallels to our Homeric passage shows how diffused the motif of divine lists was, but at the same time makes it difficult to pinpoint its diffusion path. A more fine-grained analysis of the Hittite material, however, allowed us to isolate some specific parallels that are not easily attributable to chance. Also, a look at other branches of Indo-European (in particular, the Indo-Iranian one) suggested that some concepts were possibly inherited. For instance, we have seen that celestial deities (the Sun, the Sky, the Earth) acting as witnesses of oaths is both an IE and an ANE motif. However, their co-occurrence in non-trivial contexts in Greek and Anatolian seems to be best attributable to contact. In the Greek passage we have not only a juxtaposition of concepts which seems to be either Indo-European (heaven and earth) or Near-Eastern (celestial and chthonic deities), but we also notice precise correspondences (celestial, underworld deities, *and* natural elements) with Hittite treaties, and now also with a Luwian god list. Not only does this point to the fact that the ὅρκια πιστά in Γ 276–280 have a specifically Anatolian origin (cf. also

---

monies is obviously not confined to Luwian culture, but is also found in other Levantine and Mesopotamian cultures (cf. FARAONE 1993). On this, cf. also DARDANO 2021.

38   There are no divine lists, but this could well be due to the very fragmentary nature of our only manuscript (*KBo* 16.47).

DARDANO 2021), but—if we add some further cultural data, such as the practice of cutting the throat of a sacrificial victim—it could also help us narrow the focus. This opens up the possibility of a Luwian mediation, i.e. of an actual transmission from (or through) Anatolia in the Early Iron Age, which would in turn remove the obstacle of imagining an extremely old tradition surviving the Late Bronze Age collapse in Greece. In this case, it is possible to suggest that the Greek custom described in the *Iliad* originates from Near-Eastern models *through the mediation of Anatolian cultures*, where "Anatolian" is of course meant in a linguistic sense. In order to determine the context in which this transmission might have happened, one would need to bring in further evidence, possibly from other disciplines (such as archaeology); but at this stage it seems reasonable to assume that the ceremonies in which treaties were ratified might have played an important role.[39] Further studies have the potential to support this view.

The wider implication of applying such a method of analysis is that only a case-by-case analysis of this sort will allow us to establish a taxonomy for the phraseology that Greek shares with the Indo-European languages of ancient Anatolia. Such taxonomy must make appropriate distinctions between cases of inheritance, of contact, and of independent developments, and can only be based on studies at the interface between linguistics and philology.

Appendix: Synoptic Table of Deities in Hittite Treaties

1. Treaty between Šuppiluliuma I of Hatti and Huqqana of Hayaša (*CTH* 42)
2. Treaty between Šuppiluliuma I of Hatti and Niqmaddu II of Ugarit (*CTH* 46)
3. Treaty between Šuppiluliuma I of Hatti and Aziru of Amurru (*CTH* 49)

---

39   On the transmission of cultural motifs through ceremonies, cf. Burkert (1992: 68), Karavites—Wren (1992) and Weinfeld (1973; 1990). In more recent times, d'Alfonso (2006: 325–329) suggested that the Hittite-style treaty conventions could have spread to north Syria via treaty-making ceremonies (and vice-versa); cf. also Goedegebuure (2012: 415) on possible Assyrian influence on Hieroglyphic Luwian inscriptions, Quick (2017) on Aramaic and Biblical conditional curses attached to treaties, and LEVINSON—STACKERT 2012 and STEYMANS 2013 (with references) on the possibility of Neo-Assyrian influence in biblical passages such as *Deuteronomy* 28. One should also note that Iron Age Hieroglyphic Luwian inscriptions (such as TOPADA, the re-interpreted KIZILDAĞ 4, and the newly-published TÜRKMEN-KARAHÖYÜK 1; cf. GOEDEGEBUURE et al. 2020) provide indirect evidence for vassal treaties made between a Luwian-speaking ruler and Phrygian populations (cf. D'ALFONSO 2019) and I wish to thank an anonymous reviewer for pointing out this further bibliography to me.

DIVINE WITNESSES IN GREECE AND ANATOLIA

4. Treaty between Šuppiluliuma I of Hatti and Šattiwaza of Mitanni (*CTH* 51) [divine witnesses of Mitanni are not considered here]
5. Oath of Šattiwaza of Mitanni (*CTH* 52)[40]
6. Treaty between Šuppiluliuma I of Hatti and Tette of Nuhashshi (*CTH* 53)
7. Treaty between Muršili II of Hatti and Tuppi-Teššub of Amurru (*CTH* 62)
8. Treaty between Muršili II of Hatti and Niqmepa of Ugarit (*CTH* 66)
9. Treaty between Muršili II of Hatti and Targašnalli of Hapalla (*CTH* 67)
10. Treaty between Muršili II of Hatti and Kupanta-Kuruntya of Mira-Kuwaliya (*CTH* 68)
11. Treaty between Muršili II of Hatti and Manapa-Tarhunta of the Šeha River Land (*CTH* 69)
12. Treaty between Muwattalli II of Hatti and Alakšandu of Wilusa (*CTH* 76)
13. Treaty between Hattušili III of Hatti and Ulmi-Teššub of Tarhuntašša (*CTH* 106.B.II)
14. Treaty between Tudhaliya IV of Hatti and Kuruntya of Tarhuntašša (*CTH* 106.A.1)
15. Treaty between Tudhaliya IV of Hatti and Šaušgamuwa of Amurru (*CTH* 105)
16. Treaty between Arnuwanda I of Hatti (?) and the Kaška people (*CTH* 138.1)
17. Treaty between Arnuwanda I of Hatti (?) and the Kaška people (*CTH* 139)
18. Fragment of a treaty between Šuppiluliuma I of Hatti (?) and a king of Mukši (*CTH* 136)
19. Fragment of a treaty between Šuppiluliuma I of Hatti and Šarri-Kušuh of Karkemiš (*CTH* 50)
20. Fragment of a treaty between Talmi-Teššub of Karkemiš and Šuppiluliuma II of Hatti (*CTH* 122.1)
21. Fragment of a treaty with Kizzuwatna (*CTH* 132)
22. Fragment of a treaty between Hatti and Hayaša (*CTH* 39)
23. Fragment of a treaty between Hatti and Alašiya (*CTH* 141)
24. Treaty between Tudhaliya I of Hatti with Šunaššura of Kizzuwatna

---

40 This text is generally grouped together with treaties, but it shows rather peculiar features: not only is it presented as an edict by Šattiwaza, but also it omits the provision section almost completely. One may find two divine lists, accompanying the blessings and curses sections, which are laid out in two separate sections. The presence of Mitra, Varuna, Indra, and the Nasatyas in the list of deities of Mitanni may be of particular interest to the Indo-Europeanist.

TABLE 1.1   Synoptic table of deities in Hittite treaties

		1	2	3	4	5	6	7	8	9	10	11	12	13	14	15	16	17	18	19	20	21	22	23	24
	Sun-god of Heaven	✓			✓	✓	[✓]	[✓]	[✓]	✓	✓	[✓]	✓	✓	✓		✓	✓					[✓]		
	Sun-goddess of Arinna	✓			✓	✓	[✓]	✓	✓	✓	[✓]	[✓]	✓	✓	✓						[✓]		✓		✓
	Storm-god of Heaven	✓	✓				[✓]	✓	[✓]		✓	✓		✓	✓		✓	✓					[✓]		
	Storm-god of Hatti	✓	✓		✓	✓	✓	✓	[✓]				[✓]	✓	✓						✓		[✓]		✓
	Šeri						[✓]		✓				✓												
	Hurri						[✓]		✓				✓												
	Mount Nanni						[✓]		✓				✓												
	Mount Hazzi						✓		✓				✓												
	Other Storm-gods	✓	✓							✓		✓	✓	✓	✓	✓	✓				✓	✓		✓		✓
	Lulutašši													✓	✓										
	Tutelary deities	✓			✓	✓	✓	✓	✓			✓	✓	✓	✓	✓	✓	✓		✓	✓		✓		✓
	Zithariya	✓			✓	✓			✓			✓				[✓]									
	Karzi	✓			✓	✓			[✓]			✓	✓			[✓]									
	Hapantaliya	✓			✓	✓			✓			✓	✓			[✓]									
Babylonian deities	Allatu	✓					✓	✓	✓			✓	✓			✓									
	Ea				✓	[✓]	✓	✓	✓							✓							✓		

TABLE 1.1   Synoptic table of deities in Hittite treaties (*cont.*)

		1	2	3	4	5	6	7	8	9	10	11	12	13	14	15	16	17	18	19	20	21	22	23	24
Babylonian deities (*cont.*)	Damkina				✓	[✓]																			
	Marduk	✓																							
	Hebat(s)	✓	✓		✓	✓	✓	[✓]	[✓]				✓	✓	✓					✓	✓				✓
	Enki											✓													
	Telipinu(s)				✓	✓	✓	✓	✓			✓				[✓]							✓		
	Pirwa						[✓]		✓			✓													
	Bunene							✓	[✓]							[✓]									
	Aškašepa				✓	[✓]	✓	✓	✓							✓							✓		
	Grain-deity				✓	[✓]																			
Ištar and her attendants	Ištar(s)	✓	✓		✓	[✓]	✓	[✓]	✓				✓	✓	✓	✓	✓	✓			✓		✓		✓
	Ninatta and Kulitta	✓				✓	✓	✓					✓	✓	✓	[✓]									
Protectors of Oaths	Moon God			✓	✓	[✓]	✓	[✓]	✓			✓	✓	✓	✓		✓	✓					✓		✓
	Iššara/Išhara			✓	✓	[✓]	✓	✓	✓			✓	✓	[✓]	✓			✓					✓		
	Nikkal/Ningal		✓										✓	✓									✓		
	Deity of Arusna														✓										
	War-gods	✓			✓	✓	✓	✓	✓			✓	✓	✓	✓	✓	✓	✓			✓				✓
	Yarri				✓	✓	✓	✓	✓			✓	✓	✓	✓	[✓]							✓		

TABLE 1.1　Synoptic table of deities in Hittite treaties (*cont.*)

	1	2	3	4	5	6	7	8	9	10	11	12	13	14	15	16	17	18	19	20	21	22	23	24
Zappana				✓	[✓]	✓	✓	✓			✓	✓	✓	✓	[✓]							✓		
Hasam(m)ili				✓	[✓]																			
Deities of the army	✓																							
Local deities · Hantitaššu of Hurma	✓			✓	✓	✓	✓	✓			✓	✓	✓	✓	[✓]	✓						✓		
Abara/Ayabara of Šamuha	✓			✓	[✓]	✓	✓	[✓]		[✓]	✓	✓	✓	✓	[✓]	✓						✓		
Katahha of Ankuwa	✓			✓	[✓]	✓	✓	✓			✓	✓	✓	✓	✓[a]	✓						✓		
The Queen of Katapa	✓			✓	✓	✓	✓	✓			✓	✓	✓		✓	✓			✓	✓		✓		
Ammamma of Tahurpa	✓			✓	✓	✓	✓	[✓]			✓	✓	✓	✓	✓							✓		
Huwaššanna of Hupišna	✓		✓	✓	✓	✓	✓	[✓]		✓	✓	✓	✓	✓	✓				✓[b]		✓	✓		
Tapišuwa of Ishupitta			[✓]			✓	✓	✓							[✓]						[✓]			
Hallara of Dunna	✓			✓	✓	✓	✓	✓		✓	✓	✓	✓	✓	✓							✓		
the Lady of Landa			[✓]	✓	[✓]	✓	✓	✓							[✓]						✓			

a　Here spelled ⟨Hatagga⟩.
b　Here I have followed Singer 2001: 638–640, but I wonder if, on the basis of *CTH* 122.1 (also with Karkamiš),
　　one should reconstruct "The Tutelary deity of Huwaššanna" instead of "Huwaššanna of Hupišna".

TABLE 1.1   Synoptic table of deities in Hittite treaties (*cont.*)

		1	2	3	4	5	6	7	8	9	10	11	12	13	14	15	16	17	18	19	20	21	22	23	24
Local deities (*cont.*)	Kuniyawanni of Landa			✓	✓	✓	✓	✓	✓							✓						✓			
	Nin-šenšen of Kinza			✓			✓	✓	✓													✓			
	lulaḫḫi and *ḫapiru* gods															✓	✓					✓	✓		
Mountains	Mount Lebanon			✓			✓	✓	✓							[✓]						✓			
	Mount Šariyana / Šariššiya			[✓]			✓	✓	✓							[✓]						✓			
	Mount Pišaiša			[✓]			✓	✓	[✓]							✓						✓			
Deities of the Underworld	Ereshkigal / Sun-goddess of the Earth	✓		[✓]		✓	✓	[✓]	✓		✓	✓				[✓]	✓		✓			✓	✓		
	Lelwani				✓	[✓]								✓	✓		✓						✓		
Primeval deities	Nara			✓	✓	✓	✓	✓	✓		[✓]	✓	✓			[✓]			✓			✓			
	Namšara			✓	✓	[✓]	✓	✓	✓		✓	✓	✓			[✓]			✓			✓			
	Minki/Munki			✓	✓	[✓]	✓	[✓]	✓		✓	✓	✓			[✓]			✓			✓			
	Tuhuši			[✓]	✓	[✓]	✓	✓	[✓]		[✓]	[✓]	✓			[✓]			✓			✓			
	Ammunki			[✓]	✓	[✓]	✓	✓	[✓]		[✓]	✓	✓			✓			✓			[✓]			
	Ammizzadu			[✓]	✓	✓	✓	✓	[✓]		[✓]	✓	✓			[✓]			✓			✓			
	Alalu			✓	✓	✓	✓	✓	✓		✓	✓	✓			[✓]			✓			✓			

TABLE 1.1   Synoptic table of deities in Hittite treaties (*cont.*)

		1	2	3	4	5	6	7	8	9	10	11	12	13	14	15	16	17	18	19	20	21	22	23	24
Primeval deities (*cont.*)	Anu			[✓]	✓	✓	✓	✓	✓		✓	✓				[✓]			✓			[✓]			
	Antu			✓	✓	[✓]	✓	✓	✓		[✓]	✓				[✓]			✓			[✓]			
	Apantu			[✓]			✓	✓	[✓]		[✓]					[✓]			✓			✓			
	Enlil			[✓]	✓	[✓]	✓	✓	[✓]		[✓]	✓	✓			✓						✓			
	Ninlil			[✓]	✓	✓	✓	✓	[✓]		✓	✓	✓			✓						✓			
	Bēlet-ekalli				✓	✓																			
	Kumarbi										✓	✓	✓												
	mountain-dweller gods	✓		✓	✓	✓	✓	✓	✓		✓	✓	✓	✓	✓										
	mercenary gods	✓		✓	✓	✓	✓	✓	✓		✓	✓	✓	✓	✓										
	all deities of Hatti	✓																							✓
	deities of heaven	✓																✓						✓	
	deities of the earth	✓																✓							
Natural elements	male deities			✓	✓	✓	✓	✓	✓		✓	✓	✓	✓	✓	✓			✓			✓	✓		
	female deities			[✓]	✓	[✓]	✓	✓	✓		✓	✓	✓	✓	✓	✓			✓			✓	✓		
	mountains	✓		✓	✓	[✓]	✓	✓	✓		✓	[✓]	✓	✓	✓			✓				✓			✓
	rivers	[✓]		✓	✓	[✓]	✓	✓	✓		✓	[✓]	✓	✓	✓			✓				✓			✓
	springs	[✓]		✓			✓	✓	✓		✓	✓	✓	✓	✓							✓	✓		

TABLE 1.1   Synoptic table of deities in Hittite treaties (*cont.*)

		1	2	3	4	5	6	7	8	9	10	11	12	13	14	15	16	17	18	19	20	21	22	23	24
Natural elements (*cont.*)	the Tigris					[✓]																			
	the Euphrates				✓	[✓]																			
	the (great) sea	✓		[✓]	✓		✓	✓	✓		[✓]	✓	✓	✓	✓		✓					✓	✓		
	heaven and earth	✓		[✓]	✓	✓	✓	✓	✓		[✓]	✓	✓		✓		✓	✓		✓	✓				✓
	winds			[✓]	✓	✓	✓	✓	[✓]		[✓]	✓	✓												
	clouds	✓		[✓]	✓	✓	✓	✓	✓		✓	✓	✓												

The following deities do not appear in the table:

In *CTH* 76 Mount Hulla, Mount Zaliyanu, Mount Taha, all [the deities] of the land of Wiluša, and]*appaliuna*, the underground watercourse (?) of the land of Wiluša

In *CTH* 138.1 Huwattašši (Kaskean deity)

In *CTH* 139.1 the primeval deities (just cited as a cover term)

In *CTH* 50 the gods of Karkamiš, Kubaba, Karkuhiš ... *Taruppašani.*

In *CTH* 122.1 Ku[baba, K]arḫuḫi

In *CTH* 39 ... Š]amniwa; ⌜Nergal⌝ of Hayaša, Ištar of Patteu[...]annu of Lahirhila, Zagg[a ...]arniya, Tarumu of Kam? [... the Storm-god?] of Pahhuteya. Terittuni of the plain? of Arhita, Baltaik of Tukamana, Unagašta of Parray[a], [...]huhu of Gašmiyaha, Šil[...]

In *CTH* 41.I.1 the gods of the Land of Kizzuwatna

References

ALLEN, SPENCER L. 2015, *The Splintered Divine A Study of Ištar, Baal, and Yahweh Divine Names and Divine Multiplicity in the Ancient Near East*, Boston/Berlin/Munich: de Gruyter.

ANTHONY, DAVID W. 2007, *The Horse, the Wheel, and Language: How Bronze-Age Riders from the Eurasian Steppes Shaped the Modern World*, Princeton: Princeton University Press.

ARCHI, ALFONSO 1993, *Kamrušepa and the Sheep of the Sun-God*, "Orientalia" 62/4: 404–409.

BACHVAROVA, MARY R. 2016, *From Hittite to Homer. The Anatolian Background of Ancient Greek Epic*, Cambridge: Cambridge University Press.

BARRÉ, MICHAEL L. 1983, *The God-List in the Treaty between Hannibal and Philip V of Macedonia: a study in Light of the Ancient Near Eastern Treaty Tradition*, Baltimore: Johns Hopkins University Press.

BECKMAN, GARY M. 1999, *Hittite Diplomatic Texts*, Atlanta: Scholars Press.

BECKMAN, GARY M. 2002–2005, *Pantheon. A. II. Bei den Hethitern*, "RlA" 10/3–4: 308–316.

BIANCONI, MICHELE 2015, *Contatti greco-anatolici e Sprachbund egeo-micrasiatico. Stato della ricerca e nuove prospettive*, "Archivio Glottologico Italiano" 100/2:129–178.

BIANCONI, MICHELE 2020, *Some thoughts on Anatolian Lexicon in Mycenaean Greek*, in R. Garnier (ed.), *Loanwords and Substrata*, Innsbruck: Institut für Vergleichende Sprachwissenschaft der Universität Innsbruck: 63–88.

BIANCONI, MICHELE 2021, *There and Back Again: a Hundred Years of Graeco-Anatolian*

Comparative Linguistics, in M. Bianconi (ed.), *Linguistic and Cultural Interactions between Greece and Anatolia: in Search of the Golden Fleece*, Leiden: Brill: 8–39.

BOWIE, ANGUS M. 2019, *Iliad. Book III*, Cambridge: Cambridge University Press.

BRYCE, TREVOR R. 1999, *Anatolian Scribes in Mycenaean Greece*, "Historia" 48: 257–264.

BURKERT, WALTER 1991, *Homerstudien und Orient*, in J. Latacz (ed.), *Zweihundert Jahre Homer-Forschung. Rückblick und Ausblick*, Stuttgart/Leipzig: de Gruyter: 155–181.

BURKERT, WALTER 1992, *The Orientalizing Revolution: Near Eastern Influence on Greek Culture in the Early Archaic Age*, trans. by M.E. Pinder and W. Burkert, Cambridge (Mass.)/London: Harvard University Press.

BURKERT, WALTER 2004[2], *Die Griechen und der Orient. Von Homer bis zu den Magiern*, München: C.H. Beck Verlag.

BURKERT, WALTER 2005, *Near Eastern connections*, in J.M. Foley (ed.), *A Companion to Ancient Epic*, Oxford: Blackwell: 291–301.

CAMPANILE, ENRICO 1979, *Meaning and prehistory of Old Irish* cú glas, "Journal of Indo-European Studies" 7/3–4: 237–247.

CHRISTIANSEN, BIRGIT 2012, *Schicksalsbestimmende Kommunikation. Sprachliche, gesellschaftliche und religiöse Aspekte hethitischer Fluch-, Segens- und Eidesformeln*, Wiesbaden: Harrassowitz Verlag.

COTTICELLI-KURRAS, PAOLA—GIUSFREDI, FEDERICO 2018, *Ancient Anatolian languages and cultures in contact: some methodological observations*, "JLR" 16/3–4: 172–193.

D'ALFONSO, LORENZO 2006, *Die hethitische Vertragstradition in Syrien (14.–12. Jh. v. Chr.)*, in M. Witte—K. Schmid—D. Prechel—J.C. Gertz (eds.), *Die deuteronomistischen Geschichtswerke: Redaktions- und religionsgeschichtliche Perspektiven zur „Deuteronomismus"-Diskussion in Tora und Vorderen Propheten*, Berlin/New York: de Gruyter: 303–329.

D'ALFONSO, LORENZO 2019, *War in Anatolia in the post-Hittite period: The Anatolian Hieroglyphic inscription of Topada revised*, "Journal of Cuneiform Studies" 71: 133–152.

DALLEY, STEPHANIE 2008, *Myths from Mesopotamia. Creation, the flood, Gilgamesh, and others*, Oxford: Oxford University Press.

DARDANO, PAOLA 2013, *Lingua omerica e fraseologia anatolica: vecchie questioni e nuove prospettive*, in M. Mancini—L. Lorenzetti (eds.), *Le lingue del Mediterraneo antico. Culture, mutamenti, contatti*, Roma: Carocci: 125–150.

DARDANO, PAOLA 2021, *Homeric covenantal terminology and its Near Eastern forerunners*, in M. Bianconi (ed.), *Linguistic and Cultural Interactions between Greece and the Ancient Near East: in Search of the Golden Fleece*, Leiden: Brill: 40–79.

DEL MONTE, GIUSEPPE 2003, *Antologia della letteratura ittita*, Pisa: Servizio Editoriale Universitario di Pisa.

DEVECCHI, ELENA 2015, *Trattati internazionali ittiti*, Brescia: Paideia Editrice.

DURANTE, MARCELLO 1976, *Sulla preistoria della tradizione poetica greca. Parte seconda: risultanze della comparazione indoeuropea*, Roma: Edizioni dell'Ateneo.

FARAONE, CHRISTOPHER 1993, *Molten wax, spilt wine and mutilated animals: sympathetic magic in Near Eastern and Early Greek oath ceremonies*, "JHS" 113: 60–80.

FRIEDRICH, J. 1930, *Staatsverträge des Hatti-Reiches in hethitischer Sprache*, Leipzig: J.C. Hinrichs'sche.

GARCÍA RAMÓN, JOSÉ LUIS 2011, *Sprachen in Kontakt in Griechenland und Kleinasien im 2. Jahrtausend v. Chr.*, "ZSM-Studien" 4: 23–45.

GARCÍA RAMÓN, JOSÉ LUIS 2012, *Eredità, prestiti, mutamenti comuni nel lessico e nella morfosintassi delle lingue indoeuropee: il caso di anatolico e greco*, "SILTA" 41/3: 425–439.

GASBARRA, VALENTINA—POZZA, MARIANNA 2012, *Fenomeni di interferenza greco-anatolica nel II millennio A.C.: l'ittito come mediatore tra mondo indoeuropeo e mondo non indoeuropeo*, "AION" 1 (n.s.): 165–214.

GASBARRA, VALENTINA—POZZA, MARIANNA 2019, *Percorsi lessicali nel Mediterraneo orientale antico*, Alessandria: Edizioni dell'Orso.

GERÇEK, NEBAHAT İ. 2012, *The Kaška and the Northern Frontier of Ḫatti*, Doctoral Thesis, University of Michigan.

GINEVRA, RICCARDO 2019, *Indo-european Cosmology and Poetics: Cosmic Merisms in Comparative and Cognitive Perspective*, "Archivio Glottologico Italiano" 104/1: 5–17.

GINNELL, LAURENCE 1917[3], *The Brehon laws: a legal handbook*, Glasgow: P.J. O'Callaghan.

GIORGIERI, MAURO 2001, *Aspetti magico-religiosi del giuramento presso gli Ittiti e i Greci*, in S. Ribichini—M. Rocchi—P. Xella (eds.), *La questione delle influenze vicino-orientali sulla religione greca. Stato degli studi e prospettiva della ricerca. Atti del colloquio internazionale—Roma, 22–24 maggio 1999*, Roma: Consiglio Nazionale delle Ricerche: 421–440.

GOEDEGEBUURE, PETRA—VAN DEN HOUT, THEO P.J.—OSBORNE, JAMES F.—MASSA, MICHELE—BACHHUBER CRISTOPH—ŞAHIN, FATMA 2020, *TÜRKMEN-KARAHÖYÜK I: A new Hieroglyphic Luwian inscription from Great King Hartapu, son of Mursili, conqueror of Phrygia*, "Anatolian Studies" 70: 29–43.

GOEDEGEBUURE, PETRA 2012, *Hittite iconoclasm: Disconnecting the icon, disempowering the referent*, in N. May (ed.), *Iconoclasm and Text Destruction in the Ancient Near East and Beyond*, Chicago, Illinois: The Oriental Institute of the University of Chicago: 407–452.

GOEDEGEBUURE, PETRA 2019, *The Hieroglyphic Luwian signs* *128 (*AVIS 'bird'*) = wa_x *and* *30 = *HAPA*, in A. Süel (ed.) *Acts of the IXth International Congress of Hittitology, Çorum 08–14 September 2014*, Ankara: T.C. Çorum Valiliğ: 295–316.

GURNEY, OLIVER 1977, *Some aspects of Hittite religion*, Oxford: Oxford University Press.

HAJNAL, IVO 2014, *Die griechisch-anatolischen Sprachkontakte zur Bronzezeit—Sprachbund oder loser Sprachkontakt?*, "Linguarum Varietas" 3: 105–116.

HAJNAL, IVO 2018, *Graeco-Anatolian Contacts in the Mycenaean Period*, in M.A. Fritz—J. Klein et al. (eds.), *Comparative Indo-European Linguistics. An International Handbook of Language Comparison and the Reconstruction of Indo-European*, Berlin: de Gruyter: 2036–2055.

HAWKINS, J. DAVID 2006, *The Inscription*, in G. Bunnens—J.D. Hawkins—I. Leirens (eds.), *Tell Ahmar 11. A New Luwian Stele and the Cult of the Storm-God at Til Barsib-Masuwari*, Louvain/Paris/Dudley: Peeters: 11–31.

HAWKINS, SHANE 2010, *Greek and the Languages of Asia Minor*, in E.J. Bakker (ed.), *A Companion to the Ancient Greek Language*, Chichester/Malden (MA): Wiley-Blackwell: 213–227.

HÖGEMANN, PETER 2003, *Das ionische Griechentum und seine altanatolische Umwelt im Spiegel Homers*, in M. Witte—S. Alkier (eds.), *Die Griechen und der Vordere Orient: Beiträge zum Kultur- und Relgionskontakt zwischen Griechenland und dem Vorderen Orient im 1. Jahrtausend v. Chr.*, Göttingen: Vandenhoeck & Ruprecht: 1–24.

HUNDLEY, MICHAEL B. 2014, *The God Collectors: Hittite Conceptions of the Divine*, "AoF" 41/2: 176–200.

KARAVITES, PETER—WREN, THOMAS E. 1992, *Promise-Giving and Treaty-Making: Homer and the Near East*, Leiden/New York/Cologne: Brill.

KESTEMONT, GUY 1976, *Le panthéon des instruments hittites de droit public*, "Orientalia" 45: 147–177.

KITCHEN, KENNETH A.—LAWRENCE, PAUL J.N. 2012, *Treaty, Law and Covenant in the Ancient Near East*, Wiesbaden: Harrassowitz.

KRETSCHMER, PAUL 1924, *Alakšanduš könig von Viluša*, "Glotta" 13: 205–213.

LAROCHE, EMMANUEL 1974, *Les dénominations des dieux 'antiques' dans le textes hittites*, in K. Bittel et al. (eds), *Anatolian Studies Presented to Hans Gustav Güterbock on the occasion of his 65th birthday*, Istanbul: Nederlands Historisch-Archaeologisch Instituut in het Nabije Oosten: 175–185.

LATACZ, JOACHIM 2004, *Troy and Homer. Towards a solution of an old mystery*, Oxford: Oxford University Press.

LAZZERONI, ROMANO 1987, *L'organizzazione del lessico indeuropeo: etimologia e ideologia*, "ASGM" 28: 1–13.

LAZZERONI, ROMANO 1989, *Per l'etimologia di ὅρκος: una testimonianza ittita*, "SSL" 29: 87–94.

LAZZERONI, ROMANO 1998, *La cultura indoeuropea*, Roma: Laterza.

LEVINSON, BERNARD M.—STACKERT, JEFFREY 2012, *Between the Covenant Code and Esarhaddon's succesion treaty: Deuteronomy 13 and the composition of Deuteronomy*, "Journal of Ancient Judaism" 3: 123–140.

LIVERANI, MARIO 1967, *La preistoria dell'epiteto 'Yahweh ṣĕbā'ōt'*, "AION" 17: 331–334.

LUCKENBILL, DANIEL D. 1911, *A Possible Occurrence of the Name Alexander in the Boghaz-Keuei Tablets*, "CP" 6: 85–86.

Melchert, H. Craig 2014a, *Greek and Lycian*, in G. Giannakis (ed.), *Encyclopedia of Ancient Greek Language and Linguistics*, vol. II, Leiden/Boston: Brill: 67–70.

Melchert, H. Craig 2014b, *Greek and Lydian*, in G. Giannakis (ed.), *Encyclopedia of Ancient Greek Language and Linguistics*, vol. II, Leiden/Boston: Brill: 70–71.

Metcalf, Christopher 2015, *The Gods Rich in Praise. Early Greek and Mesopotamian Religious Poetry*, Oxford: Oxford University Press.

Nenci, Giuseppe 1961, *Gli dei testimoni nei trattati ittiti e in Γ 280*, "PP" 16: 381–382.

Page, Denys 1972, *Folktales in Homer's Odyssey. The Carl Newell Jackson Lectures*, Cambridge (MA): Harvard University Press.

Pettazzoni, Raffaele 1955, *L'onniscienza di Dio*, Torino: Einaudi.

Puhvel, Jaan 1991, *Homer and Hittite*, Innsbruck: Institut für Sprachwissenschaft der Universität Innsbruck.

Quick, Laura 2017, *Deuteronomy 28 and the Aramaic Curse Tradition*, Oxford: Oxford University Press.

Rollinger, Robert 2004a, *Die Verschriftlichung von Normen: Einflüsse und Elemente orientalischer Kulturtechnik in den homerischen Epen, dargestellt am Beispiel des Vertragswesens*, in R. Rollinger—C. Ulf (edd.), *Griechische Archaik: interne Entwicklungen, externe Impulse*, Berlin: Akademie Verlag: 369–425.

Rollinger, Robert 2004b, *Hethiter, Homer und Anatolien. Erwägungen zu Il. 3, 300f. und KUB XIII Nr. 3, III 1f.*, "Historia" 53/1: 1–21.

Rutherford, Ian 2020, *Hittite Texts and Greek Religion. Contact, Interaction, and Comparison*, Oxford: Oxford University Press.

Scharfe, Hartmut 2016, *Ṛgveda, Avesta, and beyond—ex occidente lux?*, "Journal of the American Oriental Society" 136: 47–67.

Schwemer, Daniel 2006, *Das hethitische Reichspantheon. Überlegungen zu Struktur und Genese*, in R.G. Kratz—H. Spieckmann (eds.), *Götterbilder, Gottesbilder, Weltbilder. Polytheismus und Monotheismus in der Welt der Antike*, Tübingen: Mohr Siebeck: 241–265.

Singer, Itamar 1994, *'The Thousand Gods of Hatti': The Limits of an Expanding Pantheon*, in I. Alon—I. Gruenwald—I. Singer (eds.), *Concepts of the Other in Near Eastern Religions*, Leiden: Brill: 81–102.

Steymans, Hans U. 2013, *Deuteronomy 28 and Tell Tayinat*, "Verbum et Ecclesia" 34/2: 1–13.

Watkins, Calvert 1986, *The Language of the Trojans*, in M.J. Mellink (ed.), *Troy and the Trojan War. A Symposium Held at Bryn Mawr College October 1984*, Bryn Mawr: Bryn Mawr College: 45–62.

Watkins, Calvert 1995, *How to Kill a Dragon. Aspects of Indo-European Poetry*, Oxford: Oxford University Press.

Weinfeld, Moshe 1973, *Covenant terminology in the ancient Near East and its influence on the West*, "Journal of the American Oriental Society" 93: 190–199.

WEINFELD, MOSHE 1990, *The Common Heritage of Covenantal Traditions in the Ancient World*, in L. Canfora—M. Liverani—C. Zaccagnini (eds.), *I trattati nel mondo antico: forma ideologia funzione*, Roma: L'Erma di Bretschneider: 175–191.

WEST, MARTIN L. 1997, *The East Face of Helicon: West Asiatic Elements in Greek Poetry and Myth*, Oxford: Oxford University Press.

WEST, MARTIN L. 2007, *Indo-European Poetry and Myth*, Oxford: Oxford University Press.

WILHELM, GERNOT 2011, *hethiter.net/: CTH 41.1.1.*

YAKUBOVICH, ILYA 2010, *Sociolinguistics of the Luvian Language*, Leiden/Boston: Brill.

YAKUBOVICH, ILYA 2013, *Anatolian Names in -wiya and the Structure of Empire Luwian Onomastics*, in A. Mouton—I. Rutherford—I. Yakubovich (eds.), *Luwian Identities. Culture, Language and Religion Between Anatolia and the Aegean*, Leiden/Boston: Brill: 87–123.

YAKUBOVICH, ILYA 2015, *Phoenician and Luwian in Early Iron Age Cilicia*, "Anatolian Studies" 65: 35–53.

YOSHIDA, DAISUKE 1996, *Untersuchungen zu den Sonnengottheiten bei den Hethitern*, Heidelberg: Winter.

CHAPTER 2

Achaemenid Elamite and Old Persian Indefinites: A Comparative View

Juan E. Briceño Villalobos

Para J.A. y E.

∴

1 Elamite and Semitic Languages[*]

Elamite is an isolate, non-Indo-European language that was spoken in southwestern Iran at least between the 23rd and the 4th century BCE. It is an agglutinative language with a cuneiform script that represents an adaptation of the Sumero-Akkadian script.[1] Its first textual evidence is the Treaty of Narām-Sîn (EKI 2) dated around 2260–2223 BCE[2] and more texts of inscriptional nature continue to be present in southern Iran off and on until the beginning of the Achaemenid period. Old Elamite (ca. 2600–1500 BCE) and Neo-Elamite (ca. 1000–540 BCE) texts are badly documented. On the contrary, Middle Elamite (ca. 1500–1000 BCE) and Achaemenid Elamite (ca. 550–330 BCE) are better attested. While the former is usually taken as the classical period of the language, the latter—mainly found in two distinct registers: Royal Inscriptions and administrative archive—represents a partially restructured variety of Middle and Neo-Elamite carried out by Iranian scribes, as can be observed in its

---

[*] This research has been funded by the Agencia Nacional de Investigación y Desarrollo (ANID), Chile, Fondecyt de Postdoctorado 2021, Proyecto N° 3210689.

[1] This must have been developed already by the middle of the 3rd millennium BCE.

[2] Narām-Sîn was an Akkadian king, grandson of king Sargon of Akkad. Scholars have proposed that the actual Elamite king behind this treaty is king Helu or king Hita of the Awan dynasty. Moreover, most recently, it has been announced that Linear Elamite has been deciphered by François Desset along with four collaborators, Kambiz Tabibzadeh, Mathieu Kervran, Gian Pietro Basello, and Gianni Marchesi. This first phonetic script would have been devised by the 22nd century BCE—by the time of Puzur-Inšušinak, the last king of the Awan dynasty—and it would have run parallel to the cuneiform script borrowed from Mesopotamia. It has been suggested that this script might be a continuation of the still undeciphered Proto-Elamite script created by the end of the 4th millennium BCE.

© JUAN E. BRICEÑO VILLALOBOS, 2022 | DOI:10.1163/9789004508828_004

grammatical peculiarities in comparison to previous stages of the language. It must be taken into account that Achaemenid Elamite was not the sole administrative language of the Achaemenids: above all stands Imperial Aramaic, the most important administrative language of the empire, and, to a lesser extent, Achaemenid Babylonian (Late Akkadian), both being of the Semitic linguistic family.

It must also be kept in mind that the Achaemenid Royal Inscriptions are trilingual: Achaemenid Elamite (AE), Old Persian (OP), and Achaemenid Babylonian (AB). In the case of the Bīsotūn Inscription (DB), the most important and longest of all Achaemenid Royal Inscriptions, also includes an Aramaic version found in Elephantine, Egypt. Throughout this paper, I will make constant reference to the Semitic data gathered from the Royal Inscriptions, concretely from Achaemenid Babylonian (ca. 600 BCE–100 CE) and Imperial Aramaic (ca. 700–200 BCE), as long as this material provides valuable information regarding the morphology employed in the AE and OP versions.

Finally, I must point out that it has been admittedly established that the order of redaction of the three versions found in the Royal Inscriptions is as follows: Old Persian > Achaemenid Elamite > Achaemenid Babylonian. This is particularly clear in the case of the AE text, since it follows the OP syntax, with a lot of loans and calques. As opposed to the rest of the Royal Inscriptions, however, DB is a particular case, since the first version to be carved into the rock was the AE text. Hence, the OP version should have followed the AE version, although recent studies suggest that the AE version in DB would have been after an uninscribed OP version that has not come to us.

2　The Typology of Indefinites

Before embarking upon the analysis of OP and AE indefinites, I will briefly explain the linguistic typology behind my survey in the following sections. As we know, negative polarity items (HASPELMATH 1997: 33 ff.) and free-choice items (GIANNAKIDOU 2001) are two types of indefinite pronouns widely attested in the world languages.[3] On the one hand, NPIs are only licensed by non-veridical semantic operators such as negation, conditionals, interrogatives, and standard of comparison, whereas FCIs are polarity items that, being

---

3　Giannakidou (1998: 17) defines polarity as an item α that is an expression whose distribution is limited to sensitivity to some semantic property β of a context c of appearance. Most scholars nowadays take polarity as a type of semantic deficit or semantic dependency. Cf. GIANNAKIDOU—ZEIJLSTRA 2017.

of a non-episodic nature, are only grammatical in contexts providing multiple alternatives, worlds, or situations. In this regard, FCIs represent the highest levels of indefiniteness. The most typical environments that can trigger their presence are sentences that express possibility or permission (imperatives), sentences that can be interpreted generically, hypothetical and counterfactual sentences, or sentences expressing sufficient conditions, habituals, future sentences, modals verbs, etc. (HASPELMATH 1997: 48). See Table 2.1 for examples. There are mainly two types of FC indefinites: nominal and relative,[4] cf. HORN 2000: 71–107. The latter type is overly marked by domain-widening particles, such as English *-ever*, which are in charge of enhancing the expression of a wide range of possibilities, closely resembling the x alternatives displayed by nominal FC semantics. One of the most important features of FC indefinites is that they tend to avoid negative and interrogative contexts (unless non-episodic). As concerns *irrealis* indefinites, these are also non-specific as NPIs and FCI and they are, normally licensed by the future sentences, non-indicative modality, 'want' contexts habitual events, imperatives, etc. (HASPELMATH 1997: 40 ff.). In English, this type of indefinite is also rendered by the 'some'-series. Finally, existential quantifiers, which represent the lowest levels of indefiniteness, are indefinites only licensed by veridical/specific semantic contexts that refer to a speaker who presupposes the existence and unique identifiability of its referent (HASPELMATH 1997: 37 ff.). In relation with the knowledge of the speaker conveyed by these indefinites, he may (known) or may not (unknown) be able to identify the referent of the indefinite pronoun (HASPELMATH 1997: 45 ff.).

In the following sections, I will examine to what extent Old Persian relies on these types of indefinites, which follow distinct diachronic developments into Middle Persian, and how Achaemenid Elamite mirrors, in many ways, Old Iranian morphology.

---

4   In this paper, relative FC formations entail both non-specific free-relative clauses (*I will give you whatever you want*), which fill a functional slot within the main clause, and concessive conditionals (*Whatever it is, I will go*). Within the latter type, relative-correlative constructions "whoever ....he/that/this" would be included. As far as early IE languages are concerned, both types of FC indefinite relative clauses share the same morphology. For their morphological as well as semantic affinities, cf. HASPELMATH 1997: 135–136, HASPELMATH—KÖNIG 1998: 557, 606–608. In turn, in their assessment of *wh-ever* FCIs, Cheng—Giannakidou (2006: 155–156) conclude that FC relative clauses are actually definite by nature and that they lack polarity sensitivity due to the fact that they are licensed in episodic contexts, unlike nominal FCIs. Despite the validity of this assertion, I will not take into account in this paper this difference between nominal and relative FC indefinites.

ACHAEMENID ELAMITE AND OLD PERSIAN INDEFINITES 51

TABLE 2.1   The typology of indefinite pronouns

Negative polarity items (NPIS)	NEG	*I don't see **anything** on that room.*
	COND	*If **anyone** sees that, let me know.*
	INTERR	*Have you seen **anything** lately?*
	COMP	*He is faster than **anyone** else in this trial.*
Free-choice items (FCIS)	NOMINAL	*Pick up **any** card you want.* ***Anyone** can do that with the right motivation.*
	RELATIVE	*You can hire **whichever** person you see fit.* ***Whoever** pushes the bottom, he must do it now.* ***Whatever** happens, just go!*
Irrealis (IRR)		***Someone** will come to the party.* *He wants to encounter **someone** with the right attitude.* *Find me **something** that I can actually wear.*
Existential quantifiers (EQ)	unknown	*Yesterday, I think I saw **someone** of your friends, but I could not see who he was exactly.*
	known	*I have bought **something** I know you are going to like.*

3   OP *kašci* NPI/FC: MP *kas-iz* NPI and ME *akkar* NPI: AE *akkar* NPI "anyone"[5]

In principle, OP *kašci* is an animate NPI indefinite mainly attested under the scope of negation. In origin, OP *kašci*, similarly to its Indo-Iranian cognates,

---

5   I will leave for another occasion the discussion of some other attested OP and AE interrogative-indefinite formations, universal quantifiers, and polarity items such as OP *ciyā-karam* "what kind, how many" (AE *appa hamak*), OP *ada-kaị* "then, at that time" (AE *hamer*), OP *citā* "so long", AE *marrita* "all, entire", AE *appan* "ever, someday" (*EW*: 72, TAVERNIER 2018: 432), AE *unra* "each" (GRILLOT-SUSINI 2008: 56), and AE *lurika* "each" (STOLPER 2004: 77).

OAv/YAv. *kascit̰* $_{\text{FC/UNI}}$ and Ved. *káś cid* $_{\text{FC}}$, must have been a nominal FC indefinite "any", a compound of the interrogative-indefinite stem IIr. **ká-* plus the scalar focus particle IIr. **čid*.[6] It is cross-linguistically common to encounter such scalar/additive focus particles (e.g. "also, and, even") functioning as domain-widening particles along with the interrogative-indefinite stem: as shown by König (1991: 64–66) and Haspelmath (1997: 157–164), this is a very prolific strategy among the world languages for the creation of FC indefinites.[7] As we know, among early IE languages, PIE **-kʷe* also operates as a domain-widening particle together with the interrogative-indefinite stem: e.g. Lat. *quisque* and Goth. *ƕazuh*.[8] In this manner, both PIE **-kʷid* and **-kʷe* overtly mark the scalar endpoint of IE interrogatives, transforming the latter into FC indefinites.[9]

However, Indo-Iranian has modified the semantics of this inherited FC indefinite: it has turned it either into a distributive/universal pronoun "each, everyone" (Old/Young Avestan and Old Persian) or into an NPI indefinite "any" (Old Persian and Classical Sanskrit).[10] The former development is said to consist in the semantic change from a FC indefinite into a distributive/universal quantifier. Cf. Haspelmath (1997: 154–156). I take this distributive/universal reading to be derived from the FC semantics assumed by the interrogative stem along

---

6   Lubotsky—de Vaan (2011: 201) translate OP *kašci* and OP *cišci* as FC indefinites "whoever" and "whatever" respectively. In this section and in the next, I will show that there is a more fine-grained distinction at play within the indefinite frame, concretely between FC and NPI uses of these indefinites.

7   In Sabellian *-pid* (Osc. *pispid*), we find another instance of PIE **-kʷid* operating as a domain-widening particle in the formation of FC indefinites. Cf. MACHAJDÍKOVÁ—MARTZLOFF 2016: 96 ff.

8   It is plausible that the indefinite Hitt. *kuiški* also represents the union between the interrogative stem and the particle **-kʷe* (> Hitt. *-kku* "and, also; if" > *-ki*). It is with this in mind that Sideltsev—Yakubovich (2016) propose that Hitt. *kuiški* was originally a FC indefinite. The use of this particle along with non-specific relatives as well as with conditional markers has parallels in other early IE languages: HGr. ὅς κε "whoever" /εἴ κε "if", and IIr. **yá-ci/ka-ca* "whoever"/ Ved. *ced* (< **ca-íd*) /*-ca*, OAv. *-ca* "if" (BRICEÑO-VILLALOBOS 2019: 184–186). In turn, it is safe to say that particles **-kʷid* and **-kʷe* are not the only particles employed in the creation of FC indefinites among early IE languages. Notice, for instance, the focus particle Hitt. *imma* "even" (*kuiš imma* "whoever, any") (cf. SIDELTSEV 2018), the additive particle TB *-ra* "also, like" (*ketra* "whoever('s), whomever", *ket-räññe* "belonging to whomever") (cf. PINAULT 2010: 288 ff.; ADAMS 2013: 569), or the *irrealis*-modal particle Gr. ἄν (ὅς ἄν "whoever"): all of them are employed as domain-widening particles in the formation of FC indefinites.

9   Scalarity is a key feature shared by both FCIs and NPIs (HASPELMATH 1997: 164).

10 In the Rigveda, we already find instances of *káś cid* functioning as NPI, although the FC function is mostly attested for this indefinite. Additionally, we see in Classical Sanskrit that this indefinite—already covering the functions of free choice and negative polarity—has evolved into an EQ "some".

ACHAEMENID ELAMITE AND OLD PERSIAN INDEFINITES

with scalar focus particles after a multiple-alternative reading, which is a key trait of FC indefinites. This development is also observed in Lat. *quisque* ₍UNI/FC₎ "everyone, anyone" (< *$k^w$is-k^we* ₍FC₎ "anyone") or Go. *hvazuh* (< *$k^w$is-u-k^we* ₍FC₎ "anyone"). On the other hand, the semantic development from FCI into an NPI is called 'semantic weakening' or 'extension from free-choice' and, according to Haspelmath (1997: 149–150), it consists in the loss of scalarity and of non-specificity. This semantic change might also be observed in Hitt. *kuiški* ₍NPI/EXI₎ "anyone, someone", Skrt. *káś cid* ₍NPI/EXI₎ "anyone, someone", and Arm. *ok'* ₍NPI₎ "anyone".[11]

In this way, Old Persian displays the two possible developments: on the one hand, OP **kašci* ₍FC₎ "anyone" turns into OP *kašci* ₍UNI₎ "everyone, each one",[12] as in (1a), and, on the other, OP **kašci* ₍FC₎ "anyone" turns into OP *kašci* ₍NPI₎ "anyone", as in (1b). Notice that in the latter example negation is preverbal and after the indefinite, just like AE *akkar* ₍NPI₎ (*inni*) and MP *kas-iz* ₍NPI₎ (*nē*).[13] Cf. MP *kas* ₍EQ-unknown₎ "someone" and MP *ān kas* ₍EQ-known₎ "that person, someone".[14] Although

---

11   Cf. Klein (1997), De Lamberterie (2013: 43).

12   For the universal / distributive indefinite, Middle Persian employs MP *harw* "every, each, all" (< OP *haruva* "all", cf. Ved. *sárva* "whole"): *harw kas* ₍UNI₎ "everyone" (> NP *har kas* ₍FC/UNI₎ "anyone, everyone") or MP *harw tis* "everything". Observe that, in the same way as Middle Persian employs MP *harw* for creating non-specific FC indefinite relatives (e.g. *harw kē* ₍FC₎ "whoever"/ MP *harw če* ₍FC₎ "whatever"), the rest of Middle Iranian languages also make use of OIr. **harwa* as a domain-widening particle before or after the interrogative-relative pronoun: Khot. *halci*, Oss. *alči* (< OIr. **harwa-čid*), Khot. *hanu* (< OIr. **harnu*), Bactr. υαρσο (< OIr. **harwa* + ισο), and Bactr. φαρσο (<OIr. **fra-harwa* + ισο??). Additionally, notice that New Persian displays a rather odd semantic change: from universal "every" into FC "any" (HASPELMATH 1997:156). Similarly, Turkish has a *herhangi*-series, which is a compound of *her*, borrowed from Persian *har* "every" and the interrogative determiner *hangi* "which?".

13   In Middle Persian, the negative polarity function can also be performed by other indefinite formations: the bare indefinite MP *kas* can function as a NPI within non-veridical semantic contexts such as negation (BRUNNER 1977: 91) or conditionals (MP *kas* ₍NPI₎...*nē* "not anyone", MP *ka kas* ₍NPI₎ "if anyone ..."), and MP *ēč kas* ₍NPI₎ "anyone" (> NP *hič kas(-i)* ₍NPI₎ "anyone"). The first element of this compound, MP *ēč* ₍NPI₎ "any" (< OIr. **aiua-čid*), is an indefinite that is almost completely restricted to negative functions (similarly, NP *hič* ₍NPI₎ "any"). Nevertheless, MP *ēč* also contributes to the formation of FC indefinites such as *ēč kē* ₍FC₎ "whoever" (cf. *or* ₍REL₎ *ok'* ₍NPI₎ "whoever") and *ēč-ēw* ₍FC₎ "anyone". How a NPI element can aid in the expression of FC semantics must be left for future typological research. It seems, though, that the scalarity feature embedded in NPIs must play a role of some sort.

14   Also, cf. MP *kas-ēw* ₍IRR/COND₎ "someone" and NP (*yek*) *kas-i* ₍EQ/IRR/NPI₎. In combination with the relative NP *ki*, it forms non-specific indefinite relative clauses: NP *kas-i ki* "whoever", as in MP *kas kē* "whoever". With NP *har*, it forms a UNI/FC pronoun NP *har kas(-i)* "everyone, anyone". According to our data, MP *-ēw* (> NP *-e*) is certainly employed along with nominals as an indefinite article with a EQ (specific-known) function "a certain, some". However, in conjunction with other indefinites (e.g. MP *kas, tis, ēč, ēk,* etc.), MP *-ēw* marks *irrealis* as

not attested in Old Iranian, Old Indic has the indefinite Ved. *káś caná* NPI "(not) anyone" for the NPI function, the interrogative-indefinite stem plus the de-instrumental scalar focus particle IIr. **čana*.[15] For the use of OIr. **čina* alongside of the numeral 'one' with a NPI function, see section 4.

(1)[16] a. DSe_p § 5, 37
   *gāθavā **kašci** astiy dātam.*
   in place each one be-3SG put
   'Each one is put in his place'.

    b. DB_p 1, § 13, 53–54
   ***kašci** naị adaṛšnauš **cišci** θastanaị*
   anyone NEG dare-3SG anything to say
   'Not anyone dared say anything.'

    c. DB_e 12 (ex 13), 40–41
   *ak ᵐakkar aški ᵐGammata ᵐmaguš tupaka **inni***
   and anyone anything Gaumata magician regarding NEG
   lilma.k
   testify-3SG
   'And not anyone said anything about Gaumata the magician'.

In turn, Achaemenid Elamite attests the animate indefinite *akkar* [ak-ka₄-ri] "anyone", which is a compound made of the animate relative-interrogative pronoun *akka* "who? who"[17] and the delocutive animate 3rd sg. classifier -*r* (TAVERNIER 2018: 427). As it is the case for the inanimate relative-interrogative pronoun *appa* "which, what?", *akka* is indeclinable. AE *akkar* operates as a 'strong' NPI indefinite, given that all its attestations are under the direct scope of negation that is placed in a fixed preverbal position: *akkar* + NEG + V. See (1c) and (2) for examples.

---

    well as FC functions, leaving aside negative polarity uses. Notice that the indefinite marker MP -*ēw* becomes essential in the formation of the New Persian *i*-series that would eventually be employed in all functions, including the negative polarity functions, except for the comparative and FC functions, for which New Persian employs *har* "every" + indef. Cf. Haspelmath (1997: 282–284).

15   For the etymology of this focus particle and a detailed assessment of its occurrences in early Indo-Iranian, see Briceño-Villalobos (2019: 145–149).

16   For this passage, the AE and AB parallel texts are badly preserved.

17   Cf. Reiner (1969: 86); Khačikjan (1998: 27–28), Grillot-Susini (2008: 54–55), Bavant (2014: 272–274), and Tavernier (2018: 431–432).

ACHAEMENID ELAMITE AND OLD PERSIAN INDEFINITES

(2) DB$_e$ 51 (ex 63), 82
    *appan **lakkimme**[18] **akkar** uggi **inni** hutta*
    ever harm   anyone above NEG do-1SG
    '" never did harm upon anybody'

This fact is corroborated by the ME material, where the indefinite *akkar* [ak-ka₄-ra][19] (Cf. EKI 183) is attested up to five times and follows the same syntactic distribution as AE *akkar*. See (3).

(3) EKI 28A, § 5, 8[20]
    *sunkip urpubba **akkar** ... **inri**   dur[naš].*
    king=pl former=pl anyone NEG.3SG (anim.) know-3SG
    '(of) the former kings, no one knew'.

However, in the Persepolis administrative tablets, *akkar* is attested expressing an EQ "some", as in (4), similar in function to the numeral 'one' in both AE *kir* and OP *aiva*, probably due to Old Persian influence and not because of semantic change as seen above.[21] This use is also parallel to MP *kas* $_{EQ}$ "some" that also functions as an existential quantifier without MP *-iz*.[22]

(4) PF-NN 2506
    *Masa **akkar***
    Masa some
    'a certain Masa'

Now, if we turn to DB$_p$ 1, § 13, 49, we observe OP *nai... kašci haya* "not ... anyone who" (see 5a). According to Skjærvø (2009: 159), this passage represents a case of a conditional relative clause (3rd sg. perf. optative). I believe this consid-

---

18   For this passage, Aliyari Babolghani (2015) and Bae (2001)'s reading [ap-pan la-ik-ki-um-me] differ from Vallat (1977) and Grillot-Susini et al. (1993)'s [ap-pan-la-ik-ki-um-me]. The former reading is also supported by EW (73) and Tavernier (2018: 432).

19   EKI 28a -Šutruk-Nahhunte I (ca. 1190–1155 BCE): (×3) *akkar...imme /inri*, EKI 17, IRS 54-Šutruk-Nahhunte II (ca. 717–699 BCE): *akkar...inri*, and EKI 79-Tepti-Huban-Inšušnak: (ca. 550–530 BCE) *akkar...imme*.

20   Also, EKI 28A, § 11, 17.

21   See section 6.

22   However, as has been kindly pointed out by an anonymous reviewer, this discussion relies on a single occurrence in an unclear context, since *-akka* in *akka-ri* might be part of a personal name [Ma-a-sa-ak-ka₄]. Therefore, we should take due caution regarding the accountability of this form.

eration is in connection with the semantics shared by both conditionals and non-specific FC indefinite relative clauses (BRICEÑO-VILLALOBOS 2019: 181–188).[23]

(5)   a. DB$_p$ 1, §13, 48–50

naẖ   āha   martiya [naẖ Pārsa   naẖ   Māda   naẖ   amāxam
NEG be-3SG man   NEG Persian NEG Median NEG our
taumāyā] kašci   haya avam Gaumātam tayam magum
family   anyone who this Gaumata   the   magician
xšaçam dītam   caxriyā
kingship deprived of make-3SG
'There was no man, [neither Persian nor Median nor of my family],
anyone who could have despoiled that Gaumata the magus of the kingship'.

      b. DB$_e$ 12 (ex 13): 37–38

^{m}RUH^{meš}-ra inna šari   inni uttara inni ^{m}Parsira inni ^{m}Mada
man   NEG be-3SG NEG doer NEG Persian NEG Median
ak inni ^{m}NUMUN^{meš} ^{m}nuka.mi // akka ^{m}Kammada ^{m}makuš
and not family   ours   who Gaumata   magician
^{m}sunki-me e.mi   [duš-ti].
reign=from of him get-3SG
'King Darius says: there was neither men nor anyone, [neither Persian
nor Median nor of our race], who(ever) could get the reign from Gaumata the magician'

Notably, the AE parallel text in (5b) does not show the expected NPI indefinite, since the negative marker *inni* is placed before the pronominal form as part of the negative coordinator AE *ak inni* "and not, nor" (see BRICEÑO-VILLALOBOS 2020).[24] This is why we find the relative *akka* instead of the NPI *akkar*, which must always be placed before the negative marker in preverbal position: *akkar + inni + V.*

---

23   The semantic affinity between FC relatives "whoever might have ..." and conditional clauses "if anyone might have ..." is further supported by the employment of the perfect optative in the case of Old Persian. Similarly, in Middle Persian it is observed that the rel-ative *kē* "who, whoever" and the conditional conjunction *ka* "if" are often confused due to the similarity of their semantics and morphology. Cf. also Khot. *kā cu* "if anyone, who-ever". There is also a marked morphological relationship between indefinite relatives and concessive (conditional) markers. See below.

24   Avestan has similar negative coordination constructions: OAv. *nōiṯ...naēdā*, YAV. *nōiṯ... naēδa* "neither nor", YAv. *naēδa* "and not, nor".

ACHAEMENID ELAMITE AND OLD PERSIAN INDEFINITES

I admit that by simply acknowledging the NPI status of OP *kašci* acting as the antecedent of the following relative clause would be a much simpler solution to the syntax of this phrase: "not ... anyone who ...". Nevertheless, there are a few arguments in favor of considering *kašci haya* a FC indefinite relative "whoever" and I believe that this is what Horn (1904: 241) implies in his annotations to DB.[25]

Firstly, it seems that the genitive *amāxam taumāyā* "of our family" works as another descriptive adjective in the same way as the nominatives *Pārsa* and *Māda*, both modifying the nominative *martiya*, the three terms being coordinated by the asyndetic repetition of the negative markers (OP *naị...naị...naị*). Notice that in the AE version the negative coordinator *ak inni* "and not, nor" is aligned with the two previous negative markers (*inni...inni...ak inni*). This suggests that in the Old Persian version *Pārsa*, *Māda*, and *amāxam taumāyā* also function as a block, all of them modifying *martiya* and being coordinated by three negative markers. Thus, the indefinite relative OP *kašci haya* must refer back to OP *martiya*.

Secondly, from a typological perspective, we notice that the indefinite OP *kašci* happens to be present within an episodic negative context OP *naị āha* "there was no ...". Although the latter is an environment that FCIs admittedly try to avoid, it must be taken into account that *wh-ever* relatives differ from nominal FC *any* in that they can appear in episodic environments when subtriggered by a relative clause that allows them to perform grammatically with its FC nuance "anyone ₍FC₎ who" (GIANNAKIDIOU 2001: 52–54).[26] Therefore, in this case, *kašci* is a FCI subtriggered by the relative OP *haya*.

A third argument in support of the FC reading of OP *kašci haya* is based on its morphology: the union between the FC indefinite—that can also operate as a NPI—and the relative pronoun closely resembles what we see in the Middle Persian FC indefinite relative MP *ēč kē* "whoever", made up by MP *ēč* "any, at all", a NPI indefinite almost always found in negative contexts, and the interrogative-relative pronoun MP *kē* "who? who". Additionally, Middle Persian attests MP *kas kē* ₍FC₎ "anyone who" that may point as well to a similar 'indefinite plus relative' combination.

Finally, a fourth argument comes from the AB version. At the end of the clause, we find *ul amēlu* (LÚ)...*ša* "nor a man ... who", that, in principle, would go parallel to OP *naị...kašci haya* and AE *ak inni...akka*. However, AB *amēlu* (= Akk.

---

25   Horn (1904: 241 fn. 5) translates OP *kašci* "every, any", OP *kašci haya* "anyone who", and *tuvam kā haya* "thou who".

26   Cf. English, *That night John talked to **any** ₍FC₎ woman **who** came up to him* (GIANNAKIDIOU 2001: 53).

awīlum, amīlum, etc.) "man, human being" is equivalent to OP *martiya* and AE ᵐRUHᵐᵉˢ, which are placed at the beginning of each version.[27] In (6), I provide the Achaemenid Babylonian text parallel to the OP (5a) and AE (5b) versions.

(6)   DB$_b$ §12: 19b–24a

| **mamma yānu** | | **ul** | *Parsāya* | **ul** | *Madaya* [...] | **ul** | *amēlu ša* |
| anyone | NEG be | NEG | Persian | NEG | Median | NEG | man of |

zerini   ša...
lineage who

'There was not anyone, a man, neither Persian nor Median nor of my family, who ...'

If we take a look at the rest of AE *amēlu* (LÚ)[28] occurrences in the DB, it is within the scope of negation only in two occasions: one with the prohibitive negative marker *lā* and the other (this example!) with the standard negative marker *ul*. Its other occurrences are in the nominal phrase *išten amēlu* "a certain man" (cf. OP *aiva martiya*, AE *ruh kir*) and next to the relative pronoun AB *amēlu ša* "(a) man who" (cf. OP *martiya haya*, AE *ruh akka*).[29] If we check its uses in Akkadian outside DB, we witness its employment within conditional clauses almost as if it were an indefinite pronoun: *šumma amīlum* "If a man [anyone] ...".[30] Indeed, *CAD* (Mi: 53) reports that one of *amīlum*'s meanings is that of an indefinite pronoun "someone, anyone".[31] Akk. *amīlum* can function as an indefinite pronoun, especially in multiple-alternative non-episodic contexts that enable

---

27   It must be stressed that the four versions of DB are not a 100% identical. They display several disparities in word order and the dislocation of mostly similar morphological forms.

28   It should not be confused with the determinative LÚ before gentilics and words denoting occupations.

29   In some world languages such as Cheke Helo (Austronesian), the existential indefinite is formed after the generic noun and the relative pronoun: *mae ihei* "man who > someone". Cf. Boswell (2018: 101–102).

30   See Cohen (2012) for a complete discussion of conditional structures in Old Akkadian.

31   It is cross-linguistically common to find indefinites pronouns based on generic nouns. In this regard, Sumerian is particularly interesting given that it consistently employs generic nouns for the expression of indefinites: *lú* "man, someone", *lú na-me* "anyone", *níǧ* "thing, something", *níǧ na-me* "anything", etc. (JAGERSMA 2010: 231–232). Other examples of generic-noun based indefinites are Hebrew *'iš* "man, anyone", Bactr. ανδαρισο "anyone whoever" (< ανδαρο "man" + υαρσο "every"), or Bactr. ταυο κισο "anyone" (< ταυο "body" + κισο "any"), Lepcha (Sino-Tibetan) *maró* "man, someone", Pichi (IE creole) *son pɔsin* "some man = someone", etc. Cf. Haspelmath (1997: 28). Contrary to general tendency displayed by generic-noun based indefinites to be restricted to negative polarity or negative functions (such as Fr. *personne*), Akk. *amīlum* tends to be restricted to FC functions, avoiding as much as possible negative (polarity) enviroments. All this may raise the question whether

ACHAEMENID ELAMITE AND OLD PERSIAN INDEFINITES   59

FC indefinites to appear: modals, imperatives, conditionals, generics, etc.[32] So, there seems to be a tendency for *amīlum* to appear in non-negative contexts when acting as an indefinite pronoun. Although *amīlum* has other attested indefinite uses, Achaemenid Babylonian displays a very clear distribution: the indefinite AB *mamma* is always with negation, while AB *amēlu* avoids negative contexts. Moreover, as pointed out by Malbran-Labat (1994: 46), the AB version has two types of indefinite pronouns: *mamma* $_{NPI}$ and *mannu* $_{FC}$. In section 4, I will show that only the latter, which is actually an interrogative pronoun, is invested in the expression of FC indefinite relatives along with the relative *ša*, whereas the NPI *mamma* is always under the scope of negation.[33] Therefore, AB *amēlu* goes parallel to OP *martiya* and AE *ruh*, despite the fact that these two nominals are found at the beginning of their corresponding sentences. So, AB *amēlu* is modified by *Parsaya*, *Madaya* and the genitival construction *ša zerini*, much like OP *martiya* is modified by OP *Parsā*, *Madā*, and *amāxam taumāyā*.[34] In turn, in the same line, a few words before, we see *ul mamma* "not anyone"[35] and *mamma yānu* "there is not any ...",[36] the latter being the actual parallel to OP *kašci* $_{NPI}$. Thus, I believe that this analysis corresponds with my idea that negative coordination is connecting three modifiers around the word for 'man' and that OP *kašci haya* provides appositive information regarding OP *martiya*.

Hallock (1969: 771) and Bae (2001: 352) suggest that the form AE *uttara* in (5b) should be translated as "anyone". Although its meaning might be closer to "perpetrator, doer" (cf. *EW*: 1253), its correlation with OP *kašci* and AB *mamma* might make this meaning very likely, especially given that the relative AE *akka*

---

        is a genuine Akkadian strategy to employ generic nouns as indefinite pronouns or is it a non-inherent strategy borrowed from Sumerian due to language contact.

32   Although we also find *šumma mamma* "If anyone ...", the indefinite Akk. *mamma* and its variants tend to appear within the scope of negation and, to a lesser degree, they can also function as an EQ "some". Cf. also Akk. *amīlūtu* (*awīlūtum*) "mankind, human being, somebody, anybody", which similarly tends to appear in contexts that display multiple alternatives.

33   Thus, in Achaemenid Babylonian, *mamma* is a 'strong' NPI. In the same line, we evidence in earlier stages of Akkadian that Akk. *mamman* tends to avoid other non-veridical semantic contexts such as conditionals.

34   Notice that *amēlu...ša* patterns with other identical attestations in DB of this generic noun alongside the relative particle.

35   In (6), I have not included the phrase *ul Bābilāya ul mamma ina mātāti* "nor Babylonian nor anyone in the lands" since it is an AB addition not found in the other versions. See Malbran-Labat (1994) or Bae (2001).

36   Indeed, we find in Ugaritic (and other Semitic languages) existential particles along with indefinite pronouns: *'inmm /'ēnu-mimma/* "there was not anything ..." (HUNT 2007: 59). Note that, in Akkadian, indefinites tend to stand as close as possible to the beginning of the sentence.

60 BRICEÑO VILLALOBOS

TABLE 2.2 Words and phrases of (5) and (6) arranged according to their equivalent in each language

Meaning	AE	OP	AB
"man"	^{m}RUH^{meš}.ra	martiya	amēlu
"anyone"	(inni) uttara	kašci	mamma
"who"	akka	haya	ša
"there was not ..."	inni šari	naį āha	yānu
"neither Persian,	inni Parsira	naį Parsa	ul Parsāya
nor Median nor of	inni Mada	naį Mada	ul Madaya
my family"	ak inni ^{m}NUMEN^{meš} ^{m}nukami	naį amaxa taumaya	ul...ša zerini

is the only available pronominal form after a negative coordinator ak inni. Since *ak inni [akkar akka...duš.ti] with a pre-indefinite negative marker would not have been possible, the AE version resorts to the distortion of the phrase word order and turns to uttara to operate as an NPI indefinite. For the sake of clarity, I provide in Table 2.2 all words under discussion in this section organized according to their equivalent in each language.

Then, in the case of AE and AB versions, it seems clear that both AE uttara and AB mamma function as NPIs: as I already pointed out, AE uttara is under the direct scope of an extra negative marker (inni) and AB mamma is always present in negative contexts (yānu). However, there is enough evidence to suggest that OP kašci haya should be considered a FC indefinite relative. If we turn to its other attestations, we see in (1b) that negation is in preverbal position kašci $_{NPI}$ naį V, much like MP kas(-iz) nē V and AE akkar inni V, and, in (1a), we have OP kašci with a universal/distributive meaning, just as Av. kascit $_{UNI}$. Therefore, provided the fragmentary state of the language, it is safe to say that Old Persian data does not yield a unique account for this indefinite.

In Table 2.3, I provide all occurrences of the nominal animate indefinite in Achaemenid Elamite and Old Persian and their Middle Iranian counterparts.

4 OP cišci $_{NPI}$: MP tis-iz $_{NPI}$ and ME azkit $_{NPI}$: AE aški $_{NPI}$ "anything"

Attested once, OP cišci has traditionally been taken to reflect a reduplicated inanimate indefinite pronoun acting as an NPI indefinite (WaK: 158; KENT 1953: 184). See (1b) for an example. Reduplication can be defined as the prefixation or

ACHAEMENID ELAMITE AND OLD PERSIAN INDEFINITES

TABLE 2.3   OP *kašci* and AE *akkar*

Achaemenid Elamite	Old Indo-Iranian	Middle Iranian
DB$_e$ 12, ex 13, 40 *akkar* (*inni*) $_{NPI}$ "anyone"	DB$_p$ 1, § 13, 53 OP *kašci* (*nai̯*) $_{NPI}$ "anyone"	> MP *kas* (*-iz*) $_{NPI}$ (*nē*) "anyone"
Cf. ME. *akkar* $_{NPI}$	Cf. Ved. (*ná*) *kás caná* $_{NPI}$ Cf. Skrt. (*ná*) *kás cid* $_{NPI}$	
DB$_e$ 51, ex 63, 82 *akkar* (*inni*) $_{NPI}$	DB$_p$ 1, § 14, 67 ✗	
DB$_e$ ex 13, 37–38 *ak inni... akka* $_{REL}$	DB$_p$ 1, § 13, 49 OP *nai̯...*] *kašci haya* $_{FC}$	MP *kas/ēč kē* $_{FC}$ "anyone who, whoever"
DSe$_e$ 37 ✗	DSe$_p$ § 5, 37 OP *kašci* $_{UNI}$/$_{DISTR}$ "everyone, each one"	MP *harw kas* $_{UNI/FC}$ "everyone, anyone"
Cf. AE *unra* $_{UNI/DISTR}$ "everyone, each one" PF-NN 2506, PF 1846, 101 AE *akkar* $_{EQ}$ (= *kir*) "some"	Cf. OAv/YAv. *kascit̯* $_{FC/UNI}$ Cf. Ved. *kás cid* $_{FC}$	MP *kas* $_{EQ}$ "some"

suffixation of 'a complete or partial copy of the base' (BOOIJ 2005: 35) of a word for lexical or grammatical purposes. Cross-linguistically, the use of reduplication to produce FC indefinite pronouns is fairly common (HASPELMATH 1997: 23–24; 179–182). Hence, OP *cišci*, allegedly a FC indefinite,[37] would have evolved into an NPI indefinite undertaking 'semantic weakening', as discussed in section 2 for the animate indefinite. However, its Middle Iranian counterpart, MP *tis-iz* $_{NPI}$ "anything", suggests that OP *cišci* is actually the nominative-accusative neuter singular of the interrogative stem—saved for inanimate entities—plus the scalar focus particle OIr. **čid*.[38] In addition, typologically speaking, it is

---

37   The inherited FC value is attested in its Anatolian (Hitt. *kuiš kuiš* $_{FC}$, HLuw. *kwis kwis* $_{FC}$) as well as in its Italic cognates (Lat. *quis quis* $_{FC}$, Osc. *pis pis* $_{FC}$).

38   Herzfeld (1938: 355), Kent (1953: 184), and *WaK* (158) all consider that this inanimate indefinite is the result of reduplication, OIr. **čid-čid*. Similar complications to distinguish

strange indeed to find reduplicated indefinites functioning as NPIs, given that they either remain FCIs or evolve into universal/distributive indefinites.[39]

As regards Elamite, AE *aški* [áš-ki] is an inanimate indefinite, a compound formed by the nominal *aš* "part" and the numeral 'one' *ki-*: lit. "one part" (KHAČIKJAN 1998: 29). See (1c) and (7).

(7) DB$_e$ 12 (ex 13), 40–41
　　meni ^{m}taššup　appa　　^{m}unina　　aški　　inni
　　then　troops=PL　which/that　mine-1SG.(anim.)　anything　NEG
　　huttaš
　　make-3PL
　　'Then, my troops did nothing'

There are no examples of this inanimate indefinite outside the Royal Inscriptions. Hallock (1969: 670) suggests that *-ki* is a calque of OP *-ci* (< OIr. *-čid*). One argument against this assumption is the fact that the generalizing particle AE *-da* is the actual equivalent of OP *-ci*, as can be seen in AE *daeki-da*: OP *aniya-ci* "another". Furthermore, it is very likely that its connection with ME *azkit* $_{NPI}$ "anything" should dismiss this line of thinking, especially given that, although with a different spelling, ME *azkit* might be a similar compound (GRILLOT-SUSINI 2008: 57): *as/az-ki-t*: "part" + "one" + inanimate marker *-t*.[40] See (8) for an example.

(8) EKI 11Aa / MDAI XLI 36
　　azkit　　hušutta　　　ingi　　hinga.
　　anything　vengeful=inanim.　NEG-1SG　obtain-1SG
　　'I might get no punishment?'

Both ME *azkit* and AE *aški* are 'strong' NPI indefinites since their appearance in a given sentence can only be licensed by negation.[41] The same applies to

---

　　between a reduplicated form and an inanimate neuter indefinite plus a domain-widening particle are observed in Oscan *pidpid*. Cf. MACHAJDÍKOVÁ—MARTZLOFF 2016.

39　Actually, Old Persian attests a reduplicated adverbial relative of the **(H)i̯o-* stem: OP *yadā yadā* "wherever". This form, attested in XPh$_p$ 39 through emendation (SCHMITT 2014: 288), has nice parallels of relative reduplication in Classical Sanskrit *ya ya*, and Old Phrygian *yos yos*. Vedic also attest adverbial relative reduplication: Ved. *yatra yatra* "wherever", *yáthā yáthā* "in whichever way" (BRICEÑO-VILLALOBOS 2019: 163).

40　Cf. Tavernier (2018: 427) for the inanimate nominal suffix *-t*. Cf. EW (1987: 103) for a general view of *azkit*.

41　The AB version does not present parallel inanimate indefinites in these passages, although

ACHAEMENID ELAMITE AND OLD PERSIAN INDEFINITES

TABLE 2.4   OP *cišci* and AE *aški*

Achaemenid Elamite	Old Persian	Middle Iranian
DB$_e$ ex 12, 40–41	DB$_p$ 1, §13, 53	
AE *aški* (*inni*) $_{NPI}$	OP (*naị*) *cišci* $_{NPI}$	MP *tis-iz* (*nē*) $_{NPI}$
"anything"	"anything"	"anything"
Cf. ME *azkit* $_{NPI}$		Cf. MP *ēč tis* $_{NPI}$
DB$_e$ ex 25, 20	DB$_p$ 2, §25, 27–28 ✗	
aški (*inni*) $_{NPI}$		
DB$_e$ ex 28, 36	DB$_p$ 2, §28, 48 ✗	
aški (*inni*) $_{NPI}$		

OP *ciš-ci* and MP *tis-iz*[42] that operate as NPI items. In Table 2.4, I provide all Achaemenid Elamite and Old Persian inanimate indefinite occurrences as well as Middle Iranian forms.

5   OP *kā haya*: AE *akka*(-*ya*)

OP *kā* is found six times in the Old Persian corpus, most attestations being in the DB and one in the Daiva Inscription (XPh).

---

it attests the inanimate indefinite *mimma* "anything" along the relative *mala* "as much as", so as to form an inanimate FC indefinite relative, AB *mimma mala* "whatever". See section 5. In turn, in the Aramaic version, there is no parallel inanimate indefinite pronoun either. However, in other passages of DB, the Aramaic text presents the inanimate *mnd'm* $_{NPI}$ /*madda'm*/ (Syriac /*meddem*/) "anything" (X3). Cf. Syriac *kell-meddem* "everything" (< earlier Aramaic *kl* /kull/ "every"). For more information about this inanimate indefinite and its etymology, see Muraoka—Porter (1998: 172) and Gzella (2015: 26–27, 116, fn. 338). Earlier Aramaic has no common indefinite pronoun, but it employs interrogatives as head of non-specific indefinite relative clauses, similarly to Akkadian.

42   MP *tis* has similar functions as the animate indefinite MP *kas*: *tis* $_{EQ-unknown}$ "thing, something", *ān tis* $_{EQ-known}$ "that (some)thing", *tis-iz* $_{NPI}$ "anything", *ēč tis* $_{NPI}$ "anything", *tis-ēw* $_{IRR/COND/COMP}$ "something, anything", *harw tis*(*-ēw*) $_{UNI/FC}$ "everything, anything", and *tis čē* $_{FC}$ "anything that, whatever". Notably, in Turfan Middle Persian, MP$_t$ *tis-iz* $_{FC}$ "whatever" has a FC function (DURKIN-MEISTERERNST 2012: 216). Thus, MP$_t$ *-iz* and Parth. *-ž* (< OIr. **-čid*) preserve their original function as domain-widening particles employed in the formation of FC indefinites.

Although most scholars[43] agree that OP *kā* is a reflex of PIE *k^wo-H_I, I argue in this section that this assumption is typologically unsustainable and that, as has already been suggested by Kern (1891:47) and Horn (1898–1901: 121), OP *kā* forms a FC indefinite relative pronoun along with the relative pronoun OP *haya*. Therefore, *kā* would be in this case the nominative singular of the interrogative stem.

With Schmitt (2014: 198) and *contra* Hinz (1973: 25) and Back (1992: 266 fn. 18), I believe that OP *kā* cannot be considered a focus particle that performs a domain-widening function alongside *tuvam* "you". As far as early Indo-Iranian material shows, IIr. **čid* and IIr. **čā* are the only domain-widening particles consistently employed in the formation of FCI indefinites: the former is involved in the creation of nominal FC indefinites (OP *kašci*, Av. *kascit̰*) and the latter in the creation of FC indefinite relatives (cf. Av. *yō-cisca*).[44] We also should disregard Gray (1902: 60),[45] Bartholomae (1904: 422), Kent (1950: 178), Schmitt (1991: 67 fn. 37; 2014: 198), and, most recently, Brust (2018: 154)'s assertion that OP *kā* is a generalizing/ reinforcing particle. At the same time, I do not agree with Schmitt (2009, 2014: 198, 2016: 27–28) who provides "wherever (Germ. *wo immer*)" as one possible translation, considering OP *kā* (< PIE *k^wo-H_I) an instrumental form that is able to express locative semantics.[46] We should dismiss this line of thinking provided that, cross-linguistically, instrumental suffixes in early IE languages activate indefinite adverbs as NPIs, and not as FCIs.[47]

In order to explain the phonetics behind the long vowel in OP *kā*, we must take into account that long final vowels should not be interpreted as inherited, but rather as an Old Persian self-developed feature (HINZ 1973: 25). Interestingly, Rawlinson (1848: 245–246) suggests that the visarga in the interrogative form OIr. **káḥ* (< IIr. **kás*) might have been elided undertaking compensatory lengthening: **káḥ* > > OP *kā*. Similarly, Gershevitch (1988: 77) proposes that OP [*ka-a*] should be read as OP *ka* /kæ/. Be as it may, both scenarios fit with the preservation of the nominative case ending along with the enclitic -*čid* in Old Iranian sandhi forms: OP *kaš-ci*: OP *kā*, and Av. *kas-cit̰*: OAv. *kə̄*, YAv. *kō*. As regards the transcription and the transliteration of this form, OP *kā* is attested as [ka-a] in DB$_p$, transliterated as /kā or kă/, and as XPh$_p$ [*ka-ă*], transliterated as /kă/.

---

43   Chantraine (1968: 921), Frisk (1960: 632), Beekes (2010: 1264), *LIPP* (464), *WaK* (198), etc.

44   In turn, IIr. **čana* overtly marks indefinites and the numeral 'one' as NPIs.

45   Gray connects OP *kā* with the West Greek modal particle κα /kā/ with a 'generalizing' force and asserts that it is somehow related to early Greek modal particle κε with a similar function: ὅς κε "whoever".

46   Similarly, HGr. πῃ $_{NPI}$ "anywhere" (< PIE *k^we-h_I).

47   Cf. Briceño-Villalobos (2019: 111–114; 145–152, 154–155) for instrumental case indefinites in Homeric Greek and early Indo-Iranian.

ACHAEMENID ELAMITE AND OLD PERSIAN INDEFINITES 65

In the latter form, a different cuneiform sign is employed for /a/. Skjærvø (1999: 161) is the first one to propose that we are dealing with an actual etymological nominative form on account of the new sign *ă* (only employed in XPh). Schmitt (2009: 168 A[46f]), however, rejects this assumption.

Thus, a first argument against considering OP *kā* to be an instrumental indefinite form is the fact that it has no connection whatsoever with negation or any other non-veridical semantic context, whereas its so-called cognates, such as Gr. πω "yet, at all" or Lat. *quō* "to where, to anywhere",[48] operate as NPIS (BRICEÑO-VILLALOBOS 2019: 114; 188–189). Moreover, there is no evidence among early IE languages that sustain the assumption that the instrumental case plays any role within the expression of FC. To the contrary, there is plenty of evidence that indicates that the instrumental case is intimately related to the reinforcement of negation and, more importantly, to negative polarity contexts.[49]

Although Schmitt (1991: 69 fn. 37) realizes that the nominative *xšāyaϑiya* "king" should be included within the relative clause headed by the relative *haya* "who"—probably due to its disposition already as an *ezāfe*-like particle,[50] I take *kā haya* plus the subjunctive mood to embody an indefinite relative pronoun "whoever". See (9a–b) for examples.[51]

(9) a. DB$_p$ 4, § 55, 37
    ϑātiy Dārayavauš xšāyaϑiya tuvam kā xšāyaϑiya haya
    say-3SG Darius   king   you who king   -ever
    aparam āhi.
    hereafter be-2SG
    'Proclaims Darius, the king: you, whichever king you are hereafter'

   b. DB$_p$ 4, § 56, 41
    tuvam kā haya aparam imām dipim patiprsāhi.
    you   whoever hereafter this   inscription read-2SG
    'You, whoever reads this inscription hereafter'

---

48   Lat. *quō* represents a cross-over between instrumental and directive formations. See Dunkel (1997: 74), García Ramón (1997: 138), and *LIPP* (438, 465). Also the interrogative Goth. *ƕe* "how?" is a cognate of these de-instrumental forms.

49   Cf. BRICEÑO-VILLALOBOS 2019.

50   Cf. also MP *-i/-ig* < OIr. *haia-ka* (see DURKIN-MEISTERERNST 2012: 268 fn. 17). For a Persian Elamite-induced *ezāfe*, cf. Yakubovich (2020: 97–101). Nonetheless, I believe that the Aramaic disposition of the relative particle *zy* /dy/ as a linker between two elements— genitive constructions, also seen in Akkadian with the relative particle *ša*—is the real origin of Persian *ezāfe*. Cf. *DNWSIa*: 312–313.

51   Cf. Schmitt (2016: 27–29) for the figure of speech of apostrophe in these passages.

One further piece of evidence in support of the reality of this FC indefinite relative comes from Achaemenid Elamite. The Daiva Inscriptions (XPh$_e$ 38–39) attests a relative form AE *akkaya*, instead of the standard relative AE *akka* "who", the latter being, according to Bae (2001: 265), the equivalent of OP *kā*, Aram. *mn* /man/ "who?, whoever", and AB *mannu* "who?, whoever". Notably, Paper (1955: 98 fn. 21) suggests that *-ya* in AE *akkaya* may reflect the relative OIr. *$^*ịa$ found in the compound relative pronoun OP *haya* (< OIr. *$^*sa$-ịa*).[52] In the Fortification Tablets, we find other reflexes of the Old Iranian relative: AE *ia-na-a* (also *ia-né* and *i-ia-né*), a calque of the adverbial relative OP *yanai* "where, whereon" (TAVERNIER 2007: 36). Thus, according to my view, AE *akka-ya* signals the missing connection between the OP interrogative-indefinite stem and the relative pronoun taken as one morphological entity in the Elamite text. Therefore, I conclude that AE *akka* is not simply heading a standard relative clause, but a non-specific indefinite relative construction.[53]

Notably, early Akkadian (Old Babylonian and Old Assyrian) shows similar indefinite relative constructions composed by the indefinite pronoun *mam-*

---

52 In early Elamite, there is a suffix *-ya* attested in the formation of inanimate adjectives. According to Quintana (2013: 36 fn. 17), this suffix may be formed by the relative particle *-a*, which along with nominals ending in vowel would create a diphthong /-ia/, written *-ya*. The same author, however, asserts that in Achaemenid Elamite *-ya* also appears within animate adjectives such as *hakkamannušiya* "Achaemenid", *bapiliya* "Babylonian", etc. I believe that this suffix is a morphological calque from OP *-iya-* employed for the stem derivation of adjectives or nouns: e.g. OP *haxāmanišiya* "Achaemenid", OP *aϑuriya*-"Assyrian", OP *xšāyaϑiya* "king", etc. In turn, some scholars have proposed a connection of this word with AE *akka(ya)* "companion" (cf. HALLOCK 1969: 665), mainly found in the Fortification Tablets and admittedly borrowed from OP *$^*haxā$ (cf. YAv. *haxi* "companion, friend". Cf. Tavernier (2007: 199–201; 425–426). In this case, I think that the *-ya* extension found along *akkaya* "companion" is the very same suffix *-ya* employed in the creation of adjectives. Either way, I believe that this nominal has nothing to do with the *akkaya* we encounter in DB$_e$ here.

53 Since the Neo-Elamite period, there seems to be a tendency in Elamite of marking non-specific relative clauses through verbal reduplication, which has been traditionally explained as some sort of expression of plurality. Notably, in the Elamite version of this phrase, we find the reduplication of the verb *bera* "to read": DB$_e$ 45, 67: *nu akka meššin tuppi hi bebra-n-t* "you, whoever in the future reads this inscription". At first glance, the reduplicated verb *bebra* may not imply any additional semantics, but, if we take a look at DB$_e$ 47 (ex 58), we observe the simple form (*bera*) being used within a relative clause again, *akka...bera-n-r-a* [*bera*-conj.III-3rd sg.-relative particle], but, in this case, without conveying non-specific values. On the contrary, *bebra-n-t* [*bebra*-conj. III-2nd sg.] does display a multiple alternative reading along the lines of OP *tuvam kā haya* + *patipṛsāhi* whose subjunctive mood find an equivalent in the Elamite conjugation III that can express imperfective action in the present/future time. Furthermore, the other occurrence of this reduplicated *bebra* has iterative semantics: DB$_e$ 55 (ex 70): *bebra-k* [*bebra*-conj.II] "(was) written *again*".

man and the determinative-relative particle *ša*, Akk. *mamman ša* "whoever" (HUEHNERGARD 1997: 123–124, KOUWENBERG 2017: 348). However, as pointed out earlier, Achaemenid Babylonian attests the indefinite relative *mannu ša* "whoever", i.e. the interrogative plus the determinative-relative (cf. UNGNAD 1992: 38). The same compound is also found in Imperial Aramaic *mn zy /man dy/* "whoever"[54] (MURAOKA—PORTEN 1998: 172) as well as in Biblical Hebrew *mî še* "whoever"[55] (JOÜON—MURAOKA ii 1991: 536–537). In consequence, the use of the interrogative AB *mannu* "who?" (Akk. *mannum*) contrasts with that of the indefinite AB *mamma*,[56] which is exclusively attested as a NPI indefinite. Cf. Malbran-Labat (1994: 46–47). Indeed, the interrogative *mannu*, besides its function as an animate interrogative pronoun, has indefinite functions, especially when employed in indefinite relative clauses with or without the determinative-relative particle *ša*.[57] According to Waltisberg (2011: 311), headless relative clauses are either introduced by the relative particle (Akk. *ša*), or by the interrogative (Akk. *mannum*), or by the indefinite (Akk. *mamman*), the latter two strategies with or without the aid of the relative *ša*. But while AB *mamma* does not attest FC values, which seems to be the case in Old Akkadian *mamman (ša)* "whoever" (HUEHNERGARD 1997: 188, KOUWENBERG 2017: 787–788), the interrogative AB *mannu*, always accompanied by AB *ša*, is able to

---

Notice that, typologically speaking, verbal reduplication is usually identifiable with repeated, habitual, or ongoing action. Therefore, I am under the impression that Elamite marks the FC nature of the relative clause by means of verbal reduplication.

54   Cf. also Sam'al Aramaic *mz* "whatever" (< interr. *mh /mā/* "what?" + rel. *zy /dy/* "who, which") and Phoenician *m 'š* "whatever" (interr. *mh* "what?" + rel. *'š* "who, which"). Cf. Tropper (1993: 193).

55   Cf. Ugaritic *my* "who?" (Cf. SIVAN 2001: 58 ff.) and Phoenician *my* "who?" (KRAHMALKOV 2001: 108 ff.). We also find Hebr. *kol mî še* "whoever". *kol* (< Proto-Semitic **kull*, cf. Akk. *kalû* "all, everything") is a universal quantifier "everyone, all" that also participates in the formation of headless indefinite relative clauses in other Semitic languages such as Mandaic *kol man* "whoever". Notice that, as in the case of MP *harw*, which can also form headless indefinite relative clauses as in MP *harw kē/čē* "whoever/whatever" (> NP and Bal. *har ki* "whoever"), Semitic *kol* violates the typological generalization that universal quantifiers cannot become FCIS (HASPELMATH 1997: 156 fn. 13).

56   AB *mamma* is a compound made up of the Semitic interrogative base **man* and the focus particle *-ma*. It should not be confused with Akk. *mamman*, which is formed by reduplication (< **man + man*). See Delitzsch (1889: 142–144) and Faber (1988: 221–238) for an overall view of early Semitic strategies for the creation of indefinite pronouns after the interrogative stem. Overall, Akkadian indefinites are based on the interrogative stem plus the focus particle *-ma*: *mamma* (< **man* "who?" + *ma*) "anyone, someone", *mimma* (< **min* "what?" + *ma*) "anything, something", and *ayyumma* (< **ayyum* "which?" + *ma*) "whichever".

57   In Neo-Babylonian, *mannu* can sustain a distributive value "each", which meaning seems to be derived from its FC values embedded in its non-specific indefinite relative function.

introduce FC indefinite relative.[58] Therefore, it is safe to say that Achaemenid Babylonian overtly marks the difference between FC "whoever" (AB *mannu ša*) and NPI "anyone" (AB *mamma*) indefinites. Interestingly, we find the same distribution of indefinites in the Nabonidus Inscriptions (c. 556–539 BCE):[59] *mannu ša* $_{FC}$ "whoever" and *mamma/mimma* $_{NPI}$ "anyone, anything" (see GAD 1958). Consequently, the AB employment of the interrogative *mannu* in the formation of indefinite relatives instead of the indefinite *mamma* should be taken as another argument of OP *kā haya* being an indefinite relative pronoun and of the fact that OP *kā* is a (nominative) interrogative pronoun, followed by a relative, rather than an (instrumental) indefinite pronoun.[60]

Finally, let us look at the formulaic beginning of the four versions in Table 2.5. Although earlier Akkadian attests a grammaticalized form *atta*$_{masc.}$/*atti*$_{fem}$-*mannu* (you + interr.) "whoever you (are)",[61] which is usually attested in Mesopotamian ritual conjurations, Achaemenid Babylonian, along with other Semitic languages such as Old Aramaic and Achaemenid Phoenician, attests the opposite order of elements (interr. + you). We can see this in the Nabonidus Inscriptions (c. 556–539 BCE) Akk. *mannu atta*,[62] in the Nerab Inscriptions (c. 700–600 BCE) Aram. *mn 't* /*man 'attā*/,[63] and in the Tabnit Inscriptions (c. 490 BCE) Phoen. *my 't*.[64] This last array of elements certainly appears to be the one present in both Achaemenid Babylonian and Imperial Aramaic: *mannu atta*[65] and *mn 'nt* /*man 'attā*/.[66] To the contrary, Old Persian seems to follow the configuration displayed by earlier Akkadian: Akk. *atta-mannu* ("you"

---

58   The interrogative Akk. *mannu* can also express a indefinite relative without the help of the relative *ša*. Notice that in Sumerian an interrogative pronoun can also be used in the same way: *a-na* "what?, whatever", *a-ba* "who?, whoever" (JAGERSMA 2010: 230).

59   Cf. Gad (1958: 35–92) and Moran (1959: 130–140).

60   Since AE *akka* is an interrogative-relative pronoun, it is irrelevant here whether it is the interrogative or the indefinite relative that is operating when AE *akka* heads free-relative clauses acting as FC indefinite relative "whoever", in the same way as AB *mannu*.

61   Cf. Haul (2009: 128 fn. 86). This formula appears attested since Middle Babylonian texts. See *CAD* (Aii 509).

62   In Neo-Babylonian (c. 1000–600 BCE), we already find *mannu atta*: ABL 1250 r 7, *mannu atta* LÚ.A.BA *ša tassasûni* "whoever you are, scribe, who read (this)".

63   Cf. YUN 2006: 19–43.

64   Cf. KRAMALKOV 2001: 109.

65   However, there are two passages where we observe AB *atta ša*, instead of AB *mannu atta ša*.

66   As pointed out by Gzella (2015: 143–144), *'nt* instead of Old Aramaic *'t* is a feature of Achaemenid Official Aramaic, which, in contrast to other dialectal varieties of Aramaic, does present 'degeminating' spellings of long consonants: /**anta*/ (cf. Arabic *'anta*) > *'t* /*'attā*/ (Old Aramaic) > *'nt* /*'antā*/ (Achaemenid Aramaic). This degemination also occurs in the feminine form: *'ty* /*'atti*/ > /*'att*/ > /*'at*/ vs. *'nty* /*'anti*/.

ACHAEMENID ELAMITE AND OLD PERSIAN INDEFINITES

TABLE 2.5   The formula "whoever you are" in DB

	Old Persian	Achaemenid Elamite	Achaemenid Babylonian	Imperial Aramaic
you + interr. + rel.	*tuvam kā...haya* you-who?-who	*nu akka* you-who?/who		
interr. + you + rel.			*mannu atta...ša* who?-you-who	*mn 'nt...zy* who?-you-who

+ "who?"). Although is not certain that OP *tuvam kā* reflects the Akkadian idiomatic nominal phrase, it looks appealing that the Mesopotamian formulaic tradition might have caught up with DB$_p$, especially given the long literary, written tradition of Akkadian. Be as it may, the different combinations among pronouns in the four versions point again to the interrogative and not the indefinite nature of OP *kā*.[67]

But there is one last piece of evidence that may further support our line of thought: that Old Persian follows the early Akkadian formula. Notably, the AB version of XPh (line 38) attests *atta-mannu ša* "whoever you are who ...".[68] Then, XPh$_b$ *attamannu* contrasts DB$_b$ *mannu atta* and is a match with the earlier Akkadian grammaticalized idiomatic phrase (attested since Middle Babylonian) and with the Old Persian word order. Therefore, I deem that OP *tuvam kā* patterns the Akkadian formula *atta-mannu* "whoever you (are)".

Thus, I believe that the structure found in Old Persian, which does not agree with the word pattern shown by Indo-Iranian indefinite relatives (rel. + indef.): IIr.*ya-kas/kim-ča/čid* > Av. *yō-cisca, yō-kaciṭ*, Ved. *yá-káśca, yá-kimca* "whoever, whatever" (*AIGc*: 570–572), might have been induced by Semitic influence, especially Achaemenid Babylonian or Imperial Aramaic (c. 600–200 BCE), the latter being the most important and widespread administrative language in the Achaemenid Empire.

---

67   OP *kā* would not be the only interrogative attested in Old Persian. We also have OP *ciyā-karam* "how, of what sort; how many" (AE *appa hamak*) formed by the inanimate interrogative *ciyā-* and *-karam*. The latter element would be formally related to the verb OP *kar-* "to do" that can be better explained as part of a phraseological sentence, literally meaning "what (is) done". Hackstein (2004: 172–173) shows some parallels in TA $k_u yal$ formed after the interrogative pronoun *ku-* "what" plus the verbal adjective *yal* "to be done". This form would have evolved into a conjunction with causal meaning "why > because". In Ternate Malay, we find a similar grammaticalization process for this phraseological array: *binking apa* [make what] > *biki apa/kiapa* "why" (LITAMAHUPUTTY 2012:185).

68   See HERZFELD 1938.

Nevertheless, although Semitic contact might have played a role in the formation of the attested indefinite relative pattern OP *kā haya* "whoever" (interr. + rel.), I would like to suggest that there is something else behind AE *akkaya*. I believe that this form points to an inherited IE morphological form, one of whose reflexes is MP *kē* "who? INTERR, who REL". Interestingly, the *Rigveda* attests the indefinite Ved. *káya-cid* (×3)[69] "every, any", the interrogative Ved. *ká-* plus *-ya* (*AiGc*: 563, *EWAia* 307; GOTŌ 2013: 74).[70] Remarkably, this Vedic indefinite pronoun also has a distributive/universal ("every") as well as a nominal FC ("any") values.

As we know, OIr. **ká-* only performs interrogative (O/YAv. *kā̆ /kō* "who?") as well as indefinite (O/YAv. *kasciṯ*, OP *kašci* "anyone") functions, while OIr. **(sa)i̯a* > Av. *yō* and OP *haya* carries out the relative function. It has been traditionally assumed that MP *kē* derives from a fossilized genitive of the interrogative/indefinite stem **kahya*.[71] Contrary to this view and after Horn (1893: 196) and Hübschmann (1895: 142), I consider MP *kē* to be derived from the indefinite relative OIr. **kai̯a* > OP **kaya* "whoever", cognate of Ved. *káya*, which must have operated as an interrogative-relative pronoun in non-specific free-relative clauses and which, by the early Middle Persian period, would have already entailed both interrogative as well as relative functions, the latter adopted from the pronominal base OIr. **ká-*. Notably, Ved. *káya cid* FC "anyone, everyone" has a perfect match in in MP *kē-iz* "whoever" as well as Parth. *kēž* NPI/FC "anyone, whoever" (cf. TEDESCO 1945: 128–129),[72] provided that all these forms are derived from IIr. **kai̯a-čid*.

---

69   See RV 1, 129, 5; 1, 27, 8; and 8, 25, 15. This form, only attested in the genitive: Ved. *kasya*, should not be confused with the interrogative Ved. *kayā*, intr.sg. fem. "in which manner?".

70   I will not discuss in this paper whether this *-ya* actually is a reflex of the Indo-Iranian relative pronoun IIr. *ya-* or not. Suffice it to say here that the IE reflexes of **kʷo-(H)i̯o-* might point to the merger between the interrogative-indefinite stem and the anaphoric **h₁i-*. The creation of new pronominals after the union of interrogatives and demonstratives is typologically common. Some other possible cognates of **kʷó-(H)i̯-o-s* may be Gr. ποῖος, Arm. *o(v)*, Lat. *cuius*, TA *ke* (and TB *ket-ra*), etc.

71   Cf. Salemann (1895–1901: 292), Reichelt (1903: 574); Nyberg (1974: 54); Durkin-Meisterernst (2012: 214), Baghbidi (2017: 34). Similarly, Aram. *dy* REL "who, which" seems to be a fossilized genitive form (GZELLA 2011: 577).

72   While Parth. *kēž*, alongside of negation, has an NPI function "any", it can also express FC values heading non-specific indefinite relative clauses "whoever" (BRUNNER 1977: 42, *DMMPP*: 219, DURKIN-MEISTERERNST 2012: 215.) Cf. also Parth. *kadāž* "never (with neg.), whenever", similarly to MP *hagriz* "never (with neg.), whenever" (< OP *hakaram-ci*). Notice that Parth. *kēž* is the equivalent of MP *kas*: *kēž kēž* DISTR "each, everyone", *harw kēž* UNI "everyone", etc. Parthian also attests the interrogative-relative pronoun Parth. *kē* INTERR/REL "who? who".

ACHAEMENID ELAMITE AND OLD PERSIAN INDEFINITES

TABLE 2.6   OP *kā haya* and AE *akka(ya)*

Achaemenid Elamite	Early Indo-Iranian	Middle Iranian
AE *akkaya* $_{FC}$ =	OP **kaya* $_{FC}$ (< PIE **kʷo-(H)io-*) "whoever"	> MP *kē* $_{INTERR /REL /FC}$ "who?; who, whoever"
	Cf. Ved. *káya cid* $_{FC/UNI}$ "anyone, everyone"	Cf. Parth. *kē-ž* $_{NPI/ FC}$ "anyone, whoever" MP *kē-iz* "whoever"
AE *akka* $_{FC}$ "whoever"	OP *kā haya* $_{FC}$ "whoever"	
		Cf. MP *harw kē* $_{FC}$ "whoever"
	Cf. OP *kašci haya* $_{FC}$	
		Cf. MP *ēč kē* $_{FC}$ "whoever"
DB$_e$ § 44 (ex55) 63–64,	DB$_p$ 4, § 55, 37	
DB$_e$ § 45 (ex 56), 66	DB$_p$ 4, § 65, 70	
DB$_e$ § 52 (ex 64), 83,	DB$_p$ 4, § 56, 41	
DB$_e$ § 53 (ex 65), 84	DB$_p$ 4, § 64, 67	
DB$_e$ § 54 (ex 69), 94b	DB$_p$ 4, § 69, 87	
AE *akkaya* $_{FC}$ "whoever"	OP *kā haya* $_{FC}$ "whoever"	
XPh$_e$ 38–39	XPh$_p$ § 6, 46	

Thus, the interrogative-into-relative shift assumed for OIr. **ká-*, through a fossilized genitive, might be better explained as the complete absorption of the relative function by OIr. **kaia*, after relative pronoun OP *haya* (> MP *-ī*) had put aside its relative function in favor of *ezāfe*-like constructions already attested in Old Persian.[73] In the same vein, MP *kē* often appears heading non-specific relative clauses expressing a FC value. If my interpretation is sound, the former interrogative-indefinite stem OIr. **ká-* (< PIE **kʷó-*) would have only kept its indefinite function: the bare stem MP *kas* $_{EQ/NPI}$ "someone, anyone" and MP *kas-iz* $_{NPI}$ "anyone".[74] In Table 2.6, I summarize the contents of this section.

---

73   Phonetically, according to Sunderman (1989: 109–110), *hᵃya-ka-* (< OIr. **sa-ia-ka*, cf. Ved. *yaka-*) developed into MP *īg* and *hᵃya* would have developed into *ē*. Therefore, it is still possible to derive MP *kē* from **kahᵃya*, although I believe that this is less likely. Cf. On the etymological and phonetic reading of OP relatives, cf. Tavernier (1999).

74   Nonetheless, professor Agnes Korn (p.c.) has pointed out to me that genitive forms as ety-

6   OP *taya* ~FC~ : AE *appa* ~FC~ "whatever"[75]

Old Persian as well as Middle Persian place the relative pronoun in clause-initial position for expressing FC values along subjunctive verbal forms, sometimes within relative-correlative structures: OP *taya*, MP *čē*...subj.[76] See (10a–b) for an example.

(10) a. DB_p 4, §66, 75–76

utā **taya** *kunavāhi,* **avatai̯** *A.uramzdā   ucāram   kunau̯tu.*
and which do-2SG   that   Ahuramazda successful do-3SG (IMP)

b. DB_e (ex 66), 87

ak kutta **appa** *huttanti,* **huhpe** *ᵈUramazda*
and   which do-2SG that   Ahuramazda
hazzaš.ni.
to make great-2SG.opt. part.
'And whatever you shall do, may Ahuramazdā make that successful.'

If we turn to the AB version, we find the compound form AB *mimma mala* "whatever", the indefinite pronoun plus the quantitative pronoun *mala* "as

---

mological origin of Middle Persian pronominals is not at all rare: e.g. MP *man* "I" (< OP *manā*), MP *tō* "you" (< OP *tawa*), MP *amāh* "we" (< OP *amāxam*). The same can be observed in some MP demonstratives: e.g. MP *ōy* "this" (< OP *au̯ahya*). Cf. Durkin-Meisterernst (2012: 207, 213–214). As regards IE parallels, professor Ronald Kim (p.c.) has indicated to me that West Slavic displays a similar phenomenon: the shift from Proto-Slavic gen. **česo*, **čiso* to nom./acc. Cf. MEILLET 1924: 386–387.

75   In this section, I will restrict myself to AE *appa* as a FC indefinite relative "whatever" and, therefore, I will not discuss OP *aniya*...*aniya* (DB_p 1, §18, 86–87) / AE *appa-pa*...*appa-pa* (DB_e 17 (ex 18), 68–69) "some ... other", which functions as a multiple partitive construction. For its typology, see Haspelmath (1997: 177). Here, AE *appa-pa* could consist in the relative AE *appa* plus the plural animate nominal class marker, as in AE *akka-p*, or in a formation modeled after ME *akka-r*. See EW: 73 and Filippone (2016: 35–36) for a detailed discussion of these forms. Notice that we also find similar multiple partitive constructions in Middle Iranian: MP *kē*...*kē* and Khot. *kye*...*kye* "some ... other". I will not discuss either the non-specific relative OP *yaci* (DNb_p § 3, 13) "whatever" nor the interative OP *yaci*...*yaci* (DNb_p §8, 35–36) /AE *anka*...*anka* (DNb_e §8, 24–25): "whether ... or", which entails an alternative concessive conditional. See Coenen (to appear). I will leave for future research the relationship between AE *appa anka* [what if] "whenever; whatever" (cf. NP *agar-cē* [if what] "although, even if"), a possible concessive conditional from (*sap*) *appa anka* "if, when, as, because", and OP *yadi* "if" and OP *yaθā* "as, when, because, etc.".

76   Cf. Reichelt (1903: 574–575); Brunner (1977: 85), Skjærvø (2009: 256), and Durkin-Meisterernst (2012: 215).

ACHAEMENID ELAMITE AND OLD PERSIAN INDEFINITES

73

TABLE 2.7 OP *taya* and AE *appa* "whatever"

Achaemenid Elamite	Old Iranian	Middle Iranian
AE *appa* INTERR/REL/FC "what?, which, whatever"	OP *taya* REL/ FC "which, whatever"	MP *če* INTERR/REL/FC "what?, which, whatever"
DB$_e$ (ex 66), 87 DB$_e$ (ex 67), 89	DB$_p$ 4, § 66, 75–76 DB$_p$ 4, § 67, 79–80	Cf. MP *harw če* FC

much as".[77] This may be surprising as we might have expected to find either the inanimate interrogative Akk. *minû(m)* "what?", heading a non-specific relative clause together with the relative particle (interr. + rel.)—in the same way as the animate interrogative Akk. *mannu* "who?"—or an indefinite relative Akk. *mimma (ša)*[78] (indef. + rel.). Hence, this AB form sustains our assessment of taking OP *taya* and AE *appa*[79] as inanimate FC indefinite relative pronouns "whatever".[80] In turn, the inanimate interrogative-relative MP *če* "what?, which, whichever" shows similar formations, although sometimes it employs the universal quantifier MP *harw* "every" for marking the indefinite relative function. In Table 2.7, I summarize this section.

7   OP *aiva* and AE *ki*—"one, some, certain"

A marked trait of early Indo-Iranian is the almost complete absence of a *specific* indefinite (EQ "some"). In its place, the numeral 'one' OP *aiva* (< *$*(H)oi̯$-$u̯o$-. cf. Ved. *ékas* < *$*(H)oi̯$-ko-) is employed to fulfill this function. See (11) for an example. Even though Schmitt (1991: 51 fn. 36) is against considering the numeral 'one' a real indefinite determiner, I take OP *aiva* as a proper indefinite pronoun already by the Old Iranian period (cf. *WaK*: 128). This view is confirmed by the Middle Persian and Parthian data, although, in the latter, the employment of the numeral 'one' as an indefinite marker is much less common (BRUNNER 1977: 43–45).

---

77   Akk. *mala (ša)* alone can also express similar values "whoever, whatever, everyone who, etc." See Huehnergard (1997: 188). Cf. Aram. *kmst dy* "as many as".

78   Cf. The idiomatic nominal phrase Akk. *mimma šumšu*, literally "whatever the name" > "everything".

79   Nevertheless, it is observed that *appa* can also have an animate reference.

80   There is no parallel passage in the Aramaic version.

(11) DB_p 1, §11, 36

pasāva **aịva** *martiya maguš āha Gaumāta nāma.*
afterwards one/a man magician be-3SG Gaumata name
'Afterwards there was a/some man, a magus, Gaumāta by name.'

In Old and Middle Iranian, the numeral 'one' is deeply connected with the expression of indefiniteness. OP *aịva* and its derivative, the enclitic suffix MP *-ēw*,[81] can function as indefinite articles "a, a certain", much like a *specific* indefinite pronoun "some". MP *-ēw* is also involved in the formation of other types of MP indefinite formations: the indefinite MP *ēč* NPI "any"[82] and FC indefinites after interrogative pronouns such as MP *kadām-ē(w)*_FC "whoever",[83] MP *kadār-iz-ē(w)*_FC "whatever",[84] and MP *čēgam-iz-e(w)*_FC "whichever".[85] I already mentioned that MP *-ēw* also marks *irrealis* as well as FC functions along with indefinite and numeral forms (*kas, tis, ēk* and *ēč*), leaving aside negative polarity functions. The fact that MP *-iz* exclusively marks negative polarity functions strongly suggests the status of *-ēw* as a non-negative polarity marker. Therefore, whereas MP *-ēw*[86] are in charge of overtly marking FC indefinites, MP *-iz* is abundantly employed as a NPI marker.[87]

---

81 SKJÆRVØ 2009: 205.

82 According to Klingenschmitt (2000: 212), it is derived from OIr *aịua-čid*. Nevertheless, the fact that OP *-ci* yields MP *-z* should cast some doubts on this etymology. Cf. Baghbidi (2017: 50) and Bernard (2019: 43 fn. 11).

83 Cf. Ved. *katamá-*_INTERR "who or which of many", Skrt. *katama caná* NPI "(not) anyone".

84 Cf. O/YAv. *katāra* INTERR "who?", YAv. *katarasciṭ* DISTR "each of the two", Ved. *katará-* "who, which of the two?", Skrt. *katara caná* NPI "(not) anyone (of the two)".

85 Notably, MP *čē-kām-iz* [cy-k'm-c] is formed by the inanimate relative-interrogative *čē* and the verb *kām-* "to wish, to desire" along the particle *-iz*. Cf. Similar FC indefinites Lat. *quī-uīs* FC "anyone", Span. *cualquier* FC. In Middle Persian, the verb *kām-* can also function as auxiliary verb along with infinitives describing future actions. In Khwarezmian, we observe nice parallels of both phenomena: Khwar. *kām* appears as a grammatialized future particle, much like English *will*, and as an enclitic particle along interrogative stems adding an indefinite nuance, e.g. Khwar. *kd'm-k'm* "whatever" (< OIr. *katāma-kāma*).

86 Nevertheless, as mentioned before, we find MPt *-iz* (as in MPt *tis-iz* FC "anything, whatever"), MP *-iz* (as in MP *kē-iz* FC "whoever"), and Parth. *-ž* (as in *kež* FC "whoever" and *kadāž* FC "whenever") acting as domain-widening particles. Notably, in Middle Persian we find an adverbial concessive conditional sharing the same morphological element i.e. OIr. *-čid*: MP *ka-iz* "whenever" (MP *ka* "when, if"). Similar constructions can be seen in early Indo-Iranian OP *yaci* "whatever" (universal concessive conditional) and OP *yaci...yaci* "whether ... or" (alternative concessive conditional), and Ved. *yad cid* "even if; whatever" (scalar and universal concessive conditional respectively). For a detailed analysis of these forms, cf. Coenen (2021: 121–166, to appear). Furthermore, notice that NP *har cand ke* and Bal. *har či* employ the element *har*, also found in the formation of FC indefinites since Middle Persian onwards.

87 As in MP *hagriz* "ever" (< OP *hakaram-ci*).

ACHAEMENID ELAMITE AND OLD PERSIAN INDEFINITES 75

While early Indo-Iranian displays the combination between the numeral 'one' and the de-instrumental particle IIr. *čana: YAv. (nōit) aēuuō-cina $_{NPI}$ and Ved. (ná) ékaś caná $_{NPI}$,[88] Middle Persian shows the numeral 'one' along with the particle OIr. *-čid, as in MP ēč $_{NPI}$ (< OIr *aiua-čid) "any (at all)" and also in MP ēk-iz "(not) even one, anyone",[89] the latter form with negation usually found before the numeral. Nyberg (1974: 69) mentions the form MP ē-cin (ēzin), seemingly derived from OIr. *aiua čina and he regards it as equivalent of YAv. aēuuō-cina. Nevertheless, as shown above, its MP equivalent of the numeral is not MP -ēw, but MP ēk.

For its part, the Elamite numeral 'one' is ki and is mainly found along the delocutive 3rd sg. suffix -r: AE kir (Cf. PAPER 1955: 124–125; TAVERNIER 2018: 433).[90] It works as an indefinite determiner, similarly to OP aiva (REINER 1960: 225; REINER 1969: 86; QUINTANA 2013: 56), and as a member of compounds such AE da(e)ki- "another" and the aforementioned indefinite forms AE aški "anything", and ME azkit "anything". AE ki also functions along with inanimate suffixes in formations such as pel kima "within one year" or sut-kime sat-kime "each night and each day",[91] where the numeral is always in second position. Finally, in the Persepolis tablets, the numeral 'one' is found in fractions such as X ir-ma ki "X parts in 1" or X kur-ma ki "X parts in 1 handled" (GRILLOT-SUSINI 2008: 30, QUINTANA 2013: 100 fn. 57).[92] In addition, in the administrative tablets too, we find AE kir (cf. PF-NN 1431) employed as a numeral and as an indefinite determiner. Furthermore, in DB, although the collocation AE ruh

---

88   Notice that Old Avestan (Y29,6) attests nōit aēuuā "not one", negation plus the numeral 'one' in the instrumental case. Here, OAv. aēuuā functions as an NPI, although, in this case, without the aid of a de-instrumental, scalar focus particle OIr. *čina. See Briceño-Villalobos (2019) for the relationship between instrumental suffixes, PIE *-h₁ and PIE *-kʷene, and negative polarity contexts.

89   Bernard (2019) proposes that OIr. *aiua-ia-ka is the actual ancestor of MP/NP yak "one". He also deems doubtful the form MP ēk, which is traditionally taken as the correct transcription of MP ⟨'ywk¹⟩ and derived from OIr. *aiua-ka. As regards its uses, MP ēk displays functions that go parallel to those shown by the MP indefinites kas and tis: ēk $_{EQ}$ "one, some", ēk-iz $_{NPI}$ "not one, anyone", ēk $_{NPI}$ "anyone" (with conditionals), ēk-ēw $_{IRR/FC}$ "some, any", harw ēk-(ēw) "everyone", and ēk ēk $_{DISTR}$ "one by one, each".

90   As pointed out by Quintana (2013: 28 fn. 13), Achaemenid Elamite also generalizes the employment of -ra [-r (nominal class marker) + a (relative particle) as some sort of indefinite marker meaning "a, one".

91   Cf. MP kas kas, Parth. kēž kēž "each one".

92   Notice that the second position of the numeral after nominals closely resembles the one observed in MP -ē(w) "one, some". The similarity is particularly striking when we consider that MP fractions are expressed by means of MP -ēk-ēw as in MP sē-ēk-ēw "one third" (DURKIN-MEISTERERNST 2012: 220).

76 BRICEÑO VILLALOBOS

TABLE 2.8 OP *aiva* and AE *kir*

Achaemenid Elamite	Old Iranian	Middle Iranian
kir ₙᵤₘ/ₑ𝘘 "one, some"	OP *aiva* ₙᵤₘ/ₑ𝘘 "one, some, a certain"	> MP *-ēw* ₙᵤₘ/ₑ𝘘/ᵢᵣᵣ "one, some"
		Cf. MP *kadām-ē(w)* ₚ𝘤 "whoever"
		MP *kadār-iz-ē(w)* ₚ𝘤 "whatever"
		MP *čēgam-iz-ē(w)*ₚ𝘤 "whichever"
	OIr. *aiua-ka	> MP *ēk* "one"
PF 1859, 16		
inri kir ₙₚᵢ (= *akkar*) "anyone"	OIr. *(*nai*) *aiua-ka-čid* ₙₚᵢ	> MP (*nē*) *ēk-iz* ₙₚᵢ "(not) even one, any"
	OIr. *aiua-čid ₙₚᵢ	
		> MP *ēč* (*nē*) ₙₚᵢ "any (at all)"
	Cf. YAv. (*nōit*) *aēuuō-cina* ₙₚᵢ	
	Cf. Ved. (*ná*) *ékaś caná* ₙₚᵢ	Cf. Parth. *ēwiž* (*nē*) ₙₚᵢ "any"

kir "some/a certain man" closely follows OP *aiva martiya*,[93] there are instances where the numeral *kir* does not have a parallel in the OP text (e.g. DB_e 44, (ex 29), 38: *barsir kir* vs. DB_p 2, 29: *Pārsa* "(a certain/some) Persian"). This implies that somehow the use of the numeral 'one' as a specific indefinite is more consistently employed in AE version than in the OP version itself. It should be noted that this use of the numeral as an indefinite is not attested prior to Achaemenid Elamite times.

Finally, the numeral 'one' is also found along with negation, as in (12). In this case, it does not follow the Elamite word order for NPI indefinites (indef. + NEG), but the Old and Middle Iranian one as observed in negative indefinites, O/YAv. *naēcis* ₙᵢ "no one", and NPIs based on the numeral 'one', OAv. *nōit aēuuā* ₙₚᵢ, YAv. *nōit aēuua-cina* ₙₚᵢ "not (even) one", MP *nē ēk-iz* "not anyone", Parth. *nē ēwiž* ₙₚᵢ "not (a single) one".[94]

---

93   Bae (2001: 243) remarks that there is no word divider between the numeral 'one' and *martiya* in the OP version. This may imply that the indefinite nuance conveyed by the numeral 'one' is further supported by the nominal *martiya* "a man" > "someone". Also cf. AB *išten amēlu* "one man". As mentioned, Akk. *amīlu* is often employed as an indefinite.

94   The position of the negative marker with the latter two can vary, since it can also appear after the numeral in preverbal position.

ACHAEMENID ELAMITE AND OLD PERSIAN INDEFINITES

(12) PF 1859, 16

> *lipar*   *inri*   ***kir.***
> servant NEG-3SG one-3SG
> 'There is no servant.'

In Table 2.8, I summarize the uses of the numeral 'one' in both Achaemenid Elamite and Old/Middle Iranian.

8   AE *kaš kaš*

Henkelman (2008: 446, fn. 1035) has suggested that the form *kaš*, attested in some Neo-Elamite texts (EKI 85 6, 7, 8, 10:[95] *kaš kaš*) as well as in the Achaemenid administrative tablets (PF 269: 8, PF 755, 4), may represent a loan from OP *kašci*.[96] This form refers back to animate and, rarely, to inanimate objects as a resumptive pronoun. Hallock (1969: 9, 711) asserts that AE *kaš* [BI] is in substitution of the 3rd sg. dat. resumptive pronoun *hi* "to him".[97] Cf. also Stolper (2004: 77).[98] Thus, although it seems an admittedly rare formation, in some cases along with the original resumptive *hi*, AE *kaš*[99] must be taken as a resumptive pronoun of its own accord rather than an indefinite pronoun and definitely not as a substitute of *hi*. Therefore, AE *kaš* could be reckoned as another instance of the OP influence over Elamite.[100] Elamite would have acquired *kaš* from OP inventory and, after stripping this morphological loan of its original value, it would have redeployed it back into the pronominal system transformed into a resumptive pronoun.[101] In Table 2.9, I provide a summary of the contents of this last section.[102]

---

95   From the period of king Tepti-Huban-Insušnak (ca. 550–30 BCE).

96   In Achaemenid Elamite, the addition of a final *-š* is a general phenomenon observed in Old Persian loans (HENKELMAN 2008: 446 fn. 1035).

97   To be fair, *hi* can work as a demonstrative, anaphoric (or resumptive), or personal pronoun (3rd sg.). Cf. QUINTANA 2013: 40 ff.

98   However, Vallat (1987) considers *kaš* an archaic formation of the sign HI, which, therefore, should be read *hi*. Thus, in his view, *kaš* should be taken as a ghost word.

99   With reduplication in EKI 85, 6,7, 9, 10, similarly to Avestan and Old Persian reduplicated indefinites.

100   Especially if we consider the late date of the Neo-Elamite inscription where this form is attested and its presence in the Achaemenid administrative archives.

101   Cf. Tavernier (2018: 429–430).

102   Notice that MP *kas* $_{EQ}$ "some" can also mean "person", which meaning seems closer to that of a resumptive pronoun "him, her, it".

TABLE 2.9 AE *kaš*

Achaemenid Elamite	Old Iranian	Middle Iranian
PF 269:8, PF 755, 4 *kaš* RESUPT		Cf. MP *kas* EQ "some"
EKI 85 NE *kaš kaš* RESUPT "him, that one"	Cf. Av. *kaṅhe kaṅhe* FC "each and every"	Cf. MP *kas kas* DISTR, Parth. *kēz kēz* DISTR "each one, everyone"

9 Conclusions

The objective of this paper was to highlight the diachronic developments of Persian indefinites in order to track down their diverse semantic functions on each stage of the language (Old and Middle Iranian) as well as to assess how Achaemenid Elamite, in several cases, serves as a reflection of Old Iranian indefinite morphology. At the same time, we have seen that Semitic morphological data has aided us in our better understanding of AE and OP indefinite formations, especially in cases where Babylonian or Aramaic may have played a role in the creation of slightly odd phraseological patterns. In Figure 2.1, I provide a complete list of OP indefinites, their MP developments (>), their MP equivalents (=), and their AE counterparts (**bold letters**).

ACHAEMENID ELAMITE AND OLD PERSIAN INDEFINITES

OP *kašci* ₙₚᵢ "anyone" > MP *kas-iz* ₙₚᵢ "anyone". AE /ME *akkar* ₙₚᵢ "anyone"

OP *kašci* ᵤₙᵢ "each, everyone" = MP *harw kas* ᵤₙᵢ/ᴅᵢₛₜᵣ "each one, everyone". AE *unra* ᴅᵢₛₜᵣ/ᵤₙᵢ **"each, every"**

OP *cišci* ₙₚᵢ "anything" > MP *tis-iz* ₙₚᵢ "anything". AE *aški*/ ME *azkit* ₙₚᵢ **"anything"**

OP *kā haya* ꜰᴄ "whoever". AE *akka(ya)* ꜰᴄ "whoever"

OP **kai̯a* ᵢₙₜₑᵣᵣ/ꜰᴄ "who?, whoever" > MP *kē* ᵢₙₜₑᵣᵣ/ᵣₑₗ/ꜰᴄ "who? who, whoever". AE *akkaya* ꜰᴄ "whoever"

OP *taya* ꜰᴄ "whatever" = MP *čē* ᵢₙₜₑᵣᵣ/ᵣₑₗ/ꜰᴄ "what?, which, whatever". AE *appa* ᵢₙₜₑᵣᵣ/ᵣₑₗ/ꜰᴄ **"what?. which, whatever"**

OP *ai̯va* ₙᵤₘ/ ₑϙ "one, some" > MP *-ē(w)* ₙᵤₘ/ₑϙ/ᵢᵣᵣ/ꜰᴄ "one, some, any". AE *kir* ₙᵤₘ/ ₑϙ **"one, some"**/ *akkar* ₑϙ (= MP *kas* ₑϙ) **"some"**

OP **ai̯ua-ka* ₙᵤₘ "one" > MP *ēk* ₙᵤₘ/ "one, some"

OP **[nai̯] ai̯ua-ka* ₙₚᵢ "not even one" > MP [*nē*] *ēk-iz* ₙₚᵢ "not (even) one". AE [*inri*] *kir* ₙₚᵢ **"not (any)one"**

OP **ai̯ua-ci* ₙₚᵢ "any" > MP *ēč* ₙₚᵢ "any"

OP *kā-* ᵢₙₜₑᵣᵣ "who?" > MP *kas* ₑϙ "someone". AE *kaš* / ME *kaš kaš* ᵣₑₛᵤₘₚ **"him, that one"**

FIGURE 2.1 Old Persian, Middle Persian, and Achaemenid Elamite indefinites and their functions

Abbreviations

Languages

AB	Achaemenid Babylonian
AE	Achaemenid Elamite
Akk.	earlier Akkadian
Aram.	Imperial Aramaic
Arm.	Armenian
Bactr.	Bactrian
Bal.	Balochi

Skrt.	Classical Sanskrit
Gr.	Classical Greek
HGr.	Homeric Greek
HLuw.	Hieroglyphic Luwian
Hitt.	Hittite
IIr.	Indo-Iranian
Khot.	Khotanese
Khwar.	Khwarezmian
Lat.	Latin
ME	Middle Elamite
MP	Manichean Middle Persian
MP$_t$	Turfan Middle Persian
NE	Neo-Elamite
NP	New Persian
OAv.	Old Avestan
OIr.	Old Iranian
Osc.	Oscan
Oss.	Ossetic
Parth.	Parthian
Sogd.	Sogdian
Turk.	Turkish
Ved.	*Rigvedic* Vedic
YAv.	Young Avestan.

Typology/Morphology

COND	Conditional
COMP	Comparative
DISTR	Distributive
EQ	Existential Quantifier
FC	Free-Choice
FCI(s)	Free-Choice Item(s)
IND/indef.	Indefinite
INTERR/interr.	Interrogative
IRR	Irrealis
NEG	Negation
NI	Negative Indefinite
NPI(s)	Negative Polarity Item(s)
NUM	Numeral
opt.	Optative
part.	Particle

REL/rel.	Relative
RESUMPT	Resumptive
UNI	Universal Quantifier
V	Verb
✗	no correspondence

For DB, I have followed the Achaemenid Elamite and Imperial Aramaic texts in Bae (2001) and the OP text in Schmitt (2009). For the rest of the Achaemenid Royal Inscriptions, I have followed Vallat (1977). For the administrative tablets, I have made use of OCHRE: Online Cultural and Historical Research Environment. Thanks are due to prof. Stolper, as director of Persepolis Fortification Archive (PFA) Project, for letting me quote Fort. Texts. For the Middle Elamite texts, I have used König (1965). Finally, for the Achaemenid Babylonian texts, I have made use of Bae (2001), which, in turn, is an updated version of Malbran-Labat (1994).

References

ADAMS, DOUGLAS Q. 2013, *A dictionary of Tocharian B*, Amsterdam/Atlanta: Rodopi B.V. Editions.

AIGc = WACKERNAGEL, JAKOB 1896–1930, *Altindische Grammatik. Bd. III, Nominalflexion, Zahlwort, Pronomen*, Göttingen: Vandenhoeck & Ruprecht.

ALIYARI BABOLGHANI, SALMAN 2015, *The Elamite Version of Darius the Great's Inscription at Bisotun* (in Persian), Tehran: Nashr-e Markaz.

BACK, MICHAEL 1992, *Topikalisierungen in Alpersischen*, in B. Brogyanyi (ed.), *Prehistory, History, and Historiography of Language, Speech, and Linguistics Theory*, Amsterdam/Philadelphia: John Benjamins Publishing Company: 241–268.

BAE, CHUL-HYUN 2001, *Comparative studies on king Darius's Bisitun inscription*, PhD dissertation, Harvard University.

BAGHBIDI HASSAN R. 2017, *Middle Persian Historical Phonology*, Osaka: Osaka University Graduate School of Language and Culture.

BAVANT, MARC 2014, *Résultatif, diathèse et possession en basque, vieux perse et élamite*, PhD dissertation, Utrecht University.

BARTHOLOMAE, CHRISTIAN 1904, *Altiranisches Wörterbuch*, Strassburg: Verlag von Karl Trübner.

BEEKES, ROBERT S.P. 2010, *Etymological dictionary of Greek*, vol. 1–2, Boston/Leiden: Brill.

BERNARD, CHAMS 2019, *On the etymology of Persian yak 'one'*, "Wékwos" 4: 37–51.

BOOIJ, GEERT 2005, *The grammar of words: An introduction to linguistic morphology*, Oxford: Oxford University Press.

BOSWELL, FREDERICK A. 2021, *A Grammar of Cheke Holo*, PhD dissertation, Leiden University.

BRICEÑO VILLALOBOS, JUAN E. 2019, *Negation, indefinites, and polarity in early Greek and Indo-Iranian: a typological and comparative approach*, PhD dissertation, Complutense University of Madrid.

BRICEÑO VILLALOBOS, JUAN E. 2020, *Correlative negation in Old Persian*, "Poznan Studies on Contemporary Linguistics" 56/3: 451–475.

BRUNNER, CHRISTOPHER J. 1977, *A Syntax of Western Middle Iranian*, Delmar, NY: Caravan Books.

BRUST, MANFRED 2018, *Historische Laut- und Formenlehre des Altpersischen. Mit einem etymologischen Glossar*, Innsbruck: Innsbrucker Beiträge zur Sprachwissenschaft.

CAD = *The Assyrian Dictionary of the Oriental Institute of the University of Chicago*, 1968–2010.

CHANTRAINE, PIERRE 1968, *Dictionnaire étymologique de la langue grecque: histoire des mots*, Paris: Klincksieck.

COENEN, PASCAL 2021, *The Functions of Vedic cid, íd, īm, ī and sīm*, PhD Dissertation, Universitiy of Köln.

COENEN, PASCAL (to appear), *The Functions of the Old Persian Particle =ci*.

DELITZCSH, FRIEDRICH 1889, *Assyrian Grammar* (transl. By R.S. Kennedy), Berlin: H. Reuther's Verlagsbuchhandlung.

DMMPP = DURKIN-MEISTERERNST, DESMOND 2004, *Dictionary of Manichean Middle Persian and Parthian*, Turnhout: Brepols.

DNWSIa = HOFTIJZER, JABOC—JONGELING, KAREL 1995, *Dictionary of North-West Semitic Inscrptions*, Part 1 ('- L) with appendices by R.C. Steiner, A. Mosak Moshavi and B. Porten, Leiden /New York/Köln: E.J. Brill.

DUNKEL, G.E. 1997, *B. Delbrück and the Instrumental-Ablative in *-m*, in E. Crespo—J.L. García Ramón (eds.), *Berthold Debrück y la sintaxis indoeuropea hoy: Actas del Coloquio de la Indogermanische Gesellschaft, Madrid, 21–24 de septiembre de 1994*, Madrid/Wiesbaden: Ediciones de la UAM/Dr. Ludwig Reichert Verlag: 63–83.

DURKIN-MEISTERERNST, DESMOND 2012, *Grammatik des Westmitteliranischen (Parthisch und Mittelpersisch)*, Vienna: Verlag der Österreichischen Akademie der Wissenschaften.

EKI = KÖNIG, FRIEDRICH W. 1965, *Die elamischen Königinschriften*, Archiv für Orientforschung, Beihefte 16, Graz: E. Weidner.

EW = HINZ, WALTER—KOCH, HEIDEMARIE 1987, *Elamisches Wörterbuch*, Band I–II, Berlin: Verlag von Dietrich Reimer in Berlin.

EWAia = MAYRHOFER, MANFRED 1992, *Etymologisches Wörterbuch des Altindoarischen*, Band I. Heidelberg: Carl Winter Universitätsverlag.

FABER, ALICE 1988, *Indefinite pronouns in Early Semitic*, in Y.L. Arbeitman (ed.), *Fucus, A Semitic/Afrasian Gathering in Remembrance of Albert Ehrman*, Amsterdam/Philadelphia: John Benjamins Publishing Company: 221–238.

FILIPPONE, ELA 2016, *Goat-skins, Horses and Camels: How did Darius' Army Cross the Tigris?*, in C. Redard (ed.), *Des contrées avestiques à Mahabad, via Bisotun. Etudes offertes en hommage à Pierre Lecoq*, Paris: Recherches et Publications: 25–60.

FRISK, HJALMAR 1969, *Griechisches Etymologisches Wörterbuch*, Heidelberg: Carl Winter Universitätsverlag.

GAD, CYRIL J. 1958, *The Harran Inscriptions of Nabonidus*, "Anatolian Studies" 8: 35–92.

GARCÍA RAMÓN, JOSÉ LUIS 1997, *Adverbios de dirección e instrumental indoeuropeo*", in E. Crespo—J.L. García J.L. Ramón (eds.), *Berthold Debrück y la sintaxis indoeuropea hoy: Actas del Coloquio de la Indogermanische Gesellschaft, Madrid, 21–24 de septiembre de 1994*, Madrid/Wiesbaden: Ediciones de la UAM/Dr. Ludwig Reichert Verlag: 113–141.

GERSHEVITCH, ILYA 1988, *Word-Final 'a'-Vowels in Old Persian*, "East and West" 38 /1/4: 65–80.

GIANNAKIDOU, ANASTASIA 1998, *Polarity Sensitivity as (Non)Veridical Dependency*, Amsterdam/Philadelphia: John Benjamins Publishing Company.

GIANNAKIDOU, ANASTASIA 2001, *The meaning of free-choice*, "Linguistics and Philosophy" 24: 659–735.

GIANNAKIDOU, ANASTASIA—CHENG, LISA L. 2006, *(In)Definiteness, Polarity, and the Role of wh-morphology in Free Choice*, "Journal of Semantics" 23: 135–183.

GIANNAKIDOU, ANASTASIA—ZEIJLSTRA, HEDDE 2017, *The Landscape of Negative Dependencies: Negative Concord, N-Words, Split Scope*, in M. Everaert—H. van Riemsdijk (eds.), *The Blackwell Companion to Syntax*, 2nd Edition, London: Blackwell: 1–38.

GOTŌ, TOSHIFUMI 2013, *Old-Indo-Aryan morphology and its Indo-Iranian background*, Vienna: Österreichischen Akademie der Wissenschaften.

GRAY, LOUIS H. 1902, *Notes on the Old Persian Inscriptions of Behistun*, "Journal of the American Oriental Society" 23: 56–64.

GRILLOT-SUSINI, FRANÇOISE 2008, *L'Élamite. Éléments de grammaire*, Paris: Geuthner Manuels.

GRILLOT-SUSINI, FRANÇOISE—HERRENSCHMIDT, CLARISSE—MALBRAN-LABAT, FLORENCE 1993, *La version élamite de la trilingue de Behistun: une nouvelle lecture*, "Journal Asiatique" 281/ 1–2: 19–59.

GZELLA, HOLGER 2011, *Imperial Aramaic*, in S. Weninger (ed.), *The Semitic languages. An international handbook*, Berlin/Boston: De Gruyter Mouton: 574–586.

GZELLA, HOLGER 2015, *A Cultural History of Aramaic, From the Beginnings to the Advent of Islam*, Boston/Leiden: Brill.

HACKSTEIN, OLAV 2004, *Rhetorical Questions and the Grammaticalization of Interrogative Pronouns as Conjunctions in Indo-European*, in A. Hyllested—A.R. Jørgensen—J.H. Larsson—T. Olander (eds.), *Per Aspera Ad Asteriscos, Studia Indogermanica in honorem Jens Elmergård Rasmussen sexagenari Idibus Martiis anno MMIV*, Innsbruck: Innsbrucker Beiträge zur Sprachwissenschaft: 167–186.

HALLOCK, RICHARD T. 1969, *Persepolis Fortification Tablets*, Chicago: University of Chicago Press.

HASPELMATH, MARTIN 1997, *Indefinite pronouns*, Oxford: Oxford University Press.

HAUL, MICHAEL 2009, *Stele und Legende, Untersuchungen zu den keilschriftlichen Erzählwerken über die Könige von Akkade*, Göttingen: Universitätsverlag Göttingen.

HENKELMAN, WOUTER. F.M. 2008, *The other gods who are. Studies in Elamite-Iranian Acculturation based on the Persepolis Fortification texts*, Leiden: Nederlands Instituut voor het Nabije Oosten.

HERZFELD, ERNEST 1938, *Altpersische Inschriften*, Berlin: Verlag von Dietrich Reimer.

HINZ, WALTER 1973, *Neue Wege im Altpersischen*, Wiesbaden: Otto Harrassowitz.

HORN, LAURENCE R. 2000, *Any and (-)ever: Free-choice and free-relatives*, in A.Z. Wyner (ed.), *The Proceedings of the Fifteenth Annual Conference, The University of Haifa 1999*, The Israel Association for Theoretical Linguistics.

HORN, PAUL 1893, *Grundriss der Neupersischen Etyomologie*, Strassburg: Verlag von Karl J. Trübner.

HORN, PAUL 1898–1901, *Neupersische Schriftsprache*, in W. Geiger—E. Kuhn (eds.), *Grundriss der Iranischen Philologie*, Strassburg: Verlag von Karl J. Trübner: 1–200.

HORN, PAUL 1904, *The Old Persian Inscription at Behistan, transliterated with philological annotations*, in E.W. West (ed.), *Avesta, Pahlavi and Ancient Persian Studies, in honour of the late Shams-Ul-Ulama Dastur Peshotanji Behramji Sanjana MA, PhD*, Strassburg/Leipzig: Karl J. Trübner/Otto Harrassowitz: 231–262.

HUEHNERGARD, JOHN 1997, *A Grammar of Akkadian*, Atlanta, (GA): Scholars Press.

HUNT, JOEL H.—SCHNIEDEWIND, WILLIAM M. 2007, *A primer on Ugaritic. Language, Culture, and Literature*, Cambridge: Cambridge University Press.

HÜBSCHMANN, HEINRICH 1895, *Persische Studien*, Strassburg: Verlag von Karl J. Trübner.

JAGERSMA, ABRAHAM. H. 2010, *A descriptive grammar of Sumerian*, PhD dissertation, Leiden University.

JOÜON, PAUL—MURAOKA, TAKAMITSU 1991, *A grammar of Biblical Hebrew*, Volume 2, Part 3: Syntax, Roma: Editrice Pontificio Instituto Biblico.

KENT, RONALD G. 1953, *Old Persian*, New Haven, CT: American Oriental Series.

KHAČIKJAN, MARGARET 1998, *The Elamite Language*, Roma: Consiglio Nazionale delle Ricerche.

KLEIN, JARED 1997, *Indefinite Pronouns, Polarity, and Related Phenomena in Classical Armenian. A Study Based on the Old Armenian Gospels*, "Transactions of the Philological Society" 95: 189–245.

KLINGENSCHMITT, GERT 2000, *Mittelpersisch*, in B. Forssman—R. Plath (eds.), *Indoarisch, Iranisch und die Indogermanistik, Arbeitstagung der Indogermanischen Gesellschaft vom 2. bis 5. Oktober 1997 in Erlangen*, Wiesbaden: Dr. Ludwig Reichert Verlag: 191–229.

ACHAEMENID ELAMITE AND OLD PERSIAN INDEFINITES 85

KOUWENBERG, N.J.C. (BERT) 2017, *A Grammar of Old Assyrian*, Boston/Leiden: Brill.

KÖNIG, EKKEHARD 1991, *The Meaning of Focus Particles*, London/New York: Routledge.

KRAHMALKOV, CHARLES R. 2001, *A Phoenician-Punic Grammar*, Boston/Leiden: Brill.

DE LAMBERTERIE, CHARLES 2013, *Grec, phrygien, arménien, des anciens aux modernes*, "Journal des Savants" 1: 3–69.

LITAMAHUPUTTY, BATHSEBA H.J. 2012, *Ternate Malay: Grammar and Texts*, PhD dissertation, Leiden University.

LIPP = DUNKEL, GEORGE 2014, *Lexicon der indogermanischen Partikeln und Pronominalstämme*, Band II, Heidelberg: Universitätsverlag Winter.

LUBOTSKY, ALEXANDER M.—DE VAAN, MICHIEL A.C. 2011, *Old Persian*, in H. Gzella (ed.), *Languages from the World of the Bible*, Boston/Berlin: Walter de Gruyter: 194–208.

MACDONELL, ARTHUR A. 1910, *Vedic Grammar*, Strassburg: Karl J. Trübner.

MACHAJDÍKOVÁ, BARBORA—MARTZLOFF, VINCENT 2016, *Le pronom indéfini osque pitpit "quicquid" de Paul Diacre à Jacob Balde: morphosyntaxe comparée des paradigmes *kʷi- kʷi- du latin et du sabellique*, "Graeco-Latina Brunensia" 21/1: 73–118.

MALBRAN-LABAT, FLORENCE 1994, *La version Akkadienne de l'inscription trilingue de Darius à Behistun*, Roma: Gruppo Editoriale Internazionale.

MEILLET, ANTOINE 1924, *Le Slave Commun*, Paris: Librairie Anciene Honoré Champion.

MORAN, WILLIAM L. 1959, *Notes on the New Nabonidus Inscriptions*, "Orientalia (Nova Series)" 28/2: 130–140.

MURAOKA, TAKAMITSU—PORTEN, BEZALEL 1998, *A grammar of Egyptian Aramaic*, Leiden/New York/Köln: Brill.

NYBERG, HENRIK S. 1974, *A Manual of Pahlavi*, Volume 2, Wiesbaden: Otto Harrassowitz.

PAPER, HERBERT H. 1955, *The phonology and morphology of Royal Achaemenid Elamite*, Ann Arbor: The University of Michigan Press.

PINAULT, GEORGES-JEAN 2010, *On the r-Endings of the Tocharian Middle*, in R. Kim—N. Oettinger—E. Rieken—M. Weiss (eds.), *Ex Oriente Lux, Anatolian and Indo-European Studies in Honor of Craig Melchert on the occasion of his sixty-fifth birthday*, Ann Arbor: Beech Stave Press: 285–295.

QUINTANA CIFUENTES, ENRIQUE 2013, *Gramática de la lengua elamita*, Madrid: Vision Libros.

REICHELT, HANS 1903, *Das Pronomen im Mittelpersischen*, "Zeitschrift der Deutschen Morgenländischen Gesellschaft" 57/3: 570–575.

REINER, ERICA 1960, *Calques sur le vieux-perse en élamite achéménide*, "Bulletin de la Société de Linguistique de Paris" 55: 222–227.

REINER, ERICA 1969, *The Elamite Language*, in J. Friedrich—E. Reiner—A. Kammenhuber—G. Neumann—A. Heubeck (hrsg.), *Altkleinasiatische Sprachen*, Leiden/ Köln: Brill: 54–118.

RAWLINSON, HENRY C. 1848, *The Persian Cuneiform Inscription at Behistun, Decyphered and Translated; With a Memoir on Persian Cuneiform Inscriptions in General, and on That of Behistun in Particular*, "The Journal of the Royal Asiatic Society of Great Britain and Ireland" 10: i–lxxi, 1–265, 268–349.

SALEMANN, C.H. 1895–1901, *Mittelpersisch*, in W. Geiger—E. Kuhn (eds.), *Grundriss der Iranischen Philologie*, Erster Band, I. Abteilung, Strassburg: Verlag von Karl J. Trübner: 249–332.

SCHMITT, RÜDIGER 1991, *Corpus Inscriptionum Iranicarum. Part I, Inscriptions of Ancient Iran. Vol. I, The Old Persian Inscriptions. Texts I, The Bisitun Inscriptions of Darius the Great: Old Persian Text*, London: published on behalf of Corpus Inscriptionum Iranicarum by School of Oriental and African Studies.

SCHMITT, RÜDIGER 2009, *Die altpersischen Inschriften der Achaimeniden*, Wiesbaden: Reichert.

SCHMITT, RÜDIGER 2016, *Stilistik der altpersischen Inschriften: Versuch einer Annäherung*, Vienna: Austrian Academy of Sciences Press.

SIDELTSEV, ANDREI V. 2018, *Dream Syntax: Hittite imma and mān as Indefiniteness Markers*, "Zeitschrift der Deutschen Morgenländischen Gesellschaft" 168/2: 301–332.

SIDELTSEV, ANDREI V.—YAKUBOVICH, ILYA 2016, *The Origin of Lycian Indefinite Pronouns and Its Phonological Implications*, "Münchener Studien zur Sprachwissenschaft" 70/1: 75–124.

SIVAN, DANIEL 2001, *A Grammar of the Ugaritic Language*, Leiden/Boston/Köln: Brill.

STOLPER, MATTHEW W. 2004, *Elamite*, in R.D. Woodard (ed.), *The Cambridge encyclopedia of the world's ancient languages*, Cambridge: Cambridge University Press: 60–94.

SUNDERMAN, WERNER 1989, *Westmitteliranische Sprachen*, in R. Schmitt (ed.), *Compendium Linguarum Iranicarum*, Wiesbaden: Dr. Ludwig Reichert Verlag: 106–113.

SKJÆRVØ, PRODS O. 1999, *Methodological Questions in Old Persian and Parthian Epigraphy*, "Bulletin of the Asia Institute", 13: 157–167.

SKJÆRVØ, PRODS O. 2009, *Old Iranian*, in G. Windfuhr (ed.), *The Iranian Languages*, London/New York: Routledge: 43–195.

TAVERNIER, JAN 1999, *Zum altpersischen hy /hya/* "Archív Orientální", 67: 683–693.

TAVERNIER, JAN 2007, *Iranica in the Achaemenid period (ca. 550–330 B.C.). Lexicon of Old Iranian proper names and loanwords, attested in non-Iranian texts*, Leuven: Peeters.

TAVERNIER, JAN 2018, *The Elamite Language*, in J. Álvarez-Mon—G.P. Basello— Y. Wicks (eds.), *The Elamite World*, London/New York: Routledge: 416–449.

TEDESCO, PAUL 1945, *Persian čīz and Sanskrit kím*, "Language" 21/3: 128–141.

TROPPER, JOSEF 1993, *Die Inschriften von Zincirli*, Münster: UGARIT-Verlag.

UNGNAD, ARTHUR 1992, *Akkadian Grammar* (translated by H.A. Hoffner Jr.), Atlanta, GA: Scholars Press.

VALLAT, FRANÇOIS 1977, *Corpus des inscriptions royales en Elamite Achemenide*, thèse présentée pour la obtention du doctorat, Paris.

VALLAT, FRANÇOIS 1987, *Le pseudo-pronom personnel *kaš en élamite achéménide*, "Nouvelles Assyriologiques Brèves et Utilitaires (NABU)" 114: 66.

WaK = SCHMITT, RÜDIGER 2014, *Wörterbuch der altpersischen Königsinschriften*, Wiesbaden: Reichert.

WALTISBERG, MICHAEL 2011, *Syntactic Typology of Semitic*, in S. Weninger (ed.), *The Semitic Languages, An International Handbook*, Berlin/Boston: De Gruyter Mouton: 303–329.

YAKUBOVICH, ILYA S. 2020, *Persian ezāfe as a contact-induced feature*, "Voprosy Jazykoznanija" 5: 91–114.

YUN, ILSUNG A. 2006, *A case of linguistic transition: the Nerab Inscriptions*, "Journal of Semitic Studies" 51/1: 19–43.

CHAPTER 3

Phenomena of Spirantization and Language Contact in Greek Sicilian Inscriptions: The Case of ΤΡΙΑΙΝΤΑ

Marta Capano

1 Introduction

This article addresses the issue of spirantization of stops in Sicilian Greek. In order to understand the realization of this series of phonemes in Hellenistic and Roman Sicily, I contend that there are three fundamental elements to take into account: 1) comparisons with similar developments in other areas of the Greek-speaking world; 2) transliteration practices of Greek words in other languages; 3) typological evidence for the change of these sounds. After offering some considerations on relative chronology, I argue that a specific form attested in a Greek Sicilian inscription, which was hitherto regarded as the result of a *lapsus scalpri*, is in fact an authentic product of the spoken language. This form, which in my opinion is the result of language contact with Latin, should be added to the evidence for spirantization of the voiced velar stop in Sicily in the Roman period.

2 Spirantization in the Greek Phonological System in the Hellenistic and Roman Periods

Spirantization (also called fricativization) of stops is one of the well-known changes that has occurred within the history of the Greek language and it can be regarded as part of the wider process of spirantization that affected the entire consonantal system. It is not easy to identify the traces of this phenomenon, because the conservativity of writing systems obscures changes, especially when they concern the introduction of a new sound. When a linguistic change produces a phoneme that was already present in the language, and already codified in the writing system, this phoneme can be recorded quite easily, even considering the inherent tendency of writing systems to conservativism. Conversely, when a change introduces a new phoneme, or a new allophone, this new sound can go unnoticed for a long time in the written codi-

© MARTA CAPANO, 2022 | DOI:10.1163/9789004508828_005

fication. An example of the first case is the change of Ancient Greek [ɛː] > [iː] at the end of the Classical period, after which inscriptions often show etymological [ɛː] (normally ⟨η⟩) written as ι. An example of the second case is, indeed, the case of non-sibilant fricatives in Hellenistic and Roman Greek. Another difficulty for the study of spirantization in the Greek language is presented by the provenance of the material traditionally used in studies on late Greek phonology, because the regions from which this material comes might not match the areas where phenomena of spirantization are frequent. For instance, the linguistic areas in which we have an abundance of material evidence for studying spoken language, such as Egypt—with the major presence of papyri—and Attica—richer in inscriptions than other Greek speaking areas of the period—are less subject to some kinds of spirantization.[1] Before addressing in detail the consonantal sounds that underwent spirantization in Greek, we can state which ones surely did not, namely voiceless stops [p], [t], [k]. If we adopt a structuralist approach, the exclusion of voiceless stops from spirantization is little surprising, considering that the "box" of their corresponding fricative ([f], [θ], [x])—as we shall see in the next section—would be filled by the development of voiceless aspirated stops. It is well known that the voiceless aspirated stops ⟨φ⟩, ⟨θ⟩, and ⟨χ⟩—which still corresponded to [pʰ], [tʰ], [kʰ] at the beginning of the Hellenistic period—underwent spirantization by the end of the Roman period (PETROUNIAS 2001: 606–609, HORROCKS 2010: 170) in most of the Greek-speaking world, resulting ultimately in [φ], [θ], and [x]. Probably around the same time, or a little later, the same phenomenon affected also the voiced velar series, represented graphically as ⟨β⟩, ⟨δ⟩, and ⟨γ⟩, which gradually became [β] (and later [v]), [ð], and [ɣ]. This description should not give the impression that all voiced and voiceless sounds were affected at the same time, or that the change has happened in the entire Greek-speaking world—on the contrary, the phenomenon was gradual and characterized by a great areal diversity. In the next sections, I offer an outline of the process of spirantization of consonantal sounds in Greek on the basis of the epigraphic evidence and, when appropriate, literary sources, starting from voiceless aspirated stops (in the order [tʰ], [kʰ], [pʰ]) and then addressing the voiced stops ([b], [d], [g]).

---

[1] The absence of this phenomenon in areas that have greater quantities of evidence might explain the perception of scholars such as Teodorsson and Gignac (the former working on Attica and the latter on Egypt), so important for the description of phonology of Greek of the Hellenistic and Roman times, that spirantization did not affect Greek until after the 1st c. CE.

2.1 Voiceless Aspirated Stops

From a geographical point of view, spirantization is first attested in West Greek, in the Doric dialect, to be precise. Within Doric, the first phoneme to be affected by spirantization is the dental voiceless aspirated stop. Well-known literary sources, such as Aristophanes (*Thesm.* v. 81, *Pax* v. 214), Thucydides (V 77.4), and Xenophon (*Hell.* IV 4.10) represent sometimes a sibilant ⟨σ⟩ instead of the dental voiceless aspirated fricative (⟨⟨θ⟩⟩) in speeches from Doric speakers, especially in stereotypical expressions (e.g. ναὶ τὼ σιώ "for the two gods!").[2] Less than a century later, the same phenomenon appears in inscriptions from Sparta (e.g. IG V¹ 1317 and IG VI¹ 255, both from the 4th/3rd c. BCE). There are two interesting facts to notice: first, the documentation of Laconian spirantization appears earlier in Attic literary textsthan in local Laconian epigraphic records; secondly, the practice of writing σ instead of θ disappears after the 4th c. BCE, to reappear only later, during the first centuries CE (e.g. ἀνέσηκε for ἀνέθηκε in IG VI¹ 294 and IG VI¹ 307, dated from the second half of the 2nd c. CE).[3] The interpretation of this ⟨σ⟩ as an attempt to express a fricative is unanimous in the scholarship, but the contextualization of this phenomenon within the Greek language and dialectology is more controversial (cf. BUBENÍK 1983: 105–110). The spirantization of a dental segment is by no means an uncommon phenomenon in Ancient Greek, as it is attested already in Mycenean Greek (MÉNDEZ DOSUNA 1993), and it constitutes one of the most significant isoglosses for Eastern/Southern Greek (respectively in Porzig's and Risch's terms; cf. PORZIG 1954, RISCH 1955). In this paper, I will distinguish between the aforementioned case of spirantization, which goes under the name of "assibilation", and the Laconian—and later widely Greek—phenomenon, which will be called spirantization. There are two obvious reasons to do so: the first, and most important, is that the assibilation as attested in Mycenean, Arcado-Cypriot, and Attic-Ionic is conditioned by context, as it appears only before a high vowel (t > s _V[+front]), and it should ultimately be considered a case of palatalization (see also BRIXHE 1996: 45). Secondly, the areas in which the two phenomena originated are different, as assibilation seems to have spread from eastern/southern Greek dialects (Mycenean, Ionian-Attic, Arcado-Cypriot, and Lesbian), while spirantization of

---

2   For a collection and an analysis of all literary data from Aristophanes and Thucydides, see COLVIN 1999: 169–170.

3   This discontinuity might be due to the influence of κοινή spellings, as Laconians stopped using ⟨σ⟩ for ⟨θ⟩ when they perceived this as a trait of provincialism (BUBENÍK 1983: 105), but the main question is why they started to use it again. If we look at one of the later occurrences of ἀνέσεκεν for ἀνέθεκεν, in IG V¹ 308, a public inscription from 2nd c. CE Sparta, we notice that there are many other archaisms, such as Ἀρτέμιτι and Βωρσέᾳ. The inscription should be read as a proud and conscious imitation of Laconian models, with the archaizing taste of the

the dental elements, as mentioned, appears earlier in west Greek.[4] Moreover, I separate the Greek assibilation from the "Laconian" spirantization because I argue that the latter, rather than being realized as a sibilant, was uttered as a voiceless interdental fricative (cf. e.g. BUBENÍK 1983: 105). It is likely that the graphic representation of a voiceless fricative (θ < [tʰ]) overlaps with the graphic representation of a voiceless sibilant [s] by virtue of the fact that they were both continuous, fricative, coronal, and non-voiced.

In pre-Hellenistic Greek the grapheme ⟨χ⟩ still represented the voiceless aspirated stop [kʰ], which was formed by a plosive part, followed by an aspiration. Later on, there probably was a phase [kx], followed by the loss of the plosive element. If we accept this process as true, it is likely that the sequence written ⟨χχ⟩ and corresponding to [kkʰ] was one of the first contexts to undergo spirantization, because on a perception level the plosive component is still represented by the first velar, while the second element only maintains the aspiration. This stage is probably represented by readings such as Βάχχος for Βάκχος that we find around the 2nd c. BCE in Attica and in Central Greece (e.g. IG II² 1717, 1765, 1998 from Attica, SGDI II 1732, 1742, 1758 from Delphi, and IThesp 88 from Boeotia).[5] In Asia Minor, apart from some Hellenistic instances of ⟨χχ⟩ for ⟨κχ⟩ (mostly later than the 1st c. BCE), the first instances of spirantization have been found in inscriptions starting from the 2nd c. BCE, where we see frequent series of exchanges between ⟨χ⟩ and ⟨κ⟩, and cases of hypercorrections, e.g. γυναιχί for γυναικί in Sterrett, EJ 98,67.[6] The evidence, as one can see, is not abundant, and it is possible that here we are dealing here with a phenomenon that affected Hellenistic Greek only in terms of allophonic variation, and that the complete spirantization of voiceless aspirated stop did not com-

---

period. It is likely that the imitation of older inscriptions was produced by the observation of older monuments, which must have been still standing in the 2nd c. CE.

4   As for the majority of isoglosses, Mycenean is to be paired with East Greek also with regard to assibilation.

5   *Contra* Threatte (1980: 470 and 541), who does not consider spellings like βάχχος as instances of spirantization of [kʰ], but rather as another case of the assimilation [kʰkʰ] > [kkʰ], and ultimately analogous to the pronunciation [ktʰ] of ⟨χθ⟩.

6   One should notice, though, that there might be a different explanation for this kind of mistake in Asia Minor, and especially in Pisidia. As Brixhe (2016: 111) notices, Pisidic, the language spoken in the area where the inscription with the form γυναιχί comes from, did not have aspirated stops, and the words with ⟨χ⟩ from Greek into Pisidic were transcribed usually as normal velar stop. The exchange between χ and κ might be explained, instead of a case of spirantization, as a form of Greek spoken "à la Pisidienne". An inscription a few centuries later than Sterrett, EJ 98,67, IK 5 from Central Pisidia, shows ⟨κ⟩ for ⟨χ⟩ twice in the same inscription (ἐκθρόν, l. 262 and Κρόνου l. 158); in this phase the hypothesis of spirantization seems to be the most likely explanation.

pletely occur before the Roman period.[7] Some further evidence for later spirantization is offered by Latin transliterations, which will be the focus of §1.3.2.

The process of spirantization of the voiceless aspirated stops ultimately affected also the labial segment, but it is unclear when the fricatives became phonemes and the voiceless aspirated stops became allophones. It is very likely that the change was not from bilabial aspirated stop [pʰ] to labiodental fricative [f], but it went through a phase of voiceless bilabial fricative [φ].[8] This intermediate stage of spirantization is harder to isolate in texts, but it can be detected by the exchange between ⟨φ⟩ and ⟨υ⟩, or between ⟨φ⟩ and ⟨θ⟩, phenomena that are found at a much later stage than the dental or velar series. The major chronological gap between the passages [b] > [β] > [v] and [pʰ] > [φ] > [f] is also testified by the absence of confusion amongst them. In other words, when the original voiced bilabial stop ([b] = ⟨β⟩) became a bilabial fricative [β], the voiceless bilabial aspirated stop [pʰ] had not yet started the change into a bilabial fricative. Some scholars (THREATTE 1980, HORROCKS 2010) have considered spellings such as Ἐφρόνις and Ἐφραῖος, attested in Hellenistic inscriptions from Athens, as signs both of fricative pronunciation of ⟨φ⟩ and of the passage [eᵘ] > [ef] of the diphthong ⟨ευ⟩. Even if the evidence for spirantization of the original [pʰ] in Hellenistic Attica is by no means abundant we can see the first movements of a change in progress that will carry on during the Roman period. As I will demonstrate in the following sections (cf. §1.3.), there are external proofs that show that the evolution of [pʰ] had been in place already before the early Imperial period.

Spirantization—and especially the passage from bilabial stop to bilabial fricative in intervocalic position—is typologically quite common (see e.g. LAVOIE 2001: 32–36), and besides the fitting parallels in Spanish (MÉNDEZ DOSUNA 1991–1993: 103) one could also think of the process of spirantization that affected north-Italian Romance varieties, in which intervocalic stops first underwent voicing, then spirantization, and finally complete cancellation.[9] The relative frequency and typological parallels of spirantization, though, do not provide an explanation for the diffusion of the phenomenon in Greece,

---

7 KRISTOFFERSEN 2019 argues that the spirantization of Greek voiced stops happened in the Archaid period, but was limited to the creation of allophones (with the exeptions of Elean and Laconian, where it affected the phonological system). Unfortunately, Kristoffersen's article came out when the present contribution was already submitted for publication and it has not been possible to keep it fully into account.

8 Kümmel (2007: 65) notices that the intermediate phase is not necessarily required, because the passage between aspirated stop to fricative is possible simply by cancelling the plosive element, while considering pertinent the aspirated segment, which is already a fricative.

9 For a wider analysis of the cases, see KÜMMEL 2007: 65–67.

PHENOMENA OF SPIRANTIZATION AND LANGUAGE CONTACT 93

and there in fact might not have been a single process of diffusion. We shall see in the next sections that, if voiceless aspirated stops underwent spirantization earlier in west Greek, the opposite happened to voiced stops. In other words, it seems certain that the dental [tʰ] underwent spirantization before the Hellenistic period in Doric varieties, but not in the Ionic ones, and that instead the velar and labial aspirated stops underwent spirantization earlier in Attica. A prudent approach should not associate the rise of spirantization with only one dialectal branch, but instead interpret it as a potentially pan-Greek phenomenon. As previously stated, not all varieties have been equally responsive to spirantization, as for instance in Egypt, where Greek retained aspiration also in later phases. Rather than being a fact of pure conservativism, the lack of spirantization might be explained by contact with the local Egyptian language, which had aspirated stops.

2.2 Voiced Stops

If we look at what happened to the voiced stops [b], [d], and [g], which were originally represented by ⟨β⟩, ⟨δ⟩, and ⟨γ⟩ during the Classical period, we see that they underwent spirantization in many areas of the Greek world, though not everywhere and not at the same rate (see on this KRISTOFFERSEN 2019).[10] The original voiced bilabial stop, graphically represented as ⟨β⟩, seems to have undergone spirantization in the Laconian area already in the Hellenistic period, as we see from the confusion between the grapheme ⟨β⟩ and the grapheme ⟨ϝ⟩, still used in that area to indicate the velar glide. In IG VI¹ 865, from the 2nd c. BCE, ϝωρθείας is represented as Βωρθείας, which means that at that chronological stage the two sounds were already mistakable.[11] The spelling ⟨β⟩ for words that originally had a digamma appears also in the anthroponym Εὐρυβάνασσα (IG VI¹ 209, 212, 507, 573 and 574, all from the 1st c. BCE) and in the word διαβήτης (e.g. in IG VI¹ 674, 676, 680, dating to the 1st and 2nd c. CE), the title of an official in Sparta probably connected to the word ἔτος, which notoriously presents an initial digamma. As one might expect, external evidence from Laconia for the sound [w] represented by ⟨β⟩ can be found in the Latin transliteration of names with initial ⟨V⟩, as Valerius (IG VI¹ 450), but to

---

10   In Calabrian Greek and in Griko, with some diatopic differences, initial γ- is conserved as a stop before velar vowels (e.g. [ˈgonato] Bov.), but it palatalizes before [i] and [u] (e.g. [jiˈneka] Bov.), while internal intervocalic γ—but palatal vowels—changes into a fricative sound in Bovese and it is generally cancelled in Griko (e.g. [tro:] from anc. Greek. τρώγω).

11   There are more examples of the same tendency. For instance, there are nine more occurrences of exchanges between ϝωρθεία and βορθεία alone, one of which dates to the 2nd c. BCE (IG V¹ 292), with the rest dating to before the 3rd c. CE (IG V¹ 294; IG V¹ 1 301; IG V¹ 303; IG V¹ 305; IG V¹ 319; IG V¹ 341; IG V¹ 1573).

my knowledge there are no examples prior to the 1st c. CE. Conversely, there are inscriptions from Laconia where medial ⟨β⟩ is not spelled out, as in IG VI 716 (Θηαῖος for Θηβαῖος). Cases of un-spelled [b] especially before [u], are attested elsewhere in the Greek world (e.g., but there are other examples, IK Priene 398, ca. 350 BCE, with ουλήιου for ⟨β⟩ουλήιου, or IG II² 6278, 2nd c. BCE, from Attica), but it is difficult to know whether or not they are significant. In areas other than Laconia, chronology of early spirantization is more elusive, but Latin can be helpful. In general, we can say that, until the middle of the 2nd c. CE, Latin ⟨v⟩ both in initial prevocalic position and in intervocalic position, phonetically [w], is often transliterated ⟨ου⟩ (cf. 2.2.), but after the middle of the 2nd c. CE the standard increasingly changes from ⟨ου⟩ to ⟨β⟩.[12] If we consider the first occurrences of the Latin initial ⟨v⟩ transliterated with Greek ⟨β⟩, though, chronology can significantly be moved back to the 1st c. BCE, thanks to two occurrences of the phenomenon, both in public and private inscriptions. In IEleusis 296, a statue base for Livia Drusilla dated a little after 31 BCE, the name of the honorand is stated as Λιβίαν, while in IG II² 8413, an Attic private funerary monument from 16 BCE, we read the name *Vipsanius* as Βιψάνιος.[13] Some decades later, in IG II² 3242, dating to the latter part of the Augustan period, from the beginning of the 1st c. CE, we find the name Λειβία, with intervocalic ⟨v⟩ once again recorded in Greek as ⟨β⟩, once again in Attica, but this time on a public monument.[14] There are a few examples of the Latin ⟨v⟩ transliterated as Greek ⟨β⟩ in Augustan inscriptions from outside Attica, e.g. IGR I 835 from Thasos, dedicated to Livia Drusilla, so we can assume that the feature was present in other areas of the Greek world, even though it is not always documented. Considering these data, it seems to me that, although most cases of

---

12   Particularly interesting is the case of *Vibullia* mother of Herodes Atticus, that is presented as Βιβουλλία in IG II² 3604 and Οὐιβουλλία in IG II² 4063, both from Athens, in approximately coeval inscriptions (ca. 150 CE). The acceptability of spirantization for [b] in initial position is less than the intervocalic one. Other occurrences of the same name (which referred to the same person) come from honorific monuments set up in Ceos (IG XII⁵ 631) and in Elis (IvO 621) show the spelling ⟨Βιβ⟩, but they do not seem to be later than IG II² 4063.

13   The inscription can be dated with a certain precision to the last decades of the 1st c. BCE, because the individuals mentioned there have been securely identified (AIUK 2 no. 9) and, if Byrne's hypothesis is correct, it might be exactly placed in 16 BCE, during Agrippa's visit to Athens (cf. BYRNE 2003: 487–488). Another example, perhaps from the same period, might be IG II² 4141, Λιβίον, possibly for the historian Livy, but the identification is not sure and therefore the date is not certain.

14   The inscription is the rededication of the temple of Nemesis at Rhamnus to Livia, wife of Augustus, and it is usually dated to the reign of Claudius, around 45/6 CE, but recently LOZANO 2004 has proposed to predate it to 20 BCE.

PHENOMENA OF SPIRANTIZATION AND LANGUAGE CONTACT 95

Greek ⟨β⟩ for Latin ⟨v⟩ come from later than the 1st c. CE, it is nonetheless correct to date spirantization also in Attic Greek to a significantly earlier date, at least at the end of the 1st c. BCE.

Some sort of spirantization in the dental series seems to have affected the voiced dentals, with the process [d] > [ð] at least as an allophone, in the Elis region. In Elean there are several occurrences of ⟨ζ⟩ instead of ⟨δ⟩ (καὶ τᾶλλα ζίκαια for καὶ τᾶλλα δίκαια, in IED 20, 475–450 BCE), interpreted by Striano Corrochano (1989) and Méndez Dosuna (1992–1993) as cases of spirantization. The same phenomenon sporadically appears in inscriptions from Rhodes (τόζ᾽ Ἰδαμενεύς for τόδ᾽ Ἰδαμενεύς, in IG XII¹ 737, ca. 600–575 BCE) and Phlious (ζέκ[α, but the reading is uncertain, in SEG 11 275).[15] Certainly, one could object that these data are not very rich and interpret the examples above as cases of palatalization, rather than spirantization, triggered by the presence of the high vowel [i]. However, the occurrences of the grapheme ⟨ζ⟩ in place of ⟨δ⟩ also in contexts where the is no high vowel, such as in ζαμιοργία (IED 20), for which palatalization cannot be invoked as an explanation, point towards a larger usage of ⟨ζ⟩ to register the spirant pronunciation of voiced velar stop. Considering that the examples above show uniformity even in different phonological context, the chance that we are facing two separate phenomena (spirantization and palatalization) is not entirely convincing, and surely the possibility of a a number of accidental and independent mistakes is even less persuasive. More secure data on spirantization of later voiced dental stop come from Egyptian papyri, where we see exchanges between ⟨δ⟩ and ⟨ζ⟩ (e.g. ζώτε for δότε in POxy. 1927.4 and δεῦγος for ζεῦγος in PStrassb. 277.16, examples from Gignac 1976: 76). This kind of confusion between ⟨δ⟩ and ⟨ζ⟩ does not appear before the end of the 3th c. CE, and becomes more frequent after the 5th c. CE., but inscriptions of that period rarely show the same phenomenon. Moreover, on a typological point of view, scholars have often highlighted the typological markedness of the phoneme [ð] (only 7% of the languages analyzed in MADDIESON 1984 present the phoneme) and the rarity of processes of spirantization of the voiced dental segment in comparison both with velar and labial.[16] Therefore, it is possible that Greek underwent spirantization of [d] earlier than inscriptions show, or that this kind of spirantization, that did not involve aspirated stops, happened earlier in Egypt than in continental Greece.

---

15   Later, we find the same phenomenon also in Crete (IC IV 181, 2nd c. BCE), not long before spirantization becomes widespread in the Graeco-Roman world.

16   BYBEE—EASTERDAY 2019, using a dataset of 81 languages, identified 27 that presented phenomena of spirantization, of which only 3 present phenomena of spirantization for the voiced dental stop, while 9 for the labial stop and 7 for the velar stop. Noticeably, 8 languages spirantized in multiple places.

96   CAPANO

The last voiced stop that we shall consider from a general point of view, before analyzing the Sicilian situation, is [g]. The first instances of [g] > [ɣ] are found in South/Eastern Greek, as spirantization appears in Attica at the end the 4th c. BCE. (THREATTE 1980: 440). Even if from a linguistic perspective we are dealing with the "appearance" of a new phoneme, from an epigraphical viewpoint this change is made manifest through "disappearance," because spirantization of voiced velar stop is better identified by the absence of the sign ⟨γ⟩ where we expect it. In IG II² 11375, an Attic metrical inscription from the second half of the 4th c. BCE, the word ὀλίγοις is represented as ὀλίοις, and we can find more examples from Attica (THREATTE 1980).[17] Similarly, often by using occurrences of the adjective ὀλίγος, we can trace the phenomenon in Pamphylia in the 4th c. BCE (BRIXHE 1976: 58, inscr. no. 3[18]), in Arcadia and Phokis in the 3rd c. BCE (respectively IG V² 429 and FD, Fouilles de Delphes, III 3: 192), in Asia Minor in the 2nd c. BCE (for instance, but there are many examples, ὑπογραφήν with the loss of ⟨γ⟩ in IK Priene 306), and in Boeotia in the 2nd c. BCE (Ἀντί⟨γ⟩ων, in IG VII 3376). The Boeotian example is particularly interesting because it shows how fragile is our ability to deduce tendencies from mistakes in text. In a comedy of Aristophanes, two centuries before our first epigraphic record of a Boeotian ⌊g⌋ > ⌊ɣ⌋, a Boeotian character is characterized by an epichoric Greek with spirantization of [g] (ἰώγα for ἔγωγε, in *Acharn.* v. 899), in a way that must have been perceived as stereotypically Boeotian by the Athenians. Had we not had Aristophanes, we would probably have post-dated spirantization of [g] by more than a century! It is noteworthy that in Attica we mostly see omission of ⟨γ⟩ in intervocalic position and also in front of velar vowel, while we have very few examples of γ > ∅ in front of palatal vowel. I am only aware of IG II² 1472 (319/318 BCE) and IG II² 2165 (from the 2nd c. CE),

---

17   For a similar situation in contemporary Attic drama, we might consider a fragment from Plato Comicus (fr. 183 K.-A.), "ὁ δ'οὐ γὰρ ἡττίκιζεν, ὦ Μοῖραι φίλαι, / ἀλλ' ὁπότε μὲν χρείη διητώμην λέγειν / ἔφασκε διητώμην ὁπότε δ'εἰπεῖν δέοι / ὀλίγον, ⟨ὀλίον⟩ ἔλεγεν".

18   Pamphylian is notoriously difficult to classify. Many inscriptions show spirantization of [g] especially between [e] and [a], which has led scholars to keep Hellenistic Greek and Pamphylian [g] > [ɣ] > ∅ traditionally apart (SCHWYZER 1950, I 209). Nevertheless, Attic Greek shows instances of spirantization of the voiced velar in contexts similar to the Pamphylian ones (e.g. IG II² 1616 μέα for μέγα, after the middle of the 4th c. BCE; IG II² 9301 Μεαρεύς for Μεγαρεύς, ca. 362 BCE; RAUBITSCHEK, DAA 164 Παναθέναια μεάλ[α] per Παναθέναια μεγάλ[α]) as well as sporadically and later in Boeotia (SEG 31 505, from the 1st/2nd c. CE and IG VII 2542, from the late 3rd early 4th CE). Moreover, as Wallace (1983) noticed, Pamphylian also shows spirantization before palatal vowel, as in πρεῖϝυς < *pregē-wos (BRIXHE 1976, no. 87) and πρεεως (BRIXHE 1976 no. 141), equivalent to πρεῖϝυς. It seems safe to consider Pamphylian within the generally Greek process of spirantization, whether or not it originated by contact with other Greek varieties or independently in Pamphylian.

and they might be accidental and meaningless mistakes. If we compare this situation with Modern Greek, where [g] before front vowel does not merge with [g] before back vowels, as the first undergoes complete palatalization, becoming a palatal fricative (g > j_V[+front]), while the second one becomes a voiced velar fricative, we can interpret the aforementioned changes as the first movements towards this change. Already in Classical and Hellenistic Greek, at least in some areas and on a variational level, [g] followed by both front and back vowel was undergoing spirantization. The greater evidence for unspelled ⟨γ⟩ before back vowel than before front vowel can be explained on an articulatory level, because the sequence g_V[+back] is weaker and, therefore, more likely to be left unwritten.

After this outline of the spirantization of voiced and voiceless aspirated stops in Greek, it is clear that there is not a single epicenter for the phenomenon, which is instead polycentric. Data show that stops in various dialects from different parts of the Greek speaking world were undergoing spirantization before the Hellenistic koine, and that, while it is true that spirantization is more frequently attested as the koine spread through the Greek world, it would be incorrect to attribute spirantization to the koine itself. As I have described, in the Hellenistic koine voiced velar stops underwent spirantization before voiced dental stops, but in Laconia the chronology of this change was the opposite. Therefore, we have to imagine that many waves of spirantization have affected the Greek language. Moreover, the diffusion of Hellenistic Greek might have ultimately spread (not everywhere, however!) fricative pronunciations of voiceless aspirated and voiced stops as phonemes, but spirantization was not exclusively a Hellenistic feature. It is clear that, at the end of this process, the entire Greek phonological system was reorganized, as Bubeník (1983: 108) has framed, from a tripartite voiced : voiceless: voiceless aspirated to a bipartite continuous : non-continuous. Some other questions are unanswered, as for instance the issue of the phonological value of these spirantizations— in the Hellenistic period, did fricatives have a phonological value, or were they only in free variation? It is possible that Bubeník's hypothesis describes at best the phonetic realization of clusters such as ⟨σφ⟩, ⟨σθ⟩, ⟨σχ⟩, which in the Hellenistic koine might have been realized as sibilant followed by a fricative (BUBENÍK 1989: 189). On the contrary, in contexts such as after a nasal sound, it is likely that both voiceless aspirated and voiced stops were conserved longer without becoming fricative, because from a typological point of view postnasal consonants seem to resist spirantization better.

2.3 *External Evidence for Spirantization in Hellenistic Greek.*

As I have already pointed out in the previous section, on a methodological level some of the crucial pieces of evidence for spirantization are provided by other

98 CAPANO

languages, especially on the matter of transliteration of Greek words. In this section I shall analyze two cases in which comparisons with the evidence from Lycian and Latin can shed light upon the realization of voiceless aspirated stops in Hellenistic and Early Roman Greek.

2.3.1 Greek and Lycian

It has been suggested by Bryce (1986: 56) that we could use Lycian as an external confirmation of the fact that Hellenistic Greek differentiated between intervocalic and initial position ⟨β⟩, ⟨δ⟩, and ⟨γ⟩. Lycian, indeed, transliterates Δαρεῖυς as *Ñtarijeus* (MELCHERT 2008: 49) and Δεμοκλεῖδης as *Ñtemuχlida*; the latter in particular shows that the two sounds were indeed different, because the ⟨d⟩ in *Ñtemuχlida* must represent something different than what ⟨ñt⟩ stands for. Conversely, the transliteration *Ñtarijeus* for Δαρεῖυς would not make sense if Lycian ⟨d⟩ had been a stop and not a fricative. Moreover, Lycian voices voiceless stops after nasal, which explains the presence of ⟨t⟩ in the initial ⟨ñt⟩, to read as [d].[19] If we can trust the Lycian transliteration of Δεμοκλεῖδης, we have to infer that only the first dental is indeed a stop, while the second one must have a fricative pronunciation in Hellenistic Greek, at least as spoken in Anatolia. Moreover, one should keep in mind that both in Modern and Ancient Greek, as well as in Lycian, voiced stops do not become fricatives when they are immediately preceded by a nasal, and pronunciations such as [ˈðenðro] have to be explained as "orthographic pronunciations" (PETROUNIAS 2001: 606).

2.3.2 Greek and Latin

Latin is especially useful for understanding the status of voiceless aspirated stops ⟨χ⟩ and ⟨φ⟩, which, as we have seen in the previous section, are often difficult to analyze in terms of spirantization. Latin presents many ways to transliterate Ancient Greek words, and we can witness different tendencies through epigraphic texts and sometimes literary sources.[20] It should be noted that these different strategies became more rigid as time went by. It is important to consider that scribal practice during the Middle Ages can conceal changes, normalizing spelling choices, while inscriptions can often offer some important parallels to the manuscript evidence. The standard transliteration for ⟨χ⟩ in

---

19 As has been noticed, this system corresponds almost completely to present day Modern Greek, where the word *diva*, as a loanword from Italian, is transcribed ντίβα and read [ˈdiva].

20 Among the many good works that deal Latin transliteration of Greek words, to my knowledge the most complete is still BIVILLE 1990, but insightful comments are found also in ADAMS 2003: 41–43.

PHENOMENA OF SPIRANTIZATION AND LANGUAGE CONTACT

Latin is first ⟨c⟩, until the middle of the 2nd c. BCE, and then ⟨ch⟩.[21] This plosive representation was probably fairly similar to the reality of the sound as it has been in the Classical and most of the Hellenistic periods, but there are instances of a different system, with a simple aspiration (⟨h⟩, as *haus* for χάος in Varr. *De Lingua Latina* 3. fgm. 57; *haemosis* for χήμωσις in Theod.-Prisc. *Euporist.* 36; *Hristo* for Χριστός in CIL III 10934) and with a sibilant (*Eutisi* for Ἐυτυχής in CIL VIII 16980 and *cuimarsus* for κώμαρχος in Plaut. *Curc.* 286).[22] All these examples speak in favor of a late phenomenon.

Similarly to what happens to the voiceless aspirated velar, the bilabial [pʰ] is transliterated in Latin first as a ⟨p⟩, and exclusively so until the middle of the 2nd c. BCE, when it starts being transcribed with the classical ⟨ph⟩. The employment of ⟨f⟩ to transcribe ⟨φ⟩ does not appear before the 1st c. BCE, but it is already attested in three inscriptions from the Republican period (CIL I^2 2652, CIL I^2 753, and CIL I^2 1413), and it is found also in Pompeii (CIL IV 680). Finally, there are cases of later confusion between the outcomes of ancient ⟨φ⟩ and ⟨β⟩, with some consequences even in southern Italian Greek from the Middle Ages (BIVILLE 1990: 209).[23] Evidence from Pompeii seems to suggest that, before 79 CE, the pronunciation of ⟨θ⟩ was fricative, as the word λάσθη is transcribed as *lasfe* (CIL IV 2319).[24]

3 Spirantization in Sicily

In this section I will address the problem of spirantization of voiced and voiceless aspirated stops in Sicily during the Hellenistic and Roman period on the basis of the epigraphic evidence. Sicily is a particularly rich linguistic area at this chronological stage, because—besides Greek—Italic and indigenous languages were still residually spoken on the island at the end of the Classical period, while other languages, such as Punic and Latin, are also attested. Moreover, Greek in Sicily during the Hellenistic period was spoken in the form of a Doric κοινά (MIMBRERA OLARTE 2012) with characteristic features (CAPANO 2020a), but at the same time, like in most of the Greek speaking

---

21 To describe this change, one can compare *Bacas* as transliteration of Βάχχας in CIL I 581, 186 BCE, to *Achaia*, as transliteration of Ἀχαία in CIL I 626, 145 BCE. More examples are in BIVILLE 1990: 210.

22 The examples are derived from a list in BIVILLE 1990: 202–203.

23 Biville offers the interesting example of Bovese, which has *flastimáo* apparently from βλασφημεῖν.

24 Oscan spellings such as Ἀσάνα for Ἀθᾶνᾶ, Lúvfreis for Ἐλευθέριος, seem to describe the very same situation (BIVILLE 1990: 200).

world, the concurrent spread of the Hellenistic koine led to the creation of hybrid forms that endured during the Roman period. In this context, it is particularly significant to analyze the process of spirantization of the stops, because it might show distinct tendencies within the same linguistic area, and it might uncover dynamics of interactions between koine and κοινά. Unlike in section 2, in this case the material will be only epigraphic, because I could not find instances of spirantization in Sicilian literature, possibly due to the limited amount of evidence.

3.1 Voiceless Aspirated Stops in Sicily

In Sicilian Greek, aspirated stops in Classical and Hellenistic inscriptions present some difficulties, because they sometimes appear as voiceless stops, losing the aspiration. Examples of deaspiration are found in ενταδε (for ἐνθάδε) in IG XIV 28, from Imperial Syracuse and in ARENA 2002: no. 45, a defixio from Gela, 475–450 BCE. For the velar series, a similar situation is shown by Ἀρκαγάθ⟨ο⟩υ as a genitive of Ἀρχάγαθος (IGDS I 126). On the other hand, there are also instances of aspirated stops that do not appear aspirated in other Greek areas, such as Φερσεφοναι (for Περσεφόναι) in IGDS II 80, dated around the 3rd c. BCE, and Φερσεφασσα IGDS II 116 (5th/4th c. BCE).[25] Mimbrera Olarte (2012: 54) has rightly interpreted these examples as a proof of the plosive nature of ⟨φ⟩, and one might also explain them as a case of hypercorrection, which is plausible in an area where aspiration was so irregular. To this small number of cases of irregularities, I add the anthroponym Σπονγέος, for Σφογγέος, in SEG 42 833, a dedication from Buscemi, 35 CE (on which see also 2.2). The deaspiration, which can be interpreted as an assimilation of aspirated dental to the first unaspirated element, should be then reconnected with the other aforementioned examples, like ενταδε and Ἀρκαγάθου, and it is to be considered Sicilian. After this brief outline of Sicilian un-aspirated instances of normally aspirated stops, one can infer that ⟨φ⟩, ⟨θ⟩, and ⟨χ⟩ must have maintained their plosive component until at least the end of the Hellenistic period. Regarding the Roman phase, we have some interesting data, originated in most cases from contact with the Romans, or more generally of Roman origin. In ISico00578 (= CIL X 7396), a Latin inscription from Thermae Himerae, dating to the 2nd–3rd c. CE, we read the name *Epaφruitus* and in ISico356 (= CIL X 7072), from 1st/2nd c.

---

25   As Mimbrera (2008: 209) rightly states, in Sicily ⟨Θ⟩ and ⟨Φ⟩ are sometime confused (e.g. Πσιφυρō in IGDS II 76 from Akri, 5th c. BCE, corresponding to Attic ψίθυρος), that might be due to their spirantization as well as to the graphic similarities between the two letters. The early phase in which these exchanges are attested makes highly improbable that this confusion is instead a case of spirantization similar to those that I analyzed in 2.3.1.

CE Catania, the name *Eutυχis*, with graphic interference with the Greek letters χ and φ. There are no good reasons why a Greek scribe should have slipped in these three letters (considering also the Y), if one does not hypothesize that these three letters indicate sounds that do not have an immediate parallel in Latin—in other words, these inscriptions seem to exhibit evidence in favor of a conservation of the plosive and aspirated pronunciation of ⟨φ⟩ and ⟨χ⟩ in Roman Sicily.[26] This explanation must be regarded with caution, as we also have a Greek inscription from the Imperial period (IGLP 21, from Lilybaeum) in which the name *Marcus* is transliterated as Μάρχος, and here ⟨χ⟩ must have simply represented a velar stop.[27] In conclusion, the series of the voiceless aspirated stops in Sicilian Greek seem to resist spirantization more than in continental Greece, while, as we shall see in the next sections, the voiced stops seem to have undergone spirantization already in the Hellenistic period.

3.2 Voiced Bilabial Stop

As for Sicily, we have many examples of the spirantization of the bilabial voiced stop during the Hellenistic period, but we do not have earlier examples. Unfortunately, the usage of initial ϝ disappeared early from Sicilian inscriptions,[28] and it is never attested after the 5th c. BCE, and for this reason using the confusion between the grapheme ⟨β⟩ and the grapheme ⟨ϝ⟩ as a diagnostic mistake (as in Laconian inscriptions, cf. section 2.2) is not often viable approach here.[29] Nevertheless, the period immediately following the disappearance of the ϝ, it is possible to notice some occurrences of ⟨β⟩ used in place of an initial velar glide, such as the anthroponym Βειδει IGDS II 42 (4th–3rd c. BCE Syracuse).[30] This reading is also supported by another Sicilian inscription, IGDS I 126, found in

---

26   As an anonymous reviewer pointed out (and I thank them for their input), on a general level the usage of the Greek letters might be read as a sign of the absence of aspirated plosives in colloquial Latin. This consideration, which I believe is correct, of course does not invalidate the explanation that I offer in this paper.

27   One might also notice that the inscription IGLP 21 is composed of 4 words (Μάρχος Σημβρῶνις | ἥρως ἀγαθός), two of them with problematic spellings.

28   The intervocalic ϝ in Sicily was lost long before the initial ϝ, as we have very few examples of the grapheme between vowels or between a vowel and a liquid or a nasal (MIMBRERA OLARTE 2012: 84).

29   In Sicilian Doric colonies the initial [w] sound was disappearing, so the adoption of the Milesian alphabet was not the only reason for the graphic loss of ⟨ϝ⟩. The word ϝουλιαδα (ARENA 2002 no. 14, from Gela, 6th c. BCE) with a non-etymological initial ϝ, has been in fact explained as a hypercorrected form, cf. the grammar of Mimbrera Olarte (2012: 82). The possibility of reading ϝουλιαδα as Βουλιάδας, attested in Leucade, seems quite unlikely.

30   Βειδει is probably to be reconnected with forms like Ϝεῖδος in Epirus. Another possibility to explain Βειδει is to reconnect it to the anthroponym Βιδύλος, attested in Crete in the 1st c.

102

Camarina and dating to around the 2nd c. BCE. In this inscription, the anthroponym Βασία is clearly a variant of the Italic ϝασία, attested in Metaponton, Hyettia, and Lebadeia. Conversely, it has been suggested by Dubois (IGDS I 139) that the Syracusan *glossae* of the Etymologicum Magnum δερβιστήρ for δεριστήρ might indicate a fricative pronunciation of [w] that would have been somehow typical of the Syracusan area. The hypothesis is surely interesting, but the evidence seems to be a little too thin to be definitive.

As already noticed in section 2.3., the Greek transcription of Latin names is an important tool for understanding the pronunciation behind the written convention, but sometimes reasons of conservatism might conceal changes for a long time. If there are some hints for us to suspect that spirantization of bilabial stops was already happening in the Syracusan area during the 4th c. BCE, we still have some conflicting evidence from the 3rd c. BCE, as in ENT A1 (in AMPOLO 2001) the Latin name *Corovius* is transliterated as Κορ⟨ο⟩υιος, and about one century later the name *Vibius* is spelled Οὐείβιος (CURBERA 1997: 220). Unfortunately, this hypothesis has to remain speculative, because the stone is now lost and it is impossible to date the inscription with certainty. In the 2nd c. BCE, we find the first instance of a Latin name with an initial ⟨v-⟩ (at that stage surely [w]) transcribed as a ⟨β⟩, namely the name Βενοῦστα (*Venusta*) in two defixiones from Morgantina, SEG 29 930 and 931. Among the many hypercorrected ⟨β⟩ for what was clearly fricative (or at least a velar glide [w]), one can mention the confusion between ⟨β⟩ and ⟨ου⟩, as the incorrect ⟨β⟩ in Φλαβιανός, attested in ISic003236 from 1st/2nd c. CE Catania. More evidence for spirantization of the bilabial stop in Sicily can be found after the first half of the 1st c. CE, when we find the Latin name *Livius* transliterated as Λίβιος (IG XIV 488, now partially lost), and the name *Vipsanius* as Βιψάνιος (IG XIV 494). In SEG 42 833, a dedication from 35 CE found in Buscemi, we have an instructive compresence of many Latin names, amongst which I mention *Servilius* (Σερουιλίου), *Valerius Arabicus* (Βαλερίου Ἀραβικοῦ), and *Fabia* (Φαβία), in which the Latin velar glide (written as ⟨v⟩) is transcribed both as a ⟨ου⟩ and ⟨β⟩, and ⟨b⟩ is transcribed always as ⟨β⟩. Although the spelling is conservative in the name Φαβία, the name Βαλερίου surely represents a pronunciation [wale'riu], while *Fabia* might have been pronounced, at least in Greek, ['faβia]. A few centuries later, we frequently find cases of transliteration of intervocalic Latin ⟨v⟩ as ⟨ου⟩, e.g. Φλάουιος, in IG XIV

BCE (MIMBRERA OLARTE 2012: 82) or to Βῖδος, attested in Stephanus of Byzantium (MANGANARO 1997: 315). However, Βιδύλος shows a certain formal and spatial difference with Βειδει, and Βῖδος has a noticeable temporal distance, all of which makes more probable the hypothesis that Βειδει has to be explained as a coradical form to εἶδος.

PHENOMENA OF SPIRANTIZATION AND LANGUAGE CONTACT   103

278, Imperial period, from Lilybaeum, but at this chronological stage, and also later, the spelling with a β (e.g. Φλάβιος in IG XIV 455 and IMC 87) is just as acceptable.

3.3   *Voiced Dental Stop*

As seen in section 2.2, voiced stops have been the last ones to undergo spirantization, probably from after the 4th c. CE (HORROCKS 2010: 170), and even later if we consider voiced stops in postnasal position. It is not surprising that in Greek Sicilian inscriptions, to the best of my knowledge, we do not have any example of exchange between ⟨δ⟩ and ⟨ζ⟩, or between ⟨δ⟩ and ⟨θ⟩, that might be attributable to a process of spirantization. The occurrence of the name Ζόδωρος, clearly a form for Διόδωρος (e.g. in IG XIV 117, from Syracuse, probably late Imperial period), more than being an instance of spirantization of [δ] is a case of a progressive assimilation triggered by the [i], in a similar way to what happened in Ionic Greek for the name Ζεύς < *dieus. (cf. Skt. *dyauh*, etc.).

3.4   *Voiced Velar Stop*

From Classical and Hellenistic Sicily we have some evidence for deaspiration of voiceless stops, but this phenomenon cannot be explained as a spirantization and will not be explored here in detail.[31] Conversely, there is some evidence for spirantization of voiced velar stop in a decree from Nakone (NAK A, in AMPOLO 2001), dating to the 3rd c. BCE, where the word αἶγα 'goat' is spelled ⟨αια⟩, which is explainable with a fricative pronunciation of the internal ⟨γ⟩.[32] The other possible explanation for the word αἶα, i.e. the outcome [j] of intervocalic [g], provides more problems than answers, if the development g > j / V_V were true, we should imagine a first phase ['aiia], followed by a degem-

---

31   In order to have a wider image of the Sicilian Greek consonantal system, I will briefly refer here to a peculiarity of the local voiceless stops, that often present deaspiration during the Classical and Hellenistic periods. There is some evidence for exchanges between ⟨χ⟩, voiceless aspirated velar, and ⟨κ⟩, both in literary texts (e.g. δέχομαι attested as δέκομαι in Pindar, but with ⟨χ⟩ in Epicharmus) and in inscriptions (e.g. ἀνδοκεία in IG XIV 422 from Tauromenion, 2nd–1st c. BCE). These anomalies seem to correspond to the exchanges between κύτραν for χύτραν, κιτών for χιτών, mentioned by ancient grammarians for Sicily (cf. ARHENS 1843: 88). These deaspirations are not to be connected with spirantization, but rather with a typically Sicilian phenomenon concerning all voiceless aspirated stops. One might argue that deaspiration was considered a diastratically low trait of the language already in the Archaic period in Sicily, because we notice sometimes phenomena of hypercorrected aspirations, such as in IGDS I, inscriptions 22, 41, and 177.

32   It is interesting to note that even in areas where the occlusive pronunciation is sometimes retained, as in Italo-Greek, we have occurrences of fricative from the velar stop, e.g. Bov. [pi'ɣadi] from πηγάδιον.

104   CAPANO

ination. The interpretation of αἰα as a representation of the word αἶγα with a fricative [ɣ] is therefore preferred. Unless one thinks of a lapsus, there is no other possible reading for the phrase, which reads "οἱ δὲ ἱερομνάμονες τᾶι θυσ[ί]αι | θυόντω αἰ⟨γ⟩α λευκάν", "now let the hieromnamones offer a white goat as a sacrifice". We might add the additional early case of the personal name Αθōνυμος in IGDS II 32, a *defixio* from Selinous, dated to the 5th c. BCE. This personal name is explained by Bettarini (2005: 7) as the result of an assimilation from Ἀγαθόνυμος that must gave gone through the phases [aga-] > [aɣa-] > [aː]. Had the rule g > j / V_V been in place, we would have expected the form *αιαθόνυμος.[33]

One thing worth noting is that Sicily in the Classical-Hellenistic periods was a multilingual environment, while in Roman period it was mostly bilingual, with two dominant languages (cf. 2. above), and our analysis may profit from looking at these phenomena *also* through the lens of language contact. In order to exemplify this, I shall now focus on a specific case study. We have seen that the evidence for a fricative pronunciation of ⟨γ⟩ is by no means abundant, and there seems to be no hard evidence in favor of a [g] > [ɣ] development. However, as we shall see in the next section, I suggest that we have another case in a funerary inscription from Roman Syracuse. In the following section, I will use what I have so far outlined to address what I argue is an interesting case of Greek-Latin contact in Roman Sicily that, to my knowledge, has gone unnoticed so far. If my hypothesis is correct, we would have evidence of a numeral TPIAINTA, attested in a late Roman funerary inscription from Syracuse. I will argue that the form represents a case of hybridism, rather than an actual loanword, and that this phenomenon of interference can be explained as product of a community with widespread Greek-Latin bilingualism.

4 The Numeral 30. Spirantization and Language Contact

4.1 *The Linguistic Context of Hellenistic and Early Roman Sicily*
Sicily is a very interesting case of linguistic contact in the ancient world, at first between local languages—such as Elymian—and then imported languages, like Greek and Punic. There have been many insightful studies on Greek in contact with local languages in Classical and Hellenistic Sicily, but by the initial period of Roman domination (2nd c. BCE), although Punic was still spoken, at least to a certain extent (AMADASI GUZZO 2012), Elymian and Oscan had

---

33   An alternative explanation, offered by Mimbrera (2012: 53), considers the name Αθōνυμος as the result of an apocope for Αθανώνυμος, is not more convincing.

PHENOMENA OF SPIRANTIZATION AND LANGUAGE CONTACT

disappeared. Starting from the late 3rd c. BCE, there is yet another context for linguistic contact in Sicily, when Latin was first introduced to the island after the Romans took control. There have been many important contributions on the topic of Greek-Latin contact in Sicily, concerning, for example, grammar and lexicon (TRIBULATO 2012), onomastics (KORHONEN 2011), and formulae (CAPANO 2020a). Linguists do not agree on how much cultural contact and proximity are necessary to cause language change, but it is generally agreed that there is permeabity amongst linguistic systems (HICKEY 2010) and that language contact can happen also in a situation of little contact among speakers. However, if we consider the Sicilian linguistic landscape in the Roman period, we see that the interactions among Greek and Latin speaking populations were very intense, to the point of being described as "intimate" by some scholars (JOSEPH 2010, who borrowed the image from BLOOMFIELD 1933). Greek and Latin coexisted in Sicily for at least 9 centuries, and most of that time they did so while sharing a political system, a social life, and, in the latest period, a religion, Christianity. In my recent work (CAPANO 2020a and 2020b), I consider all these as external factors for linguistic change, that resulted in phenomena of interference, loanword, code shift, and creation of hybrid forms. Here, after having analyzed the process of spirantization in Sicily, I will offer some new evidence on language contact in Sicily.

4.2 *Spirantization and Language Contact: A Hybrid Numeral in Syracuse*

The form TPIAINTA is attested on a funerary monument found in the Catacombs of Syracuse and dated to the 3rd–4th c. CE, IG XIV 75 (cf. fig. 3.1).[34] The inscription, 6 lines long and roughly cut on a stone that appears to be a reused Corinthian capital, reads:

Ἐνθάδε
κῖτε Ἀντ-
ωνῖνος
ἐτῶν τρια-
ίντα
κ(ατάθεσις) π(ρὸ) δ' εἰ(δῶν)

Here lies Antoninos, 30 years old. His deposition (was) 4 days before the Ides.

---

34   The photo of the inscription comes from the volume by BISCONTI—BRACONI 2013, *Incisioni Figurate della tarda antichità*, published by Pontificio Istituto di Archeologia Cristiana (PIAC), and it is reproduced here with the authorization of PIAC, which I thank.

FIGURE 3.1
The inscription of Antoninos

In an attempt to interpret the numeral in lines 4–5, Carini (1875: 123, no. XXVII) suggested to integrate [κο] in order to restore the regular τρια[κο]ντα, which is attested elsewhere in Sicily, but there is no sign of material loss of the inscribed surface of the stone. One could assume, as WESSEL (1989 no. 1378) must have done by accepting the reading τριάκοντα, that we are dealing with a *lapsus scalpri*, or—in other words—with an error in the transcription from the arranged text during the engraving process. However, there is an additional problem to this interpretation. As is clearly visible in the image published by Sgarlata (2013: 522 fig. 7), and as Wessel carefully noticed, there is an ⟨ι⟩ at the beginning of line 5. This form TPIAINTA is hitherto unattested in Greek, but I argue that here we are not dealing with an error of the stonecutter. Rather, we can explain this form through language contact, and therefore validate its authenticity. If we consider the aforementioned example of αἶα (for αἶγα) as a true case of spirantization already in the 3rd c. BCE, it would not be surprising that, almost 6 centuries later, there is another epigraphical example of loss of voiced velar stop in internal position. I argue that the numeral TPIAINTA represents in fact τριαγίντα '30', where ⟨γ⟩ is not spelled out because it corresponded to a voiced fricative velar in internal position, in the same way as ⟨γ⟩ was missing from the word αἶγα. But what to make of -γίντα? In Ancient Greek, numerals between 30 and 90 were formed by the addition of the proparoxytone suffix -κοντα to the stem; this means that, for instance, the "regular" word for 'thirty' is τριάκοντα, which was indeed restored by Wessel (τρια[κο]{ι}ντα, with the expunction of ι). As shown by Mimbrera Olarte (2012: 180), Doric Greek

Sicily presents only one form for '30', i.e. τριάκοντα, that also has the derivative τριακοστῷ 'the thirtieth'. Interestingly, while the numeral '30' seems quite stable, there is variation in the Sicilian names for 'forty', which is attested as τετρώκοντα, τεσσεράκοντα, and τεσσαράκοντα, the last of which originated during the Hellenistic period.

It is well known that numerals have gone through a series of phonetical changes between Imperial and Medieval Greek, so much that the Byzantine and Modern Greek developments of the numeral '30' is τριάντα (HOLTON—HORROCKS et al. 2019: 1252). In this case, though, we witness the fact that the development does not match this tendency. One might argue that the inscription of Ἀντωνῖνος is indeed a step towards the form τριάντα, reached by the assimilation of voiceless [t] between sonorants, but this does not explain the presence of ι at the beginning of line 5. However, the number becomes completely transparent if we entertain the possibility that it is a case of linguistic contact with Latin, in which the numeral '30' is represented by *triginta*, which appears rarely in Latin inscriptions because of the tendency of Roman epigraphy to use numbers (e.g. XXX) rather than numerals. It is a well-known fact that, during their development, Romance languages underwent major changes in the denomination of the tens, which must have been *trienta, *quadranta, *quinquanta at some stage of Late Latin, but at this stage, during the 3rd–4th c. CE, there is no reason to believe that the Latin numeral 30 had already underwent a change. If we look for contemporary evidence for the numeral '30', spelled out in Latin, we can see AÉ 1976 no. 52, a funerary inscription from Rome dating to 300–350 CE, or a funerary inscription from Dalmatia, from the 4th c. CE.

It is then reasonable, I argue, to interpret TPIAINTA as [tria'yinta] from a phonetical point of view—but it is legitimate to read in it a product of language contact? We know that Syracuse, and similarly Catania, had a lively bilingual society (KORHONEN 2012, 2018), not only within the same city (where Greek speaking families live in the same spaces as Latin speaking families) but even within the same family.[35] In this context, one can explain τριαίντα as a hybrid form between Greek τριάκοντα and Latin *triginta*, where the first part comes from the Greek τρια-, but the suffix is the regular Latin *-ginta*. Since by the 3rd–4th c. CE spirantization must have become widespread, it is, after all, regular that *τριγίντα would have been pronounced, and thus written, without the

---

35   To mention a case outside Catania and Syracuse, which are more studied, *Claudius Theseus* in Messina shows that within the same household one could have some funerary inscriptions in Greek and some others in Latin, even in the same generation (KORHONEN 2016: 117).

velar segment. If all the above is correct, τριαγίντα is the reflex of a local pronunciation (with spirantization) of the voiced velar stop not only of Greek, but also of Latin. Unfortunately, at the moment we do not have good parallels in Latin inscriptions, but we can hope that new inscriptions will show independent evidence for this Sicilian pronunciation of stops, especially in the Latin speaking community in Syracuse. The evidence for this phenomenon is very little, therefore I will not argue that we are dealing with a case of linguistic change, but instead with a phenomenon of variation. In this case, the interference between Latin and Greek resulted in a hybrid form that is not uncommon in areas of linguistic contact.[36] Hybrid words might have never reached the standard of the language (that is the case of hybrid creations in child speech, as studied by MATRAS 2009: 23–25), or even spread widely. I argue that, in the same way as morphemic loanwords might be favored by the transparency and easiness in identifying the morpheme, the hybrid form τριαίντα might be facilitated by the identifiability of the suffix *-ginta*, which also appeared in *viginta*,[37] *quadriginta*, *quinquaginta*, etc. In other words, the speakers were able to isolate the suffix and therefore to reproduce it in other contexts and, because the passage [g] > [ɣ] already happened before the Roman period, it is likely that the Greek pronunciation of the Latin suffix in Sicily presented the spirantization of [g]. There is little need to say that loanwords are not restricted to a particular area of the lexicon and, more broadly, linguistic contact can affect any part of the language, though not with the same probability.[38] Furthermore, numbers are generally considered to be part of the core lexicon, which is less likely to be borrowed, but there are cases of loans of numerals; for instance one can think of the numeral [pantʃ], '5', attested in the Abruzzo region in Italy, from Romani (Indo-Aryan) varieties spoken in the area (PELLIS 1936), or of the loanword of the Semitic numerals 'one' (masc.), 'two', and 'six' into Hurrian (CECCHINI

---

36   To give an example from the formation of the Hellenistic Κοινή, one could think of Arcadic ἰαρής 'priest', a compromise form between Arcadic ἱερής and Doric ἱαρεύς, or, in Sicily, the personal name Ἰρήνα, a hybrid form between Dor. Ἰράνα and Ion. Ἰρήνη, found e.g. in ISic000997, from 3rd–4th c. CE Syracuse. One should keep in mind that phenomena of hybridization can happen within the utterances (CROFT 2003: 49), without affecting the entire language: in this case of ἰαρής and Ἰρήνη, as well as in τριαίντα, we are not referring to any mixed language, but only to a case of a language shift within the word, that is, the creation of a new hybrid form.

37   It should be noted the more common and standard form for '20' is *viginti*, from which e.g. Italian *venti* also originates, but *viginta* is also attested, e.g. Tac. *Ann.* 12, 23. 1 as a variant, and in epigraphic texts, e.g. AÉ 2016, 1938 and EDCS 69100228, both from Africa and dated between the second half of the 5th CE and the first half of the 6th c. CE.

38   For some attempts to create schemes on borrowability, see MORAVCSIK 1978; on hierarchies of borrowability, see THOMASON—KAUFMANN 1988 and MATRAS 2009.

1981: 106–109; DOMBROWSKI—DOMBROWSKI 1991).[39] One might argue that the examples of loss of ⟨γ⟩ as instances of spirantization are too rare, but, on the contrary, I suspect that the scarce evidence could be explained by the fact that the development of a fricative did not merge with any other phoneme in Ancient Greek. In other words, in the Greek language during the Roman period, [ɣ] was not in complementary distribution with any other phoneme. The development of a new phoneme—on an internal level—might induce the stonecutter to preserve the original grapheme for the new phoneme, and—on an external level—prevents the linguist from detecting the change through the exchange between two letters, as happens, for instance, between ⟨η⟩ and ⟨ι⟩.

5   Conclusion

This contribution aimed to shed light on an elusive matter, the development of fricative sounds from voiceless aspirated and voiced stops in Greek. All scholars easily admit that such a change must have happened,[40] but very few have examined the material to determine where and when this phenomenon took place. I have tried to delineate the temporal and spatial coordinates of spirantization of stops for most of the Greek-speaking world during the Hellenistic and early Roman periods, but I am aware that this kind of phenomenon is better observed within micro-contexts, ideally within a small area. I nevertheless have attempted to describe the bigger picture that is needed for better understanding the Sicilian situation, because no linguistic area is entirely an island, not even Sicily (whose connectivity with other areas of the Mediterranean is becoming increasingly clear). There are good reasons to believe that in Sicily the voiced stops [g] and [b] underwent spirantization in the Hellenistic period, before the 3rd and before the 2nd c. BCE respectively, while the voiced dental stop might have started to become fricative at a substandard level during the Imperial period. Voiceless aspirated stops probably retained their plosive component in Sicily longer than in other areas of the Hellenistic world, and did not become fricative before the late Imperial period. One might object that the evidence is too thin to support the theory, but I believe that spirantization can be detected by small hints, as written texts by nature tend to even out variation and divergence from the norm. Inscriptions, together with papyri, provide our

---

39   For an extensive case of loanword of numeral, one can refer to the Thai language, that derives them from Middle Chinese and, for numerals in literary and poetic style, from Sanskrit (SUTHIWAN—TADMOR 2009: 605).

40   Of course, arguing otherwise would mean neglecting the Modern Greek evidence!

best evidence—much more so than literary sources—for language contact, which most of the time can be detected thanks to patent traces of language A in language B (by loanwords, phonetic and morphosyntactic interference, codeswitching ...). In this paper, I have argued for a further case of interference between Latin and Greek, within a substandard context. Moreover, as I hope I have shown with the case of τριαίντα, not all linguistic features that a linguist might identify on the stone should be taken as a fruitful innovation. A mistake, even when it is not accidental and entails linguistic meaning, might very well be a short-lived innovation, a product of a variation that does not turn into change, or a change that does not live long. After all, not all linguistic changes have success!

References

AIUK 2 = Lambert, Stephen 2018, *Attic Inscriptions in UK Collections*, Athens: British School at Athens.

Amadasi Guzzo, Maria Giulia 2012, *Phoenician and Punic in Sicily*, in O. Tribulato (ed.), *Language and Linguistic Contact in Ancient Sicily*, Cambridge: Cambridge University Press: 115–131.

Ampolo, Carmine (ed.) 2001, *Da un'antica città di Sicilia. I decreti di Entella e Nakone. Catalogo della mostra*, Pisa: Scuola Normale Superiore.

Arena, Renato 2002[2], *Iscrizioni greche arcaiche di Sicilia e Magna Grecia* vol. II: *Iscrizioni di Gela e di Agrigento*, Alessandria: Edizioni dell'Orso.

Battistoni, Filippo 2006, *The ancient* pinakes *from Tauromenion: some new readings*, "ZPE" 157: 169–179.

Bettarini, Luca 2005, *Corpus delle defixiones di Selinunte: edizione e commento*, Alessandria: Edizioni dell'Orso.

Biville, Frédérique 1990, *Les emprunts du latin au grec. Approche phonétique*, Louvain/Paris: Édition Peeters.

Brixhe, Claude 1976, *Le Dialecte Grec de Pamphylie: Documents et Grammaire*, Paris: Librarie d'Amerique et d'Orient Adrien-Maisonneuve.

Brixhe, Claude 1996, *Phonétique et Phonologie du grec ancien*, Louvain-La-Neuve: Peeters.

Brixhe, Claude 2016, *Stèles et langue de Pisidie*, Nancy: Association pour la diffusion de la recherche sur l'Antiquité.

Bubeník, Vit 1983, *The Phonological Interpretation of Ancient Greek: A Pandialectal Analysis*, Toronto/Buffalo/London: University of Toronto Press.

Bubeník, Vit 1989, *Hellenistic and Roman Greece as a Sociolinguistic Area*, Amsterdam/Philadelphia: John Benjamins.

Buck, Carl D. 1955, *The Greek Dialects: Grammar, Selected Inscriptions, Glossary*, Chicago: University of Chicago Press.

Bybee, Joan—Easterday, Schelece 2019, *Consonant strengthening: A crosslinguistic survey and articulatory proposal*, "Linguistic Typology" 23/2: 263–302.

Byrne, Sean G. 2003, *Roman Citizens of Athens*, Studia Hellenistica 40, Leuven/Dudley (MA): Peeters.

Capano, Marta 2020a, *Il greco di Sicilia fra età ellenistica e tarda antichità. Risultati dell'analisi di un corpus epigrafico*, Tesi di dottorato discussa all'Università degli Studi di Napoli "L'Orientale".

Capano, Marta 2020b, *Dissertation Summary. The Greek language in Sicily between the Hellenistic Period and Late Antiquity. A contribution from an epigraphic corpus*, "Journal of Greek Linguistics" 20/2 1–15.

Carini, Isidoro 1876, *Rassegna archeologica*, "AAS" 3.1: 121–125.

Cecchini, Serena M. 1981, *sty ı in Ugaritico* "Orientalia" 50: 106–109.

Colvin, Stephen C. 1999, *Dialect in Aristophanes: The Politics of Language in Ancient Greek Literature*, Oxford: Oxford University Press.

Croft, William 2003, *Mixed languages and acts of identity: an evolutionary approach*, in Y. Matras,—P. Bakker (eds.), *The Mixed Language Debate: Theoretical and Empirical Advances*, Berlin/New York: Mouton de Gruyter: 41–72.

Curbera, Jaime 1997, *The Persons Cursed on a Defixio from Lilybaeum*, "Mnemosyne" IV 50/2: 219–225.

Dombrowski, Franz A.—Dombrowski, Bruno W.W. 1991, *Numerals and Numeral Systems in the Hamito-Semitic and Other Language Groups*, in A.S. Kaye (ed.), *Semitic Studies in Honor of Wolf Leslau on the Occasion of his 85th Birthday, November 14, 1991*, Wiesbaden: Harrassowitz: 340–381.

Gignac, Francis T. 1976–1981, *A Grammar of the Greek Papyri of the Roman and Byzantine Periods. 2 vols*, Milano: Istituto Tipografico Cisalpino.

Gignac, Francis T. 1991, *Phonology of the Greek of Egypt, influence of Coptic on the*, in A.S. Atiya (ed.), *The Coptic encyclopedia*. Volume 8, New York: Macmillan Publishers: 71–96.

Girgis, Wahib A. 1966, *Greek loan words in Coptic (Part II)*, "Bulletin de la Société d'Archéologie Copte" 18: 71–96.

Grossman, Eitan 2018, *Did Greek Influence the Coptic Preference for Prefixing? A Quantitative-Typological Perspective*, "Journal of Language Contact" 11/1: 1–31.

Grossman, Eitan 2015, *No case before the verb, obligatory case after the verb in Coptic*, in E. Grossman—M. Haspelmath—T.S. Richter (edd.), *Egyptian-Coptic linguistics in typological perspective*, Berlin: de Gruyter: 203–225.

Grossman, Eitan—Richter, Tonio S. 2017, *Dialectal variation and language change: The case of Greek loan-verb integration strategies in Coptic*, in E. Grossman—P. Dils—T.S. Richter—W. Schenkel (eds.), *Greek Influence on Egyptian-Coptic: Con-*

tact-induced change in an ancient African language. DDGLC Working Papers I. Lingua Aegyptia, Studia Monographica 17, Hamburg: Widmaier Verlag: 207–236.

JOSEPH, BRIAN D. 2010, *Language Contact in the Balkans*, in R. Hickey (ed.), *The Handbook of Language Contact*, Chichester/Malden (MA): Wiley-Blackwell: 618–633.

HOLTON, DAVID—HORROCKS, GEOFFREY—JANSSEN, MARJOLIJNE—LENDARI, TINA—MANOLESSOU, IO—TOUFEXIS, NOTIS 2019, *The Cambridge Grammar of Medieval and Early Modern Greek. Nominal Morphology*, Cambridge: Cambridge University Press.

HORROCKS, GEOFFREY 2010, *Greek: A History of the Language and its Speakers*, Malden (MA)/Oxford/Chichester: Wiley-Blackwell.

IED = MINON, SOPHIE 2007, *Les Inscriptions éléennes dialectales (VIe–IIe siècle avant J.-C.), Vol. I, Textes*, Geneva: Drotz.

IEleusis = CLINTON, KEVIN 2005–2008, *Eleusis. The Inscriptions on Stone. Documents of the Sanctuary of the Two Goddesses and Public Documents of the Deme*, Athens: Βιβλιοθήκη της εν Αθήναις Αρχαιολογικής.

IGDS I = DUBOIS, LAURENT 1989, *Inscriptions grecques dialectales de Sicile (vol. I)*, Rome: Publications de l' École Française de Rome.

IGDS II = DUBOIS, LAURENT 2008, *Inscriptions grecques dialectales de Sicile. (vol. II)*, Rome: Publications de l' École Française de Rome.

IK Central Pisidia = HORSLEY, GREG H.R.—MITCHELL, STEPHEN 2000, Bonn: Habelt Verlag.

IK Priene = BLÜMEL, WOLFGANG—MERKELBACH, REINHOLD 2014, *Die Inschriften von Priene. 2 vols*, Bonn: Habelt Verlag.

ISic = [http://sicily.classics.ox.ac.uk/inscriptions/]

IThesp = ROESCH, PAUL 2007–2009, *Les Inscriptions de Thespies (IThesp), Fasc. I–XII*, Lyon: Maison de l' Orient et de la Méditerranée Jean Pouillou.

KORHONEN, KALLE 2011, *Language and Identity in the Roman Colonies of Sicily*, in R. Sweetman (ed.), *Roman Colonies in the First Century of Their Foundation*, 7–31, Oxford: Oxbow Books Ltd: 7–31.

KORHONEN, KALLE 2012, *Sicily in the Roman Imperial period: Language and society*, in O. Tribulato (ed.), *Language and Linguistic Contact in Sicily*, Cambridge: Cambridge University Press: 326–369.

KORHONEN, KALLE 2016, *Questioni del bilinguismo siciliano antico in lunga durata*, "Linguarum Varietas" 6: 115–120.

KRISTOFFERSEN, TORE R. 2019, *The Phonological Status of Voiced-Stop Spirantization in Ancient Greek Dialects*, "Die Sprache" 53/1: 85–113.

KÜMMEL, MARTIN J. 2007, *Konsonantenwandel. Bausteine zu einer Typologie des Lautwandels und ihre Konsequenzen für die vergleichende Rekonstruktion*, Wiesbaden: Reichert Verlag.

LAVOIE, LISA M. 2001, *Consonant Strength: Phonological Patterns and Phonetic Manifestations*, New York/London: Garland Publishing, Inc.

LEJEUNE, MICHEL 1972, *Phonétique historique du mycénien et du grec ancien*, Paris: Éditions Klinsieck.

LOZANO, FERNANDO 2004, *Thea Livia in Athens: Redating IG II² 3242*, "ZPE" 148: 177–180.

MADDIESON, IAN 1984, *Patterns of sounds*, Cambridge: Cambridge University Press.

MANGANARO, GIACOMO 1997, *Nuove tavolette di piombo iscritte siceliote*, "PdP" 52: 306–348.

MATRAS, YARON 2009, *Language Contact*, Cambridge: Cambridge University Press.

MELCHERT, H. CRAIG 2008, *Lycian*, in R.D. Woodard (ed.), *The Ancient Languages of Asia Minor*, Cambridge: Cambridge University Press: 46–55.

MÉNDEZ DOSUNA, JULIAN 1991–1993, *On ⟨Z⟩ for ⟨Δ⟩ in Greek Dialectal Inscriptions*, "Die Sprache" 35: 82–114.

MÉNDEZ DOSUNA, JULIAN 1993, *A note on Myc. a-ze-ti-ri-ja, Att. σβέννυμι, and palatalization*, "Die Sprache" 35: 208–220.

MIMBRERA OLARTE, SUSANA 2012, *Fonética y morfología del dorio de Sicilia (siglos vii-i a.c.)*, Madrid: Consejo Superior De Investigaciones Científica.

MIMBRERA, SUSANA 2012, *Sicilian Greek Before the Fourth Century BCE*, in O. Tribulato (ed.), *Language and Linguistic Contact in Ancient Sicily*, Cambridge: Cambridge University Press: 191–222.

MORAVCSIK, EDITH 1978, *Universals of language contact*, in J.H. Greenberg (ed.), *Universals of human language*, Stanford: Stanford University Press: 94–122.

PELLIS, UGO 1936, *Il rilievo zingaresco a L'Annunziata di Giulianova (Teramo)*, "Bollettino dell'Atlante Linguistico Italiano" 2/2: 61–85.

PETROUNIAS, ELEUTHERIOS B. 2007, *Pronunciation during the Hellenistic Period*, in A.-F. Christidis, (ed.), *A History of Ancient Greek: From the Beginnings to Late Antiquity*, Cambridge: Cambridge University Press: 599–609.

PORZIG, WALTER 1954, *Sprachgeographische Untersuchungen zu den altgriechischen Dialekten*, "IF" 61: 147–169.

RAUBITSCHEK DAA = RAUBITSCHEK, ANTHONY 1949, *Dedications from the Athenian Akropolis. A Catalogue of the Inscriptions of the Sixth and Fifth centuries B.C. With the collaboration of Lilian H. Jeffery*, Cambridge (MA): Archaeological Institute of America.

RISCH, ERNST 1955, *Die Gliederung der griechschen Dialekte in neuer Sicht*, "MH" 12: 61–76.

SCHWYZER, EDUARD 1950, *Griechische Grammatik / auf der Grundlage von Karl Brugmanns Griechischer Grammatik von Eduard Schwyzer; 2. Bd. vervollständigt und herausgegeben von Albert Debrunner; 3. Bd.: Register von Demetrius J. Georgacas*. München: C.H. Beck.

SGARLATA, MARIARITA 2013, *Parole e immagini nelle catacombe di Siracusa*, in F. Bisconti—M. Braconi (eds.), *Incisioni figurate nella tarda antichità*, Città del Vaticano: Pontificio Istituto di Archeologia Cristiana: 511–523.

STERRETT, JOHN ROBERT S. 1888, *An Epigraphical Journey in Asia Minor*, Papers of The American School of Classical Studies at Athens 2, Boston: Damrell and Upham.

STRIANO CORROCHANO, ARACELI 1989, *Rodio* ετραΤεν, "Emerita" 57/1: 103–111.

SUTHIWAN, TITIMA—TADMOR, URI, 2009, *Loanwords in Thai*, in M. Haspelmath—U. Tadmor (eds.), *Loanwords in the World's Languages: A Comparative Handbook*, Berlin: Mouton De Gruyter: 599–616.

TEODORSSON, SVEN TAGE 1978, *The Phonology of Attic in the Hellenistic Period*, Göteborg: Acta Universitatis Gothoburgensis.

THOMASON, SARAH G.—KAUFMAN, TERRENCE 1988, *Language Contact, Creolization, and Genetic Linguistics*, Berkeley/Los Angeles: University of California Press.

THREATTE, LESLIE 1980, *The Grammar of Attic Inscriptions. Vol. 1 Phonology*, Berlin/New York: Walter De Gruyter.

TRIBULATO, OLGA (ed.) 2012, *Language and Linguistic Contact in Ancient Sicily*, Cambridge: Cambridge University Press.

WESSEL, KARL 1989, *Inscriptiones Graecae Christianae veteres Occidentis. Inscriptiones Christianae Italiae, Subsidia, 1*, Bari: Edipuglia.

CHAPTER 4

Egyptian Greek: A Contact Variety

Sonja Dahlgren

1   Introduction*

In this paper I explore whether the Greek form used in Egypt in the Roman period could be considered a contact variety. This means it would be an independent variety separate from the standard Greek as we know it from literary sources that could be called Egyptian Greek.[1] I will use Greek documentary texts from Egypt formerly analysed in Dahlgren (2017) as evidence as many of them have orthographic variation representative of spoken language.[2] From the form of the misspellings it can be inferred that they represent phonological and phonetic transfer from Egyptian-Coptic, which can be verified by similar misspellings of Greek loanwords in native Coptic texts (DAHLGREN 2017). This paper focuses on language use from the Roman period (1st c. CE) onward, due to the fact that before this there seems to have been no widespread societal bilingualism and Greek phonological development (in Egypt) was not yet as advanced (see e.g. VIERROS 2012: 39–53; 107–117; CLARYSSE 2010: 64; HORROCKS 2010: 165–170). From the beginning of the Roman period, phonological variation intensifies in general, partly tied to the emergence of Coptic

---

*   I would like to thank Eitan Grossman, Ben Molineaux, Marja Vierros and the reviewer Sofia Torallas Tovar (who revealed her identity) and the anonymous reviewer for their comments, in many respects improving the clarity and contents of this paper. The writing of this article was funded by the project Digital Grammar of Greek Documentary Papyri (PapyGreek, ERC-2017-STG 758481).

1   A thorough introduction to the centuries long interaction between the Greeks and the Egyptians is available in TORALLAS TOVAR 2010.

2   The texts were written by a group of scribes that might have been apprentices, in the middle of their Greek education, with e.g. very fluent handwriting (such as that of experienced writers of private letters) but with shaky grammar and orthography (BAGNALL 2007: 16–17, 21). They have been assumed to have been school exercises (BAGNALL 2007: 21; FEWSTER 2002: 235) or drafts of documents later to be rewritten more carefully (PINTAUDI—SIJPESTEIJN 1993: 13). The collection includes abbreviations for horoscopes, petitions, bills, decrees, notes in relation to bills or deliveries, provisions regarding the priests in the temple etc. (PINTAUDI—SIJPESTEIJN 1993: 11–12). The fact that the Greek education of the scribes was unfinished is an advantage here, as that allowed the transfer elements of their native language (L1) to seep through (DAHLGREN 2017: 17).

© SONJA DAHLGREN, 2022 | DOI:10.1163/9789004508828_006

and partly to the phonological development of Greek itself (DAHLGREN 2017: 28–34). Because the Greek front vowel qualities started to raise (HORROCKS 2010: 167–170), the documentary texts from this period show new phenomena compared to the misspellings in the centuries prior to the Roman period. Furthermore, the variation is extended to the transfer of Coptic vowel qualities and stress system (DAHLGREN 2016, 2017). This means that the number of second language (L2) Greek speakers with a linguistic background connected to Egyptian-Coptic must have increased in the Roman period. Leiwo (2018, 2020) argues that the contact features were accelerated because of the intense multilingualism the Roman economic activity brought, prosperous business facilitated by an excellent road network in Roman Egypt. Another factor contributing to this may be an increase in literacy rates by native language (L1) Egyptians due to the gradual emergence of the Coptic script at this time, a far easier writing system than the consonantal, and otherwise complex, Demotic Egyptian script prior to it (e.g. BAGNALL 1993: 235–238; FEWSTER 2002: 225–226; RICHTER 2009: 415). Fournet (2020: 42–75), on the other hand, brings the question back to multilingualism: while Greek only had one version of Koine throughout Egypt, Coptic had several, quite different dialects. Might this have been the reason to favour Greek in legal documents?

The main part of this paper focuses on phonological phenomena, but I will also touch upon some variation in morphosyntax, some of which is directly caused by Egyptian transfer on the phonetic-phonological level. The Greek language went through important phonological changes from the Roman period onward, including the famous iotacism i.e. the raising and fronting of Greek front vowels discussed in many studies of Greek phonology (e.g., GIGNAC 1976, HORROCKS 2010: 167; TORALLAS TOVAR 2010: 261–262 with many examples). However, as so many of the Greek primary sources from the first centuries CE come from Egypt, language contact should at least be examined as a cause behind the more creative spellings. Many of the Egyptian transfer phenomena are observed in this paper through the analysis of the Narmouthis Greek ostraca (O.Narm., 2nd–3rd c. CE) conducted in DAHLGREN 2016 and 2017, which includes ca. 100 nonstandard Greek (orthographic) variants compared to ca. 500 similar nonstandard variants of Greek loanwords in native Coptic texts, from several collections from 3rd to 12th century CE. However, Narmouthis Greek ostraca were not the only texts with nonstandard variation in phonology and morphology, so comparable evidence from other Greek texts is also given in this paper,[3] contributing to a wider understanding of Egyptian

---

3 Texts are taken from several collections of Greek in Papyrological Navigator (online platform, ca. 70 000 texts).

EGYPTIAN GREEK: A CONTACT VARIETY

Greek. Egyptian Greek as a contact variety has been studied on a smaller scale in DAHLGREN 2016 and DAHLGREN 2017: 148–161. In this paper, I will compare the structural variation of Egyptian Greek with other similar contact varieties of conquest-induced (colonial) prestige varieties such as Indian English, the Celtic varieties of English and Finland Swedish; I will also explore the possibility of creolisation.

The paper is organised as follows. In Section 1.1 I will outline a theoretical framework on the beginning of societal-level bilingualism in Roman Egypt. In Section 2, I will go into details about phonological and morphological variation in Egyptian Greek: 2.1 deals with phonological variation, 2.2. with phonetic variation, which partly causes morphological variation, and 2.3 with morphological variation. In Section 3, I will present other contact varieties similar to Egyptian Greek. Finally in Section 4, I discuss various future avenues of research, focusing on the possible creolisation of Egyptian Greek in later periods.

1.1 *Beginning of Societal Bilingualism*

Egyptian and Greek were in contact for a long period of time. The earliest Greek presence in Egypt dates to 7th c. BCE and concerns trade in Naukratis (FISCHER-BOVET 2008: 33). From the Hellenistic period onward the presence of Greeks in Egypt strengthened. Alexander the Great conquered Egypt in 332 BCE and established Greek as the official language of the government, creating pressure for the Egyptian scribal class to learn Greek (CLARYSSE 1993: 186–188; 200–201). However, there does not appear to have been wide-spread bilingualism on a societal level before the Romans arrived. During the Ptolemaic period, the priestly and scribal classes, to whom literacy was restricted before the Hellenistic period, learned Greek in order to gain more prestigious employment in the administration.[4] Thus doing, they were able to maintain their elite position in the society. The sons of the scribal officers learned Greek to be able to carry on their fathers' occupation, but it is unclear how extensive the use of the two languages was (VIERROS 2014: 234–235). In the Roman period even official language policy very liberally allowed for the use of two languages even regarding legal matters, so long as both participants understood the languages used (TORALLAS TOVAR fortch.; see also CRESPO 2007 on Greek usage e.g. as the language of the court and the attitudes of the Egyptian priests on Greek language use, and the conscious effort of the Ptolemies to

---

4   Of course, there were mixed marriages from early Ptolemaic period onward (3rd c. BCE), even if not very numerous (CLARYSSE 1992: 51–52), so presumably at least some of the offspring born out of these would have been bilingual. Bilingualism was also more vividly present in cities among the Egyptians than the Greeks (TORALLAS TOVAR 2010: 258).

promote the use of Koine). This must speak for a situation in which multiple languages were used in the society on a regular basis, even if Torallas Tovar cautiously points out that absolute evidence of the actual linguistic situation is difficult to attain, despite these sources of information. Furthermore, even after the Roman conquest, Greek remained the language of the army.[5] Therefore, through the army, people from various linguistic backgrounds used Greek on a regular basis to converse with one another (linguistic backgrounds consisting of e.g. Aramaic, Arabic, Dacian, Egyptian, Latin, Nabatean, Thracian, Syrian etc.; FOURNET 2003). It seems that an L2 variety of Greek started to develop in the 2nd century CE because at about this time, the same type of nonstandard variants are suddenly found in papyri from Fayyum oasis to Eastern Desert garrisons, mostly involving phonological variation (see also LEIWO 2018, 2020 for an analysis of 2nd c. variation in the Eastern Desert). In texts coming from different parts of the realm, there was more widespread variation in the word-final unstressed vowel reduced to schwa and stress-related /o, u/ variation according to the Coptic stress system, as well as iotacism that resulted from consonant-to-vowel coarticulation (DAHLGREN 2016; DAHLGREN 2017: 148–160). Similar variation appeared in at least three corpora linked to Fayyum, one of the most bilingual regions in Roman Egypt, and the Roman army. One of these is the O.Narm. corpus, written by L1 Egyptian temple scribes (BAGNALL 2007, FEWSTER 2002: 222–223). The P.Fay. corpus, also studied in this paper, is also from Fayyum; this is a collection of private letters written by an army veteran, Lucius Bellienus Gemellus. We do not know his L1, but his surname is Umbrian, so it could have been Latin; judging by his linguistic idiosyncrasies,[6] it was not Egyp-

---

5 Although Latin seems certainly to have been the official language of the army, it is very clear that much of what could be considered 'official' correspondence and text production continued to be written in Greek. This seems to have been the case even when the writer clearly was someone other than whoever the document concerned. Among what was continuously written in Greek was especially receipts, but also correspondence in general. By all accounts, it seems that there was a tradition or a policy to write at least receipts for goods in Greek as some of the receipts have bilingual transfer from Latin inflectional system and alphabet to Greek; therefore, some of the writers were at least used to writing Latin, and might have been Latin speakers. Of course such policies may have varied between individual record keepers, and some receipts were indeed written in Latin, although these seem to be in the minority. Overall, there seems to have been a linguistic flexibility in place regarding army business records, but mostly Greek was used, even in situations in which the writer seems to have been a Latin speaker (ADAMS 2003: 599–608).

6 In addition to the very regular variation of ⟨i, ei⟩ and ⟨y, oi⟩, frequent also to native Greek writers due to the contemporary phonological development in which these formerly separate phonemes merged, Gemellus also had a habit of consistently choosing the nonstandard graphemic variant ⟨oi⟩ to depict the phonemic /y/ and vice versa. This occurred even with

EGYPTIAN GREEK: A CONTACT VARIETY

tian (GIGNAC 1976: 48; LEIWO 2017). The third corpus is O.Claud., from Mons Claudianus, where there lay a Roman garrison; the writer of these private letters was an L1 Egyptian produce seller with L2 Greek correspondents in the army (LEIWO 2005, 2010 and 2017). As can be seen from the map below (Fig. 4.1), the distance between the Fayyumic corpora and that in the Eastern Desert, in Mons Claudianus, is not small.

The distance alone goes toward proving that the nonstandard (phonological) features that appeared in all these texts were not regional semi-standards but part of an L2 variety because the writers were too far apart for the linguistic variants to be considered instances of local varieties. Certainly, some (mainly) orthographic variation did occur, such as the graphemic marking of word-final schwa with ⟨o⟩ especially in Fayyum, when it mostly was marked with ⟨e⟩ elsewhere; these were more direct instances of dialectal Coptic phonological/orthographic transfer (DAHLGREN 2017: 122–124, 150–151). But the more generally spread nonstandard variants occurring in different corpora with a distance between them could easily have been diffused by the connection between government scribes and army personnel, the corner stones of any colonial conquest. According to Leiwo (2018, 2020), all letter writers along the military roads linking Roman garrisons were somehow connected to the Roman army. The majority of these letter writers were soldiers, which itself constitutes a connection to Fayyum: this was where soldiers of the Roman army possessed plots of land in the fertile ground of the oasis, along with the Greek immigrants that resided there before the Romans (DAHLGREN 2017: 27). Naturally, the soldiers might have been in touch with civilians for various reasons, including commerce (LEIWO 2020); all these contacts would have made the spread of a contact variety easy.

Traditionally, Greek-Egyptian contact has been studied from the point of view of bi- and multilingualism (GIGNAC 1976; PAPACONSTANTINOU 2010, VIERROS 2012). However, some research has contributed to assigning the variation found in Greek in Egypt to transfer effects from Egyptian (GIGNAC 1991; HORROCKS 2010: 112), implying a more general societal L2 usage. Greek nonstandard usage in Egypt displays typical tendencies of a contact variety, especially with respect to phonology (details in Section 3). I briefly survey the types of variation found in Egyptian Greek, and then provide comparisons of similar types of contact varieties elsewhere in space and time.

---

such frequent words as υἱῶι ⟨ʰyiōi⟩ 'son (dat.)' (written οιειωι ⟨oieiōi⟩). Gemellus also seemed to follow the Fayyumic Coptic dialectal practice of depicting word-final schwa with ⟨o⟩, while it was usually written with ⟨e⟩ in other dialects (DAHLGREN 2017: 150–151). Clearly, Gemellus was a man who liked to follow the standard, even if this was, in fact, nonstandard.

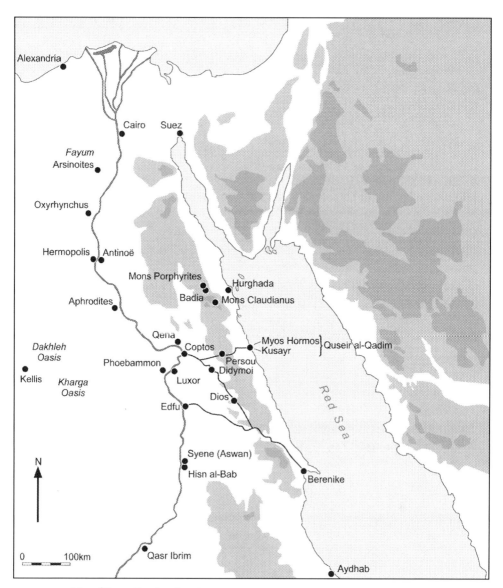

FIGURE 4.1 Map of Egypt. Bouchaud et al. 2017

2 Features of Contact Phonology

L2 Greek in Egypt displayed orthographic variation that is compatible with descriptions of Coptic phonology, including the loss of voicing contrast in plosives, the underdifferentiation of /y, u/, the stress-related allophonic variation of /o, u/, and the reduction of word-final vowel to schwa (GIRGIS 1966;

EGYPTIAN GREEK: A CONTACT VARIETY

GIGNAC 1976; DAHLGREN 2016; DAHLGREN 2017). Parallel evidence of the same phonological phenomena is found in Greek loanwords in Coptic, in Coptic texts (GIGNAC 1991; DAHLGREN 2017: 114–138). Many misspellings also display a tendency to consonantal coarticulation on vowels, an aid for (native language) speech perception utilised in many consonant-rich languages to give immediate information on consonant quality through the altered quality of vowels (e.g. TRAUNMÜLLER 1999; DAHLGREN 2017; DAHLGREN 2020 regarding Egyptian Greek). Coptic as an Afroasiatic language had word formation based on a so-called 'consonantal skeleton', which consisted of 1–4 consonants forming the basic lexical root, an abstract phonological entity,[7] while vowels were used to form grammatical categories (see e.g. LAYTON 2000: 152 for the root and pattern formation and LOPRIENO—MÜLLER 2012: 119–120 for the diachronic development of this in Egyptian). Therefore, clearly distinguishing between the manner and place of articulation of consonants would have been more important for Coptic than Greek. All these features are basic elements of phonological contact: simplifying and merging structures or transferring features that are linguistically significant for L1 but redundant in L2. The linguistic outcome of the language contact depends e.g. on how early and/or long the contact is and whether loanwords are received in oral or written form (e.g. HAUGEN 1950; WEINREICH 1979: 18–19, 28; DOHLUS 2005; ANDERSSON et al. 2017).

Orthographic variation is, of course, largely a reflection of spoken language, but it does display different transfer phenomena, divided into phonological, phonetic and morphological, described in sections 2.1, 2.2 and 2.3, respectively. In Egyptian Greek, almost all of the phonological and phonetic transfer is tied to the transfer of the Egyptian stress system on the L2 Greek, with different phonetic, phonemic, and even morphologically impacted outcomes depending on the position of the nonstandard variant in the word. According to Matras (2009: 87, 233), prosody is the most difficult aspect of the foreign language to learn after reaching maturity and the foreign accent is most persistent regarding prosody. Before going into morphological transfer, I will shortly introduce the phonological and phonetic variation in Egyptian Greek, deriving from the phonological system of Egyptian-Coptic. The examples given here of the phonological and phonetic variation and the vowel reduction system of Coptic have been analysed in detail in DAHLGREN 2017 and 2020.

---

7   The basic lexical root was an abstract phonological entity, which was formed into a word with inflectional affixes, which conveyed deictic markers and grammatical functions such as gender, number, tense etc. In earlier stages of Egyptian these were mostly suffixes (LOPRIENO—MÜLLER 2012: 119–120).

2.1 Variation on the Phonological Level: Underdifferentiation of Foreign Phonemes and Stress-Related Allophonic Variation[8]

This section deals with what can be said to be purely phonological in nature: foreign phoneme underdifferentiation resulting in merger of L1 and L2 phonemes, and stress-related phoneme distribution. One of the most easily noticeable features of Egyptian Greek is the underdifferentation of Greek voiced stops as voiceless because Egyptian-Coptic did not have this opposition (LOPRIENO 1995: 40–43). This concerned /k, g/ and /t, d/ more than /p, b/ because it seems that Coptic had /b/ so it was recognised for Greek as well (GIGNAC 1976: 64; LOPRIENO 1995: 40–46). The nonstandard spelling of *atelpʰos* in (1) is one of the many examples of this, the standard /d/ having been replaced with /t/.

(1) ατελφω *atelpʰō* < ἀδελφῷ *adelpʰō* 'brother (dat.)' (O.Narm.: 103)

Underdifferentiation also concerned the variation between /y/ and /u/, as in (2) and (3), and again for the same reason: this contrast did not occur in Egyptian-Coptic (e.g. PEUST 1999: 201 for Coptic vowel qualities).

(2) πουρου *pourou* /puru/ < πυροῦ *pyroú* /py'ru/ 'wheat (gen.)' (O.Narm. 42 & 46)

(3) ἥμισου *ʰêmisou* < ἥμισυ *ʰêmisy* 'half (n.nom./acc.)' (O.AbuMina. 157; 7th c. CE)

The near-phonetic spelling *pourou* is one of the earliest variants for this, and limited almost exclusively to Fayyum and early Roman period. This limited usage fits Haugen's (1950: 216–217) description of a *pre-bilingual period*, descriptive of societal bilingualism, with the first small groups of bilinguals taking up foreign and loanwords and the rest of the (L1) speakers repeating them in a form that is heavily integrated into L1. The later unrounding of /y/ to [i] and concurrent advancement of societal bilingualism, with more speakers able to produce the foreign phonemes, probably fixed this problem (DAHLGREN 2017: 68–76; 80–81). Regardless, there are a few quite late attestations of *ʰêmisy* writ-

---

8 The absolute amount of attestations for the various nonstandard, phonological/phonetic-based misspellings is presented in Dahlgren (2017: 148–161). The frequency of them has been calculated statistically in DAHLGREN—KEERSEMAEKERS—STOLK (forthc.). Generally, the number of attestations per orthographic nonstandard spellings range from a few hundred to

EGYPTIAN GREEK: A CONTACT VARIETY

ten as *ʰêmisou*, one of the few remnants of /y, u/ variation after the early Roman period. Perhaps some nonstandard variants were frozen into a particular form with more usage, but that is merely speculation until further proof of some frequencies can be found.

Another example of variation in the round vowels concerns /o/ and /u/. Coptic had no unstressed /o/ or /ɔ/; these had allophonic variation with /u/ in unstressed positions (PEUST 1999: 211–213, 250–254). Consequently, unstressed /o/ was often replaced in Greek loanwords and L2 Greek with /u/. Sometimes, also /o/ that was originally stressed in Greek seems to have been treated as unstressed due to Coptic stress transfer. In (4), the genitive marker /u/ has been retained but the Greek original stressed /o/ replaced with ⟨ou⟩ /u/, showing such contact-induced change of a stress position—it appears to be placed on the second syllable. This also happened vice versa: Greek original stressed /u/ was replaced with /o/ as in (5). In Coptic, stress was usually placed on one of the two last syllables, so the stress position of penultima is in accordance with Coptic stress rules, only marked with a (nonstandard) grapheme that codes for the stressed round vowel in Coptic (DAHLGREN 2017: 153; DAHLGREN 2020).

(4) λουγου *lougou* /lugu/ < λόγου *lógou* /lugu/ 'word (gen.)' (PSI 8 884.2, Oxyrhynchites 390 CE)

(5) κομιονται *komiontai* < κομιοῦνται *komioúntai* /komiuntai/ 'to take care of' (BGU 4 1123.6, Alexandria 30 BCE–14 CE)

2.2 Variation on the Phonetic Level: Word-Final Schwa and Consonant-to-vowel Coarticulation

This section concentrates on phonetic transfer, which is, in fact, the most frequent type of variation in Egyptian Greek (DAHLGREN 2017: 165–166), containing variation within the vowels /a, e, o/ and variation related to iotacism.

Variation related to /a, e, o/ has been analysed by Gignac (1991) as resulting from the contact with Coptic, which did not have all three phonemes in any one of its dialects. This no doubt caused problems for perceiving all the distinctions in Greek words. Furthermore, Coptic regularly used these graphemes (mostly ⟨e⟩) for marking schwa (DAHLGREN 2016; 2017: 62–65; PEUST 1999: 250

---

several thousands, depending on the phenomenon (e.g. stop variation, /y, u/ /o, u/ and /a, e, o/ variation), with the several variants related to iotacism running as high as tens of thousands of attestations.

onward), offering further proof for the unspecific phonemic nature of at least ϵ ⟨e⟩ in any of the Coptic dialects. It seems, from several examples, that it was used to depict a phonetic schwa in L2 Greek production as well, which would have resulted from the transfer effect of it from Egyptian-Coptic. Unfortunately for Greek production, these examples often involve verb mood marking, so that it becomes unclear whether an infinitive or an imperative is meant in a given context. Consider e.g. examples (6) and (7) which each have nonstandard orthography for what seem to be imperative forms, but easily confusable with infinitives (see further LEIWO 2010, 2017 and DAHLGREN—LEIWO 2020). Note that the Egyptian-influenced reduction of word-final vowels to schwa is tied to the word-final -*n* often deleted in Egyptian Greek (GIGNAC 1976: 111). This is an instance where the transfer of the phonetic level influenced morphology, further discussed in Chapter 4.

(6) κερασεν *kerase*(*n*) < κέρασον *keraso*(*n*) 'to mix (aor.imp.)' (O.Narm. 115)

(7) πεμψεν *pempse*(*n*) from πέμψον *pempso*(*n*) 'to send (aor.imp.)' (O.Claud. 2: 2nd c. CE)

The occurrence of the word-final schwa in Coptic is connected to the stress system of Coptic, which, of course, is a phonological feature of a language. However, as Coptic was a stress-timed language (DAHLGREN 2017: 133–138; see Auer (2001) for a stress type typology), much like English it reduced the qualities of unstressed vowels, and vowel reduction is a phonetic phenomenon. This tendency to vowel reduction in unstressed positions had two manifestations: full schwa, reaching its target (the word-final schwa as in (6–7)) and consonant-to-vowel coarticulation, which was the manifestation of an incomplete schwa word-medially. In the latter, the vowel quality retains some properties of the surrounding consonants due to insufficient time between two consonants to reach the target i.e. schwa (FLEMMING 2009: 79–86; 89–91). Much of what is concidered iotacism in Egyptian Greek is, in fact, a result of contact-induced consonant-to-vowel coarticulation i.e. contextually conditioned vowel reduction.

Due to Egyptian influence, especially front vowels were susceptible to consonant-to-vowel coarticulation, fronting the vowel quality near front consonants such as dentals or nasals (mostly /n/), and retracting the vowel quality near consonants that have that ability, such as bilabials (FLEMMING 2009: 82–84; 92) or back consonants such as velars, uvulars and pharyngeals. The bilabial at the beginning of the word is responsible for the variation in (8), retracting [e̞] to [e].

EGYPTIAN GREEK: A CONTACT VARIETY

(8) μετροπολι *metropoli* < μητροπόλει *mētropólei* [metropoli] 'the city (dat.)'
     (O.Narm. 110)

This phenomenon is studied within Coptology regarding the bivalency of
Coptic *eta* [e] written either with ⟨i⟩ /i/ or ⟨a⟩ /a/—variation follows the
consonantal environment (PEUST 1999: 229–230; DAHLGREN 2017: 106–112).
Coptic texts can have variation within the full range of [i, e, ɛ, æ, a] but in L2
Greek, variation seems to be limited to [i, e, ɛ], as in (9). In *lɛbɛnous*, the bilabial /b/ has affected both the /i/ in the first syllable and the /a/ in the second
syllable, retracting the quality of the first and raising that of the latter.[9]

(9)   λεβενογ[c] *lɛbɛnous* < λίβανος *líbanos* 'frankincense' (P.Hamb.Bil.1, 3rd–
     4th cent. CE)

There are thousands of examples of the phenomenon in the Greek documentary papyri; unfortunately, a full statistical analysis of the exact amount of the
attestations related to iotacism following the consonantal environment instead
of free variation is beyond the scope of this article. However, even these prelim-
inary results should affect how we look at iotacism, the raising and fronting of
Greek original υ, οι, ει, η /y, oi, ei, e:/ to [i], as in Modern Greek.

2.3 Variation on the Morphological level: Greek Inflection of Egyptian Personal Names and Cases

In this section, I look at variation in morphology, taking as a test case the inflection of personal names and irregular nouns, both of which are bound to be
affected by L2 usage. Names are less standardised in general (ANDERSON 2007:
3–5), and irregular forms are difficult to remember by L2 users, often ending in
analogous formations (see e.g. case studies on Russian/Estonian (EHALA 2012)
and English/German bilinguals (WAGNER 2017)).

The variation related to Greek cases has been extensively studied before.
Stolk (2015) noticed that case syncretism was tied to the merger of the semantic
roles of genitive and dative, while the development was also affected by the
phonological development of Greek (cf. GIGNAC 1976: 208; HORROCKS 2010:
115–117 and 180–181). However, not all case variation was caused by Greek-
internal reasons. Leiwo (2003: 5–8) studied the case marking in the Narmouthis
Greek ostraca in connection with the preposition *pros* in a collection of appar-

---

9 Bilabials cause a 'trough' effect on adjacent vowels, and especially high vowels are lowered in
   quality; cf. Flemming (2009: 82–84, 92).

ent tax receipts, which in the context required the accusative case (O.Narm. 1–19)[10]. The distribution of the cases marked in a nonstandard way varied apart from one aspect: there was an attempt to mark the first element of the phrase correctly (cf. also VIERROS 2012: 140–154).

The failure to produce standard case-marking was plausibly contact-induced variation as Egyptian had no cases;[11] however, it had prepositions.[12] In Greek, a preposition could have different meanings depending on the case in which the complement was; in Egyptian, too, the meaning of a preposition could vary, but only the context helped in understanding the meaning—the object, the noun, was always uninflected. It is therefore understandable for the scribes to have faltered in choosing—and remembering—the correct case endings demanded by the prepositions at hand. However, although it at first glance seems as though the scribes' use of the Greek cases is completely chaotic, there is, when given a thorough examination, some very interesting variation to be found on the individual level of the writers. This is especially clear concerning the Greek inflection of Egyptian personal names.

The Greek inflectional system of Egyptian personal names was somewhat artificial and did not quite follow the Greek noun declension categories. Egyptian names ending with a vowel received a Greek ending of -*s*, the names that ended with a consonant were moulded into the Greek form by adding -*is* or -*ês* (both [is]) to the end (there was a tendency to end names ending in a dental sound with a suffix of -*ês* PESTMAN 1993: 485).[13] The system is displayed in Table 4.1 below.

---

10   Leiwo (2003: 5–8) on O.Narm. 1–19 tax receipts: *pros* 'to' + noun in the accusative. 18 texts out of the 19 preserve the first word after the preposition (the texts start with the preposition). Out of these, the first word is in the accusative 11 times if the first word, 3 times if the constituent occurs later in the text; in the nominative (most usual due to L1 impact) 2 times if the first word, 3 times on a later occurrence; genitive 4 times if the first word, 4 times if it occurs later; and dative (which was merging with the genitive) 1 time if it was the first word, 3 times if it occurred later.

11   Coptic is typically not described as having cases (see e.g. LAYTON 2000) and e.g. the functions of accusative and dative are described through direct/indirect objects. Grossman (2014) presents a different view: not only does Grossman consider Coptic having cases, he also notices that there is a dichotomy found in African languages. This involves having no case before the verb, and obligatory case after the verb. He also finds that there is an overt nominative marker, differing from the accusative and the citation form, and obligatorily marking highly accessible postverbal subjects. See also Grossman (2018) for some analysis about the diachronic formation of cases.

12   However, according to Grossman (2014: 208), e.g. *nci/nče*, which is normally described as a preposition by some Coptologists, is rather a nominative marker, so the situation is less than clear here as well.

13   -*ês* was written with *eta* indicating a historically long /e/ but, by the Roman period, was often pronounced as [i], which, no doubt, further added to the confusion in spelling.

EGYPTIAN GREEK: A CONTACT VARIETY

TABLE 4.1   The inflection of Egyptian names in Greek

Egyptian names ending in a vowel	Egyptian names ending in a consonant	Egyptian names ending in a dental sound
-s, -tos, -ti, -n	-is, -ios, -ei, -in	-ês, -oû, -êi, -ên
Pana + s	Petosir + is	Pekhut + ês
Pana-s	Petosir-is	Pekhut-ês
Pana-NOM	Petosir-NOM	Pekhut-NOM
Pana-tos	Petosir-ios	Pekhut-oû
Pana-GEN	Petosir-GEN	Pekhut-GEN
Pana-ti	Petosir-ei	Pekhut-êi
Pana-DAT	Petosir-DAT	Pekhut-DAT
Pana-n	Petosir-in	Pekhut-ên
Pana-ACC	Petosir-ACC	Pekhut-ACC

Regardless of the system in place, Egyptian names are often not inflected as might be expected. One can see how, for instance, in the two following texts by a single scribe, almost all the nouns and articles are inflected precisely as the context requires, but the inflection of the Egyptian names varies considerably in its adherence to the written standard. The preposition *peri* in this context requires the subsequent nouns and articles to be inflected in the genitive; the most problems in these three texts are seen in the Egyptian names ending in *-is* in the Greek form, although all the regular nouns ending in *-is* are inflected precisely as they should be.

O.Narm. 71. 2nd–3rd c. CE

δ.
περὶ μη-
νύσεως Θ-
ερμοῦθις ἡ
καὶ Σαραπιάς ˙
περὶ Πετοσῖρις
ὁ καὶ Σαραπίωνος
μήνυσας ˙ -----------
οἰκίας Πεκῦσις---
μὴ πρὸ μήνυσας Ἀ[κ-

128   DAHLGREN

η[ς καὶ Ἀκε]ποννις·---
 ---]μήνυσας τὸν
  ---]ην ὡς συν
   ---] ὕλην.

[1] *d peri*   *mênys-eôs*   *Thermuth-is*
  4 concerning-PREP laying.of.information-SG.GEN Thermuth-NOM
  hê   *kai*
  ART.FEM.SG.NOM and

[2] *Sarapia-s* *peri*   *Petosir-is* *ho*   *kai*
  Sarapia-NOM concerning-PREP Petosir-NOM ART.MASC.SG.NOM and
  Sarapiôn-os
  Sarapiôn-GEN

[3] *mêny-sas*   *oiki-as*
  laying.of.information-PST.PTCP.MASC.SG.NOM house-SG.GEN
  Pekys-is *mê pro*
  Pekys-NOM not before-PREP

[4] *mêny-sas*   *Akê-s* *kai*
  laying.of.information-PST.PTCP.MASC.SG.NOM Ake-NOM and
  Akeponn-is----
  Akeponn-NOM

[5] *mêny-sas*   *ton*
  laying.of.information-PST.PTCP.MASC.SG.NOM ART.MASC.SG.ACC?
  (*---êin ôs syn---*) *hylê-n.*
  (---? ? with-PREP) forest-SG.ACC

'Concerning Thermuthis a.k.a. Sarapias filing a complaint; concerning
Petosiris a.k.a. Sarapion who filing a complaint; concerning the house of
Pekysis; Akeponnis, not having filed a complaint before ... filing a com-
plaint the ...'[14]

As we can see from this example, the writer of this document did not have
a problem with inflecting *mênysis*, a noun ending with *-is*, on the first line;

---

14 The translation is mine into English, from the original translation into Italian provided by
  PINTAUDI—SIJPERSTEIJN 1993.

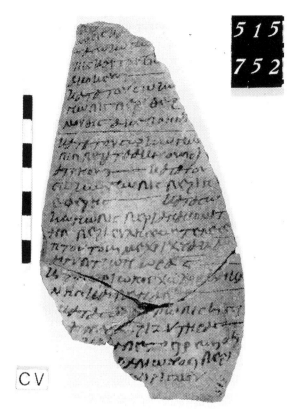

FIGURE 4.2 OGN I: 72, The Cairo Egyptian Museum
PICTURES TAKEN FROM THE ORIGINALS BY
DR. ANGIOLO MENCHETTI

neither did he have a problem with inflecting *Sarapiôn* on the second line. All the other names, as well as the articles, seem to be in the nominative, however, not only the ones ending *-is*; also the one connected to *Sarapiôn*. Perhaps the ending *-os* was taken as a nominative ending?

O.Narm. 72. 2nd–3rd c. CE

    περὶ [..]
    κασις κα-
    τὰ Σωκωνῶ-
    πις καὶ τοῦ εἰσ-
    ακοκεύς -------
    κατὰ τοῦ Σωκω-
    νῶπις περὶ Θερ-

μοῦθις Ἀκεπονννι ⟍ς′ ·

κατὰ τοῦ Σωκωνῶ-
πις περὶ Τααkηους Φ-
ατρηους ·--- κατὰ τοῦ
Σωκωνῶπις περὶ Ν-
εφερῆς ·-- κατὰ Σω-
κωνῶπις περὶ ἀνακομιτ-
ῆς, περὶ συλήσεως · τέλεσε-
ν τούτους μέχρι Χυὰκ ᾱ
Αἰγυπτίων ὥρᾳ ς ·---
κατὰ Ὠρίωνος χωλοῦ καὶ Κα-
μῆς καὶ Πενας · --
   κατὰ Σωκ[ω]νῶπις καὶ Σερ-
   ήνου [π]ερὶ ζυτηρᾶς· ---
   κατὰ Πετοσίρεως ὁ καὶ
   [Σα]ραπίωνος περὶ
   το]υ χιρισμοῦ.

[1] *peri*   *Kas-is*   *kai* *tou*   *kata*
     concerning-PREP Kas-NOM and ART.MASC.2SG.GEN against-PREP
     Sôkônôp-is   *kai*
     Sokonop-NOM and

[2] *tou*   *eisakok-eus;*   *kata*
     ART.MASC.2SG.GEN court.official-SG.NOM against-PREP
     tou   *Sôkônôp-is*
     ART.MASC.2SG.GEN Sokonop-NOM

[3] *peri*   *Thermuth-is*   *Akeponn-is;*   *kata*
     concerning-PREP Thermuth-NOM Akeponn-NOM against-PREP
     tou
     ART.MASC.2SG.GEN

[4] *Sôkônôp-is*   *peri*   *Taakê-us*
     Sokonop-NOM concerning-PREP Taake-GEN
     Phatrê-us;   *kata*
     Phatre.GEN_Taakês.daughter.of.Phatrês against.PREP

EGYPTIAN GREEK: A CONTACT VARIETY 131

[5] *tou   Sôkônôp-is   peri   Nepherê-s;*
    ART.MASC.2SG.GEN Sokonop-NOM concerning-PREP Nefere-NOM
    kata   Sôkônôp-is
    against-PREP Sokonop-NOM

[6] *peri   anakomitês   peri   sylêseôs;*
    concerning-PREP recovery-SG.GEN concerning-PREP robbery-SG.GEN
    tele-sen
    to.complete-IMP.2SG

[7] *toutous   mekhri Khyak   a Aigypti-ôn*
    ART.MASC.PL.ACC by   Eg.month._Feb-Mar 1 Egyptians-GEN
    hôra-i   s;
    in.hour-DAT 6

[8] *kata   Hôriôn-os   khôl-ou   kai Kamê-s   kai*
    against-PREP Horion-GEN limping-SG.ADJ.GEN and Kame-NOM and
    Pena-s;
    Pena-NOM

[9] *kata   Sôkônôp-is   kai Serên-u   peri*
    against-PREP Sokonop-NOM and Seren-GEN concerning-PREP
    zytêra-s
    payment.of.beer-SG.GEN

[10] *kata   Petosir-eôs   ho   kai Sarapiôn-os*
    against-PREP Petosir-GEN ART.MASC.SG.NOM and Sarapion-GEN
    peri
    concerning-PREP

[11] *tou   khirism-ou.*
    ART.MASC.SG.GEN administration-SG.GEN

'Concerning ... Kasis against Sokonopis and *eisagogeus*; against Sokonopis concerning Thermuthis daughter of Akeponnis; against Sokonopis concerning Taakes daughter of Hatres; against Sokonopis concerning Nepheres; against Sokonopis concerning recovery from the robbery. Execute these on 1st Choiak of the Egyptians, on the 6th hour. Against Horion the lame and Kames and Ponas; against Sokonopis and Serenos regarding the beer tax; against Petosiris a.k.a. Sarapion concerning administration.'

TABLE 4.2   Nouns ending in -is

Inflection of Egyptian names ending in -is	Inflection of third declension noun *polis* (*poli-*)	Inflection of third declension noun *elpis* (*elpid-*)	Inflection of third declension noun *kharis* (*kharit-*)
-is, -ios, -ei, -in	-s, -os, -i, -n	-s, -os, -i, -a	-s, -os, -i, -n
Petosir-is	poli-s	elpi -s	khari-s
Petosir-NOM	city-NOM	hope-NOM	grace-NOM
Petosir-ios	pole-ôs	elpid-os	kharit-os
Petosir-GEN	city-GEN	hope-GEN	grace-GEN
Petosir-ei	pole-i	elpid-i	kharit-i
Petosir-DAT	city-DAT	hope-DAT	grace-DAT
Petosir-in	pol -in	elpid-a	khari-n
Petosir-ACC	city-ACC	hope-ACC	grace-ACC

Notice, again, the declension of *sylêsis* on line six, and the names *Taakès* on line four, *Hôriôn* on line eight, *Serênos* on line nine and *Sarapiôn* on line ten. Still, none of the names ending in -*is* are inflected according to the Greek standard for Egyptian names; in this context, the preposition *kata* also requires a genitive. *Petosiris* on line ten is, admittedly, marked by genitive case, but not the one intended for this type of an Egyptian name, but rather inflected after the model of a regular (although irregular) noun ending in -*is*, like *polis*.

In a third text, (O.Narm. 73), the Greek type names (e.g. *Sarapamôn* on line three) are inflected in the genitive as dictated by the preposition and context. In all three texts, all but one of the Egyptian names ending in -*is* are left in the nominative despite the need pressed by the preposition to inflect the names in the genitive in this context; still the scribe had no problems in inflecting other nouns ending in -*is* according to the standard. On the other hand, all the names that follow the standard Greek declension system, e.g. *Sarapiôn*, ending in -*ôn*, are inflected exactly as they should be.

There are various ways one might try to explain this. It might be the case that Egyptians were unwilling to inflect names of their own culture, seeing as they were not, in fact, treated in that manner in their own language. This, however, leads to the question why they bothered to render the names in the Greek form at all, then. Most of the Egyptian names in the O.Narm. corpus are in the Greek nominative form, not in the original Egyptian basic form from which the Greek type was transcribed and produced into the Greek nomin-

EGYPTIAN GREEK: A CONTACT VARIETY

TABLE 4.3   Inflectional endings for Greek nouns ending in -is as perceived by a L2 learner

Inflection of Egyptian names ending in -is	Inflection of third declension noun *polis*	Inflection of third declension noun *elpis*	Inflection of third declension noun *kharis*
-is, -ios, -ei, -in	-is, -eôs, -ei, -in	-is, -dos, -di, -da	-is, -tos, -ti, -in
Petosir-is	pol-is	elp-is	khar-is
Petosir-NOM	city-NOM	hope-NOM	grace-NOM
Petosir-ios	pol-eôs	elpi-dos	khari-tos
Petosir-GEN	city-GEN	hope-GEN	grace-GEN
Petosir-ei	pol-ei	elpi-di	khari-ti
Petosir-DAT	city-DAT	hope-DAT	grace-DAT
Petosir-in	pol-in	elpi-da	khar-in
Petosir-ACC	city-ACC	hope-ACC	grace-ACC

ative form in the first place (e.g. Petosir + -is). Also, one could think this to be part of the general development of dropping /i/ in the endings -ios (HOR-ROCKS 2010: 175) as the /o/ in, for example, in the genitive form of the name *Sokonopis* (*Sokonopios*), is indeed in an unstressed syllable. This, however, does not explain the nonstandard usage, either, as surely this would also have affected regular nouns with the same ending. Perhaps the inflectional categories for Egyptian names simply proved too much for the Egyptian scribes. As we can see from the examples in Table 4.2, there was much to remember if the Egyptian name inflectional system was to be remembered alongside the standard categories, as these provided one with quite enough variation in themselves.

Of course, keeping in mind the Egyptian scribes of O.Narm. were not necessarily fluent bilinguals, but rather L2 Greek learners only using Greek for work or education, they might not have remembered all the possible noun inflectional rules and language historical exceptions, if taught in the first place. In that case, to them the inflectional endings of nouns in -is probably looked like in the examples in Table 4.3 above, with a reinterpretation of the morpheme boundary.

The situation looks quite different now. First of all, these 'alternative' inflectional endings of *elpis* and *kharis* are similar to the ones used for inflecting Egyptian names ending in a vowel, for example *Panas* from table 4.1: NOM -*s*, GEN -*tos*, DAT -*ti*, ACC -*n* (Table 4.4).

TABLE 4.4   Comparing 'alternative' *kharis* to the inflection of Egyptian
names ending in a vowel

Inflection of Egyptian name ending in a vowel	Inflection of third declension noun
Pana + s	*kharis*
-s, -tos, -ti, -n	-is, -tos, -ti, -in

TABLE 4.5   Comparing alternative *polis* to the inflection of Egyptian
names ending in a consonant

Inflection of Egyptian names ending in -*is*	Inflection of third declension noun *polis*
-is, -ios, -ei, -in	-is, -eôs, -ei, -in

The alternative inflection of *polis*, on the other hand, now looks quite similar to the Egyptian name inflectional type for names ending in a consonant (-*is*) (Table 4.5).

The inflection of *polis* is an irregular one due to language historical reasons—one can see its inflection differs from the other two -*is* ending nouns from the third declension. It was, however, a frequently occurring word, so probably quite well remembered: a proof of sorts of this is the genitive inflection of *Petosiris*, *Petosireôs*, on line ten in O.Narm. 72—if the scribes did remember one of the possible inflectional types for names ending in -*is*, this would have been a strong candidate. According to the Egyptian name inflectional rules, *Petosiris* inflected in the genitive would have been *Petosirios*. There are similar slips toward the standard inflectional form with Egyptian names ending in -*ês*. Following the inflectional pattern of, for example, *Periklês* or *Heraklês*, very famous names indeed, many Egyptian names ending in -*ês* were inflected in this fashion, like the genitive form *Taakêus* of *Taakês* on line four, text two; the Egyptian inflection for this would have been *Taakeu*. The Egyptian inflection for -*ês* ending names was the same as for the Greek first declension -*ês* ending names such as *Persês* ('Persian') or *Hermês*, which had a slightly different type of inflection from *Periklês*, and from the other third declension model for -*ês* ending nouns, which had a different accusative ending of -*ê*/-*ên* instead

EGYPTIAN GREEK: A CONTACT VARIETY

TABLE 4.6 Comparing the inflection of Egyptian names ending in *-ês* to the inflection of *Periklês*

Inflection of Egyptian names ending in *-ês*	Inflection of third declension name Periklês
-ês -ou, -êi, -ên	-s, -ous, -i, -a
Pekhut-ês	Periklê-s
Pekhut-NOM	Perikles-NOM
Pekhut-ou	Perikle-ous
Pekhut-GEN	Perikles- GEN
Pekhut-êi	Perikle-i
Pekhut-DAT	Perikles-DAT
Pekhut-ên	Perikle-a
Pekhut-ACC	Perikles- ACC

of *-a*. However, for some reason these were not often confused with each other. Instead, the *Periklês* model was favoured. Maybe the famous men had pressed one inflectional type strongly into the minds of the scribes? See Table 4.6 for a comparison of the forms.

Quite like the *-ês* ending nouns' inflection, for some reason the standard Greek inflection for *-os* ending names did not seem to cause a lot of problems to the Egyptian scribes. The second declension model for the *-os* ending nouns was highly regular and contained such basic level words as *logos* ('word'). This was nothing like the confusing variety of *-is* ending nouns which probably got confused with the inflection for vowel ending Egyptian names; the problem was that the inflectional types for both the vowel ending Egyptian names and the consonant ending Egyptian names were taken from the Greek third declension, the different endings reflecting the different third declension Greek noun stems. Once again: the Egyptian names ending in a vowel (*-s* ending in the Greek nominative form) received an inflectional type matching that of the noun *kharis*, which had a stem ending in a consonant; the Egyptian names ending in a consonant (*-is* ending in the Greek nominative form), on the other hand, received an inflection matching (roughly) that of *polis*, a Greek noun whose stem in the nominative originally ended, despite appearances, in a vowel (Table 4.7).

TABLE 4.7 Comparing the inflectional endings of Egyptian names to the third declension nouns

Egyptian names ending in a vowel	Third declension noun	Egyptian names ending in a consonant	Alternative third declension noun
Pana + s	*kharis*	Petosir + is	*polis*
-s -tos, -ti, -n	-s, -tos, -ti, -n	-is -ios, -ei, -in	-is, -eôs, -ei, -in
Pana-s	khari-s	Petosir-is	pol-is
Pana-NOM	grace-NOM	Petosir-NOM	city-NOM
Pana-tos	kharit-os	Petosir-ios	pol-eôs
Pana-GEN	grace-GEN	Petosir-GEN	city-GEN
Pana-ti	kharit-i	Petosir-ei	pol-ei
Pana-DAT	grace-DAT	Petosir-DAT	city-DAT
Pana-n	khari-n	Petosir-in	pol-in
Pana-ACC	khari-ACC	Petosir-ACC	city-ACC

There was no special inflection type for Egyptian names ending in *-ôn*, so these were inflected in the standard third declension manner following, for instance, the inflection of *Poseidôn*. Quite a few of the Greek gods' names were of this form, so scribes writing Greek were probably very familiar with this inflection type. It should come as no surprise, then, that names ending in *-ôn* were very often inflected precisely according to the standard, like in all these three texts: see, for instance, the genitive form *Sarapamônos* for *Sarapamôn* in O.Narm. 73, line three.

The reinterpretation of the morpheme boundary is not unique to Egyptian Greek but probably a frequent feature in any language contact situation; analogous reformations are behind even some of the verb forms in Modern Greek. To give another example related to Greek, it also takes place in Cappadocian Greek, a Greek variety formerly spoken in Turkey (nowadays only spoken in Greece, by descendants of immigrants from Cappadocia). For example, in the contact-induced analogical remodelling of the medio-passive paradigm as an agglutinative inflection, based on the 3sg, in complete accordance with Watkins' Law (JANSE 2009: 101–102).

3 Similar Contact Varieties: Indian English, Irish and (Highland) Scottish Varieties of English, Finland Swedish

Egyptian Greek matches Matras's theory of system convergence (2009: 223–226; see further analysis in DAHLGREN 2017: 73–74): speakers do not maintain two separated systems of phonological sub-components but instead use one phonemic inventory and distribution for both languages. There were very few loanwords from Egyptian, and typically to language contacts of this type, these were mostly technical or local terms such as month names (κάκις *kákis* < Coptic ⲕⲁⲕⲉ *kake*; also βᾶρις *báris* (TORALLAS TOVAR 2004; see also THOMASON 2001: 69 on loanword principles)). Besides technical terminology, the contact mostly involves phonological transfer, while Coptic has loanwords from almost all Greek grammatical categories (RICHTER 2009: 406 ff.). This asymmetry makes Egyptian Greek similar to other contact varieties such as Indian English or Irish and (Highland) Scottish English, and Finland Swedish.

It is generally accepted that borrowing of language structures is easier between typologically similar languages, while, in principle, anything can occur in language contact (THOMASON 2001; AIKHENVALD 2007). It is also accepted that the prestige language does not borrow much from the indigenous language (e.g. THOMASON 2001). Regardless, L2 learners can change the language: sometimes structural transfer occurs from the indigenous language to the prestige one, creating a new variety (THOMASON 2001: 63). Thomason (2001: 74–75) talks about the type of transfer that usually occurs with shift-induced transfer, but elaborates that this type of transfer can also occur without language shift, such as in Indian English. Typically, it starts with phonology and syntax, instead of borrowing, which starts with lexicon. In case of a contact variety (L2 version of the target language, (TL_2)), there may be some lexical transfer but structural transfer dominates.

Thomason's description seems to fit Egyptian Greek remarkably well but also several other contact varieties that have arisen from conquest scenarios, and include a societal prestige language, that of the conquerors. These include well-studied cases like Indian English, Irish and (Highland) Scottish Englishes, and Finland Swedish. All of these contact varieties share some common properties. All these contact situations were associated with prestigious languages of conquerors. They involve typologically dissimilar languages. The contact is long, often several hundred years. The contact has remained relatively stable with strong cultural attachment to the original culture of the indigenous language (maintenance of culture and religion; Egyptian, Indian Native languages, Finnish) on the other hand, and language shift, often aided by urbanisation on the other (Irish) (THOMASON 2001: 15–26); cultural shift can occur without language shift, of course, toward urbanisation and industrialisation. Learning of the L2 has benefits for speakers, e.g. employment opportunities (cf. THOMASON 2001: 15–26), which has made the language socially attractive for many L2 speakers, using what is essentially a TL_2 variety (THOMASON 2001: 75). Most importantly, the variation seems to be mostly phonological, and furthermore much of it is stress-related transfer: for example, from the transfer effect of the Egyptian stress system, there followed vowel reduction that profoundly changed what Greek words must have sounded like in their native form. These types of contact effects create the uniquely distinguishable sounds of the contact varieties.

3.1 Indian English

Indian English, like Egyptian Greek, has a rather long history of development. It was used extensively from the middle of 19th century onward, but the contact in larger scale started earlier with the East India Company, which was given a royal charter and consequently started to establish trade centres in India. This brought in English merchants and started the interaction with both the Moghul emperors of a number of Indian states and the local Indians in general. Further along came British missionaries, bringing with them the chance for education. The British army also had a role in spreading the English language by attracting many Indian soldiers (especially Sikhs), in which context English spread quickly (MUKHERJEE 2007: 164). The situation is in many ways similar to the Hellenistic Egypt after Alexander's conquest.

English is still an official language in government, along with Hindi, and a high language in the society of India (SAILAJA 2009: 1–6). There are some loanwords in the Indian English variety from the native languages, not used elsewhere in other colonial and post-colonial varieties of English. These include some numerals (one *lakh* = 100,000),[15] some political and administrative vocabulary (e.g. *dharna* 'a sit-in'; SAILAJA 2009: 73), and e.g. the verb *air-dash*, created by Indian politicians, which means to go from one place to another very quickly (often by airplane). (SAILAJA 2009: 73–77). Some others (quite few), technical words specific to India, have landed in English permanently: e.g. *jungle* and *verandah*[16] (DURKIN 2014: 386–389; SAILAJA 2012:

---

15   These are taught to children at school (mathematic revision). https://nroer.gov.in/nroer _team/file/readDoc/55b23f2881fccb054b6be25f/.

16   *Jungle* (first surviving written record 1776) comes from Hindi *jangal*, in turn deriving from Sanskrit *jangala-s*. The origin of the word is unknown but it has come to the English language through Hindi. Similarly, *verandah* (Hindi *varanda*) seems to have originated from Portuguese *varanda* 'long balcony or terrace' (originally of uncertain origin, possibly

EGYPTIAN GREEK: A CONTACT VARIETY

362).[17] Mainly, however, transfer from indigenous Indian languages has been phonological: Indian English has a distinct Indian accent (SAILAJA 2012: 360). English alveolar stops /d, t/ are realised as retroflex stops [ɖ], [ʈ], and pronunciation in general is according to spelling (full) vowels (['sæniti] vs. ['sænəti]); stress patterns are syllable-timed (DETERDING 2010: 392–395; SAILAJA 2012). The transfer of the stress system is the biggest cause behind the usage of full vowels: not many syllable-timed languages reduce vowels in the same way as (BrE) English as a stress-timed language does (cf. e.g. AUER 2001: 1391–1393). Many Hindi speakers, by contrast, engage in extensive English code-switching, and Hindi has borrowed vocabulary from English (SAILAJA 2009: 62).

Indian English, as much as it sounds like a L2 variety, is the native language of almost 200,000 Indians: according to the 1991 census report, there were 178,598 Indians, approximately 0.021% of the total population, who have English as their first language. This is in addition to English constantly remaining the prestige language of the society, and the numbers pertaining to L2 or L3 speakers of English are much higher: 64,602,299 (8.0%) and 25,440,188 (3.1%), respectively. In the 2001 census in India, the numbers had risen further: 226,449 L1 English speakers (0.02%), 86,125,221 L2 speakers and 38,993,066 L3 speakers, the total of all these speakers reaching up to 12.18% speakers of English in the population (TROPF 2004: 11–15; 20; 36).[18] No doubt the increasing number of speakers is related to the prestige position of English in the Indian society, with an increasing number of parents opting for (private) English schooling for their children in order to increase their employment opportunities (TROPF 2004: 16). The kind of work facilitated by English-language education includes e.g. government jobs, business, and education, not unlike the situation in Hellenistic Egypt.

3.2 *Irish and (Highland) Scottish Varieties of English*

Irish and (Highland) Scottish varieties of English offer fruitful comparisons to Egyptian Greek. Much of the transfer is again on the phonological level from the indigenous languages to English, and the replacement of the English phonemes by the (originally) L1 ones and the transfer of the stress system of Irish

---

     related to Spanish *baranda* 'railing' (ultimately from Vulgar Latin **barra* 'barrier, bar')). The word became a part of English through its usage in India (first surviving written record 1711). The Online Etymology Dictionary, accessed 7th August 2020.
     https://www.etymonline.com/word/jungle
     https://www.etymonline.com/search?q=verandah.

17   Durkin lists ca. 40 loanwords entering English, but many of these have uncertain origins in the general South Asian linguistic area.

18   http://www.censusindia.gov.in/2011-documents/lsi/ling_survey_india.html.

(under focus here) and Gaelic onto English are behind the uniquely recognisable character of these varieties. As in Indian English, the history of the contact is a longstanding one.

Irish English was created by the Norman invasion of the late 12th century, Tudor conquest and colonisation of 16th century and by mid-19th century English was a majority language in the country (e.g. HICKEY 2007). As in Indian English, some (comparable to) technical vocabulary of e.g. local natural elements have found their way in the English varieties, but these are mainly used locally. Such are e.g. *glen* 'valley', *loch* '(sea)lake', etc. in Ireland and Scotland. Very few loanwords have been borrowed from the languages to English globally, but among the few are e.g. *whisk(e)y*, a phonetic spelling of *uisce beatha* (in Irish, *uisge-beatha* in (Scottish) Gaelic), 'water of life';[19] and e.g. *bog*. There is some syntactic transfer such as reduplication (*at all at all*) and recent past construction (*I was after doing the laundry when I saw the news*; also in Highland Scottish English due to Gaelic influence), using reflexive pronoun for emphasis (*Is it yourself who did this?*) etc. Nevertheless, while these features might seem peculiar or unidiomatic to speakers from other English varieties, the Irish/(Highland) Scottish varieties are mostly recogniced by their distinct phonological features. For instance, in Irish English (standard BrE and AmE) English dental fricatives [θ, ð] are realised as dental stops [t̪, d̪] (*three -tree*), and there is an epenthetic schwa after liquids (*filᵊm*); furthermore, stress patterns are transferred from Irish with stress being placed on the first syllable (e.g. HICKEY 2004, 2007).

Some of these features apply similarly to the Highland Scottish variety of English, originally deriving from the Northern Irish dialect. Some of the features that derive from Gaelic are the same in Scots, which is the main source of variation in Lowland Scottish English.

Scottish English is a continuum of Scots in the Lowlands at the other end, and Standard Scottish English (SSE) at the other (STUART-SMITH 2008: 48). SSE is phonetically similar to Scots in all varieties, although the lexical distribution of phonemes comes close to standard English varieties in some places (MAGUIRE 2012: 57). (Standard Scottish) English is the prestige language in contact with both Scots and Gaelic (MAGUIRE 2012: 62).

The shared phonological transfer features from Gaelic include, among others, dental production of /t/, /d/ and /n/, bilabial pronunciations of /f/ and /v/, and retroflex approximant pronunciations of /r/ that retract the following

---

19   Online Etymology Dictionary, accessed 7th August 2020.
       https://www.etymonline.com/word/whiskey.

alveolar consonants (*horse* [hɔɹ̝s]). On the side of morphosyntax, there is the extended use of progressive aspect and e.g. emphatic use of reflexive pronouns (as in Irish). Many of these features are even more pronounced in Highland Scottish English due to the shift to English having been not only rapid but more recent in that context; hence, there are also many more transfer features extant in the variety. Gaelic has, for example, left traces of vowel quantity (allophonic in SSE) and pre-aspiration of voiceless stops (*happen* [haːhpən]) in Highland Scottish English (MAGUIRE 2012: 63).[20]

Like Irish, also Gaelic makes use of the epenthetic schwa after liquids (in Scots, unlike Gaelic, this is restricted to the sequences /lm, rm, rn, rl/, in words such as *girl* [girᵊl], *film* [filᵊm] and a connection to Gaelic is uncertain; MAGUIRE 2012: 62). Also stress placement is distinctly word-initial. As with Indian English, the contact situation is also typically asymmetric with the dominant language of the society receiving (almost) only phonological transfer from the indigenous language, and the indigenous language simplifying, as in the case of Irish, grammatically due to the influence of the dominant one. This will largely be because of lack of usage: there are very few L1 speakers of Irish or Gaelic in either country, to the extent that almost all Irish teachers in Ireland are L2 speakers. Many of the speakers of Irish also engage in code-switching into English (e.g. study by HICKEY 2009).

3.3 Finland Swedish

The language contact with Swedish and Finnish started in the 16th century. Swedish was the main language of the government while most Finnish people spoke Finnish in their everyday lives. After the Russian conquest (1809), Swedish at first remained the only official language until 1863 when Finnish was added alongside it; after Finnish independence in 1917, Finnish has dominated as the language of the government but Swedish remains an official language of the government alongside Finnish. There are a few Finnish calques in Finland Swedish, e.g. *leverlåda* < *maksalaatikko*, literally 'liver box', meaning a liver-based casserole. In Sweden, the same dish is called *korvkaka* (lit. 'sausage cake'). Another delicacy, if ordered in Sweden by its Finland Swedish name, can cause some confusion among the staff, as the cinnamon roll, called *kanelbulle* ('cinnamon bun') in Sweden, has the unfortunate name of *örfil* in Finland Swedish,

---

20   Gaelic was spoken throughout Scotland until the beginning of the 19th century, after which it was restricted to the Highlands and Western Isles. Nowadays it is even more restricted to Western Isles and isolated pockets in the Highlands. In the Highlands, English has and is replacing it, and in the Lowlands, it has been replaced by Scots (MAGUIRE 2012: 53).

deriving from Finnish *korvapuusti* (lit. 'slap on the ear'). But again, phonology is the most distinctive difference between the varieties.

There are some phonemic differences from the Swedish variety, including the realisation of *sj* as [ʂ] and [ɕ ~ ʃ] when it is velar and palatalised in Sweden. The most noticeable feature of Finland Swedish is the loss of tonality, causing certain minimal pairs to only be understood from context. These include /ˈandɛn/ 'duck' vs. /ˌandˈɛn/ 'spirit' [ˈandɛn], with the latter one having a secondary stress in Swedish spoken in Sweden (KURONEN 2000: 17–24; KURONEN— LEINONEN 2001). By contrast, Finnish has taken a high number of loanwords from Swedish, while hardly any have entered from Finnish to Swedish. Nowadays, there is much code-switching to Finnish among the younger L1 Finland Swedish speakers.

Why are the contact situations so similar? Why is there mostly phonological transfer? Explanations are partly sociolinguistic, partly typological. The conquering group will change the societal situation to serve its own purposes for administration, education, etc. There is no need for the dominant group to learn the indigenous language well because the society will function largely on its terms. The indigenous population, by contrast, will learn the L2 if they want to be employed in administration, education etc.; there will be marriages, friendships etc. between the groups (see CLARYSSE 1992: 51–52 regarding the Egyptian Greek situation). With enough L2 speakers of the shared language, inadvertent transfer of the perceptually easiest level of the language will occur (phonology and phonetics). Phonological level might be the easiest to copy because it is the most salient, and contains less processing than morphosyntactic patterns. An exception to the rule is Cappadocian Greek, where Turkish agglutinative noun morphology has in some dialects even replaced the inherited Greek flexion (THOMASON 2001: 63–64). Importantly, however, Greek was not a prestige language in the area where it was originally spoken (Janse p.c.).

4   Discussion and Conclusions

It is important to keep in mind that Egyptian Greek comes to us through written level only so there is no definite proof of how far spread the variation presented in this paper was, because not every writer would let the features of spoken language penetrate through to the written one (some statistics are available, however, proving e.g. consonant-to-vowel coarticulation beyond chance level (DAHLGREN—KEERSEMAEKERS—STOLK forthc.)). This is the situation now in modern English and French, for example, where some writers let slip the occasional phonetic spelling and imperfect inflection, but most try to adhere to the written standard (if the nonstandard spellings are not intentionally used in puns or word play, for example). However, the same type of variation repeats itself in different parts and periods of Egyptian Greek, with parallel evidence of the same phonological phenomena in Coptic, so it is probable that there was at least a semi-standard of Greek influenced by Egyptian spoken in Egypt. To compare what we know of this proposed contact variety with other similar ones, Egyptian Greek perhaps most resembles Irish English in that the phonemic features derive from the indigenous language, and Indian English in being so heavily affected by stress transfer from the indigenous language. In Egyptian Greek the simplification of grammar was probably related to the fact that most of the users of this TL_2 were of Egyptian-origin, and therefore themselves spoke a language which was less fusional than Greek. In Irish English, the process is different but the result the same: there are very few L1 speakers of Irish left, and this has allowed English, the L1 language of the majority of all Irish users, to tamper with the inflectional patterns of Irish, because English is mophosyntactically less complex. Simplification is one of the most frequent phenomena in language contact according to a rich literature of contact linguistics (HAUGEN 1950, WEINREICH 1953, THOMASON—KAUFMAN 1988, THOMASON 2001, MATRAS 2009; recent statistical study by SINNEMÄKI—DI GARBO 2018), so this is not surprising. We do not know what would have happened to Egyptian Greek without the Arab conquest of 641 CE, which limited Greek usage and had Egyptians shift to Arabic (RICHTER 2009: 417–432).

If Greek had continued to be used, would it have stayed the same, a prestigious contact variety similar to Indian English and Irish English, or would it have evolved in time as Finland Swedish when prestige effect had changed after some centuries of usage? The latter might not have required the independence of Egypt from Greek but merely a long enough coexistence of the languages in contact as in Indian English, English still being used after independence. Or would Egyptian Greek have eventually advanced into a creole? Sometimes, contact varieties can develop into creoles without the intermediate phase of pidgins (cf. KOUWENBERG—SINGLER 2018). There is some evidence mainly deriving through the study of Greek effect on Coptic that could contribute to the study of Egyptian Greek as a mixed language. According to Reintges (2004: 70), Coptic represented a bilingual language variety, with two parent languages, Greek and Egyptian. This idea of a profoundly mixed language has been rejected by other scholars (e.g. ZAKRZEWSKA 2017), at least partly; Zakrzewska concedes that from a sociolinguistic point of view, for example considering the abrupt emergence of Coptic in the literary use, this corresponds with a constructed linguistic variety intended for in-group communica-

144 DAHLGREN

TABLE 4.8 Coptic integration of the Greek loanverb

Bohairic	Manichaean Lycopolitan	Sahidic
a-f-er-keleuin	*a-f-r-keleue*	*a-f-keleue*
PST-3SGM-do-command	PST-3SGM-do-command	PST-3SGM-command

tion (ZAKRZEWSKA 2017: 134; 140–141). However, some evidence of a language use drawing from two pools is available.

In (2.2) I discussed the variation between infinitive and imperative in Greek due to the confusion laid over the forms by the phonetic variation. The situation with imperative/infinitive verb inflection was further complicated by Coptic having the (mostly) same form for imperative and infinitive (LAYTON 2000: 155; DAHLGREN 2017: 119–120; DAHLGREN—LEIWO 2020). Furthermore, there is a longstanding debate over whether Coptic borrowed Greek verbs in the infinitive or the imperative form because of different representations of them in Coptic dialects, as in Table 4.8.

Bohairic has the form *a-f-er-keleuin and Sahidic a-f-keleue for* 'he commanded', the form constituting a light verb construction (Coptic *(e)r-* ('to do') as an auxiliary, and a Greek verb in its original form). However, the Bohairic verb form looks like a Greek infinitive and the Sahidic one like an imperative. According to Grossman and Richter, both verb forms were actually borrowed in the infinitive. However, due to a combination of phonetic erosion and morphological reduction with some of the dialects (e.g. Sahidic) first dropping the Coptic auxiliary *(e)r-* as the verb started to feel 'own' i.e. more integrated to native Coptic, the Greek infinitive ending *-n* would have been dropped, leading to a form looking like the imperative (GROSSMAN—RICHTER 2017: 208–223). I argue that instead of the form being more integrated into L1 morphology through 'acceptance', the process would have been initiated by the reduction of the word-final syllable, which was a typical Coptic feature, visible also in L2 Egyptian Greek production (see above in 2.2). After that, more integration would have followed easily as part of the verb already looked more like a native word (DAHLGREN 2018).

Fayyumic Coptic documents offer more evidence of the profound effect Greek had on Coptic. 8th century Fayyumic letters use Greek phrases with Coptic meanings, for example phrases such as *tirênê nek* 'peace be with you', the Greek loanword *eirênê* fully integrated into Coptic morphology without any marking of the foreign element. Furthermore, the phrase was never used in Greek. There was also heavy truncation of Greek words, the forms matching the shorter form of Coptic words; for instance *apókrisis* 'separation' being much shortened to *apokres* (BOUD'HORS 2017: 425–431; 437–438). The form of the original word this much altered, this might suggest that Greek was no longer a prestigious language in the Fayyum as there was no attempt to preserve the foreign pronunciation.

It is a typical feature of creoles to truncate words so that the semantically less transparent grammatical morphemes are reduced, as well as to include items from the lexifier language, retentions from the substrate languages and internal creations (MATRAS 2009: 281). The phrase *tirênê nek* might have come about this way, even if Greek was not exactly a lexifier language for Coptic. There were also often many spelling forms for the same word (*holokottinos/holokottn/holok* etc.). The unsystematic misspellings indicate that the orthography was based on the phonetic form of the word, which seems to have been fully integrated to Coptic, rather than being a learned phonological or orthographic form. This is compatible with a systemic convergence. To what extent was the same morphosyntax used? If Greek and Coptic shared forms and phrases, we could talk about mixed language(s). In relation to prefixation in Coptic, Grossman (2018) finds that it is unlikely that Greek affected Coptic morphosyntactic changes, such as the change from (dominant) suffixation in Egyptian to prefixation in Coptic. The extent of the mixing in each language should offer interesting new avenues of research. Was the simultaneous simplification of structures an ongoing phenomenon due to L1 impact with advancing bilingualism during the Roman period, or only L2 usage? Frequency of any structural changes according to typical patterns of creolisation is one factor that might prove creolisation, so more statistical studies are needed of the different linguistic aspects of Egyptian Greek. The form of Egyptian Greek resemples the first stage of creolisation, comparable to e.g. Hawai'i Creole with phoneme replacement (e.g. full vowels instead of schwa (*commA*), stress transfer and simplified grammar (compare Indian English), and furthermore semantic change of English-original words (SAKODA—SIEGEL 2004; DRAGER 2012). Context helps where grammatical function disappears (compare Finland Swedish loss of tonality): Coptic had a more strict word order than Greek (see e.g. GROSSMAN 2014), which might have helped to distinguish verb mood variation from infinitive in Egyptian Greek, for example, if there was transfer of the syntactic level as well as the others. This could have lead to the chain effect of *phonology > phonetics > morphology > syntax*, where the phonological system of Coptic created phonetic features that eliminated the distinction of Greek cases and verb mood by their word-final vowels, and consequently forced word order to change (cf. HORROCKS 2010: 108–109; 172–174) in order to preserve references, all beginning with stress transfer. Although I here offer more questions than answers, perhaps with the help of new technologies[21] at our disposal, future studies will offer answers to these questions.

References

The Greek documentary papyri can be found by their abbreviations in the *Checklist of Editions of Greek, Latin, Demotic and Coptic Papyri, Ostraca and Tablets* (*Web edition*). http://library.duke.edu/rubenstein/scriptorium/papyrus/texts/clist.html.

Greek and Coptic Text Editions

BGU = *Aegyptische Urkunden aus den Koeniglichen Museen zu Berlin: Griechische Urkunden*. 1912, Berlin: Königliche Museen zu Berlin.

O.Claud. 2 = BINGEN, JEAN—BÜLOW-JACOBSEN, ADAM—COCKLE, WALTER E.H.—CUVIGNY, HÉLÈNE—KAYSER FRANÇOIS—VAN RENGEN, WILFRIED (eds.) 1997, *Mons Claudianus: Ostraca graeca et latina, Vol. 2: Nos. 191–416.*, Cairo: Institut français d'archéologie orientale.

O.Claud. 4 = BÜLOW-JACOBSEN, ADAM (ed.) 2009, *Ostraca graeca et latina*, Vol. 4: Nos. 632–896.ed., Cairo: Institut français d'archéologie orientale.

O.Frangé 8 = BOUD'HORS, A.—HEURTEL, C. 2010. *Les ostraca coptes de la TT 29. Autour du moine Frangé. vol. 1 Textes*, Bruxelles: CReA-Patrimoine.

O. Narm. = PINTAUDI, ROSARIO—SIJPERSTEIJN, PIETER J. 1993, *Ostraka Greci da Narmuthis* (OGN I), Pisa: Giardini editori e stampatori in Pisa.

P. Hamb.bil. 1 = DIEBNER, BERND J.—KASSER, RODOLPHE (eds.) 1989, *Hamburger Papyrus bil. 1. Die alttestamentlichen Texte des Papyrus Bilinguis 1 der Staats- und Universitätsbibliothek Hamburg: Canticum canticorum (coptice), Lamentationes Ieremiae (coptice), Ecclesiastes (graece et coptice)*, Genève: Cramer.

PSI = VITELLI, GIROLAMO—NORSA, MEDEA (eds.) 1927, *Papiri greci e latini*, Firenze: Enrico Ariani.

Bibliography

ADAMS, JAMES N. 2003, *Bilingualism and the Latin language*, Cambridge: Cambridge University Press.

AIKHENVALD, ALEXANDRA Y. 2007, *Grammars in Contact: A Cross-Linguistic Perspective*, in A.Y. Aikhenvald—R.M.W. Dixon (eds.), *Grammars in Contact. A Cross-Linguistic Typology*, Oxford: Oxford University Press: 1–66.

---

21   There are new searchable databases that allow searches of the orthographic level i.e. misspellings, that are linked to the Papyrological Navigator: Trismegistos Text Irregularities and Paratypa, developed in the project Digital Grammar of the Greek documentary papyri.

ANDERSON, JOHN M. 2007, *The Grammar of names*, Oxford: Oxford University Press.

ANDERSSON, SAMUEL—SAYEED, OLLIE—VAUX, BERT 2017, *The phonology of language contact*, Oxford Handbooks Online.

AUER, PETER 2001, *Silben- und akzentzählende Sprachen*, in M. Haspelmath,—E. König—W. Oesterreicher—W. Raible (eds.), *Language typology and language universals. An international handbook*, Berlin: De Gruyter: 1391–1399.

BAGNALL, ROBERT S. 2007, *Reflections on the Greek of the Narmouthis Ostraca*, in M. Capasso—P. Davoli (eds.), *New archaeological and papyrological researches on the Fayyum, Proceedings of the International Meeting of Egyptology and Papyrology, Lecce, June 8th–10th 2005, 14–21. Papyrologia Lupiensia* 14, Galatina (Lecce): Congedo.

BAGNALL, ROBERT S. 1993, *Egypt in Late Antiquity*, Princeton: Princeton University Press.

BOUCHAUD, CHARLÈNE—MORALES, JACOB—SCHRAM, VALERIE.—VAN DER VEEN, MARIJKE 2017, *The earliest evidence for citrus in* Egypt, in V. Zech-Matterne—G. Fiorentino (eds.), *AGRUMED: Archaeology and history of citrus fruit in the Mediterranean: Acclimatization, diversifications, uses*. Naples: Publications du Centre Jean Bérard (généré le 17 août 2020).

BOUD'HORS, ANNE 2017, *Greek loanwords in Fayyumic documentary texts*, in E. Grossman—P. Dils—T.S. Richter—W. Schenkel (eds.), *Greek influence on Egyptian-Coptic. Contact-induced change in an ancient African language* (DDGLC Working Papers 1. Lingua Aegyptia, Studia Monographica 17), Hamburg: Widmaier Verlag: 423–439.

CLARYSSE, WILLY 2010, *Bilingual Papyrological Archives*, in A. Papaconstantinou (ed.), *The Multilingual Experience in Egypt, from the Ptolemies to the Abbasids*, Farnham: Ashgate: 47–72.

CLARYSSE, WILLY 1993, *Egyptian scribes writing Greek*, "CdÉ" 68: 186–201.

CLARYSSE, WILLY 1992, *Some Greeks in Egypt*, in J.H. Johnson (ed.), *Life in a Multicultural Society: Egypt from Cambyses to Constantine and Beyond*, Chicago: The Oriental Institute: 51–52.

CLARYSSE, WILLY 1987, *Greek Loan-words in Demotic*, in S.P. Vleeming (ed.), *Aspects of Demotic Lexicography. Acts of the Second International Conference for Demotic Studies Leiden, 19–21 September 1984*, Studia Demotica I., Leuven: Peeters: 9–33.

CRESPO, EMILIO 2007. *The linguistic policy of the Ptolemaic kingdom*, in M.V. Chatzopoulos—V. Psilakakou (eds.), *Phones charakter ethnikos: actes du ve Congres International de Dialectologie Grecque: (Athenes 28–30 septembre 2006)*, Ἀθήνα: Κέντρον Ἑλληνικῆς καὶ Ρωμαϊκῆς Ἀρχαιότητος τοῦ Ἐθνικοῦ Ἱδρύματος Ἐρευνῶν Βασιλέως Κωνσταντίνου: 35–50.

DAHLGREN, SONJA 2016, *Towards a definition of an Egyptian Greek variety*, "Papers in Historical Phonology" 1/1. 90–108.

DAHLGREN, SONJA 2017, *Outcome of long-term language contact: Transfer of Egyptian phonological features onto Greek in Graeco-Roman Egypt*, University of Helsinki, doctoral dissertation.

DAHLGREN, SONJA 2018, [review to] Grossman, E.—Dils, P.—Sebastian, T.R.—Schenkel, W. (eds.), 2017, *Greek influence on Egyptian-Coptic*. Lingua Aegyptia, Studia Monographica 17, "Journal of Greek Linguistics" 18/2: 281–291.

DAHLGREN, SONJA 2020, *The system of Coptic vowel reduction: Evidence from L2 Greek usage*, in N. Kuznetsova—C. Anderson (eds.), *The dynamics of vowel reduction and loss: phonetic mechanisms and outcomes for phonology and morphology*, "Italian Journal of Linguistics" 32/1: 209–226.

DAHLGREN, SONJA—LEIWO, MARTTI 2020, *Confusion of form or phoneme?*, in D. Rafiyenko—I.A. Seržant (eds.), *Postclassical Greek. Contemporary Approaches to Philology and Linguistics*. Trends in Linguistics. Studies and monographs. [TiLSM] 335, Berlin/Boston: de Gruyter Mouton: 283–301.

DAHLGREN, SONJA—KEERSMAEKERS, ALEK—STOLK. JOANNE (*forthcoming*), *Language contact in historical documents: the identification and co-occurrence of Egyptian transfer features in Greek documentary papyri*.

DRAGER, KATIE 2012, *Pidgin and Hawai'i English: An overview*, "International Journal of Language, Translation and Intercultural Communication" 1: 61–73.

DETERDING, DAVID 2010, *Variation across Englishes: Phonology*, in A. Kirkpatrick (ed.), *The Routledge handbook of World Englishes*, Oxon/New York: Routledge: 385–399.

DOHLUS, KATRIN 2005, *Phonetics or phonology: Asymmetries in loanword adaptations—French and German mid front rounded vowels in Japanese*, "ZAS Papers in Linguistics" 42: 117–135.

DURKIN, PHILIP 2014, *Borrowed words: A history of loanwords in English*, Oxford: Oxford University Press.

EHALA, MARTIN 2012, *Transfer, hybridization and analogy in L2 usage: The case of Estonian object marking*, "International Journal of Bilingualism" 16/1: 159–174.

FISCHER-BOVET, CHRISTELLE 2008, *Army and Society in Ptolemaic Egypt*, Ph.D. dissertation, Stanford University.

FEWSTER, PENELOPE 2002, *Bilingualism in Roman Egypt*, in J.N. Adams—M. Janse—S. Swain (eds.), *Bilingualism in ancient society: Language contact and the written text*, Oxford: Oxford University Press: 220–245.

FLEMMING, EDWARD 2009, *The phonetics of schwa vowels*, in D. Minkova (ed.), *Phonological weakness in English. From old to present-day English*, New York: Palgrave Macmillan: 78–98.

FOURNET, JEAN-LUC 2003, *Langues, écritures et culture dans les praesidia*, in H. Cuvigny (ed.), *La route de Myos Hormos. L'armée romaine dans le désert Oriental d'Égypte*. Vol. 2, Cairo: Institut français d'archéologie orientale du Caire: 427–500.

FOURNET, JEAN-LUC 2020, *The Rise of Coptic*, Princeton: Princeton University Press.

GIGNAC, FRANCIS T. 1976, *A grammar of the Greek papyri of the Roman and Byzantine periods. Vol. I Phonology*, Milano: Istituto editoriale cisalpino—La goliardica.

GIGNAC, FRANCIS T. 1991, *Phonology of the Greek of Egypt, influence of Coptic on the*, in A.S. Atiya (ed.), *The Coptic encyclopedia*, Volume 8, New York: Macmillan Publishers: 71–96.

GIRGIS, WAHIB A. 1966, *Greek loan words in Coptic (Part II)*, "Bulletin de la Société d'Archéologie Copte" 18: 71–96.

GROSSMAN, EITAN 2018, *Did Greek Influence the Coptic Preference for Prefixing? A Quantitative-Typological Perspective*, "Journal of Language Contact" 11/1: 1–31.

GROSSMAN, EITAN 2015, *No case before the verb, obligatory case after the verb in Coptic*, in E. Grossman—M. Haspelmath—T.S. Richter (edd.), *Egyptian-Coptic linguistics in typological perspective*, Berlin: de Gruyter: 203–225.

GROSSMAN, EITAN—RICHTER, TONIO S. 2017, *Dialectal variation and language change: The case of Greek loan-verb integration strategies in Coptic*, in E. Grossman—P. Dils—T.S. Richter—W. Schenkel (eds.), *Greek Influence on Egyptian-Coptic: Contact-induced change in an ancient African language*, Hamburg: Widmaier Verlag: 207–236.

HAUGEN, EINAR 1950, *The Analysis of linguistic borrowing*, "Language" 26/1: 210–231.

HICKEY, RAYMOND 2007, *Irish English: History and Present-Day Forms*, Cambridge: Cambridge University Press.

HICKEY, RAYMOND 2004, *A Sound Atlas of Irish English*, Volume 1, Berlin: de Gruyter: 57–60.

HICKEY, TINA 2009, *Code-switching and borrowing in Irish*, "Journal of Sociolinguistics" 13/5: 670–688.

HORROCKS, GEOFFREY C. 2010, *Greek: A history of the language and its speakers*, Oxford: Wiley-Blackwell.

KOUWENBERG, SILVIA—SINGLER, JOHN V. 2018, *Creolization in Context: Historical and Typological Perspectives*, "Annual Review of Linguistics" 4: 213–232.

KURONEN, MIKKO 2000, *Vokaluttalets akustik i sverigesvenska, finlandssvenska och finska*, Studia Philologica Jyväskyläensia 49. University of Jyväskylä, doctoral dissertation.

KURONEN, MIKKO—LEINONEN, KARI 2001, *Fonetiska skillnader mellan finlandssvenska och rikssvenska*, in L. Jönsson—V. Adelswärd—A. Cederberg—P.A. Pettersson—C. Kelly (eds.), *Svenskans beskrivning 24. Förhandlingar vid Tjugofjärde sammankomsten för svenskans beskrivning*, Linköping: Linköping University Electronic Press: 125–138.

LAMBDIN, THOMAS O. 1958, *The bivalence of Coptic Eta and related problems in the vocalization of Egyptian*, "Journal of Near Eastern Studies" 17/3: 177–193.

LAMBERT, JAMES 2014, *Indian English slang*, in J. Coleman (ed.), *Global English Slang: Methodologies and Perspectives*, London: Routledge: 126–134.

LAMBERT, JAMES 2018, *Anglo-Indian slang in dictionaries on historical principles*, "World Englishes" 37/2: 248–260.

LAYTON, BENTLEY 2000, *A Coptic grammar. With Chrestomathy and glossary. Sahidic dialect*, Wiesbaden: Harrassowitz Verlag.

LEIWO, MARTTI 2003, *Scribes and Language Variation*, in L. Pietilä-Castrén—M. Vesterinen (eds.), *Grapta Poikila I. Papers and Monographs of the Finnish Institute at Athens* Vol. VIII, Helsinki: Foundation of the Finnish Institute at Athens: 1–11.

LEIWO, MARTTI 2005, *Substandard Greek. Remarks from Mons Claudianus*, in N.M. Kennel—J.E. Tomlinson (eds.), *Ancient Greece at the turn of the millennium. Recent work and future perspectives. Proceedings of the Athens Symposium 18–20 May 2001*, Athens: Canadian Archaeological Institute at Athens: 237–261.

LEIWO, MARTTI 2010, *Imperatives and other directives in the letters from Mons Claudianus*, in T.V. Evans—D.D. Obbink (eds.), *The language of the papyri*, Oxford: Oxford University Press: 97–119.

LEIWO, MARTTI 2017, *Confusion of mood and tense in Greek private letters of Roman Egypt*, in M. Janse—K. Bentein (eds.), *Linguistic variation and change: Tense, aspect and modality in Ancient Greek*, Leiden: Brill: 242–260.

LEIWO, MARTTI 2020, *L2 Greek in Roman Egypt. Intense language contact in Roman military forts*, "Journal of Historical Sociolinguistics" 6/2: 1–31.

LOPRIENO, ANTONIO—MÜLLER, MATTHIAS 2012, *Ancient Egyptian and Coptic*, in Z. Frajzyngier—E. Shay (eds.), *The Afroasiatic languages*, Cambridge: Cambridge University Press: 102–144.

MAGUIRE, WARREN 2012, *English and Scots in Scotland*, in R. Hickey (ed.), *Areal Features of the Anglophone World*, Berlin: Mouton de Gruyter: 53–78.

MATRAS, YARON 2009, *Language contact*, Cambridge: Cambridge University Press.

MESSERI, GABRIELLA—PINTAUDI, ROSARIO 2001, *Corrigenda ad OGN I*, "Aegyptus" 81: 253–282.

MUKHERJEE, JOYBRATO 2007, *Steady states in the evolution of New Englishes: Present-day Indian English as an equilibrium*, "Journal of English Linguistics" 35/2: 157–187.

PAPACONSTANTINOU, ARIETTA (ed.) 2010, *The Multilingual Experience in Egypt, from the Ptolemies to the 'Abbāsids*, Farnham: Ashgate Publishing, Ltd.

PESTMAN, PIETER W. 1993, *The archive of the Theban Choachytes (second century B.C.): A survey of the Demotic and Greek papyri contained in the archive*, Leuven: Peeters.

PEUST, CARSTEN 1999, *Egyptian Phonology. An Introduction to the Phonology of a Dead Language*, Göttingen: Peust und Gutschmidt.

REINTGES, CHRIS R. 2004, *Coptic Egyptian as a bilingual language variety*, in P. Bádenas de la Peña—S. Torallas Tovar—E.R. Luján—M.Á. Gallego (eds.), *Lenguas en contacto: el testimonio escrito*, Madrid: Consejo superior de invastigaciones científicas: 69–86.

RICHTER, TONIO S. 2009, *Greek, Coptic and the 'language of the Hijra': the rise and decline of the Coptic language in late antique and medieval Egypt*, in H.M. Cotton—

R.G. Hoyland—J.J. Price—D.J. Wasserstein (eds.), *From Hellenism to Islam: Cultural and linguistic change in the Roman Near East*, Cambridge: Cambridge University Press: 401–446.

Sailaja, Pingali 2012, *Indian English: Features and sociolinguistic aspects*, "Language and Linguistics Compass" 6/6: 359–370.

Sailaja, Pingali 2009, *Indian English*, Edinburgh: Edinburgh University Press.

Sakoda, Kent—Siegel, Jeff 2004, *Hawai'i Creole: Phonology*, in B. Kortmann—E.W. Schneider, in collab. with K. Burridge, R. Mesthrie, C. Upton (eds.), *A handbook of varieties of English: A Multimedia Reference Tool*. Vol. 1: Phonology, Berlin: Mouton de Gruyter: 729–749.

Sinnemäki, Kaius—Di Garbo, Francesca 2018, *Language structures may adapt to the sociolinguistic environment, but it matters what and how you count: A typological study of verbal and nominal complexity*, "Frontiers in Psychology" 9: 1–22.

Stolk, Joanne V. 2015, *Case variation in Greek papyri. Retracing dative case syncretism in the language of the Greek documentary papyri and ostraca from Egypt (300 BCE–800 CE)*, doctoral dissertation chapter, University of Oslo, Department of Philosophy, Classics, History of Art and Ideas.

Stuart-Smith, Jane 2008, *Scottish English: Phonology*, in B. Kortmann—C. Upton (eds.), *Varieties of English 1. The British Isles*, Berlin: Mouton de Gruyter: 48–70.

Thomason, Sarah G. 2001, *Language contact. An introduction*, Edinburgh: Edinburgh University Press.

Thomason, Sarah G.—Kaufman, Terence 1988, *Language contact, creolization, and genetic linguistics*, Berkeley, CA: University of California Press.

Torallas Tovar, Sofía 2010, *Greek in Egypt*, in E.J. Bakker (ed.), *A companion to the Ancient Greek language*, Oxford: Wiley-Blackwell: 253–266.

Torallas Tovar, Sofía 2004, *Egyptian lexical interference in the Greek of Byzantine and Early Islamic Egypt*, in P.M. Sijpesteijn—L. Sundelin (eds.), *Papyrology and the History of Early Islamic Egypt*, Leiden: Brill: 163–198.

Torallas Tovar, Sofía (*forthcoming*), *Greek and Egyptian: Did linguistic policies exist in Graeco-Roman Egypt*, in E. O'Connell (ed.), *Egypt and Empire*, London.

Tropf, Herbert S. 2004, *India and its languages*, Munich: Siemens AG.

Vierros, Marja 2014, *Bilingualism in Hellenistic Egypt*, in G.K. Giannakis (ed.), *Encyclopedia of Ancient Greek Language and Linguistics*, Leiden: Brill: 234–238.

Vierros, Marja 2012, *Bilingual notaries in Hellenistic Egypt. A study of Greek as a second language*, Brussel: Koninklijke Vlaamse Academie van België voor Wetenschappen en Kunsten.

Wagner, Thomas 2017, *L2 irregular verb morphology: Exploring behavioral data from intermediate English learners of German as a foreign language using generalized mixed effects models*, "Studies in Second Language Learning and Teaching" 7/3: 535–553.

WEINREICH, URIEL 1979 [1953¹], *Languages in contact. Findings and problems*, The Hague: Mouton Publishers.

ZAKRZEWSKA, EWA D. 2017, *"A bilingual language variety" or "the language of the Pharaohs"? Coptic from the perspective of contact linguistics*, in E. Grossman—P. Dils—T.S. Richter—W. Schenkel (eds.), *Greek Influence on Egyptian-Coptic: Contact-induced change in an ancient African language*, Hamburg: Widmaier Verlag: 115–161.

CHAPTER 5

Substrate Matters

Franco Fanciullo

I would like to start with a personal anecdote. Many years ago, as a young student, I was asked during a Historical Linguistics (in Italy, "Glottologia") examination whether the Messapic language had the sound that in the Greek alphabet is represented by the digamma. I should have known, but I could not remember. Thinking on my feet, I reasoned that in present (Romance) Salento dialects, in some places more than others, [v] can sometimes undergo deletion: for example, Lat. vīvu ('alive-M') / vīva ('alive-F') can become ['iu] / ['ia], ūva ('grapes') can become ['ua]. "Chorographic" (i.e., geographic) congruence, the importance of which was particularly stressed by Merlo, is perhaps the best-known of the three criteria outlined by Ascoli to diagnose the existence of a substrate phenomenon. Therefore, I answered that Messapic did not have such a sound. It was a mistake, of course,[1] but one that taught me a valuable lesson. I was, in fact, directly experiencing the fallacy of the chorographic criterion (which, to be fair, is not always futile): diatopic congruency cannot correspond *eo ipso* to phonetic-phonological congruency, though (in our case) the present inhabitants of Salento do seem to largely descend from ancient Messapians. There is, indeed, no evidence of any mass extermination during or after the Roman conquest. On the contrary, the modern place name *Tuturano* (an ancient settlement a little south of Brindisi), for instance, is the outcome of a Latin praedial form (something like [PRAEDIU] *T(HA)OTOR-ĀNU) which derives from the Messapic gentilitial name *ϑaotor* or similar and suggests that the owner of the *praedium* was a Latin-Messapic Mr *Θaotor*.

I can add that, just as "chorographic" congruency does not work properly retrospectively, it does not work properly prospectively either: Salento *regional Italian* does not show any sign of [v]-deletion, though this deletion is well attested in Salento *dialects*. On the other hand, as anyone interested in studying Italo-Romance dialects knows well, the allophones [bb] and [ddʒ] (which are always geminated unless they occur after a consonant) in regional central and southern Italian is correctly attributed to the influence of the dialects, that

---

1 As, e.g., nominative *deivas* (< *deiwo-s*) = *deus* in inscription nr. 81 (from San Cataldo near Lecce) in PISANI 1964 easily testifies.

© FRANCO FANCIULLO, 2022 | DOI:10.1163/9789004508828_007

is to say, after all, to a type of substrate conditioning: c.-s. It. [bb]*ene* ≠ stand. It. [b]*ene*, that is /'bɛne/ 'well' in both systems; c.-s. It. *li*[bb]*ra* ≠ stand. It. *li*[b]*ra* (3rd pers. of the verb *librare* 'to balance'), that is /'libra/ in both systems (but c.-s. It. *li*[bb]*ra* = stand. It. *li*[bb]*ra* 'libra [pound]', that is /'libbra/ in both systems); c.-s. It. [ddʒ]*irare* ≠ stand. It. [dʒ]*irare*, that is /dʒi'rare/ 'to turn' in both systems; c.-s. It. *ma*[ddʒ]*o* ≠ stand. It. *ma*[dʒ]*o*, that is /'madʒo/ 'sg. of [*re*] *magi* = the three wise men' in both systems (but c.-s. It *fu*[ddʒ]*i* = stand. It. *fu*[ddʒ]*i* 'you run away', that is /'fuddʒi/ in both systems).[2] In the same way, we have to ascribe to the Sicilian dialect, which characteristically has [rr-] or [ʈʈ-] as allophones of /r-/ at the beginning of the word (see [rr]*osa* or [ʈʈ]*osa* 'rose' = /'rosa/), the same allophone that we find in Sicilian regional Italian (see e.g. Sic. reg. It. *la* [rr]*ivoluzione* [rr]*ussa* 'the Russian revolution').

Against the opinion of the so-called "substratophobes" (but, at the same time, without any uncritical acceptance of the opinion of the so-called "substratomaniacs"), it is likely that the current, manifold interaction between dialects and standard Italian is somewhat comparable to the interaction between Latin and all the other languages that Latin superimposed during its spread. In fact, not only can we expect that in similar situations we find, *ceteris paribus*, similar solutions, but also, much more importantly, we have written evidence that, just as an Italian can more or less recognise where another Italian comes from on the basis of (some) of his pronunciation (which, in any case, is a sort

---

2   Generally speaking, in the most conservative phonology of central and southern dialects, [b] was the post-consonantal pronunciation (while [v] was the *non*-postconsonantal one) of /b/ (issued from the collision of Lat. B and V), regardless of the kind of the preceding C, which could then be also another [b]: e.g., central-southern ⌐*z-boltá(re)*¬ 'to turn; to sprain', with /sb-/ from *EX-VOLV[I]TĀRE (where /s-/ < EX- selects [b]), but also central-southern ⌐*abbento*¬ 'rest', with *abb-* from ADVENTUS (where *d from AD- selects [b], after which *-*db-* > -*bb-*). It is precisely with this [bb], final result of etymological */db/, that, in the interaction between central and southern dialects (where [b] as stop is possible only if in postconsonantal position; gemination is only a peculiar aspect of postconsonantal position: the consonant in second position is preceded by a copy of itself) and standard Italian (where [b] can appear not only after a consonant, including gemination, but also between vowels and at the beginning of the word), central-southern speakers replaced the non-postconsonantal [b] of Italian: at first, in the Italianisms that little by little had entered the various dialects, then in regional Italian with a central-southern substrate (more details in FANCIULLO 1997). As for [ddʒ] as a central-southern pronunciation of /dʒ/: generally (more details in e.g., FANCIULLO 2018a), Tusc. / It. /dʒ/ corresponds etymologically, in central-southern dialects, to a /j/ (pronounced [j] in non-postconsonantal, [j] in postconsonantal position), while geminated [ddʒ] is, in these dialects, the continuation of Lat. -BJ- and -VJ-. Precisely this last, geminated, [ddʒ] has, in the interaction between central-southern dialects and Italian, taken the place of non-postconsonantal /dʒ/ (= It. not geminated [dʒ]): at first, in Italianisms that had entered the various dialects, then in regional Italian with a southern substrate.

SUBSTRATE MATTERS

of substrate conditioning), the same happened among the Romans. Regarding *proprii quidam et inenarrabiles soni* (Quintilian, *Institutio Oratoria* 1,5,33), thanks to which *nonnumquam nationes deprehendimus*, that is to say, the way in which we guess the geographical origin of our interlocutor (since *sonis homines ut aera tinnitu dinoscimus*, ib., 11,30), the reader might consult FANCIULLO 2018b: 202 ff.[3]

As a consequence, the always present, very complex interaction between Italian and dialects urges us to be very prudent when we are talking about substrate. As FILIPPONIO 2015 first noticed,[4] the opinion expressed in Adams 2007: 368 is rather hasty. According to Adams, one can expect to find linguistic interference in situations of bilingualism, but the interference "will disappear once the substrate language is dead". In principle Adams is right; but the effects of original interference will persist. To remain in the field of Italo-romance, the first-phase Roman dialect, a high-Southern type of Italian dialect, acted as a substrate for the second-phase Roman dialect (from 16th century), which is a sort of out-of-Tuscany Tuscan dialect. The first-phase Roman dialect disappeared some 400 years ago, but some of its effects (and not only phonetic ones) are still present in the contemporary dialect: e.g., [bb] for [b] = /b/ and [ddʒ] for [dʒ] = /dʒ/ in non-post-consonantal position; the assimilation of type *mo*[nd]*o* 'world' (lat. MUNDU) > *mo*[nn]*o*; the different morphemes *-amo, -emo, -imo*, 1st pl. of present indicative, different according to conjugation, *vs.* the sole Tuscan morpheme *-iamo* for all conjugations.

When we talk about **substrate** (cf. FANCIULLO 2018b), we must keep in mind that it is a label for at least two concepts:

a) "substrate" as a specific and unavoidable sub-field of contact linguistics;
b) "substrate" as a specific theory of linguistic change, formalized in the second half of the 19th century and in vogue until at least the mid-20th.

---

3   Here I discuss some documentary evidence, e.g., the case of an *eques romanus* who was sitting near Tacitus at the circus, who, after talking a while without identifying him, asked him whether he was *italicus* [...] *an provincialis* (Tacitus came from northern Italy or from Gallia Narbonensis: according to his manner of speaking he did not seem to be *Romanus*). At the indirect answer of the writer (*nosti me et quidem ex studiis*), the other asked at once: *Tacitus es an Plinius?*—Pliny was also not *Romanus* as he came from Como, in northern Italy (anecdote in Plinius, *Epistulae* 9,23). In *Historia Augusta, Sev.* 15,7, one can read about the "terrible" African accent in the Latin of Septimius Severus' sister: she was from Leptis Magna, in modern Libya. I add here that, one century before, the poet Statius commended another Severus, Lucius Septimius, ancestor of the emperor and also from Leptis Magna, on his becoming, in Italy, as *Italus* as an *Italus*, having retained nothing of African Latin and ways of life (*non sermo Poenus, non habitus tibi, externa non mens*: in *Silvae* 4,5,45–46).

4   Note 34 p. 116.

It is my conviction that the debate between "substratomaniacs" and "substratophobes", so lively and so readily rekindled, originates from the lack of this distinction.

G.I. Ascoli was the first who formulated a substrate-centred theory of linguistic change, which is based on three criteria:

i)   "chorographic" (i.e. geographic): the diatopic distribution of L_1 (the vanishing language overwhelmed by an incoming language) and L_2 (the incoming language which takes the place of L_1) must be the same;

ii) "intrinsic" (i.e. structural): there must be a structural correspondence between the element x of L_2 that is to be attributed to L_1 and the element y of L_1 that is considered to be the trigger to x of L_2;

iii) "extrinsic": if various languages share the same substrate, an element x in a L_2 will be due to substrate phenomenon if it is found in all languages which share that substrate.

To assert a (phonological *in primis*) legacy from L_1 to L_2, it is necessary to satisfy all of these criteria, although for iii) in particular, it is possible that there might not be enough data.

Ascoli's criteria were quite reasonable[5] in a phase in which the aim of linguists was to describe in detail **how** sound changes happen (see e.g. the formulation of Verner's law, which took place in the same period) but in which there were not yet adequate instruments to explain **why** (even today it is difficult to explain why languages change). In Ascoli's time, Romance linguistics was a long way off from its present state. It had not yet dealt with *la faillite de l'étymologie phonétique* (as per Gilliéron's formulation), and it had not yet ascertained that the more details you collect, the more difficult it is to reduce linguistic changes to mere equations. Indeed, Romance languages provide much more data than languages with restricted *corpora*, on which 19th- and 20th-century linguistics (in particular, Indo-European linguistics) had been established. It is not a coincidence, then, that "geo-linguists" like Rohlfs, a data collector for AIS, were the first and most passionate "substratophobes".[6]

---

5   Their aim is very clear: to counteract indiscriminate use of substrate principle, which was not uncommon even among Ascoli's followers. Merlo, for instance, did not hesitate to "reverse", so to speak, above all the second criterion, choosing from modern Romance varieties certain elements which, being unexpected because they differ from standard utterances, he considered sure indications of past languages, for which documentary evidence is totally lacking (FANCIULLO 2018b: 206).

6   See e.g. ROHLFS 1925.

SUBSTRATE MATTERS   157

On this basis, I think that Ascoli's criteria are no longer useful today: not because they are wrong *per se*, but because they were conceived in a different theoretical framework. Of course, I have nothing against criterion i. (it would be nonsensical, for instance, to look for traces of Celtic in Calabria), nor against criterion iii. (although sufficient evidence might be lacking). However, we ought to remember what I said earlier about the tendency of Salento dialects to delete [v]: these dialects not only did not inherit this tendency from Messapic (L_1), but also they did not influence regional Italian (L_2). This example concretely demonstrates that substrate phenomena in L_1 and L_2 have no necessary cause-effect relationship. Moreover, it is more difficult to explain what structural congruency means. Unlike most scholars, I am convinced that we must not necessarily expect to find in L_2 a "copy" of what was in L_1. Of course, some "copying" phenomena do appear (recall the southern Italian pronunciation [bb] and [ddʒ] for standard Italian /b/ = [b] and /dʒ/ = [dʒ] or the geminated pronunciation [rr] or [ʈʈ] in Sicilian regional Italian, all of which depend on dialect influence), but if one knows reasonably well both L_1 and L_2, one often discovers that a substrate heritage undergoes exaptation because of the new context, which is certainly different from the previous one. Sometimes, substrate may prevent the transfer of certain phenomena from L_1 to L_2, or promote the development of traits that are opposite to the ones in L_1.

Let's take a look at an example of exaptation. In southern Italy, Potenza has a dialect of northern Italian origin which was transplanted to southern Italy during the Middle Ages and, as a consequence, is nowadays deeply influenced by the surrounding southern Italian dialects. In other words: the present-day Potenza dialect is a southern Italian dialect with a northern Italian linguistic substrate. In this dialect, the morpheme -*árə* of *awtsárə* 'you lift / lift!', *kandárə* 'you sing / sing!', *purtárə* 'you carry / carry!', second person plural of the present indicative and of the imperative (i.), constitutes a minimal pair with the morpheme -*átə* of *awtsátə* 'lifted', *kandátə* 'sung', *purtátə* 'carried', of the past participle (ii.). In i) one may notice, under a southern Italian veneer (-*r*- < -*ð*- < -*d*-), the northern-Italian heritage of the dental lenition (-*d*- < Lat. -T-). Since in northern Italian dialects the lenition of -T- affects both the morpheme of the second person plural and the morpheme of the past participle, in the Potenza dialect we should expect to find -*r*- < -*ð*- < -*d*- not only in i), where we actually see it, but also in ii), where instead it is missing. However, we do not have in the present-day Potenza dialect a case of failed intrinsic evidence (or failed structural congruency). Rather, we have a sort of morphophonological polarization. In fact, some generations ago we had -*árə* as the morpheme of the past participle in the Potenza dialect as well, cf., e.g., the original past participle > noun *strašš̌ənárə* 'sort of homemade pasta' (properly: ⌜*strascinati*⌝, the past participle plural of *straššəná* 'to drag'), where the preservation of the original ending has been favoured by the trans-categorization verb > noun. In other words, in order to allow the distinction between the second person plural and the past participle, the Potenza dialect preserved the northern Italian outcome in the second person plural, but adopted the southern morpheme for the past participle. In fact, it should be noted that, generally and notwithstanding the lenition of -T-, the morphemes of second person plural (e.g.: Ligurian *cantè* < *cantadi* < CANTĀTIS; ROHLFS, GrammStor. § 531) and past participle (e.g.: Ligurian *-ao* < -ĀTU; ib. § 620) actually remain different in northern Italian dialects as well.

Now let us look at an example of reverse substrate reaction. One might think that, just as [bb] = /b/ and [ddʒ] = /dʒ/ (which is in southern regional Italian, as seen above, definitely a direct heritage from dialect substrate), the voiced segment [ddz-] in cases such as [ddz]*appa* 'hoe', [ddz]*io* 'uncle', [ddz]*òccolo* 'hoof', [ddz]*ùcchero* 'sugar' (where standard Italian has [tts-]: [tts]*appa* ecc.), is also a **direct** dialectal heritage in Salento regional Italian. That is to say, according to Merlo's thinking and terminology, this outcome suggests the inability of the Salento glottis to utter voiceless [tts]. On the contrary, Salento dialect also has [tts] ([tts]*appa*, [tts]*íu*, [tts]*wèkkulu*, [tts]*úkkaru*). The pronunciation ⌊ddz-⌋, missing in the dialect but compulsory in the regional Italian of the same area, is a perhaps unconscious but precise distancing of the regional Italian phonetics from dialectal phonetics, which is perceived as "rough" and consequently avoided.[7]

The lesson is clear. On the one hand, as the interaction between (Regional) Italian and Italian dialects shows, we have to deal with substrate as a linguistic heritage from L_1 to L_2 (a. above). On the other hand, however, this does not at all mean that, when we find in a language peculiar features (*in primis* of phonetic nature) that are different from the ones we were expecting, we have to automatically conjecture that they are what remains of earlier languages which have disappeared and about which we know nothing. Such use of substrate is typical of a "substratomaniac" approach, such as for instance that adopted by Merlo. When he commented on some unexpected voiced outcomes (from Latin voiceless stops) from the Potenza dialect[8] whose northern Italian origin had not yet been detected, Merlo wrote: "Meglio ritenere la sonora basilisca una anomalia, un caso sporàdico, e dichiararla singolarmente, indipendentemente. *Forse là, in*

---

7 For more details and examples, see FANCIULLO 2018b.

8 These were collected by Salvioni (1912, 532 ff.): *cuvuzz* CUCŪTIA 'pumpkin' and *giuove* JŎCU 'game', *frittara* -ĀTA 'omelette' and *asciura* -ŪTA 'gone out [f.]', *savé* *SAPĒRE 'to know' and *cevuddara* CEPŬLLA + -ĀTA 'broad beans and onions [cipolle] soup'...

SUBSTRATE MATTERS

quel punto, non v'eran Sanniti, ma altre genti, e chi sa quali genti!" (MERLO 1920: 242 ff.; the italics are mine). That is, if in the Potenza dialect we do not find the voiceless outcomes that we usually find in southern dialects, it means that, in the area where modern Potenza lies, ancient people did not speak Italic ("Samnite") languages but other, hard to classify, languages.[9]

As for contacts between Latin and pre-Latin languages, though it is obvious that pre-Latin elements may have survived in the Romance languages, it is not easy to establish which ones and in which form, especially because we have only (when we have it at all!) incomplete knowledge of L_1-triggers (*e.g.*, varieties of Celtic in northern Italy, Etruscan in Tuscany, varieties of Oscan and Umbrian in central and southern Italy). We have seen that "chorographic" congruence alone may be very ambiguous, now confirming (the case of [bb] for /b/ and [ddʒ] for /dʒ/),[10] now disproving (the case of [v] in modern Salento dialects) Ascoli's first criterion. The claim of structural congruence (that is, the claim that one finds in L_2 a "copy" of what comes from L_1) might also be ambiguous, because the substrate feature may be reused in L_2 in a new framework.

That said, let us now turn our attention to a very well-known phenomenon, which is attested in most present day central and southern Italian dialects—though not everywhere with the same characteristics. It concerns the assimilation of the nasal + stop clusters, which is total in the case of nasal + voiced stop > geminated nasal and partial in the case of nasal + voiceless stop > nasal + voiced stop. Let us consider whether and how this trait can depend on similar phenomena in Italic (Umbrian, Oscan) languages. In his sharp review of the whole problem in the paper entitled, "L'influsso delle lingue sabelliche sul latino *ossia la sostratite*[11] *superata*" (the italics are mine), Seidl (2015) rejects any connection between modern and ancient (Italic) assimilations on the basis of a very strict adherence to Ascoli's evidence:

A) both assimilations (total and partial) have documentary evidence in the Umbrian language of the Iguvine Tables, but Gubbio, which is the epicentre of the ancient assimilation process, today lies outside the modern area of the phenomena (SEIDL 2015: 47); thus, Ascoli's first criterion fails.

---

9   Cf. also fn. 5.

10 We may add, for instance, [wó] for [wɔ́] (*s*[wɔ́]*no* 'sound') and [jé] for [jɛ́] (*p*[jɛ́]*de* 'foot') in the Italian varieties spoken in Campania and elsewhere: the utterance of metaphonic dialectal diphthongs [wó] and [jé] has been transferred to non-metaphonic diphthongs of Italian, [wɔ́] and [jɛ́].

11 *Sostratite* = "substratitis" (as if substratitis were a disease).

160   FANCIULLO

B)   if, on the contrary, the modern epicentre of total and partial assimilations
     coincides with the area of the ancient Sabellians, ancient Sabellic variet-
     ies do not, however, show any documentary evidence of partial assimila-
     tion (ib.); thus, Ascoli's second criterion fails.

Seidl supports his observance of Ascoli's criteria by arguing that Sabellic (i.e.,
Italic) languages are a "well-documented" substrate (p. 75; at p. 76, however,
these languages become a less secure, "relatively well-documented" substrate).
Nevertheless, one might ask: is our knowledge of the Italic languages enough
to ascertain what really happened between these languages and Latin?

Here I offer a divertissement based on an article of mine currently in press.
Suppose one has, for a modern Romance dialect (let's call it dialect-*x*), documentary evidence similar to that which we have for *Restsprachen* such as
ancient Italic languages; and suppose one has to decide whether dialect-*x* has
or does not have assimilation of nasal + stop only on the basis of the following
forms:[12]

i)   *miŋgúćću* = hypocoristic of 'Domenico', something like '[*Do*]*men*[i]*cuc-
      cio*',
ii)   *mbíere* 'drink',
iii) *kwántu* QUANTŌ 'how much',
iv)   *kwándu* QUANDŌ 'when',
v)   *kwánnu* *[HOC]QU[E] ANNŌ 'this year'.

The answer would seem to be rather simple. Conservation of -*nt*- in *kwántu*
(iii), -*nd*- in *kwándu* (iv), distinguished from / opposed to etymological -*nn*-
in *kwánnu* (v), and -*mb*- in *mbíere* (ii), which we would surely trace back to
IM-BIBERE: all of this would suggest that we are dealing with the case of a dialect without any kind of assimilation, neither total nor partial. However, what
about *miŋgúćću* = '[*Do*]*men*[i]*cuccio*' (i), with [ŋg] for [ŋk], with partial assimilation? To solve this problem, we would point out that, in *miŋgúćću*, the voicing
affects a **secondary** cluster (*miŋgu*- < *men*[i]*ku*-), and would invoke a lenition of
intervocalic [k] before [i]-deletion, since the **primary** cluster in *kwántu* would
remain unaffected. This answer, however, would be very far from the facts. We
know dialect-*x* much better than any *Restsprache* because it is still spoken and
we know that it actually is a variety with almost mandatory assimilation for
-*mb*- (both as a primary cluster and from -NV-: *mmúkka* IN + BUCCA adverb
'in mouth' with *mmukkáre* 'to feed' and 'to bite', *kjúmmu* PLUMBU 'lead', *mmer*-

---

12   The words, typical of everyday language, are not *exempla ficta*, but real forms: they belong
      to the central Salento dialect of Cellino San Marco.

SUBSTRATE MATTERS

tikáre 'to overturn [of means of transport]' *INVERTICĀRE, *mmištíre* 'to guess right' and 'to hit the mark' INVESTĪRE ...); the assimilation for *-nd-* is much less mandatory (*túnnu* [RO]TUNDU 'round' but *ránde* GRANDE 'big', *spunnáre* *EXFUNDĀRE 'to break through' but *mmundáre* MUNDĀRE 'to weed [in agriculture]', *tánnu* 'then', from a *TANDŌ which was analogical on QUANDŌ, but *kwándu* 'when', *pènnula* ⌈*pèndola*⌉ = string of tomatoes hanging for conservation' but *mèndula* = ⌈*mèndola*⌉ 'almond' ...);[13] and as for partial assimilation (i.e., voicing of post-nasal voiceless stops), dialect-*x* totally lacks it (*ámpa* VAMPA 'blaze', *sántu* m. / *sánta* f. SANCTU 'saint', *ránku* 'cramp' < *CRANCU for CAN-CRU / CANCER etc.). What, then, can we say about *mbí(e)re* 'to drink' (without *-mb-* > *-mm-* assimilation) and the anthroponym *mingúćću* 'Menicuccio' (with partial assimilation *-ŋk-* > *-ŋg-*)? Only a thorough knowledge of both dialect-*x* and the larger context where dialect-*x* is spoken allows us to state that these forms, though actually present in our dialect, are misleading: *mbí(e)re* 'to drink' is not derived from IM-BIBERE, but rather from (*a*)*bbíere* (which, from *AD-BIBERE, is the most common form in Salento dialects), where *-bb-* > *-mb-* via a late dissimilation.[14] Instead, *mingúćću* 'Menicuccio', with partial assimilation and, moreover, suffix *-úćću* (and not, as expected, *-úttsu*: e.g., in dialect-*x*, *jaḍḍúttsu* ⌈*gall-uccio*⌉ = 'cockerel'), is actually a form from outside, specifically from Naples (the ancient capital city), which is not surprising when dealing with an anthroponym.

If a handful of forms (i.e., the ones in i–v), chosen with more or less the same randomness as the Sabellic forms that have come down to us, can lead us, as we have just seen, to a very incorrect idea of the linguistic system of which they are a part, then points A) and B) above demand some remarks as well.

Regarding A): Gubbio, the epicentre of ancient assimilations, is nowadays more or less ten kilometers **outside** the modern assimilation area, which, according to Seidl, goes against Ascoli's "chorographic" congruence. But in modern north-eastern Umbria (where Gubbio is located) there occurred, between the Middle Ages and the modern period, the confluence of quite a few different linguistic tides (from Tuscany, from northern Italy, and from Rome, at least). As a consequence, the linguistic conditions of modern Gubbio, more than twenty centuries later, may scarcely be regarded as the straight continuation of linguistic conditions in ancient Gubbio. Regarding B): in ancient times

---

13   Regarding the reasons why in dialect-*x* the assimilation of -MB- / -NV- is almost mandatory, while that of -ND- is not as much (reasons in any case directly or indirectly referable to the standardizing pressure of Italian), see FANCIULLO *forthcoming*.

14   That is to say that the rule *-bb-* > *-mb-* (but also *-dd-* > *-nd-* and *-gg-* > *-ŋg-*) acted after the rule *-mb-* > *-mm-* (but also *-nd-* > *-nn-* and *-ŋg-* > *-ŋŋ-*).

Gubbio was the epicentre of the two kinds of assimilation (total: nasal + voiced stop > geminated nasal; partial: nasal + voiceless stop > nasal + voiced stop), but today such an epicentre seems to correspond to the area once inhabited by the Samnites—which would go against Ascoli's structural congruence. However, we have seen above that one cannot expect a "copy" from the pattern L_1 to appear in its replica in L_2, because the substrate heritage may have acted as a trigger to or have been involved in processes which were not present in L_1 (for more details, see Fanciullo 2018b). For instance, the modern, smaller area in which partial assimilation takes place lies entirely **within** the modern, relatively larger area of total assimilation; this may suggest that, whatever its origin, total assimilation is chronologically prior to partial assimilation, for which it might have, so to speak, paved the way. In this framework, that total assimilation is genuinely due to substrate and that partial assimilation, instead, is a Romance innovation triggered by the total one, might not be "linguistic fiction."

To be clear: it is not my intention to champion the direct continuation between modern southern-Italian assimilations and those in Italic languages. I am only trying to prove that meticulous adherence to Ascoli's criteria, as demanded by Seidl, is not intrinsically conclusive, and does not provide arguments for or against the derivation of the later assimilations from the former. And it is not conclusive, because we know very well the point of arrival, the modern Italo-Romance dialects, but we do not know equally well the possible starting point, the Italic languages, which are for us *Restsprachen*, i.e languages for which we have only random documentary evidence.

Conversely, as we lack compelling arguments, we can leave aside both the *a priori* affirmation and the meticulous denial of the role of substrate heritage in present-day central and southern Italo-Romance assimilations, and examine them in their diachrony on the basis of the (much or little) evidence we have about them.

Against the traditional point of view of "substratomaniacs", the Romance geographical distribution of the total assimilations (-MB-/-NV- > -*mm*- and -ND- > -*nn*-) seems to have changed over time. If nowadays -MB-/-NV- and -ND- assimilations cover the whole of central and southern Italy,[15] in Varvaro's reconstruction the two assimilations appear as an expanding phenomenon, which imposes itself first in Rome (from the 13th century), then in Naples (from the

---

15   The assimilation -MB- / -NV- > -*mm*-, from a "linea [line] Pitigliano (Toscana)—Orvieto—Nocera Umbra—Treia (Marche)" southwards; the assimilation -ND- > -*nn*-, from a line north of Lazio—Umbria—Ancona, southwards (ROHLFS, GrammStor., §§, respectively, 254 and 253). Southern Calabria, the north-eastern triangle of Sicily and, here and there, Salento are left out (ib.).

SUBSTRATE MATTERS

14th–15th centuries), and arrives in Lucania and northern Calabria presumably not before the 16th century.[16] Though Varvaro's reconstruction is based on archival documents, where one cannot exclude that the standardizing influence of Latin (graphic maintain of ⟨mb⟩ and ⟨nd⟩) can almost partially conceal the real conditions (i.e., potential cases of assimilation), his observations, on the whole, hit the mark. But a few, though important, earlier cases of assimilation escaped Varvaro's notice. These predate, and sometimes considerably, the 13th century, and are documented in areas where, according to Varvaro's reconstruction, the phenomenon should have arrived much later: e.g., λινουάμμακον instead of λινοβάμβακον (neuter of Gr. λινοβάμβακος '[made] of linen and βαμβάκιον = cotton') in a Byzantine document of 1191 from Gallipoli (Salento),[17] *plummeo* instead of *plumbeo* (*plummeo nostro sigillo*) in a Latin document of 1095 from Oria (again in Salento), and finally a chronologically very noteworthy *bennere* instead of *vendere* 'to sell' in a Latin document from Cava (Campania) that dates to 826. All of this suggests that the "geometric" modern setting has followed a much less straightforward medieval distribution of assimilations.[18] On the other hand, one must consider that, in all the literature for or against the origin from substrate of such assimilations, no author deals with the parallel assimilation -NG^{a,o,u}- > [ŋŋ], which is, instead, the precise pendant of -MB-/-NV- > -*mm*- and -ND- > -*nn*- in modern Southern-Italian varieties. Presumably nobody said anything about -NG^{a,o,u}- > [ŋŋ] because this assimilation:

– does not seem to have any documentary evidence in the Sabellic languages, unlike -*mm*- < *-*mb*- and -*nn*- < *-*nd*-;

– in modern central and southern Italo-Romance varieties, it is highly recessive, and therefore not much observable: the segments [mm] (< -MB-/-NV-) and [nn] (< -ND-), though "anti-Italian" originally, do not differ at all from etymological [mm] and [nn] of standard Italian (and of the dialects), while the dialectal [ŋŋ] (< -NG^{a,o,u}-) is completely alien to Italian—therefore, it is especially subject to standardizing pressures (nowadays, it is fairly widespread in Sicily dialects and desultory in Calabria and Salento dialects).[19]

---

16   VARVARO 1979 = 2004: 191.

17   We have here a *Romance* phonetic utterance emerging in the transcription of a Greek word in a *Greek* text (Greek does not actually show total assimilation), which is not surprising in the situation of widespread bilingualism of Norman southern Italy.

18   For instance, it is peculiar that, against the quoted λινουάμμακον instead of λινοβάμβακον in the Gallipoli diploma of 1191, the present Romance dialect of Gallipoli does **not** show total assimilation; for a wider discussion, with more details and references to previous bibliography, see FANCIULLO 2004: 64–71 and FANCIULLO *forthcoming*.

19   ROHLFS, GrammStor. § 255, with examples such as Sic. *lòŋŋu* 'long', Sic. and Cal. (*g*)*aŋŋa* ('*ganga*') 'molar tooth', Salent. *saŋŋu* 'blood' and so on.

We obtain a very clear-cut outline where modern assimilations:

- appear to have a rather well-balanced structure: on the one hand, total assimilation affects not only /b/ and /d/, but also /g/; on the other hand, partial assimilation (voicing of /p, t, k/ when preceded by nasal) is geographically "included" within the area in which total assimilation take place, and the latter **may** then have triggered the former;
- show a considerable diachronic depth, from the point of view of the documentary evidence, and particularly of Campanian *bennere* instead of *vendere* (which goes back to 826). This depth seems to be confirmed by individual cases in the following centuries (see above);
- along the chronological axis, according to Varvaro's reconstruction, their previous distribution was rather more limited than the present one, even if their spread seems to have happened in a slightly more complex way than Varvaro proposed; of course, even if these assimilations had an Italic origin, this spread would rather be a Romance phenomenon, no more directly attributable to a possible pre-Latin influence;
- ultimately stimulate questions within a much larger and articulated framework. Among them, the question as to whether these assimilations are of Sabellic origin is merely one, and perhaps not even the most important.

References

ADAMS, JAMES N., 2007, *The regional diversification of Latin 200 BC–AD 600*, Cambridge: Cambridge University Press.

AIS = JABERG, KARL—JUD, JAKOB 1928–1940, *Sprach- und Sachatlas Italiens und der Südschweiz*, Zofingen: Ringier.

FANCIULLO, FRANCO 1997, *Raddoppiamento Sintattico e ricostruzione linguistica nel Sud italiano*, Pisa: Edizioni ETS.

FANCIULLO, FRANCO 2004, *Dialetti e non solo*, Alessandria: Edizioni dell'Orso.

FANCIULLO, FRANCO 2018a, *Frammento di fonologia diacronica fra Corsica, Toscana e sud-Italia (a proposito degli esiti di lat. J, DJ, $G^{e,i}$)*, "L'Italia Dialettale" 79: 97–128.

FANCIULLO, FRANCO 2018b, *Problemi di sostrato. Sicuro che i suoi effetti debbano manifestarsi in copia conforme?*, "Lingua e Stile" 53/2: 199–218.

FANCIULLO, FRANCO (*forthcoming*), *Problemi di sostrato: i nessi di nasale + occlusiva fra italici antichi e moderni italiani*, in E. Benelli—S. Marchesini—P. Poccetti (eds.), *Proceedings of the Meeting "Per una definizione delle lingue e delle culture sabelliche / Defining Sabellian Languages and Cultures" (Rome, 8–9 February 2018)*, Roma: Fabrizio Serra.

FILIPPONIO, LORENZO 2015, *Il sostrato celtico e la fonologia galloromanza e galloitalica. Materiali e metodi*, in L. Filipponio—Ch. Seidl (eds.), *Le lingue d'Italia e le altre.*

Contatti, sostrati e superstrati nella storia linguistica della Penisola, Milano: Franco Angeli: 95–127.

FILIPPONIO, LORENZO—SEIDL, CHRISTIAN (eds.) 2015, *Le lingue d'Italia e le altre. Contatti, sostrati e superstrati nella storia linguistica della Penisola*, Milano: Franco Angeli.

MERLO, CLEMENTE 1920, *Fonologia del dialetto di Sora (Caserta)*, "Annali delle Università Toscane" 4–5: 121–282.

PISANI, VITTORE 1964, *Le lingue dell'Italia antica oltre il latino*, Torino: Rosenberg & Sellier.

ROHLFS, GERHARD 1925, *Der Stand der Mundartenforschung in Unteritalien (bis zum Jahre 1923)*, "Revue de Linguistique Romane" 1: 278–323.

ROHLFS, GrammStor. = ROHLFS, GERHARD 1966–1969, *Grammatica storica della lingua italiana e dei suoi dialetti*, 3 volumes, Torino: Einaudi.

SALVIONI, CARLO 1912, *Per la fonetica e la morfologia delle parlate meridionali d'Italia*, Milano: L.F. Cogliati, reprinted as M. Loporcaro—L. Pescia—R. Broggini—P. Vecchio (eds.), *Salvioni, C. Scritti linguistici* in 5 volumes, Bellinzona, Edizioni dello Stato del Cantone Ticino, 2008, II volume: 525–559.

SEIDL, CHRISTIAN 2015, *L'influsso delle lingue sabelliche sul latino ossia la sostratite superata*, in L. Filipponio—Ch. Seidl (eds.), *Le lingue d'Italia e le altre. Contatti, sostrati e superstrati nella storia linguistica della Penisola*, Mailand: Franco Angeli: 53–79.

VARVARO, ALBERTO, 1979, *Capitoli per la storia linguistica dell'Italia meridionale e della Sicilia. I, Gli esiti di -ND-, -MB-*, "Medioevo Romanzo" 6: 189–216.

VARVARO, ALBERTO 2004, *Identità linguistiche e letterarie nell'Europa romanza*, Roma: Salerno Editrice.

CHAPTER 6

Natural Language Use and Bilingual Interference: Verbal Complementation Patterns in Post-Classical Greek

Victoria Fendel

1 Introduction

Interferences are idiolectal structures resulting from a language user inadvertently drawing on two rather than one language when putting their ideas into words (GROSJEAN 2001: 6; ADAMS 2003: 426; MYERS-SCOTTON 2006: 242). Interferences are one-off occurrences, they are not regionalisms that recur (CHAMBERS—TRUDGILL 1998), they are not interlanguage features that recur (SELINKER 1972), they are not a diachronic change in the making (STOLK 2015), they are language errors that result from the current situation related to aspects such as the learner's ability and nervousness in the midst of situational pressures (BIBER—CONRAD 2009). Interferences are part of someone's idiolect. An idiolect is one person's language variety influenced by their language biography, that is the number of factors that have impacted on how a person uses language (HAMERS—BLANC 2000: 26 and 40; ADAMS 2003; GOGLIA 2005: 50–58; Y. BUTLER—HAKUTA 2006: 116–117; ELSPASS 2012: 165). The way to find interferences in a corpus language is to establish a pattern for the item in question and define and contextualise the outliers. This is what this article does in order to evaluate two instances of γράφω ὅτι *grafō* *ʰoti* + deontic verb form in the early fourth-century letter P.Kell.1.65, from the village of Kellis in the Egyptian Oasis Magna.

This article details the verb profile of the lemma γράφω *grafō* in classical and post-classical literary and documentary sources (see similarly for different verbs JIMÉNEZ LÓPEZ 2006; JIMÉNEZ LÓPEZ 2016). A verb profile is the number of patterns that a verb can appear in. Each pattern is considered a unique form-function pairing (a construction). A function is associated with each frame that the verb appears in. Language users seem to have a certain awareness of the close association of, for example, certain verbal items with specific constructions according to experimental research (GOLDBERG 1995: 36).

The verb profile of γράφω *grafō* in classical and post-classical literary and documentary sources shows three clearly defined form-function pairings and

© VICTORIA FENDEL, 2022 | DOI:10.1163/9789004508828_008

related contexts. These are labelled the collocation, the idiom and the formula of γράφω *grafō* below. Drawing on literary and documentary data helps establish which structures are 'out of place' in the papyri and which ones are not. This makes it possible to distinguish between variations, e.g. archaisms, classicisms, modernisms, regionalisms, and idiosyncracies, and deviations, which are not supported by the verb profile.

Deviations can result from the confusion of Greek patterns, second-language-acquisition-related errors (e.g. the overgeneralisation of patterns or the insertion of memorised chunks of language without attention to the context), or bilingual interference. In the French-English pair 'j' ai peur' and 'I have fear', rather than 'I am scared', one would classify 'I have fear' as modelled on the French expression rather than using native English morpho-syntax (HEINE—KUTEVA 2005: 100–103). Yet, the influence of Language 1 (L1 hereafter) on Language 2 (L2 hereafter) can be more subtle, in that only a pattern is copied, rather than every word (MATRAS—SAKEL 2007).

Questions to ask specifically with regard to γράφω ὅτι *grafō ʰoti* + deontic verb form in P.Kell.1.65 include: (i) Are the three constructional contexts observed in the post-classical papyri attested in earlier literary Greek? If not, we may be dealing with a formulaic pattern specific to a colloquial epistolary context. (ii) Does the verb profile of γράφω *grafō* support insubordinate complements? If not, we have to consider options such as colloquialism, bilingual interference, and internal confusion of patterns. (iii) Does γράφω *grafō* change meaning and/or adopt new meanings in the post-classical period, similar to e.g. καταλαμβάνω *katalambanō* 'to visit' and παρακαλέω *parakaleō* 'to ask', which adopt new meanings and / or patterns and for which applying the classical pattern would result in incomprehensible or nonsense translations in postclassical texts? In essence, the article seeks to answer the question of whether the instances of γράφω ὅτι *grafō ʰoti* + deontic verb form in P.Kell.1.65 result from bilingual interference, internal confusion, the intrusion of oral syntax into writing, or whether they constitute a minor use pattern that is grammatical and idiomatic in Greek (HEINE—KUTEVA 2005: 44–62).

The article shows that for the verb profile of γράφω *grafō* the concepts of collocation, idiom and formula (i) reflect the fact that there are no one-to-one form-function pairings in the complementation patterns of γράφω *grafō*, but rather that there are clusters of forms that map onto a function (apparently guided by the parameters ±object and factive / prospective), and (ii) that these clusters of patterns are clearly linked to a pragmatic context, which is particularly obvious in letters, which are divided into free, semi-formulaic (i.e. discourse markers and hedges) and formulaic contexts (i.e. the epistolary frame). The verb profile of γράφω *grafō* does not support the combination of γράφω ὅτι *grafō ʰoti* + deontic verb form in P.Kell.1.65. However, it shows (i) that there is a small number of comparable examples from the same region or other thoroughly bilingual areas of the country, and (ii) that the letter shows an interesting treatment of personal names along with ungrammatical deviations in the areas of discourse markers and semi-formulaic expressions. Moreover, the intended function seems to be that of an urgent request or a plea, a function that is attested for a frame with γράφω *grafō* in the literary sources only occasionally and appears clearly more commonly in the post-classical documentary sources.

As a word of caution, theoretically, cognitively speaking, the difference between bilingual interference and other types of deviations lies with the interaction of two languages in a uniquely produced structure as opposed to processes that are motivated by drawing on one language only. In reality, this difference is often difficult to pin down conclusively. Thus, we can either accept a lot of false positives or false negatives. The present article takes the cautious approach of leaning towards accepting false negatives rather than including false positives, in that there may be cases which could be identified as bilingual interference if supplementary data emerged in future.

The remainder of the article is divided into five sections. Section 2 addresses the circumstances in later Roman and early Byzantine Egypt from different angles. Section 3 introduces the grammatical framework of Construction Grammar and details the concept of verb profiles. Section 4 addresses the empirical data. Section 5 considers the relevance of language teaching and learning in communities of practice to the topic. Section 6 provides a short summary and conclusion.

2 Egypt in the Later Roman and Early Byzantine Periods

The period of interest is the later Roman and early Byzantine periods in Egypt. By this time, Greek and Egyptian had coexisted in Egypt for over a millennium entering into varying relationships with each other. Especially over the course of the Ptolemaic period, the Greek language and alphabet had gained in prominence not least because the language of the country's administration was Greek. Egyptian retreated into the less official spheres. This is evident, for example, in the requirement that Demotic contracts have Greek subscripts summarising their content in Ptolemaic times (DEPAUW 2009) or that Roman citizens' wills conform to the Roman format for wills under Roman law during Roman times, thus were written in Latin (GAREL—NOWAK 2017). The following three paragraphs give an intentionally very condensed overview of the socio-political, sociocultural and sociolinguistic circumstances in the later Roman and early Byzantine periods.

A brief word of warning about terminology needs to be prefixed here. Over the course of its history, Egyptian has been written with different yet related writing systems, that is, generally speaking, the graphemes used were abstracted away from the hieroglyphic script in order to facilitate writing Egyptian on materials other than stone. The name of the writing system used for the everyday language is, as a rule amongst Egyptologists, used to refer to the stage of Egyptian in the final stages of the language. Thus, we call the same language, Egyptian, Demotic during the Ptolemaic and early Roman periods and Coptic during the later Roman and Byzantine periods. These labels are only labels for different stages of the same language and reflect changes in the writing system; the language, Egyptian, itself developed continuously over the millennia.

Socio-politically speaking, the *Constitutio Antoniniana* in AD 212 heralded a new era. Legally, from AD 212 onwards, every inhabitant of the Roman empire was a citizen (JÖRDENS 2012). Thus, the legal distinction between the Roman and non-Roman formats of wills fell out of use. Societally, in the Ptolemaic and Roman periods, Greek-Egyptian double names became a common practice to show one's status in society (DEPAUW—COUSSEMENT 2014). These naming practices show a high degree of fluidity between the once distinct spheres of the Greek and Egyptian parts of the population (KRAUS 2000; TORALLAS TOVAR 2004a: 164; TORALLAS TOVAR 2010a: 255). Economically, villages and smaller towns and gradually also larger cities like Alexandria faced a decline in building activity indicating economic depression (KEENAN 2007; KISS 2007; VAN MINNEN 2007). The military economy seems to have sustained slightly longer, in that it could withstand large-scale attacks until the arrival of the Sassanids in the early seventh century (FOSS 2003; SÄNGER 2011). By and large, a socio-political restructuring seems to have been in progress. Governmental institutions were losing power and clerical institutions filled the gap (WIPSZYCKA 2007; QUACK 2017a; FOURNET 2019, ch. 4). Additionally, smaller local groups could now form more independent close-knit social networks (MILROY—MILROY 2012) than with stricter government control in place. One example of such a group is the village community of Kellis whose letters form part of the bilingual corpus under investigation.

Socio-culturally speaking, the later Roman and early Byzantine periods see the shift to Christianity especially with the Edicts of Milan (AD 313) and Thessalonica (AD 380), which granted Christianity an official status and made it the official religion of the Roman Empire. The new religion seems to have radiated out from the urban centres in particular (DEPAUW—CLARYSSE) 2013) and seems to have replaced the inherited Egyptian polytheistic religion comparatively quickly (HOUSTON et al. 2003). Clerical superiors took over in many spheres of life, not least in the administrative and educational ones. What crystallises in this period is the thorough mixture of the Greek and Egyptian cultures in everyday life. This is evident, for example, in the large number of loanwords referring to everyday objects, both in Greek and in Egyptian: βάις *bais* from ⲃⲁ / ⲃⲁⲉ *ba* / *bae* 'branch of a palm tree' and ⲯⲩⲭⲏ, ⲯⲩⲭⲟⲟⲩⲉ *psukʰē* / *psukʰooue* from ψυχή *psukʰē* 'spirit, soul' (FÖRSTER 2002; TORALLAS TOVAR 2004a, 2004b, 2007, 2017). Matras (2015) argues that the borrowing of inflectional morphology would indicate a shift in linguistic identity due to its essential status in communicative settings. However, a renegotiation of linguistic identity does not seem to have taken place in Egypt as functional morphology (especially inflectional morphology) is not borrowed.[1] This ties in with the observation that the Greek and Egyptian words referring to the same concept are often retained alongside each other but take on different functional specialisations: Classical Egyptian 𓇋𓏏𓆑 *jt*—Demotic *it*—Coptic ⲉⲓⲱⲧ (S) *eiōt* / ⲓⲱⲧ (B) *iōt* vs πατήρ *patēr* ⲡⲁⲧⲉⲣ *pater* 'father'. While the Egyptian lexeme was used in everyday life, the Greek lexeme was reserved for the religious and epistolary spheres.

Socio-linguistically speaking, Matras (2009, ch. 3) considers essential for a language to succeed in a multilingual setting (i) a fully functional writing system, (ii) educational backing and (iii) political backing. Bagnall's (1993; 236–237) claim that there was no native writing system for the Egyptian language between the mid-second and fourth centuries has been proved wrong by Quack (2017b: 61) and Choat (2006, 1: 178–187; 2012: 584–585), who show that a fully functional alphabetic Egyptian writing system existed from around AD 100 already. However, a difference exists between the widely taught and fully established Greek alphabet and the emergent Coptic alphabet. A similar kind of inequality exists with regard to educational backing. With the government no longer providing funding to the temples in the later Roman period (CRIBIORE 2001: 22–23; HOUSTON et al. 2003; TORALLAS TOVAR 2010b: 32–33), access to learning the Egyptian script became more limited. Monasteries largely took over in the Greek educational sphere and thus provided continuing access to acquiring the Greek alphabet (CRIBIORE 2001: 23–24; CHOAT

---

1 Occasionally, the definite article is borrowed with the noun, for example Hdt.Hist.2.143 πίρω-μις *pirōmis* from ⲣⲱⲙⲓ *rōmi* 'man' and P.Cair.Masp.3.67303 (Aphrodito, AD 553) πκωμ *pkōm* from ⲕⲱⲙ *kōm* 'wooden wagon-box' (TORALLAS TOVAR 2004a: 192). Yet the definite article therein becomes part of the word in Greek rather than being borrowed as a definite article. One-offs also exist, for example the possessive pronoun *pa-* in P. Neph. 12.11 ἀσπάζομαι ˚Ωρ πα Ταϳμουρώ· *aspazomai ʰōr pa Tahmourō* 'I greet Hor, the one from Tahmouro'. Yet these seem to be code-switches, that is unnaturalised imports, rather than borrowings, that is naturalised imports (HOFFMANN 1991: 99–100; MYERS-SCOTTON 2006: 253–260).

NATURAL LANGUAGE USE AND BILINGUAL INTERFERENCE

2009: 347–349; BUCKING 2012). Finally, political backing refers to the acceptability of a language up to the highest registers, that is the administrative and official ones (ADAMS 2003: 593–597; CRESPO 2007: 40–41; PALME 2009; SILK—GEORGAKOPOULOU 2009). Depauw (2012) cites the example of the stele of Cornelius Gallus (29 BC) on which Greek, Latin and Hieroglyphic inscriptions appear but no Demotic ones. He argues that the everyday Egyptian language (Demotic) had been denied official status. The inclusion of hieroglyphs is to be seen as an instance of the emblematic acceptance of Egyptian culture in the country. The trilingual stele shows a clearly different power triad than the trilingual Rosetta stone dating from the beginning of the Ptolemaic period (196 BC) (WALLIS BUDGE 1929). It features inscriptions in Hieroglyphic, Demotic and Greek. Also relevant is the remark on Greek summaries of Demotic contracts from above. Apparently, the Demotic language no longer fared well in the official sphere.

3   Construction Grammar and Verb Profiles

3.1   *Construction Grammar*

Cognitive grammars, such as Construction Grammar, rest on the concept that the human brain relies on a network of associations between forms and functions when processing language. Any formal difference is linked to a functional difference (GOLDBERG 1995: 3). By not positing underlying structural or semantic levels, as for instance Lexical-Functional Grammar does, Construction Grammar is a monostratal theory of grammar (GOLDBERG 1995: 7). For example, formally, the difference between 'to be afraid to' and 'to be afraid of' is the change in the final particle triggering the subsequent change in the form of the complement of the particle, that is an infinitive after 'to' and an ing-form after 'of'. While 'to be afraid to', semantically speaking, involves a certain intentionality, 'to be afraid of' does not (GOLDBERG 1995: 3).

A construction 'is posited in the grammar if and only if something about its form, meaning, or use is not strictly predictable from other aspects of the grammar' (GOLDBERG 1995: 13). Thus, constructions are not the only thing to be considered and they have to be meaningful. Constructions exist at all structural levels, for instance, the clause, the phrase or the sentence. The change in meaning between 'to be afraid of' vs 'to be afraid to', to use this example, is to be attributed to the constructional change rather than to polysemy of the verb phrase or lexical changes (GOLDBERG 1995: 18). By contrast, there is no functional difference between 'try to' vs 'try and' in English (GRIES—STEFANOWITSCH 2004: 122–123). Hence, no construction can be posited.

3.2   *Verb Profiles*

This article applies the general idea of verb profiles to the Greek verb 'to write' (GROSS 1984; HANKS 1996; HANKS 1996; HARTMANN et al. 2013). The concept of verb profiles encompasses the fact that most verbs appear in more than one syntactic and consequently semantic environment. For example, English 'to tell':

(1)   Henry always tells **the truth.**   – nominal

(2a) Henry told Paul **that he went rowing yesterday.**   – clausal, factive, syndetic

(2b) Henry told Paul **he went rowing yesterday.**   – clausal, factive, asyndetic

(2c) Henry told Paul: **'I went rowing yesterday.'**   – clausal, factive, independent

(3a) Henry told Paul **to go rowing.**   – infinitival, prospective

(3b) Henry told Paul **that he (should) go rowing.**   – clausal, prospective, syndetic

(3c) Henry told Paul: **'Go rowing!'**   – clausal, prospective, independent

(1) to (3) show a range of nominal, phrasal and clausal options with English *to tell*. Some of these are semantically almost equivalent, some of them show significant semantic differences. To the right of each pattern shown in (1) to (3), its structural and semantic properties are indicated. These are used to class patterns into three categories.

Factive vs prospective refers to the semantics of the complement with regard to the surrounding context (SCHULZ 2003). An event / entity described by a complement is either known or not yet known in the context, thus the complement is either anaphoric or cataphoric. Complements referring to known entities / events, that is anaphoric ones, are factive; complements referring to unknown entities / events, that is cataphoric ones, are prospective.

Syndetic vs asyndetic refers to the formal linkage between a verb and its clausal complement (BENTEIN 2015). The linkage can be achieved by means of a subordinating conjunction such as English 'that' or Greek ὅτι *hoti*, yet linkage can also be achieved without this formal feature. The valency requirements of the verb, such as 'to tell somebody something' above, achieve linkage in these cases.

Dependent vs independent refers to the syntactic encoding of the pragmatic status of a clausal complement. A complement clause can take the form of a dependent clause, which is often clear in the adjustment of pronouns and moods for instance, or an independent clause (MARNETTE 1996: 2–3 for relevant features). In the case of an independent clause taking on the function of a verbal complement, only the pragmatics of the structure reveal this relationship, whereas in the case of a dependent clause functioning as a complement of the verb, the form of the clause indicates the relationship.

Clausal vs phrasal vs nominal refers to the morpho-syntactic structure of the complement (KROEGER 2004). As shown above, the complement slot of a verb can be filled by a clause, a phrase or a noun / pronoun. These changes in the morpho-syntactic structure of the complement affect semantic changes in the verb as shown above.

However, the differences between environments cannot only be conditioned syntactically and semantically but also extra-linguistically, that is differences could be idiolectal, sociolectal, dialectal or register-related. For example, for English 'to give', there seem to be syntactic constraints on (GOLDBERG 1995: 2) and semantic consequences to changing the complementation pattern. Lakoff and Johnson (1980, 130) argue regarding distransitive 'to teach somebody something' vs periphrastic 'to teach something to somebody' that the transfer is conceptualised as achieved and effective in the ditransitive but not in the periphrastic construction. For English 'to begin', there seem to be dialectal differences between complementation patterns. Mair (2002: 115–121) finds modernday dialectal differences between British English and American English for 'begin' / 'start' + infinitive vs -ing. This is a change in progress according to Mair.

For Greek, extralinguistic factors impact on the choice of complementation pattern as Bentein (2017) has shown for finite vs infinite complementation patterns, with the latter being more formal than the former, and Hult (1990) for syndetic vs asyndetic complementation patterns, with the latter being more informal than the former.

4   Empirical Data

4.1   *Data Samples*
The article is based on four data samples: (i) the Classical Attic literary corpus of Xenophon, (ii) the post-classical Koine literary corpus of Plutarch, (iii) the post-classical documentary corpus of letters on papyrus dating from the fourth

to mid-seventh centuries (excluding those from bilingual archives), and (iv) the post-classical documentary corpus of bilingual papyrus archives dating from the fourth to mid-seventh centuries. Data samples (i) to (iii) listed above are used as the control group, whereas data sample (iv) is the data sample investigated in this article, as it contains the relevant instances of γράφω ὅτι *grafō ʰoti* + deontic verb form in P.Kell.1.65.

The corpus of letters belonging to bilingual papyrus archives dating from the fourth- to mid-seventh centuries encompasses the archives of Apa Paieous and Apa Nepherous, who were successive abbots of the monastery of Hathor (KRAMER et al. 1987; HAUBEN 2002) in the Herakleopolite nome, the archive of Apa John, most likely to be identified with the desert monk identified in literary sources (BUTLER 1898: 213; WILCKEN 1927; ZUCKERMAN, 1995; FOURNET 2009: 437; CLACKSON 2010: 93) in the Hermopolite nome, and the archive of the village of Kellis, which consists of smaller sub-archives of several prominent writers, in the Daklah oasis in the western desert (GARDNER et al., 2014; GARDNER et al., 1999; WORP—WHITEHORNE 1995). All these capture the linguistic situation in the fourth century. The final archive of the corpus is the large archive of the nobleman and landowner Dioscoros of Aphrodito in the Antaiopolite nome (FOURNET 2019: 10–14; FOURNET—MAGDELAINE 2008).

The fourth-century archives primarily represent the networks of prominent figures in the clerical sphere, be that in a monastery or in the desert. The letters addressed to them are primarily requests for help and support and thus offer a glimpse at the surrounding demographics. The fourth-century archive from Kellis represents a most likely Manichaean sphere. Yet, the village archive of Kellis is also different from the other archives, in that it consists of several sub-archives, thus the recipient of the letters is not always the same unlike in the other fourth-century archives. The sixth-century archive represents the surroundings of an influential, educated landowner. The letters addressed to him are requests, reports and complaints.

The reason why the debate about the recipients', that is the archive owners', linguistic profile is irrelevant here is that they are not the people whose linguistic output can be studied. An archive is basically someone's mailbox. It contains everything this person received, but unlike modern mailboxes, nothing this person wrote. Thus, archives represent a one-dimensional view of their social networks. In theory, letters written by the archive owner will have been part of the recipients' archives, yet these are often either lost or impossible to securely identify.

Searches for the lemma γράφω *grafō* have been carried out in the *Thesaurus Linguae Graecae* (TLG hereafter) and the *Duke Database of Documentary Papyri*

NATURAL LANGUAGE USE AND BILINGUAL INTERFERENCE   175

TABLE 6.1   Table head

Collocation			Idiom			Formula			Misc.
Nominal	Clausal	Other	Infinitival	Participial	Other	Clausal	Participial	Other	

(DDbDP hereafter)[2] as well as in the bilingual letter corpus. The results have
been archived in .excel sheets using the table head shown in Table 6.1.

The category 'Miscellaneous' contains all the instances that are (a) nouns
('scribe', etc.), (b) passive, (c) without a direct object of any kind, or (d) too
damaged to be analysed.

4.2   *Collocation, Idiom, Formula*

The terms collocation, idiom and formula are chosen here to refer to three
clusters of complementation patterns of a verb. While these terms have been
used with many meanings in the research literature, they are chosen here (i)
because they represent the concept that items have a lexical affinity to one or
the other item, (ii) because they represent the concept that complementation
patterns are not always transparent and modular (CRISTOFARO 2008), and (iii)
they represent the concept that contextual / pragmatic factors influence the
form of the complementation pattern. The term 'collocation' is reserved for the
most common pattern of a verb; the term 'idiom' is used for a less common
but nevertheless contextually unrestricted pattern; the term 'formula' is used
for complementation patterns that are limited to specific pragmatic contexts,
such as epistolary formulae or fixed expressions.

The three patterns with γράφω *grafō* are exemplified below with instances
that are not part of the bilingual corpus under investigation.

Collocation
(a) nominal:

(4)   Plu.Biogr.et Phi.Lysander.20.1.6
       καὶ   συνελθὼν   ἐδεῖτο   γράψαι   περὶ   αὐτοῦ   πρὸς   τοὺς
       kai   sunelthōn   *edeito*   **grapsai**   *peri*   *autou   pros   tous*
       and   after.gathering   he.asked   **to.write**   about   him   to   the

---

2   The tool finds the lemma less reliably than the TLG, thus instances might have been missed.

176 FENDEL

ἄρχοντας   ἑτέραν   ἐπιστολὴν ὡς οὐδὲν   ἠδικημένον   οὐδ'
ark^hontas ^heteran epistolēn ^hōs ouden ēdikēmenon   oud'
leaders   another letter   as not   having.been.wronged nor
ἐγκαλοῦντα.
egkalounta
complaining
'And after gathering, he (sc. Pharnabazos) asked to write another letter
about him to the leaders as he had not been wronged nor was he complaining.'

(b) clausal

(5)   Xen.Hist.Anabasis.2.3.1.1
ὃ   δὲ   δὴ   ἔγραψα ὅτι βασιλεὺς ἐξεπλάγη   τῇ   ἐφόδῳ,
^ho de   dē   **egrapsa** ^hoti basileus exeplagē   tē   ep^hodō
it and surely **I.wrote** that king   had.been.expelled the plan
τῷδε   δῆλον   ἦν.
tōde   dēlon   ēn
to.him obvious it.was
'And I wrote it (i.e.) that the king had been expelled by means of the plan,
(as) was obvious to this man.'

Idiom
(a) infinitival:

(6)   Xen.Hist.Hellenica.6.3.12.5
βασιλεὺς μὲν   γὰρ δήπου   ἔγραψε πάσας τὰς ἐν τῇ   Ἑλλάδι πόλεις
basileus men gar dēpou   **egrapse** pasas tas en tē ^helladi poleis
king   but for certainly **wrote**   all   the in the Greece cities
αὐτονόμους   εἶναι·
autonomous einai
independent to.be
'For the king wrote / ordered that all the cities in Greece (should) be
autonomous.'

NATURAL LANGUAGE USE AND BILINGUAL INTERFERENCE

(b) participial:

(7) Plu.Biogr.et Phil.Lysander.23.1.5
πρός τε   τοὺς ἐν Ἀσίᾳ φίλους ἔγραψεν   αἰτεῖσθαι κελεύων   παρὰ
pros te   tous en Asia pʰilous **egrapsen** aiteistʰai keleuōn   para
to   and the in Asia friends **he.wrote** to.ask   ordering from
Λακεδαιμονίων στρατηγὸν Ἀγησίλαον ἐπὶ τὸν πρὸς   τοὺς βαρβάρους
Lakedaimoniōn stratēgon Agēsilaon epi ton pros   tous barbarous
Spartans   general   Agesilaos for the against the   barbarians
πόλεμον.
polemon
war
'He also wrote to the friends in Asia ordering (them) to ask of the Spartans
(that) Agesilaos (be) the general for the war against the barbarians.'

Formula
(a) clausal:

(8) P.Flor.2.189.9–16 (AD 267, Theadelphia, Arsinoites, Heroninus archive)
ἀλλ' ἐπὶ οὖν ἡ   ἀνάγκη   κατεπίγει ὡς καὶ σὺ   οὐδὲ ἀγνοεῖς,
all' epi oun ē   anagkē   katepigei ʰōs kai su   oude agnoeis
but as now the necessity presses as too you   not not.know
γράφω σοι   φίλτατε ὅπως τῇ ιγ ἀπὸ   νυκτὸς ἀποστείλη[ς] τὰ
grapʰō soi   pʰiltate ʰopōs tē ig apo   nuktos aposteilē[s] ta
I.write to.you beloved that the 13 during night you.send   the
κτήνη   καὶ τοὺς κοφίνου[ς   πρὸς] ἐμὲ ἵνα μὴ ὡς πάρυσυ
ktēnē   kai tous kopʰinou[s pros] eme ʰina mē ʰōs parusu
livestock and the baskets   to   me that not like a.year.ago
ὑπ[ηρε]ασῶμεν καὶ νῦν τὸ   αὐτὸ [πάθω]μεν.
up[ēre]asōmen kai nun to   auto [patʰō]men
we.serve   and now that same we.suffer
'But as (ἐπεί) the necessity presses (κατεπείγει), as you too know very well,
I am writing to you, dear friend, in order that on the 13th during the night
you send the livestock and baskets to me in order that we do not do service[3] like a year ago (πέρυσι) and undergo the same now.'

---

3 The verbal lemma is not listed in Liddell-Scott-Jones (1996), Lampe (1961) or Trapp—Höran-
der (2001). However, the nominal lemma ὑπηρεσία seems to have lost its original meaning
related to rowing in the post-classical period and retained the meaning of 'service'.

178 FENDEL

(b) participial:

(9) BGU.12.2184.verso (501–600, Hermopolis, Taurinos archive)
γράφω σημαίνων καὶ παρακαλῶν τὰ πρακτέα   παρ᾽ αὐτῆς κα[…]
grapʰō sēmainōn kai parakalōn ta praktea   par᾽ autēs ka[…]
I.write reporting and asking   the to.be.done by her   …
τούτου μανθάνειν ᵽ̣
toutou mantʰanein
this   to.learn
'I am writing (thereby) reporting and asking (you) to learn the things to
be done by her …'

Overview tables providing numeric data about the three complementation patterns and their subcategories are given in Tables 6.2 to 6.5.

TABLE 6.2   Xenophon, historiography, 5th / 4th centuries BC, TLG, lemma γράφω (searches: June 2020)—
98 passages in total

Collocation			Idiom			Formula			Misc.
Nominal	Clausal	Other	Infinitival	Participial	Other	Clausal	Participial	Other	
34	5	∅	9	∅	∅	3	1	∅	
39			9			4			46
≈ 40%			≈ 9%			≈4%			≈47%

NB: The sample contains 11 instances of the verb in the middle voice. These are disregarded for the analysis.

TABLE 6.3   Plutarch, historiography, 1st / 2nd centuries AD, TLG, lemma γράφω (searches: June 2020)—36
passages in total

Collocation			Idiom			Formula			Misc.
Nominal	Clausal	Other	Infinitival	Participial	Other	Clausal	Participial	Other	
14	1	∅	∅	1	∅	1	2	∅	
15			1			3			17
≈42%			≈3%			≈8%			≈47%

NB: The sample contains 1 instance of the verb in the middle voice. This is disregarded for the analysis.

NATURAL LANGUAGE USE AND BILINGUAL INTERFERENCE

TABLE 6.4 DDbDP, s.v. LEX γράφω, language: Ancient Greek, provenance: known, AD 250–700 (searches: June 2020)—256 passages in total

Collocation			Idiom			Formula			Misc.
Nominal	Clausal	Other	Infinitival	Participial	Other	Clausal	Participial	Other	
47	21	3[a]	7	1	1[b]	30	2	13	
71			9			45			131
≈28%			≈3.5%			≈17.5%			≈51%

a These are two instances of ^{h}oti recitativum (SB 14.11957.9–11 and CPR 7.57.12–14) and one instance of an accusative for a dative case (Stud. Pal. 20.111.4–7).

b This is a participial instance with a particle added (Stud. Pal. 3(2).2.132.1–5).
  NB: The sample contains 2 instances of the verb in the middle voice. These are disregarded for the analysis.

TABLE 6.5 Private letters belonging to bilingual papyrus archives, 4th to mid-7th centuries AD, language: Ancient Greek (searches: June 2020)—61 passages in total

Collocation			Idiom			Formula			Misc.
Nominal	Clausal	Other	Infinitival	Participial	Other	Clausal	Participial	Other	
13	1	5[a]	1	2	2[b]	5	1	3	
19			5			9			28
≈31%			≈8%			≈15%			≈46%

a These are two instances of ^{h}oti recitativum (P. Kell. 1.71.48–49, P. Neph. 18.18–19), one participial instance (P. Kell. 1.74.24–28), one instance of a lack of case endings (P. Herm. 7.6–8) and one instance of confusion of Greek patterns (P. Kell. 1.5.18–24).

b These are two instances of an accusativum cum infinitivo structure (P. Cair. Masp. 1.67067.1–2 and 2–4).
  NB: The sample contains 1 instance of the verb in the middle voice. This is disregarded for the analysis.

The proportions in the tables show (i) that all three patterns already existed in classical and post-classical literature, and (ii) that the formula in particular is attested significantly more often in the documentary texts, a situation that can be explained by its function (an urgent plea directed at an addressee). What is not obvious from the tables above but only from inspecting every relevant instance one by one is that the idiom appears not only least frequently but is also the one pattern that has a liking for the passive voice of the governing verb. These instances are not part of the data sample as mentioned and are counted in the large category 'Miscellaneous'.

180 FENDEL

4.3   *Outliers*

The category 'Other' for the collocation, idiom and formula in Tables 6.2 to 6.5 contains instances that deviate from the established norm in each category. The category 'other' is empty for the literary texts, as can be expected, but contains register-related variations up and down as well as potential instances of bilingual interference in the documentary samples. The relevant instances for the collocation and idiom are all register-related variations and are therefore only listed in the footnotes to the tables.

The relevant instances for the formula are more interesting. The 13 relevant instances in the DDbDP sample consist of 6 instances with the optative after ἵνα *hina*, which can be interpreted as a classicism, thus a variation upwards (all in P.Panop.Beatty.1, AD 298, Panopolis, official letter), and 3 instances of syndetic parataxis with καί, which can be interpreted as a colloquialism, thus a variation downwards (CPR 30.17.8–9, AD 643–644, Hermopolis, private letter; P.Herm.5.2–4, AD 317–323, Hermopolis, private letter; P.Paramone.14.8–10, AD 500–699, Arsinoites, letter). The remaining 4 instances represent an unexpected mismatch between the subordinator and the following verb, that is ὅτι *hoti* with the imperative or subjunctive and ὅπως with the imperative.

The 3 instances in the category 'Other' of the formula in the bilingual corpus of private letters consist of one instance of asyndetic parataxis (the subjunctive), which can be interpreted as a colloquialism, thus a variation downwards (P.Neph.12.18–19, AD 350–370, Hathor / Herakleopolite nome), and two instances of an unexpected mismatch between the subordinator and the following verb, that is ὅτι *hoti* with the imperative or subjunctive.

All six instances showing an unexpected mismatch between the subordinator and the following verb are listed below.

(a) DDbDP:

(10)   O.Trim.2.531.15–19 (350–370, Trimithis, Oasis Magna)

γράφω   δὲ σοί,   ὦ   ἀδελφὲ Πανᾶ, ὅτι   ὅσα
grapʰō de soi   ō   adelpʰe Pana ʰoti ʰosa
I.write but to.you oh brother Pana **that** everything.that

ἐνεχειρησάμην   σοὶ   [ταχέ]ως ποίησον ἕως πέμψω   ἐφ' ὑμᾶς
enekʰeirēsamēn soi   [takʰe]ōs poiēson ʰeōs pempsō   epʰ' ʰumas
I.entrusted   to.you quickly do   until I.will.send to you

καὶ μὴ ἀμελήσητε ἐν οὐδενί.
kai mē amelēsēte en oudeni
and not forget   in nothing

NATURAL LANGUAGE USE AND BILINGUAL INTERFERENCE   181

'I am writing to you, brother Panas, that you may do quickly whatever I have entrusted to you until I send (a message) to you all, so you do not forget[4] in any way.'

(11) P.Ross.Georg.3.1.8–9 (270, Alexandria)
νῦν   οὖν   ὑμ[ῖ]ν   γράφω   ὅτ[ι]   ἐν τάχει   ὅ   ποιεῖται   πέμψατέ
nun oun   ʰum[i]n grapʰō   ʰot[i]   en takʰei   ʰo   poieitai pempsate
now thus to.you   I.write that   in speed which is.done send
μοι   τὸ   ἐραιοῦν   κολωβειν   ἵ\να/   ἐντός μου   αὐτ[ὸ]   εὕρω.
moi   to   eraioun kolōbein   ʰ\na/   entos mou aut[o]   ʰeurō
to.me the woollen tunic   in.order.that with me   it   I.find
'Now, I am writing to you that quickly you may send to me the woollen (ἐρεοῦν) tunic (κολόβιον), which is being done, in order that I find it with me.'

(12) SB 3.7244.4–7 (226–275, Arsinoites, Fayyum)
γράφω σοι,   ὅτι   μὴ   ἀμελήσῃς   ὑπάγειν   [πρὸς]   Παμοῦθιν,   ὅτι
grapʰō soi   ʰoti   mē   amelēsēs   ʰupagein   [pros] Pamoutʰin ʰoti
I.write to.you that not you.forget go   to   Pamouthis as
ἐκ   λ( )   ἕνεκα   τῶν ἀρουρῶν εἰς μίσθωσιν ἢ   αὐτὸν ἢ   τοὺς παρὰ
ek   l( )   ʰeneka   tōn arourōn eis mistʰōsin ē   auton ē   tous para
from l( ) regarding the arourae for rent   or him   or the from
Πρωτ[άρχο]υ ἢ   τὸν ἀραβατοξότην {καὶ} τὸ   κέρμα μετεβεβλ[ή]καμεν
Prōt[arkᵏo]u ē   ton arabatoxotēn {kai} to   kerma metebebl[ē]kamen
Protarchos   or the Arab.archer   and   the coin   we.exchanged
ὁμοῦ.
ʰomou
together
'I am writing to you that you shall not forget to go to Pamouthis, because since ... we have paid (?) in total a coin in rent for the arourae either to him or to those from Protarchos or to the Arab archer (ἀραβοτοξότην).'

(13) P.Giss.103.6–9 (300–399, Oasis Magna)
ἀναγκαίω[ς δὲ   γράφω σοι   ὅ]πως   ταχέως   ἡ[μᾶς   κατάλ]αβε
anagkaiō[s de   grapʰō soi   ʰo]pōs takʰeōs   ʰē[mas katal]abe
necessarily but I.write to.you that   quickly us   visit

---

4   The reason for the change from the singular imperative to the plural subjunctive is unclear. It parallels however the change from initial σοί to later ὑμᾶς.

182   FENDEL

πρὸ   τοῦ ε [...
pro   tou e [
before the e [
'Out of necessity I am writing to you that you may quickly visit us before
...'

(b) Bilingual corpus:

(14) P.Kell.1.65.5–8 (301–325, Kellis, Oasis Magna)

ἔγραψά σοι   πρὸ   τούτου ὅτι· **τήρησον** τὸν τόπον μου ὅ   ἐστιν
egrap*ˢ*a soi   *pro*   *toutou* ʰ*oti tērēson* ton topon mou* ʰ*o*   *estin*
I.wrote to.you before this   **that guard**   the place my   that is
ἐπὶ   μισθῷ ὄν.
epi   *mistʰō on*
under rent   being
'I wrote to you before that you shall guard my place which[5] is being rented
out.'

(15) P.Kell.1.65.30–34 (301–325, Kellis, Oasis Magna)

θαυμάζω   δέ· ἔγραψά σοι   ὅτι· πέμψῃς   τὸ
tʰaumazō   *de egrap*ˢ*a soi*   ʰ*oti pemp*ˢ*ēs*   *to*
I.am.surprised but **I.wrote to.you** that you.may.send the
μαρφόρτιόν μου καὶ ⟦ουκε⟧ τὸ χιτώνιον, καὶ οὐκ ἠμέλησέ
marpʰortion mou kai [⟦*ouke*⟧] *to kʰitōnion kai ouk ēmelēse*
coat   my   and [|not|] the tunic   and not it.mattered
σοι· πέμψῃς   μοι.
soi   *pemp*ˢ*ēs*   *moi*
to.you you.may.send to.me
'I am surprised (that) I wrote to you that you may send my coat (μαφόρ-
τιον) and tunic, but you did not care. Send (it) to me (sc. now)!'

Noticeably, all six instances come from thoroughly bilingual areas of Egypt, that
is the Oasis Magna, the Fayyum and the metropolis of Alexandria, and date
from the third and fourth centuries, that is a period of time when, as we have
seen, laxer norms and rules were in place and thus flexibility and freedom were
higher.

---

5 The writer seems insecure about the correct form of the relative construction (τόπον is mas-
culine, ὅ is neuter).

One can discount P.Giss.103.6–9 (ὅ]πως (...) κατάλ]αβε) on the basis that (i) only part of the verb is preserved and (ii) that even if the reconstruction is correct, the common orthographic interchange between long and short /e/ means that a regular subjunctive after ὅπως may be hidden underneath a spelling variation. O.Trim.2.531.15–19 displays a non-contiguous sequence of 'I write', 'to you' and 'that' (with ὦ ἀδελφὲ Πανᾶ intervening). P.Ross.Georg.3.1.8–9 displays 'to you' preceding 'to write', unlike in the other instances. In O.Trim.2.531.15–19 and P.Ross.Georg.3.1.8–9, syntactic elements are moved into the preverbal position in the ὅτι *hoti* clause, potentially for reasons of focus.

By contrast, in SB 3.7244.4–7, P.Kell.1.65.5–8 and P.Kell.1.65.30–34, 'I write / wrote to you that' forms a contiguous sequence and the verb phrase in the subordinate clause immediately follows ὅτι *hoti*. Thus, the insertion of a memorised chunk of language could explain these instances. However, it cannot explain the instances in O.Trim.2.531.15–19 and P.Ross.Georg.3.1.8–9.

Generally speaking, there are three ways to analyse the pattern γράφω ὅτι *grafō* *hoti* + deontic verb form. Importantly, the same pattern can result from very different processes (MITHUN 2019) as well as from a combination of several processes (CRISTOFARO 2016).

(i) There is the pattern dubbed insubordination, that is the combination of a prototypical subordinator with an independent clause (EVANS 2007; MITHUN 2008; see e.g. CRISTOFARO 2016). It appears with ὅτι *hoti* + indicative to a limited extent (*oti recitativum*) and ἵνα *hina* + subjunctive to a significant extent in Greek (WINTER 1955; HULT 1990; LEVINSOHN 1999; SIM 2011). However, ὅτι *hoti* + subjunctive / imperative would still need an additional step in this analysis.

(ii) One could argue with the insertion of acquired pieces (or chunks) of language without knowledge of their syntactic requirements when embedded (BYBEE 2010). This analysis applies most often to formulaic structures and fixed expressions which have a specific pragmatic function, such as 'You know' in English (ERMAN 2001) or 'I want you to know that' in Greek (JAMES 2008; PORTER—PITTS 2013). Yet, this analysis fails for two instances mentioned above as explained due to their non-contiguous structure.

(iii) Bilingual interference could have played a role. Coptic does not distinguish between prospective and factive complement clauses morphologically (ⲭⲉ *dʲe* appears in both), thus the choice of the wrong subordinator in the sense of the overgeneralisation of one subordinator (ὅτι *hoti*), could be explained. Furthermore, Coptic does not make a morphological distinction between dependent and independent clauses, thus the imperative / subjunctive after ὅτι *hoti* could be accounted for (LAYTON 2011, vol. 20, para. 338.a.ii).

What sets the two passages from the bilingual letter corpus apart from the other instances is (i) that they are a repetition and thus a re-instantiation of a past request, (ii) that they appear both in the same letter, that is they seem to be part of one writer's idiolect, and (iii) that this letter contains not just these two but another eight instances where bilingualism seems to have impacted. The instances relate to the morphosyntactic treatment of personal names and the morphosyntactic linking of discourse units. The morphosyntactic treatment of Egyptian personal names in Greek is a thorny issue (BRUNSCH 1978; KRAMER et al. 1987, 4: 38; ANDERSON 2007: 169–170 and 287; MUHS 2010). It will suffice here to say that the lack of inflectional endings is at the very least unexpected in Greek (FEWSTER 2002: 238–239; VIERROS 2003: 16–17; PAPATHOMAS 2007: 720–721; TORALLAS TOVAR 2010a: 262). The linkage of discourse units is by comparison more syndetic in Greek than it is in Coptic where linkage is often achieved pragmatically rather than morphosyntactically (e.g. HASZNOS 2006).

Going back to the fact that the same surface level structure can be caused by different processes or a combination of processes, one could conjecture that several processes may have interacted resulting in the two structures in P.Kell.1.65. The use of acquired chunks of language especially in a recurring fixed expression, the lack of distinction between factive and prospective as well as dependent and independent complement clauses in Coptic and finally the availability of insubordinate patterns with ὅτι *hoti* and ἵνα *hina* may all have interacted. Given the bilingual setting and the large number of linguistic structures that seem to have been influenced by bilingualism in the same letter, it seems likely that bilingual interference played a role, even if only a reinforcing one.

5   Language Teaching and Learning in Communities of Practice

Experimental research regarding language learners' acquisition of verbal complementation patterns in modern multi-language settings shows that there are facilitating factors to learners acquiring patterns. These include (i) a high frequency of occurrence of the relevant pattern with the verb in question, (ii) the existence of a parallel in the learners' L1, and (iii) an awareness of the constructional surroundings of the verb in question. A well-researched language pair is L1 Spanish and L2 English.

Frequency of occurrence and the existence of a parallel in the L1 are relevant to the complementation by means of an infinitive vs a gerund in English. The gerund, which does not exist in Spanish and is low frequency in English, loses out (SCHWARTZ—CAUSARANO 2007). An L1 parallel was also found to be relevant to mastery of the presence vs absence of 'that' after verbs such as 'say' and 'think', an alternation where no preference can be detected for native speakers. The L2 speakers will accept the zero 'that' option more easily where there is a Spanish parallel. Overall, the correct application of the pattern seems to be related to the degree of language proficiency rather than the level of instruction (VANPATTEN 2011; LLINÀS-GRAU—BEL 2019). Frequency effects are particularly prominent with the basic verbs of a language, that is the most frequent verbs. L2 learners tend to overuse them while overextending their semantic scope (VIBERG 2002 on L1 English L2 Swedish).

The relevance of the constructional surroundings of a verb ties in with the verb-island hypothesis (TOMASELLO 2003). This hypothesis claims that in child language acquisition every verb and its syntax are acquired separately, put differently, that every verb is an island. Valenzuela Manzanares and Rojo Lopez (2008) find this hypothesis to apply to second-language acquisition too. However, L2 speakers do not always recognise the form of a construction. Constructions that modify what learners acquire as the basic verb meaning and are without a Spanish counterpart pose specific problems (MARTINEZ VAZQUEZ 2004).

The facilitating factors explored, i.e. (i) a high frequency of occurrence of the relevant pattern with the verb in question, (ii) the existence of a parallel in the learners' L1, and (iii) an awareness of the constructional surroundings of the verb in question, map onto the three factors found to be relevant to the structure γράφω ὅτι *grafo* ᴴ*oti* + deontic verb form in P.Kell.1.65. Section 4.3 concluded that the use of acquired chunks of language, the lack of distinction between factive and prospective as well as dependent and independent complement clauses in Coptic and the availability of insubordinate patterns with ὅτι ᴴ*oti* and ἵνα ᴴ*ina* may all have shaped the structures in P.Kell.1.65.

Firstly, chunking depends on the frequency of occurrence of a piece of language (a chunk). Only frequently co-occurring items that form a unit with one semantic or pragmatic function will be memorised as invariable chunks. Secondly, bilingual interference is often linked to an L1 (near-)parallel, which interferes with the expected structure in the L2. If there is no L1 parallel, the language user can transpose a structure word by word (polysemy copying) into the target language (direct interference). Transposition by means of identifying a functional pivot (pivot matching), however, is based on similarities between languages (indirect interference). Thirdly and finally, insubordination is one example of a constructional environment in which the construction as a whole carries the meaning rather than any one constituent.

Looking beyond the structure and considering the external context of the deviating structures discussed in Section 4.3, it appears that all the relevant instances come from a limited number of thoroughly bilingual areas, that is the Oasis Magna, the Fayyum and the city of Alexandria. As regards language acquisition, these communities form communities of practice, that is 'groups of people who share a concern or a passion for something they do and learn how to do it better as they interact regularly' (UNWIN et al. 2007; WENGER-TRAYNER—WENGER-TRAYNER 2015: 1). One of the best examples of a community of practice is a school. For example, Clarysse (1993, 188) found that in texts from the Ptolemaic period Egyptian scribes preferred a pen made of rush, whereas Greek scribes preferred a pen made of reed. Apparently, two different scribal traditions, two communities of practice, existed. Another example of several communities of practice existing is Quack's (2017b) detailed analysis of local writing systems being developed in Egypt during the Roman period.

In Kellis (Oasis Magna), the Manichaean community seems to have had an educational superior, the Teacher, around whom a community of practice centred (see e.g. P. Kell. Copt. 20.24–26). The Teacher is mentioned in P. Kell. Copt. 19, 20, 24, 25, and 29; P. Kell. Copt. 31 is written by the Teacher (GARDNER 2006). The Teacher seems to have been mobile rather than residing in one school. Thus, a community of practice influenced by him may have been as large as the Oasis Magna. In the Fayyum and the city of Alexandria, evidence suggests that schools existed in monastic contexts. Thus, communities of practice could have existed here too.

A specific practice, which could be linguistic or extra-linguistic (such as writing materials), is usually exchanged in a community of practice. This explains the cluster of deviating but similar instances in the Oasis Magna. Thoroughly bilingual areas could have Egyptian-Greek schools (CRIBIORE 1999), such that both languages were used alongside each other in an educational setting. This explains the higher incidence of bilingual interference in such areas. Both these observations taken together further support the hypothesis that in the deviant patterns in P.Kell.1.65 bilingual interference played a role.

6   Summary and Conclusion

This article has evaluated two instances of γράφω ὅτι *grafō ʰoti* + deontic verb form in the early fourth-century letter P.Kell.1.65 from the village of Kellis in the Egyptian Oasis Magna. The letter belongs to a bilingual, Greek-Coptic papyrus archive, documenting the interactions between members of a largely Manichaean community in the eastern desert. This community seems to have had certain linguistic peculiarities, both with regard to their use of the epistolary formulae (CHOAT 2007; CHOAT 2010) and with regard to their use of semi-formulaic / fixed expressions (WORP 2011; FENDEL 2019).

In order to decide whether the deviant instances in P.Kell.1.65 resulted from the confusion of Greek patterns, second-language-acquisition-related errors, or bilingual interference, the article detailed the verb profile of the lemma γράφω *grafō* in classical and post-classical literary and documentary sources. The verb profile falls into three form-function pairings termed here the collocation, the idiom and the formula. The instances in P.Kell.1.65 represent the formula of γράφω *grafō*, functionally speaking, but seem to be a mixture of the collocation and the formula, structurally speaking.

Section 2 provided a broad overview of the situation in early Byzantine Egypt from a socio-political, socio-cultural and socio-linguistic perspective. Coptic seems to have gained in importance vis-à-vis Greek as compared to earlier periods of their coexistence. Section 3 introduced the idea of a verb profile by means of English 'to tell' and showed how the division into a collocation, an idiom and a formula in a verb profile emerges. Section 4 established the verb profile of γράφω *grafō* based on (i) the Classical Attic literary corpus of Xenophon, (ii) the post-classical Koine literary corpus of Plutarch, (iii) the post-classical documentary corpus of letters on papyrus dating from the fourth to mid-seventh centuries (excluding those from bilingual archives), and (iv) the post-classical documentary corpus of bilingual papyrus archives dating from the fourth to mid-seventh centuries.

Based on the verb profile, Section 4 evaluated the status of the deviant instances in P.Kell.1.65. It appears (i) that there is a small number of comparable examples from the same region or other thoroughly bilingual areas of the country, and (ii) that P.Kell.1.65 shows an interesting treatment of personal names along with ungrammatical deviations in the areas of discourse markers and semi-formulaic expressions. Therefore, it was suggested that the structure γράφω ὅτι *grafō ʰoti* + deontic verb form has resulted from a combination of bilingual interference (with an L1 model), chunking of frequently recurring pieces of language, and the availability of insubordination in Greek. Section 5 showed that these three mechanisms (chunking, bilingual interference, and insubordination) map onto factors found to facilitate the acquisition of verbal complementation patterns in modern languages (i.e. a high frequency of occurrence, the existence of an L1 parallel, and an awareness of the constructional environment). The accumulation of the deviant pattern, γράφω ὅτι *grafō ʰoti* + deontic verb form, in and around the Oasis Magna could point to a bilingual community of practice. The figure of the Teacher mentioned in the letters from Kellis adds further weight to this hypothesis. This also ties in with the above-mentioned linguistic peculiarities in Kellis and the Oasis Magna pointing to a close-knit social network.

References

ADAMS, JAMES 2003, *Bilingualism and the Latin language*, Cambridge: Cambridge University Press.

ANDERSON, JOHN 2007, *The grammar of names*, Oxford: Oxford University Press.

BAGNALL, ROGER 1993, *Egypt in late antiquity*, Princeton: Princeton University Press.

BENTEIN, KLAAS 2015, *Minor Complementation Patterns in Post-classical Greek (I–VI AD): A Socio-historical Analysis of a Corpus of Documentary Papyri*, "Symbolae Osloenses" 89: 104–147. https://doi.org/10.1080/00397679.2015.1095012.

BENTEIN, KLAAS 2017, *Finite vs. non-finite complementation in Post-classical and Early Byzantine Greek: Towards a pragmatic restructuring of the complementation system?*, "Journal of Greek Linguistics" 17: 3–36. https://doi.org/10.1163/15699846-01701002.

BIBER, DOUGLAS—SUSAN CONRAD 2009, *Register, genre, and style*, Cambridge: Cambridge University Press.

BRUNSCH, WOLFGANG 1978, *Untersuchungen zu den griechischen Wiedergaben ägyptischer Personennamen*, "Enchoria" 8: 1–142.

BUCKING, SCOTT 2012, *Towards an archaeology of bilingualism*, in A. Mullen—P. James (edd.), *Multilingualism in the Graeco-Roman Worlds*, Cambridge: Cambridge University Press: 225–264.

BUTLER, CUTHBERT 1898, *The Lausiac history of Palladius*, Cambridge: At the University Press.

BUTLER, YUKO—KENJI HAKUTA 2006, *Bilingualism and Second Language Acquisition*, in T. Bhatia—W. Ritchie (edd.), *The Handbook of Bilingualism*, Oxford: John Wiley & Sons: 114–144. https://doi.org/10.1002/9780470756997.ch5.

BYBEE, JOAN 2010, *Language, usage and cognition*, Cambridge: Cambridge University Press.

CHAMBERS, JACK—TRUDGILL, PETER 1998, *Dialectology*, 2nd ed. Cambridge Textbooks in Linguistics, Cambridge/New York: Cambridge University Press.

CHOAT, MALCOLM 2006, *Belief and cult in fourth-century papyri*, Turnhout/Sydney: Brepols.

CHOAT, MALCOLM 2007, *Epistolary formulae in early Coptic letters*, in N. Bosson—A. Boud'hors (edd.), *Actes du huitième Congrès international d'études coptes*, Leuven: Peeters: 667–678.

CHOAT, MALCOLM 2009, *Language and Culture in Late Antique Egypt*, in P. Rousseau—J. Raithel (edd.), *A Companion to Late Antiquity*, Chicester/Malden: John Wiley & Sons: 342–356.

CHOAT, MALCOLM 2010, *Early coptic epistolography*, in A. Papaconstantinou (ed.), *The Multilingual experience in Egypt, from the Ptolemies to the Abbasids*, Farnham: Ashgate: 153–178.

CHOAT, MALCOLM 2012, *Coptic*, in Ch. Riggs (ed.), *The Oxford handbook of Roman Egypt*, Oxford: Oxford University Press: 581–593.

CLACKSON, SARAH 2010, *Coptic or Greek? Bilingualism in the papyri*, in A. Papaconstantinou (ed.), *The multilingual experience in Egypt: From the Ptolemies to the Abbasids*, Farnham: Ashgate: 73–104.

CLARYSSE, WILLY 1993, *Egyptian Scribes writing Greek*, "Chronique d'Égypte" 68: 186–201. https://doi.org/10.1484/J.CDE.2.308932.

CRESPO, EMILIO 2007, The *linguistic policy of the Ptolemaic kingdom*, in M. Chatzopoulos—V. Psilakakou (edd.), *Phōnēs charaktēr ethnikos: actes du ve Congrès international de dialectologie grecque (Athènes 28–30 septembre 2006)*, Athens: Kentron Hellēnikēs kai Rōmaïkēs Archaiotētos, Ethnikon Hidryma Ereunōn, 35–49.

CRIBIORE, RAFFAELLA 1999, *Greek and Coptic Education in Late Antique Egypt*, in S. Emmel (ed.), *Ägypten und Nubien in spätantiker und christlicher Zeit: Akten des 6. Internationalen Koptologenkongresses, Münster, 20.–26. Juli 1996*, 6, Wiesbaden: Reichert, 279–286.

CRIBIORE, RAFFAELLA 2001, *Gymnastics of the mind: Greek education in Hellenistic and Roman Egypt*, Princeton/Oxford: Princeton University Press.

CRISTOFARO, SONIA 2008, *A constructionist approach to complementation: Evidence from Ancient Greek*, "Linguistics" 46: 571–606. https://doi.org/10.1515/LING.2008.019.

CRISTOFARO, SONIA 2016, *Routes to insubordination*, in N. Evans—H. Watanabe (edd.), *Insubordination*, Amsterdam: John Benjamins: 393–422.

DEPAUW, MARK 2009, *Bilingual Greek-Demotic Documentary Papyri and Hellenization in Ptolemaic Egypt*, in P. Van Nuffelen (ed.), *Faces of Hellenism. Studies in the History of the Eastern Mediterranean (4th century B.C.–5th century A.D.)*, Leuven: Peeters: 120–139.

DEPAUW, MARK 2012, *Language use, literacy and bilingualism*, in Ch. Riggs (ed.), *The Oxford Handbook of Roman Egypt*, Oxford: Oxford University Press: 493–506.

DEPAUW, MARK—CLARYSSE, WILLY 2013, *How Christian was Fourth Century Egypt? Onomastic Perspectives on Conversion*, "Vigiliae Christianae" 67: 407–435. https://doi.org/10.1163/15700720-12341144.

DEPAUW, MARK—COUSSEMENT, SANDRA 2014, *Identifiers and identification methods in the ancient world: Legal Documents in Ancient Societies III*, Leuven: Peeters.

ELSPASS, STEPHAN 2012, *The use of private letters and diaries in sociolinguistic investigation*, in J. Conde-Silvestre—J. Hernández-Campoy (eds.), *The Handbook of Historical Sociolinguistics*, Malden (MA): John Wiley & Sons: 156–169.

ERMAN, BRITT. 2001, *Pragmatic markers revisited with a focus on you know in adult and adolescent talk*, "Journal of Pragmatics" 33: 1337–1359. https://doi.org/10.1016/S0378-2166(00)00066-7.

EVANS, NICHOLAS 2007, *Insubordination and its uses*, in I. Nikolaeva (ed.), *Finiteness: theoretical and empirical foundations*, Oxford: Oxford University Press: 366–431.

FENDEL, VICTORIA 2019, *The paradox of Kellis (Western Egyptian Desert)*, "Journal for Graeco-Roman Studies" 58: 101–133. https://doi.org/10.23933/jgrs.2018.58.3.101.

FEWSTER, PENELOPE 2002, *Bilingualism in Roman Egypt*, in J.N. Adams—M. Janse—S. Swain (eds.), *Bilingualism in Ancient Society: Language contact and the written text*, Oxford: Oxford University Press: 220–245.

FÖRSTER, HANS 2002, *Wörterbuch der griechischen Wörter in den koptischen dokumentarischen Texten*, Berlin: Mouton de Gruyter.

FOSS, CLIVE 2003, *The Persians in the Roman near East (602–630 AD)*, "Journal of the Royal Asiatic Society" 13: 149–170.

FOURNET, JEAN-LUC 2009, *The multilingual environment of late antique Egypt: Greek, Latin, Coptic, and Persian documentation*, in R. Bagnall (ed.), *The Oxford Handbook of Papyrology*, Oxford: Oxford University Press: 418–451.

FOURNET, JEAN-LUC 2019, *The rise of Coptic: Egyptian versus Greek in late antiquity. Rostovtzeff Lectures. Princeton*, Oxford: Princeton University Press.

FOURNET, JEAN-LUC—MAGDELAINE, CAROLINE (eds.) 2008, *Les archives de Dioscore d'Aphrodité cent ans après leur découverte: histoire et culture dans l'Egypte byzantine: actes du Colloque de Strasbourg, 8–10 décembre 2005*, Paris: De Boccard.

GARDNER, IAIN 2006, *A letter from the teacher: Some comments on letter-writing and the Manichaean community of IVth century Egypt*, in L. Painchaud—P.-H. Poirier (eds.), *Coptica—Gnostica—Manichaica: Mélanges offerts à Wolf-Peter Funk*, Québec: Les Presses de l'Université Laval: 317–323.

GARDNER, IAIN—ALCOCK, ANTHONY—FUNK, WOLF-PETER—HOPE, COLIN—BOWEN, GILLIAN 1999, *Coptic documentary texts from Kellis*, Oxford: Oxbow.

GARDNER, IAIN—ALCOCK, ANTHONY—FUNK, WOLF-PETER—HOPE, COLIN—BOWEN, GILLIAN 2014, *Coptic documentary texts from Kellis*, Oxford: Oxbow.

GAREL, ESTHER—NOWAK, MARIA 2017, *Monastic Wills: The Continuation of Late Roman Legal Tradition?*, in M. Choat—M. Giorda (eds.), *Writing and Communication in Early Egyptian Monasticism*, Leiden/Boston: Brill: 108–128.

GOGLIA, FRANCESCO 2005, *Communicative strategies in the Italian of Igbo-Nigerian immigrants in Padova (Italy): a contact linguistic approach*, Manchester: University of Manchester.

GOLDBERG, ADELE 1995, *Constructions: a construction grammar approach to argument structure*, Chicago/London: University of Chicago Press.

GRIES, STEFAN—STEFANOWITSCH ANATOL 2004, *Extending collostructional analysis*, "International Journal of Corpus Linguistics" 9: 97–129.

GROSJEAN, FRANCOIS 2001, *The bilingual's language modes*, in J. Nicol (ed.), *One mind, two languages: bilingual language processing*, Malden, Mass./Oxford: Blackwell: 1–22.

GROSS, GASTON 1984, *Lexicon-grammar and the Syntactic Analysis of French*, in *Proceedings of the 10th International Conference on Computational Linguistics*, Stroudsburg, PA, USA: Association for Computational Linguistics: 275–282, https://doi.org/10.3115/980431.980549.

HAMERS, JOSIANE—BLANC, MICHEL 2000[2], *Bilinguality and bilingualism*, Cambridge/New York: Cambridge University Press.

HANKS, PATRICK 1996, *Contextual Dependency and Lexical Sets*, "International Journal of Corpus Linguistics" 1: 75–98.

HARTMANN, IREN—HASPELMATH, MARTIN—TAYLOR, BRADLEY (eds.) 2013, *Valency Patterns Leipzig. Online database*, Leipzig: Max Planck Institute for Evolutionary Anthropology.

HASZNOS, ANDREA 2006, *A Case Where Coptic is more Syndetic than Greek*, "Acta Antiqua Academiae Scientiarum Hungaricae" 46: 91–97. https://doi.org/10.1556/AAnt.46 .2006.1-2.11.

HAUBEN, HANS 2002, *Aurêlios Pageus, alias Apa Paiêous, et le monastère mélitien d'Hathor*, "Ancient Society": 337–352.

HEINE, BERNDT—KUTEVA, TANIA 2005, *Language contact and grammatical change*, New York: Cambridge University Press.

HOFFMANN, CHARLOTTE 1991, *An introduction to bilingualism*, London: Longman.

HOUSTON, STEPHEN—BAINES JOHN—COOPER JERROLD 2003, *Last Writing: Script Obsolescence in Egypt, Mesopotamia, and Mesoamerica*, "Comparative Studies in Society and History" 45: 430–479.

HULT, KARIN 1990, *Syntactic variation in Greek of the 5th century* A.D., Göteborg: Acta Universitatis Gothoburgensis.

JAMES, PATRICK 2008, *Retention and retreat: complementary participles and infinitives with verbs of perception and declaration in the Roman and Byzantine documentary papyri*, Thesis, University of Cambridge. https://doi.org/10.17863/CAM.31210.

JIMÉNEZ LÓPEZ, MARIA 2006, *Persuadir en griego: el marco predicativo de* πείθω, in E. Crespo—J. de la Villa,—A Revuelta (eds.), *Word Classes and Related Topics in Ancient Greek. Proceedings of the Conference on "Greek Syntax and Word Classes,"*, Louvain-la-Neuve: Peeters: 163–191.

JIMÉNEZ LÓPEZ, MARIA 2016, *Funciones semánticas alternantes y diátesis verbal: el caso de* παρασκευάζω, in E. Borrel Vidal—P. Gómez Cardó (eds.), *Omnia mutantur: Canvi, transformació y pervivència en la cultura clàssica, en les seves llengües i en el seu llegat*, Barcelona: Universidad de Barcelona Edicions: 199–210.

JÖRDENS, ANDREA 2012, *Status and Citizenship*, in Ch. Riggs (ed.), *The Oxford Handbook of Roman Egypt*, Oxford: Oxford University Press: 247–259.

KEENAN, JAMES 2007, *Byzantine Egyptian villages*, in R. Bagnall (ed.), *Egypt in the Byzantine world, 300–700*, Cambridge: Cambridge University Press: 226–243.

KISS, ZSOLT 2007, *Alexandria in the fourth to seventh centuries*, in R. Bagnall (ed.), *Egypt in the Byzantine world, 300–700*, Cambridge: Cambridge University Press: 187–206.

KRAMER, BÄRBEL—SHELTON, JOHN—BROWNE, GERALD 1987, *Das Archiv des Nepheros und verwandte Texte*, Mainz am Rhein: Philipp Von Zabern.

KRAUS, THOMAS 2000, *(Il)literacy in non-literary papyri from Graeco-Roman Egypt: Fur-*

ther aspects of the educational ideal in ancient literary sources and modern times, "Mnemosyne" 53: 322–342. https://doi.org/10.1163/156852500510633.

KROEGER, PAUL 2004, *Analyzing Syntax: A Lexical-Functional Approach*, Cambridge: Cambridge University Press.

LAKOFF, GEORGE,—JOHNSON, MARK 1980, *Metaphors we live by*, Chicago/London: University of Chicago Press.

LAMPE, GEOFFREY 1961, *A Patristic Greek lexicon*, Oxford: Clarendon Press.

LAYTON, BENTLEY 2011[3], *A Coptic grammar: with chrestomathy and glossary: Sahidic dialect*, Wiesbaden: Harrassowitz.

LEVINSOHN, STEPHEN 1999, *Ὅτι Recitativum in John's Gospel: A Stylistic or a Pragmatic Device?*, "Work Papers of the Summer Institute of Linguistics, University of North Dakota Session 1999" 43: 1–14.

LIDDELL, HENRY—SCOTT ROBERT—JONES HENRY 1996[9], *A Greek-English lexicon*, Oxford: Clarendon Press.

LLINÀS-GRAU, MIREIRA—BEL, AURORA 2019, *On the Acceptance of the Null That by Bilingual Catalan/Spanish L2 Learners of English*, "Languages" 4: 1–16.

MAIR, CHRISTIAN 2002, *Three changing patterns of verb complementation in Late Modern English: a real-time study based on matching text corpora*, "English Language and Linguistics" 6: 105–131.

MARNETTE, SOPHIE 1996, *Réflexions sur le discours indirect libre en français médiéval*, "Romania" 114: 1–49. https://doi.org/10.3406/roma.1996.2193.

MARTINEZ VAZQUEZ, MONTSERRAT 2004, *Learning Argument Structure Generalizations in a Foreign Language*, "Vigo International Journal of Applied Linguistics" 1: 151–165.

MATRAS, YARON—SAKEL, JEANETTE 2007, *Investigating the mechanisms of pattern replication in language convergence*, "Studies in Language", 31/4: 829–865. https://doi.org/10.1075/sl.31.4.05mat.

MATRAS, YARON 2009, *Language contact*, Cambridge: Cambridge University Press.

MATRAS, YARON 2015, *Why is the borrowing of inflectional morphology dispreferred?*, in F. Gardani—P. Arkadiev—N. Amiridze (eds.), *Borrowed Morphology*, Berlin/Boston: Mouton de Gruyter: 47–80.

MILROY, JAMES—MILROY, LESLEY 2012[4], *Authority in language: investigating standard English*, London: Routledge.

VAN MINNEN, PETER 2007, *The other cities in Later Roman Egypt*, in R. Bagnall (ed.), *Egypt in the Byzantine world, 300–700*, Cambridge: Cambridge University Press: 207–225.

MITHUN, MARIANNE 2008, *The Extension of Dependency Beyond the Sentence*, "Language" 84: 69–119.

MITHUN, MARIANNE 2019, *Sources and mechanisms*, in G. Kaltenböck—K. Beijering,—M. Sansiñena (eds.), *Insubordination: theoretical and empirical issues*, Berlin/Boston: Mouton de Gruyter: 29–54.

MUHS, BRIAN 2010, *Language contact and personal names in early Ptolemaic Egypt*, in D. Obbink—T. Evans (eds.), *The language of the papyri*, Oxford: Oxford University Press: 187–197.

MYERS-SCOTTON, CAROL 2006, *Multiple voices: an introduction to bilingualism*, Malden, MA: Blackwell Pub.

PALME, BERNHARD 2009, *The Range of Documentary Texts: Types and Categories*, in R. Bagnall (ed.), *The Oxford Handbook of Papyrology*, Oxford: Oxford University Press: 358–394.

PAPATHOMAS, AMPHILOCHIOS 2007, *Höflichkeit und Servilität in den griechischen Papyrusbriefen der ausgehenden Antike*, in B. Palme (ed.), *Akten des 23. Internationalen Papyrologenkongress, Wien, 22.–28. Juli 2001*, Vienna: Verlag der Österreichischen Akademie der Wissenschaften: 497–512.

PORTER, STANLEY—PITTS, ANDREW W. 2013, *The Disclosure Formula in the Epistolary Papyri and in the New Testament: Development, Form, Function, and Syntax*, in S. Porter—A.W. Pitts (eds.), *The Language of the New Testament: Context, History, and Development*, Leiden/Boston: Brill: 421–438.

QUACK, JOACHIM 2017a, *On the Regionalization of Roman-Period Egyptian Hands*, in J. Cromwell—E. Grossman (eds.), *Scribal Repertoires in Egypt from the New Kingdom to the Early Islamic Period*, Oxford: Oxford University Press: 184–211.

QUACK, JOACHIM 2017b, *How the Coptic script came about*, in E. Grossman—P. Dils—T. Richter—W. Schenkel (eds.), *Greek influence on Egyptian-Coptic: Contact-induced change in an ancient African language*, Hamburg: Widmaier: 27–96.

SÄNGER, PATRICK 2011, *The Administration of Sasanian Egypt: New Masters and Byzantine Continuity*, "Greek, Roman, and Byzantine Studies" 51: 653–665.

SCHULZ, PETRA 2003, *Factivity: its nature and acquisition*, Tübingen: Max Niemeyer.

SCHWARTZ, MICHAEL—CAUSARANO, PEI-NI 2007, *The role of frequency in SLA: an analysis of gerunds and infinitives in ESL written discourse*, "Arizona Working Papers in SLA and Teaching" 14: 43–57.

SELINKER, LARRY 1972, *Interlanguage*, "International Review of Applied Linguistics" 10: 209–231.

SILK, MICHAEL—GEORGAKOPOULOU, ALEXANDRA 2009, *Standard languages and language standards: Greek, past and present*, Farnham: Ashgate.

SIM, MARGARET 2011, *Marking thought and talk in New Testament Greek: new light from linguistics on the particles "hina" and "hoti."*, Cambridge: James Clarke.

STOLK, JOANNE 2015, *Case variation in Greek papyri. Retracing dative case syncretism in the language of the Greek documentary papyri and ostraca from Egypt (300 BCE–800 CE)*, PhD thesis, Univeristy of Oslo.

TOMASELLO, MICHAEL 2003, *Constructing a language: a usage-based theory of language acquisition*, Cambridge, Mass./London: Harvard University Press.

TORALLAS TOVAR, SOFÍA 2004a, *Egyptian lexical interference in the Greek of Byzantine and early Islamic Egypt*, in P. Sijpesteijn—L. Sundelin (eds.), *Papyrology and the history of early Islamic Egypt*, Leiden: Brill: 163–198.

Torallas Tovar, Sofía 2004b, *The context of loanwords in Egyptian Greek*, in P. Bádenas de la Pena—S. Torallas Tovar—E. Luján—M. Ángeles Gallego (eds.), *Lenguas en contacto: El testimonio escrito*, Madrid: Consejo Superior de Investigaciones Científicas: 57–67.

Torallas Tovar, Sofía 2007, *Egyptian loanwords in Septuaginta and the papyri*, in B. Palme (ed.), *Akten des 23. Internationalen Papyrologenkongresses, Wien, 22.–28. Juli 2001*, Vienna: Verlag der Österreichischen Akademie der Wissenschaften: 687–692.

Torallas Tovar, Sofía 2010a, *Greek in Egypt*, in E. Bakker (ed.), *A Companion to the Ancient Greek Language*, Oxford: John Wiley & Sons: 253–266.

Torallas Tovar, Sofía 2010b, *Linguistic Identity in Graeco-Roman Egypt*, in A. Papaconstantinou (ed.), *The Multilingual Experience in Egypt, from the Ptolemies to the Abbasids*, Farnham: Ashgate: 17–43.

Torallas Tovar, Sofía 2017, *The Reverse Case: Egyptian Borrowing in Greek*, in E. Grossman—P. Dils—T. Richter—W. Schenkel (eds.), *Greek Influence on Egyptian Coptic: Contact induced change in an ancient African language*, Hamburg: Widmaier: 97–113.

Trapp, Erich—Hörandner Wolfram 2001, *Lexikon zur byzantinischen Gräzität: besonders des 9.–12. Jahrhunderts*, Wien: Verlag der Österreichischen Akademie der Wissenschaften.

Unwin, Lorna—Hughes, Jason—Jewson, Nick 2007, *Communities of practice: critical perspectives*, London: Routledge.

Valenzuela Manzanares, Javier—Rojo López, Anna 2008, *What can language learners tell us about constructions?*, in S. De Knop—Teun De Rycker (eds.), *Cognitive approaches to pedagogical grammar: A volume in honour of Rene Dirven*, Berlin: Mouton de Gruyter: 197–230.

Vanpatten, Bill 2011, *Stubborn syntax: How it resists explicit teaching and learning*, in C. Sanz—R. Leow (eds.), *Implicit and explicit language learning: conditions, processes, and knowledge in SLA and bilingualism*, Washington, DC: Georgetown University Press: 9–21.

Viberg, Åke 2002, *Basic Verbs in Second Language Acquisition*, "Revue francaise de linguistique appliquée" 7: 61–79.

Vierros, Marja 2003, *Everything is Relative. The Relative Clause Constructions of an Egyptian Scribe Writing Greek*, in M. Vesterinen—L. Pietilä-Castrén (eds.), *Grapta Poikila*, Helsinki: Finnish Institute at Athens: 13–23.

Wallis Budge, Ernest 1929, *The Rosetta Stone in the British Museum*, London: Harrison & Sons.

Wenger-Trayner, Etienne—Wenger-Trayner, Beverly 2015, *Introduction to communities of practice, Resources for social learning,* https://wenger-trayner.com/resources/.

WILCKEN, ULRICH 1927, *Urkunden der Ptolemäerzeit (ältere Funde)*, Berlin: Mouton De Gruyter.

WINTER, PAUL 1955, *Ὅτι Recitativum in Luke 1 25, 61, 11 23*, "The Harvard Theological Review" 48: 213–216.

WIPSZYCKA, EWA 2007, *The institutional church*, in R. Bagnall (ed.), *Egypt in the Byzantine world, 300–700*, Oxford: Oxford University Press: 331–349.

WORP, KLAAS 2011, *(διa)φυλάσσω + DAT.: A linguistic regionalism in inscriptions from Christian Egypt?*, "Analecta Papyrologica" 23–24: 237–239.

WORP, KLAAS—WHITEHORNE, JOHN 1995, *Greek papyri from Kellis*, Oxford: Oxbow.

ZUCKERMAN, CONSTANTINE 1995, *The Hapless Recruit Psois and the Mighty Anchorite, Apa John*, "The Bulletin of the American Society of Papyrologists": 183–194.

CHAPTER 7

Where Does Dionysus Ὕης Come From?

Laura Massetti

1 Dionysus's Disappearence and Dionysus Ὕης*

The Greek god Dionysus is "the divine stranger *par excellence* of the ancient world" (WEAVER 2004: 35). As such, he is the protagonist of several theoxeny myths[1] in which he is refused hospitality, the most well-known of which is the Pentheus story, preserved *in extenso* in Euripides' *Bacchae*. After this refusal, an epiphany of the god effects a punishment. At the same time, the motif of Dionysus's refusal is often crossed and merged with that of the *disappearing god*. As a consequence of being offended, the god disappears with disastrous consequences for the world.[2] After searching for the disappeared one, the other gods manage to restore his/her place among the deities by means of a sacrifice.

In the case of Dionysus, a subgroup of narratives involving both the theoxeny-theme and the *disappearing-god* one is set during the god's childhood and go as follows. Dionysus is persecuted by someone, such as a powerful sovereign.[3] In order to escape from him, he plunges into the sea, where he receives help from a female deity. He is later able to come back and take revenge on the perpetrator(s) of his persecution. One of the earliest attestations of such an account is found in the sixth book of the *Iliad*:

---

* This paper was written in the framework of the project 'Family Myths. Phraseology and Inherited Indo-European Thematic Structures in Greek Myth'. This project has received funding from the European Union's Horizon 2020 research and innovation programme under the Marie Sklodowska-Curie grant agreement No. 793479. A special thank goes to Esther Manfredi, who carefully read and reviewed my article. I am responsible for all remaining mistakes.

1 Cf. KEARNS 2016.

2 On the motif of the 'disappearing god' cf. BURKERT 1979, 123–148. For comments on Greek stories involving Dionysus's disappearance, cf. OTTO 1965; KERÉNYI 1976. For the link between these narratives and the mystery cults cf. GRAF—JOHNSTON 2007; COLE 2007; FARAONE 2010, 2013.

3 For comments on these stories cf. OTTO 1965; KERÉNYI 1976. For the link between these narratives and the mystery cults cf. GRAF—JOHNSTON 2007; COLE 2007; FARAONE 2010, 2013.

© LAURA MASSETTI, 2022 | DOI:10.1163/9789004508828_009

WHERE DOES DIONYSUS ΥΗΣ COME FROM?

Il. 6.130–140

οὐδὲ γὰρ οὐδὲ Δρύαντος υἱὸς κρατερὸς Λυκόοργος
δὴν ἦν, ὅς ῥα θεοῖσιν ἐπουρανίοισιν ἔριζεν·
ὅς ποτε μαινομένοιο Διωνύσοιο τιθήνας
σεῦε κατ' ἠγάθεον Νυσήϊον· αἳ δ' ἅμα πᾶσαι
θύσθλα χαμαὶ κατέχευαν ὑπ' ἀνδροφόνοιο Λυκούργου
θεινόμεναι βουπλῆγι· Διώνυσος δὲ **φοβηθεὶς**
δύσεθ' ἁλὸς κατὰ κῦμα, Θέτις δ' ὑπεδέξατο κόλπῳ
δειδιότα· κρατερὸς γὰρ ἔχε τρόμος ἀνδρὸς ὁμοκλῆ.
τῷ μὲν ἔπειτ' ὀδύσαντο θεοὶ ῥεῖα ζώοντες,
καί μιν τυφλὸν ἔθηκε Κρόνου πάϊς· οὐδ' ἄρ' ἔτι δὴν
ἦν, ἐπεὶ ἀθανάτοισιν ἀπήχθετο πᾶσι θεοῖσιν

No, for not even the son of Dryas, mighty Lycurgus, lived long, he who strove with heavenly gods; he drove down over the sacred mount of Nysa the nurses of raging Dionysus, and they all together let their wands fall to the ground, struck with an ox-goad by man-slaying Lycurgus; but **Dionysus fled, and plunged beneath the wave of the sea, and Thetis received him, who was filled with fear, in her bosom,** for mighty **terror** had got hold of him at the man's shouts. Then at Lycurgus did the gods who live at their ease grow angry, and the son of Cronos made him blind; and he lived not for long, since he was hated by all the immortal gods.

MURRAY—WYATT 1924

Ancient commentators, logographers and lexicographers connected Lycurgus's persecution with the figure of 'Dionysus of the rain' (Gk. Ὗης) and with the *Hyades*, Dionysus's 'rainy' nurses, cf.

Pher. fr. 96 D

Ὗης ἐπίθετον Διονύσου, ὡς Κλείδημος· ἐπειδή, φησίν, ἐπιτελοῦμεν τὰς θυσίας αὐτῷ καθ' ὃν ὁ θεὸς ὕει χρόνον· ὁ δὲ Φερεκύδης τὴν Σεμέλην Ὗην λέγει καὶ τὰς τοῦ Διονύσου τροφοὺς Ὑάδας.[4] Ἀριστοφάνης δὲ συγκαταλέγει ξενικοῖς θεοῖς τὸν Ὗην.

Hyes: **epithet of Dionysus**, as Kleidemos says: because we make sacrifices to him according to the time in which **the god makes it rain** (lit. 'the god

---

4   Cf. also *Schol. Arati Phaen.* 172 M Ἡ δὲ προσωνυμία ἐστὶν, ὅτι τὸν Διόνυσον ἀνεθρέψαντο "Their name is (Hyades) because they raised Dionysus."

198   MASSETTI

rains'). Pherecydes calls **Semele** *Hye*; and **the nurses of Dionysus** *Hyades*. Aristophanes classifies *Hyes* among the foreign gods.[5]

Schol. 25 *in Il.* 18.486 H.

Καλοῦνται δὲ Ὑάδες ἢ αἴτιοι ὄμβρων καὶ ὑετῶν καθίστανται. [...] Αὗται θρέψα-σαι τὸν Διόνυσον [...] Λυκοῦγος δὲ μέχρι τῆς θαλάσσης συνεδίωξε τὸν Διόνυσον. [...] Φερεκύδης, καθάπερ προείρηται, τὰς Ὑάδας Δωδωνίδας Νύμφας φησὶν εἶναι, καί, Διονύσου τροφούς. Ἃς παρακαταθέσθαι τὸν Διόνυσον τῇ Ἰνοῖ διὰ τὸν τῆς Ἥρας φόβον. Καθ' ὃν καιρὸν καὶ αὐτὰς Λυκοῦργος ἐδίωξε

They (scil. a group of stars) are called *Hyades* **or are thought to cause rain and precipitations.** [...] They raised Dionysus [...] **Lycurgus chased Dionysus up to the sea.** [...] As already stated, Pherecydes says that the **Hyades** are the Nymphs from Dodona and **nurses of Dionysus.** They gave custody of Dionysus to Ino because **they were afraid of Hera.** On that occasion **Lycurgus chased them too.**

Hyg. Astr. 2.21

Hyades Pherecydes Atheniensis **Liberi nutrices esse demonstrat** [...] *Hae dicuntur* **a Lycurgo fugatae,** *et praeter Ambrosiam* **omnes ad Thetim pro-fugisse,** *ut ait Asclepiades.*

Hyades: Pherecydes of Athens attests that they were **Liber's nurses** [...] It's commonly said that **they were made to run away by Lycurgus** and all of them, except Ambrosia, as Asclepiades reports, **fled to Thetis.**

It has long been proposed that Dionysus's name might be etymologically re-lated to the semantic field of 'water' and 'humidity', since the god is associ-ated with the notion 'fertility' and 'watery/moist fruits'.[6] According to Peters (1989: 217–220), this very connection might lie at the basis of Dionysus's name, which he understands as *$Dih/i̯e$-hnūso-* (with a first member to Gk. δίε/ομαι and a second member to Gk. νῦσα 'spring', reflecting *$snuh_2$-ti-h_2).[7] However,

---

5   Phot. *Lex.* (p. 616.11 Porson) = *Etym. Gen.* B (*Etym. Magn.* 775.2) = *Suid.* (4.683.1 Adler).

6   For the association between Dionysus and the liquid element in Cornutus see FILONI 2018: 528–530, 560, 575.

7   Similarly, Janda (2000: 259–273) has proposed a *Transponat* [*Dih_1-e-$snuh_2$-ti-o-*] '(the one) who makes the water flow'. On the variants of Dionysus's name, Thess. Διεννυσ°, Cycl.-Ion. Διεννυσ° and Myc. *$Diu̯ohnūso$-, all reshaped on Διὸς νῦσος* cf. GARCÍA RAMÓN 1987: 185–186. Different etymological interpretations for the name of the god have also been proposed by

WHERE DOES DIONYSUS ΥΗΣ COME FROM?

the Greek sources about Dionysus *Hyes* do not allow us to recover a clear link between Dionysus's disappearance and the rain. In this paper, I focus on the figure of Dionysus *Hyes* and the Lycurgus's episode, by cross-referencing (a) a Greek tradition, which displays comparable narrative patterns as *Iliad* 6.130–140; (b) Greek rituals involving the search for and the invocation of disappeared Dionysus. I argue that, from a thematic point of view, the narrative concerning young Dionysus's escape parallels an Anatolian ritual-mythological text in a remarkable way, namely: CTH 671, "Sacrifice and Prayer to the Storm-god of Nerik". Through this analysis the paper aims to show that the reference to the Anatolian myth and ritual provides the missing link between Dionysus 'of the rain' and the Lycurgus episode.

2   Myths of Disappearence and the Agrionia Festivals

As already anticipated, the main events of *Iliad* 6.130–140 resemble those of several other 'Dionysiac' stories.[8] In this context, I would like to shortly present one Greek narrative avatar, namely: Perseus's persecution against Dionysus and his nurses in Argos. In this connection, I will also endeavour to point out how the main events of Dionysus's persecution(s) parallel the ritual gestures of the *Agrionia* festivals. The *Agrionia*, "a (spring) festival in the Dorian and Aeolic area, which is a festival of dissolution and inversion, with a women's uprising, madness and cannibalistic fantasies" (BURKERT 1985: 163–165), is often con-

---

DUNKEL 1995: 12–13: *Diu̯oh-nūso-* (thematized) 'son of the Sky-god' < **Diu̯oh-suHnu(h₁)*-, SZEMERÉNYI 1974: 572, and BLANC 2001: 139. MACEDO 2012: 39–40, leads the second compound member °*hnūso-* to an IE root **sneu̯H-* 'to turn', as Dionysus is the 'dancing god' *par excellence*.

8 For parallels between *Il.* 6.130–141, *Il.* 1.590–594, 18.394–405 (in both cases Hephaestus disappears in the depth of the sea) cf. FARAONE 2013. The two Iliadic parallels display macroscopic phraseological similarities. Significantly, one ancient commentator (*Schol.* 16 *in Il.* 6.130 D.) merges the two episodes: Ὁ δὲ ὑπὸ δέους εἰς τὴν θάλασσαν καταδύνει, καὶ ὑπὸ Θέτιδος καὶ Εὐρυνόμης ὑπολαμβάνεται. Ὁ οὖν Λυκοῦργος οὐκ ἀμισθὶ δυσσεβήσας, ἔδωκε τὴν ἐξ ἀνθρώπων δίκην. [...] Τῆς ἱστορίας πολλοὶ ἐμνήσθησαν, προηγουμένως δὲ ὁ τὴν Εὐρωπίαν πεποιηκὼς Εὔμηλος. In commenting on *Iliad* 6, the scholiast mentions Thetis and Eurynome as helpers of Dionysus, although there is no mention of Eurynome in *Iliad* 6. However, Eurynome and Thetis figure as helpers of Hephaestus in *Il.* 18.398, cf. Εὐρυνόμη τε Θέτις θ' ὑπεδέξατο κόλπῳ "Eurynome and Thetis received me into their bosom." Given the mention of Eumelos and the *Europia*, it is possible that the commentator is referencing Eumelos's version. Other possible narrative avatars for Dionysus's persecution are: Ino and Melicertes, Perseus or Acrisius persecuting Dionysus and Semele in Brasiae (Paus. 3.24.3–4), Hypsipyle/Thoas and Oinoe (A.R. *Arg.* 1.619–627).

nected with stories about Dionysus's persecution. The story featuring Perseus attacking Dionysus can be recognized as one of these myths. It is preserved by a few sources. According to an anonymous Iliadic commentator, 'Perseus kills Dionysus', cf.

Schol. in Hom. Il. 14.319

[…] ὅτι Διόνυσον ἀνεῖλεν εἰς τὴν Λερναίαν ἐμβαλὼν λίμνην

Because he (: Perseus) **killed Dionysus,** by throwing him **into** Lerna's **lake**

Moreover, in his *Periegesis*, Pausanias locates the tomb of the maenad Chorea and the collective grave of the other maenads, who had fought against Perseus, close to the temple of Zeus Nemeios and Tyche in Argos:

Paus. 2.20.4

τὸ δὲ μνῆμα τὸ πλησίον Χορείας μαινάδος ὀνομάζουσι, Διονύσῳ λέγοντες καὶ ἄλλας γυναῖκας καὶ ταύτην ἐς Ἄργος συστρατεύσασθαι, Περσέα δέ, ὡς ἐκράτει τῆς μάχης, φονεῦσαι τῶν γυναικῶν τὰς πολλάς· τὰς μὲν οὖν λοιπὰς θάπτουσιν ἐν κοινῷ, ταύτῃ δέ—ἀξιώματι γὰρ δὴ προεῖχεν—ἰδίᾳ τὸ μνῆμα ἐποίησαν[9]

The tomb near this (: the temple of Tyche) they call that of the maenad Chorea, **saying that she was one of the women who joined Dionysus in his expedition against Argos, and that Perseus, being victorious in the battle, put most of the women to the sword.** To the rest they gave a common grave, but to Chorea they gave separate burial because of her high rank

As underlined by Auffarth (2006), "the battle of Perseus against Dionysus and his host of women could be an aetiology for the *Agrionia* in Argos". Indeed, the festival involved the simulation of four main ritual gestures, which may nicely correlate with the main facts/events of the tale. Plutarch provides a variety of examples of the individual ritual gestures from the Agrionia festival of Orchomenos, namely:

(a) The 'pursuit' and/or simulation of the killing of Dionysus and/or Dionysus's nurses, cf.

---

9   Cf. also Paus. 2.22.1, 23.7–8.

WHERE DOES DIONYSUS ΥΗΣ COME FROM?

Plut. *Aet.* 263eff.

καὶ γίνεται παρ' ἐνιαυτὸν ἐν τοῖς Ἀγριωνίοις φυγὴ καὶ δίωξις αὐτῶν ὑπὸ τοῦ Διονύσου ξίφος ἔχοντος. ἔξεστι δὲ τὴν καταληφθεῖσαν ἀνελεῖν, καὶ ἀνεῖλεν ἐφ' ἡμῶν Ζωΐλος ὁ ἱερεύς.

Also every year in the Agrionia (scil. of Orchomenos, Boeotia) there takes place their (the maenads') **flight and their pursuit** by the priest of Dionysus carrying a knife. **It's possible to kill the one who falls behind**, and the priest Zoilus **killed one** on occasion of a festival of ours.

(b) The search for the god, who has 'run away' and **(c)** the identification of his hiding place, cf.

Plut. *Quaest.* 717

οὐ φαύλως οὖν καὶ [b] παρ' ἡμῖν ἐν τοῖς Ἀγριωνίοις τὸν Διόνυσον αἱ γυναῖκες ὡς ἀποδεδρακότα ζητοῦσιν, εἶτα παύονται [c] καὶ λέγουσιν ὅτι πρὸς τὰς Μούσας καταπέφευγεν καὶ κέκρυπται παρ' ἐκείναις

It is not an accident that [b] **in the Agrionia, as it is celebrated here, the women search for Dionysus as though he had run away**, then desist [d] and say that **he has taken refuge with the Muses and is hidden among them**

MINAR—SANDBACH—HELMBOLD 1961

(d) The sacrifice: in discussing the analogies between the Greek traditions about 'disappeared Dionysus' and the Egyptian ones about 'disappeared Osiris', Plutarch mentions a chthonic sacrifice in honor of the Greek god,[10] which was performed in Argos.[11] He does not frame this ritual in an 'Agrionia-context'; however, it is legitimate to imagine that the ritual was connected with a local Dionysiac story, in which the god had plunged into waters, perhaps that of Dionysus's death due to Perseus's persecution or another of his *katabaseis*.

Plut. *De Iside* 35

Ἀργείοις δὲ βουγενὴς Διόνυσος ἐπίκλην, ἐστίν· ἀνακαλοῦνται δ' αὐτὸν ὑπὸ σαλ-πίγγων ἐξ ὕδατος, ἐμβάλλοντες εἰς τὴν ἄβυσσον ἄρνα τῷ Πυλαόχῳ τὰς δὲ σάλ-

---

10 For the 'chthonic' traits of this sacrifice cf. BACHVAROVA 2016: 86–95.

11 For comments to Plutarch's *De Iside* cf. GRIFFITHS 1970, NAGY 2013. On the *interpretatio Graeca* of the Egyptian account cf. HERRMANN 1957. On Osiris and Dionysus cf. FRATEAN-TONIO 2011.

πιγγας ἐν θύρσοις ἀποκρύπτουσιν, ὡς Σωκράτης ἐν τοῖς περὶ Ὁσίων εἴρηκεν. (Socr. Arg. fr. 5.10) [...] καὶ θύουσιν οἱ Ὅσιοι θυσίαν ἀπόρρητον ἐν τῷ ἱερῷ τοῦ Ἀπόλλωνος, ὅταν αἱ Θυιάδες ἐγείρωσι τὸν Λικνίτην.

... while **among the Argives** Dionysus bears the name 'born of a bull', and **they summon him** with trumpets **from the water after throwing a lamb into the deep for the Gate-Keeper,** but they cover the trumpets with thyrsus-rods as Socrates has said in his work *Concerning the Holy Ones.* [...] while the Holy Ones offer a secret sacrifice in the temple of Apollo, whenever the Thyiades **wake the god of the sacred basket.**

The above mentioned ritual gestures correlate with the main events of the myths associated with the *Agrionia*, as shown in the following table:

Ritual gestures (similar / complementary)	Mythical event
(a) [PURSUIT] / [KILLING]—[DIONYSUS + NURSES]	[AGGRESSION]—[MAENADS] Lycurgus **attacks** / Perseus **kills** Dionysus and his nurses
(b) [SEARCH FOR THE HIDDEN GOD]	[GOD]—[HIDE] in [WATER] Dionysus **hides** (Lycurgus) / **dies** (Perseus) **in the sea**
(c) [IDENTIFICATION of HIDING PLACE]	[GODDESS'S HELP] Thetis (Lycurgus) / (?)
(d) [SACRIFICE]	[COMPENSATION] Lycurgus is blinded / Institution of the *Agrionia* (?)

3   Summary

To sum up: the narrative of Perseus killing Dionysus and his nurses in Argos is the narrative avatar of *Iliad* 6.130–140 (Lycurgus kills Dionysus's nurses and compels the god to hide in the depth of the sea). Moreover, this very account is likely to be the aetiological myth of the Argive *Agrionia*. As parallels from other *Agrionia* festivals show, the main events of Dionysus's persecutions match the ritual gestures of the festival: pursue/killing, search for the disappeared god, identification of his hideout and, most likely, a sacrifice, which aimed at bring-ing back the god among mortals and immortals.

Even though the reference to the Argive tradition and festival helps us frame the episode of *Iliad* 6 *e Graeco ipso*, i.e., within other Greek narrative and ritual avatars, it is still unclear why ancient Greek sources connected Lycurgus's episode with 'Dionysus of the rain'. The answer to this question must be sought elsewhere.

4 An Anatolian Parallel: "Sacrifice and Prayer to the Stormgod of Nerik" (CTH 671)

The ritual sequence of the Greek *Agrionia* strikingly parallels that of an Anatolian ritual and mythological text: CTH 671, "Sacrifice and Prayer to the Stormgod of Nerik".[12] The city of Nerik, founded by the Hattic speakers of Narak and later taken over by Ḫattušiliš I, worshipped a local Storm-god (ᴰU ᵁᴿᵁ*Nerik*). This deity was believed to be the son of ᴰ*Wuruntemu* and the Sun-goddess of Arinna. The text of CTH 671 can be dated to New Hittite (NH, cf. HAAS 1970: 141) and its origin is probably non-Indo-European. Indeed, it exhibits a prominent Hattic component, namely: Hattic theonyms and a non-Anatolian invocation of the Storm-god. Just like the Greek *Agrionia* festival, the Hittite ritual aims at restoring the place of the disappeared god to the world.[13] The cause of the god's disappearance is referred to in the 'mythological section' of the text, which, however, is only partially preserved. In following the sequence of information provided by the Hittite text, I will first of all focus on the ritual section in this context.

4.1 *The Sacrifice*
The text opens with a chthonic sacrifice to the Storm-god, cf.

> §1 (Vs. 2–4)
> *nu-kán* I UDU ᴰU ᵁᴿᵁ*Ne-ri-ik* BAL-[*an-ti* III UDUᴴᴵᴬ
> A]NA ᴰEREŠ.KI.GAL ᴰ*Ú-ru-zi-mu-ia* DINGIRᴹᴱˢ *uk-tu-ri-ia-aš-ša* BAL-*an-ti* UDUᴴᴵᴬ-*kan ḫa-at-te-eš-ni* GAM-*an-da ḫu-u-kán-zi* [...]

> (scil. the GUDU-priest) **sacrifices one sheep to the Storm God of Nerik and [... sheep] to the EREŠH.KI.GAL goddess, to (the god) Uruzimu, and to the eternal deities. They slaughter the sheep down in a pit.**

---

12 I print the text as edited by HAAS 1970. On CTH 671, cf. also DEIGHTON 1982: 74–84 and FREU—MAZOYER 2007: 344–349.

13 The main events of CTH 671 partially match those of other *mugawar*-texts (: invocations of the disappeared gods, cf. BURKERT 1979: 123–142; ATTERER 2011). However, CTH 671 exhibits two major differences on a narrative and on a ritual level. On a narrative level,

4.2 The God Disappears

As the following selected passages make clear, the Storm-god went down into a pit and should now be summoned from the river Maraššanta, cf.

§3 (Vs. 12)
ᴰU ᵁᴿᵁNe-ri-ik-wa-za-kán ša-a-it
nu-wa-ra-aš-kán ḫa-at-te-eš-ni GAM-an-da pa-a-it [...]

The god of Nerik is **angry** and went down **into a pit**

§5 (Vs. 26–28)
na-ak-ki-ia-iš-wa-kán ⁱᴰ[Ma-ra-aš-š]a-an-ta-za pár-ki-ia [...]
ḫa[l-l]u-u-wa-za ḫ[u-u-u]n-ḫu-e-eš-na-za UGU e-ḫu EGIR-pa-wa-[za

O noble (one), **rise from the Maraššanta River** [...] come up **from the deep wave.**

4.3 The God Hides

The river Maraššanta is probably imagined as a way to the underworld. Indeed, in performing the over mentioned sacrifice, the priest summons a number of underworld deities and invites them to open the gate to the Dark Earth (: the underworld),[14] cf.

§4 (Vs. 18–21)
ḫal-zi-ia-an-du-wa-ra-[an .....]x-wa-za-kán
GE₆-i KI-pi na-a-ú
ú-id-du-wa-ra-aš [... GE₆-aš] KI-aš
ᴳᴵˢKÁ.GALᴴᴵᴬ a-pa-ši-el ḫi-es-du
pí-ra-an-wa-aš-ši-ia [.... ú-i]d-du
ᴰU ᵁᴿᵁNe-ri-ik [... ú-i]d-du

Let them summon [him ...]. Let him turn himself [...] to the Dark Earth. Let him come [...]. **Let him open the gates of the Dark Earth** [...]. Before him/it [let ...]. Let them [bring(?)] the Storm God of Nerik up from the Dark Earth [...]

the so-called 'search motif' (: the gods make several attempts to find the disappeared god) is not preserved in the text. On a ritual level, the chthonic sacrifice is found only in this text, not in other *mugawar*.

14   On the 'dark earth' and its connection with the netherworld in Greece and in the Near East cf. Oettinger 1989–1990, Dardano 2013: 142–143.

WHERE DOES DIONYSUS ΥΗΣ COME FROM?

§7 (Vs. 38)
[ᴰ]*Ú-ru-un-te-mu-u*[*n* ... ᴳᴵˢKÁᴴᴵᴬ *a-pa-ši-la*] GE₆-*aš* KI-*aš ḫé-e-eš-du*

Wuruntemu (: chthonic deity) [...]. May (s)he open [the gates] of the Dark Earth.

4.4 *The Feelings of the God and His Divine Helper*

Let's now turn to the mythological section of the text. This part of CTH 671 seems to make brief reference to the facts that led to the disappearance of the Storm-god. The god is said to have descended into a pit because of a negative feeling: while in §3 (Vs. 12), he is described as angry (Hitt. ᴰU ᵁᴿᵁ*Ne-ri-ik-wa-za-kán ša-a-it* "The god of Nerik **is angry**"), in §11 he is said to have been 'scared'. This negative feeling is reminiscent of Dionysus's fear in *Iliad* 6, cf.

§11 (Rs. 1–4)
[*A-NA* DUMUᴹᴱˢ-MELUTTI
i]*š-ḫa-nu-wa-an-ti iš-ḫar-wa-an-ti li-li*[*škit*] [...]
[ᴰU ᵁᴿᵁ*Ne-ri-ik-ma-aš-kán*] DINGIRᴸᴵᴹ
pí-ra-an ú-i-ri-te-eš-ta [...]
ᴳᴵˢ*d*]*a-ḫa-an-ga-za ar-ḫa* [*i-ia-a*]*n-ni-eš*
a-ru-na-aš-ša-aš IX-*aš wa-ap-pu-ú-i* GAM-[*an pa-a-it*]
[*na-ak-k*]*i-ia-aš-aš* ÍD-[*aš wa-ap-pu*]*-wa-aš kat-ta-an pa-a-it* ᴰ*Ú-ru-zi-mu-za* [...]

Because of the bloody, bloodstained mortals he disappeared [...] The Storm-god of Nerik got scared of the deity [...] he went down to the shore of the nine seas, down to the bank of the noble river. Wuruntemu ...

In CTH 671 the disappearance of the Storm-god is connected with the river Maraššanta, which is described as "close to the soul of the Storm God of Nerik". In particular, the Storm-god is said to have once changed the course of the river. So, in order to favor the return of the disappeared deity, the Storm-God of the Sky asks the river to swear an oath: he shall never alter his course. A last passage from the mythological section preserves a few interesting phraseological details. The text concludes with the return of the disappeared god: while he was deserting the world of the living he slept and had 'sweet dreams in the bosom of the goddess Teš(i)mi'.[15] Once again, the reference to the 'bosom of a female

---

15   On the name and nature of the goddess cf. OTTEN 1950: 122–126; SOYSAL 1998: 60; TA-
      RACHA 2009: 56.

goddess' strikingly recalls the image of a scared Dionysus, who finds shelter 'in Thetis's bosom' (*Il.* 6.136), cf.

§18 (Rs. 56–59)
ᴰTe-ši-mi-wa-kán a-aš-ši-ia-an-ti gi-nu-wa ša-ni-iz-zi-uš ti-eš-ḫu-uš šu-up-pa-ri-ia-an-za e-eš-ta a-ra-a-i ᵁᴿᵁ*Ne-ri-qa-aš* ᴰU-*aš* ᴰ*Te-ši-mi-eš*(?!)-*wa-ta* GEŠTIN-*aš mu-re-eš mi-li-it ma-a-an kán-kán-an-za*

In the bosom of the beloved goddess Tesimi (lit. in the beloved bosom) you dreamt (lit. slept) sweet dreams. **Stand up**, Storm-god of Nerik; Tesimi for you hangs here a winegrape (which is as sweet as) honey.

4.5   *The God Returns*

Finally, when the Storm-god comes back to the city of Nerik, mild rain falls from the sky. The Anatolian text thus provides a direct link between the disappearance-return of the god and the atmospheric phenomenon 'rain'. This particular connection is missing in the Greek tradition concerning Dionysus *Hyes*, cf.

§19 (Rs. 60)
e-ḫu ᵁᴿᵁ*Ne-ri-qa-aš* ᴰU-*aš ne-pí-ša-za-kán* GAM *me-e-uš ḫé-e-uš ú-it*

Come, Storm-god of Nerik, **mild rain came from the sky**

As for the Greek texts discussed above, the set of correlations between the ritual gestures and the main events of the Anatolian story can be summarized as follows:

Ritual gestures (similar / complementary)	Mythical event
(a) [CAUSE of NEGATIVE FEELING]	[FEAR], [ANGER] the Storm-god of Nerik got scared (*wiritešta*) He is angry (*šait*)
(b) [HIDING in WATER]	[INVOCATION] from [WATER] The Storm-god hides in the Maraššanta river (ⁱᴰ*Maraššantaza parkiya*)
(c) [IDENTIFICATION of HIDING PLACE]	[GODDESS'S HELP] The Storm god sleeps in the bosom of the goddess Teš(i)mi (ᴰ*Tešmi⸗wa⸗kan āššiyanti ginuwa*)
(d) [SACRIFICE]	[COMPENSATION] Sheep is slaughtered into a pit Invocation of the god and the Gate-keeper

5   Conclusions

It has now become clear that the Anatolian text CTH 671 and some Dionysiac myths and rituals share a series of similarities, namely:

- The disappearance of the god is connected with a traumatic event, which troubles the deity: Dionysus and the Storm-god of Nerik experience 'fear' and/or 'anger', cf. Gk. φοβηθείς (var. χολωθείς) ... δειδιότα· κρατερὸς γὰρ ἔχε τρόμος "scared (var. enraged) ... filled with fear, for mighty terror" (*Il.* 6.135–137); Hitt. ᴰU ᵁᴿᵁ*Ne-ri-ik-wa-za-kán ša-a-it* "the god of Nerik is angry", Hitt. ᴰU ᵁᴿᵁ*Nerik-ma-aš-kan*] DINGIRᴸᴵᴹ *piran wiritešta* [...] "The Storm-god of Nerik got scared of the deity" (CTH 671);
- Both Dionysus and the Hittite Storm-god conceal themselves or die in the water, cf. Gk. δύσεθ' ἁλὸς κατὰ κῦμα "he plunged into the sea-wave" (*Il.* 6.136); Hitt. ᴰU ᵁᴿᵁ*Ne-ri-ik-wa-za-kán* ... *ḫa-at-te-eš-ni* GAM-*an-da pa-a-it* "the god of Nerik ... went down into a pit" (CTH 671).
- The ritual which aims at 'restoring' the place of the god involves an invocation of the deity from the water (a pit or a river), cf. Gk. ἀνακαλοῦνται δ' αὐτὸν ... ἐξ ὕδατος (Plut. *De Iside* 35); Hitt. UDU.ᴴᴸ·ᴬ-*kán ḫa-at-te-eš-ni* GAM-*an-da ḫu-u-kán-zi* (CTH 671). Water is often imagined as a way to the netherworld; as a consequence, rituals of the 'return' also involve a chthonic sacrifice to the Gate-keepers of the Underworld, cf. Gk. ἐμβάλλοντες εἰς τὴν ἄβυσσον ἄρνα τῷ Πυλαόχῳ (Plut. *De Iside* 35); Hitt. UDU.ᴴᴵ·ᴬ-*kan ḫa-at-te-eš-ni* GAM-*an-da ḫu-u-kán-zi* ... GE₆-*aš*] KI-*aš* ᴳᴵˢKÁ.GALᴴᴸ·ᴬ *a-pa-ši-el ḫi-eš-du* "they slaughter the sheep down into a pit ... Let him (the Gate-keeper) open the gates of the Dark Earth" (CTH 671);
- During their absence from the world, the Greek and the Hittite gods seek refuge with a female goddess, who lovingly receives the god(s) in her bosom, like a mother, cf. *Il.* 6.136 Θέτις δ' ὑπεδέξατο κόλπῳ "and Thetis received him in her bosom", or like a lover, cf. ᴰ*Tešmi⸗wa⸗kan āššiyanti ginuwa* [...] *ēšta* "in the bosom of Tesmi, your beloved (you slept)" (CTH 671).

In the light of these correspondences it is remarkable that both Dionysus and the Storm-god of Nerik share a connection with the rain: Lycurgus's persecution is connected with 'Dionysus of the Rain' (Ὕης), while the rain comes after the Storm-god of Nerik has come back.

These parallels might thus constitute a case of mythological/ritual borrowing from the Ancient Near East to Greece through the mediation of Hittite. The connection between Dionysus and the rain is unclear within Greek, but it makes sense in the light of the proposed thematic matches. Not only did Dionysus assume the same leading role as the Hittite Storm-god within a disappearance-myth, he also took over a connection with the atmospheric phenomenon, which originally belonged to an Anatolian atmospheric deity.

Finally, the comparison between Dionysus and the Storm-god of Nerik may count as a further parallel between the Greek god and an Anatolian deity. As underlined by Taylor (2003) and Bachvarova (2008), Dionysus seems to share a number of traits and associations with some Anatolian deities, such as HLuw. "Tarḫunza (Storm-god) of the vineyard" (cf. CLuw. *Winiyanta-*, Bo 2447 iv 16). The common traits between Dionysus and the Storm-god of Nerik can thus count as a further case of Greek-Anatolian 'religious contact' reflected in the rituals and literary texts of two neighbouring traditions.

References

ATTERER, MARIA 2011, *Typologische Analyse hethitischer Mythen. Schlange und Wetter-gott*, Hamburg: Verlag Dr. Kovač.

AUFFARTH, CHRISTOPH 2006, *Agrionia*, in H. Cancik—H. Schneider (edd.), Chr. F. Salazar (trans.), *Brill's New Pauly*, online: http://dx.doi.org.ezp-prod1.hul.harvard.ed u/10.1163/1574.9347_bnp_e108780 (access: 06/19/19).

BACHVAROVA, MARY R. 2008, *Sumerian Gala Priests and Eastern Mediterranean Return-ing Gods: Tragic Laments in Cross-Cultural Perspectives*, in A. Suter (ed.), *Lament: Studies in the Ancient Mediterranean World and Beyond*, Oxford: Oxford University Press: 18–52.

BACHVAROVA, MARY R. 2016, *From Hittite to Homer. The Anatolian Background of Ancient Greek Epic*, Cambridge: Cambridge University Press.

BLANC, ALAIN 2001, Διόνυσος *(ion-att.)*, Διώνυσος *(Hom.)*, in A. Blanc—Ch. de Lamberterie—J.L. Perpillou (edd.), *Chronique d'étymologie grecque n° 6*, "RPh" 75: 139.

BURKERT, WALTER 1979, *Structure and History in Greek Mythology and Ritual*, Berkeley and Los Angeles: University of California Press.

BURKERT, WALTER 1985, *Greek Religion* (orig. *Griechische Religion der archaischen und Klassische Epoche*), Cambridge, MA: Harvard University Press.

BURKERT, WALTER 1997, *Homo necans. Interpretationen altgriechischer Opferriten und Mythen*, 2. Auflage, Berlin: de Gruyter.

COLE, SUSAN G. 2007, *Finding Dionysus*, in D. Ogden (ed.), *A companion to Greek Reli-gion*, Oxford/Malden: Wiley-Blackwell: 327–341.

DARDANO, PAOLA 2013, *Lingua omerica e fraseologia anatolica: vecchie questioni e nuove prospettive*, in: M. Mancini—L. Lorenzetti (edd.), *Le lingue del Mediterraneo antico. Culture, mutamenti, contatti*, Roma: Carocci: 125–150.

DEIGHTON, HILARY J. 1982, *The 'Weather-God' in Hittite Anatolia. An examination of the archaeological and textual sources*, Oxford: B.A.R.

DOLCETTI, PAOLA 2004, *Testimonianze e frammenti: Ferecide di Atene*, Alessandria: Edizioni dell'Orso.

DUNKEL, GEORGE E. 1995, *More Mycenaean survivals in later Greek: ὦνος, ὦμος, ζωμός, Διώνυσος, and κῶμος*, in H. Hettrich (ed.), *Verba et structurae. Festschrift für Klaus Strunk zum 65. Geburtstag*, Innsbruck: Institut für Sprache und Literatur der Universität Innsbruck: 1–21.

FARAONE, CHRISTOPHER A. 2010, *Rushing and Falling into Milk. New Perspectives on the Golden Tablets*, in R. Edmonds (ed.), *Further along the Path: Recent Studies in the Orphic Gold Leaves*, Cambridge: Cambridge University Press: 304–324.

FARAONE, CHRISTOPHER A. 2013, *Gender Differentiation and Role Models in the Worship of Dionysus: The Thracian and Thessalian Pattern*, in A. Bernabé (ed.), *Redefining Dionysus*, Berlin: de Gruyter: 120–134.

FILONI, ANDREA 2018, *Alle fonti di Cornuto*, "Aitia" 8/2: Online (published 31.12.2019).

FRATEANTONIO, CHRISTA 2011, *'Das hat nichts mit Osiris zu tun'. Zur Verweigerung des Dionysos/Osiris-Synkretismus bei Pausanias*, in R. Schleisier (ed.), *A different god? Dionysos and Ancient Polytheism*, Boston/Berlin: de Gruyter: 447–464.

FREU, JACQUES—MAZOYER, MICHEL 2007, *Les débuts du Nouvel Empire Hittite. Les Hittites et leur histoire*, Paris: L'Harmattan.

GARCÍA RAMÓN, JOSÉ LUIS 1987, *Sobre las variantes Διεννυσος, Δινυσος y Διννυσος del nombre de Dioniso: Hechos e hipótesis*, in J.T. Killen—J.L. Melena—J.-P. Olivier (edd.), *Studies in Mycenaean and Clasical Greek presented to John Chadwick*, "Minos" 20/22: 183–200.

GRAF, FRITZ—JOHNSTON, SARAH I. 2007, *Ritual Texts for the Afterlife. Orpheus and the Bacchic Gold Tablets*, second edition, London/New York: Routledge.

GRIFFITHS, JOHN G. 1970, *Plutarch's De Iside et Osiride*, Cambridge: Univ. of Wales Press.

HAAS, VOLKERT 1970, *Der Kult von Nerik. Ein Beitrag zur hethitischen Religionsgeschichte*, Roma: Päpstliches Bibelinstitut.

HAAS, VOLKERT 1994, *Geschichte der hethitischen Religion*, Leiden/New York, NY/Köln: Brill.

HAAS, VOLKERT 2006, *Die hethitische Literatur, Texte, Stilistik, Motive*, Berlin/Boston: de Gruyter.

HERRMANN, SIEGFRIED 1957, *Isis in Byblos*. "ZÄS" 82: 48–55.

JANDA, MICHAEL 2000, *Eleusis: das indogermanische Erbe der Mysterien*, Innsbruck: Institut für Sprachen und Literaturen der Universität Innsbruck.

KEARNS, EMILY 2016, *Theoxenia. Oxford Classical Dictionary*, online: https://oxfordre .com/classics/classics/view/10.1093/acrefore/9780199381135.001.0001/acrefore-978 0199381135-e-6380. (Uploaded: March 2016, consulted: 01.06.2020).

KERÉNYI, KARL 1976, *Dionysos: Archetypal Image of Indestructible Life*, Princeton, NJ: Princeton University Press.

MACEDO, JOSÉ MARCOS 2012, *Breve nota sobre a etimologia de Dioniso*, "Synthesis" 19: 29–41.

MINAR, EDWIN L.—SANDBACH, FRANCIS H.—HELMBOLD, WILLIAM C. (transl.) 1961, Plutarch. *Moralia, Volume IX: Table-Talk, Books 7–9. Dialogue on Love*, Cambridge, MA: Harvard University Press.

MURRAY, AUGUSTUS T. (transl.)—WYATT, WILLIAM F. (rev.) 1924, *Homer. Iliad, Volume I: Books 1–12*, Cambridge, MA: Harvard University Press, 1924.

NAGY, GREGORY 2013, *Comments on Plutarch's Essay on Isis and Osiris*, online: http://nrs.harvard.edu/urn-3:hlnc.essay:Nagy.Comments_on_Isis_and_Osiris.1999-. (Uploaded: 28.08.2013, consulted 20.12.2019).

OETTINGER, NORBERT 1989–1990, *Die 'dunkle Erde' im Hethitischen und Griechischen: Alfred Heubeck zum Gedächtnis (20.7. 1914–24.5. 1987)*, "WO" 20/21: 83–92.

OTTEN, HEINRICH 1950, *Die Gottheit Lelvani der Boğazgöy-Texte*, "JCS" 4: 119–136.

OTTO, WALTER Fr. 1965, *Dionysos: Myth and Cult* (orig. *Dionysos: Mythus und Kultus*), Bloomington/London: Indiana University Press.

PETERS, MARTIN 1989, *Sprachliche Studien zum Frühgriechischen*, (unpubl.) Habilitationsarbeit, Vienna.

SOYSAL, OğUZ 1998, *A forgotten Hittite fragment of the KI.LAM Festival*, "JCS" 50: 59–65.

SZEMERÉNYI, OSWALD 1974, *The origin of the Greek Lexicon: Ex oriente lux*, "JCS" 94: 144–157.

TAYLOR, PATRICK J. 2003, *Studies in Ancient Anatolian Language and Culture*, Ph.D. Dissertation, Harvard University.

TARACHA, PIOTR 2009, *Religions of Second Millennium Anatolia*, Wiesbaden: Harrassowitz.

WEAVER, JOHN B. 2004, *Plots of Epiphany: Prison-Escape in Acts of the Apostles*, Berlin: de Gruyter.

CHAPTER 8

Alignment Change and Changing Alignments: Armenian Syntax and the First 'Death' of Parthian

Robin Meyer

1 Introduction

It is no secret to historical linguists and Indo-Europeanists that Classical Armenian, although occupying its own branch on the Indo-European family tree, is a language heavily influenced by its Iranian neighbours, chief amongst which Parthian. After Hübschmann's establishment of the fact that Armenian is not an Iranian language,[1] great progress has been made over the course of the twentieth century in the separation, categorisation, and analysis of Iranian and native elements in the Armenian lexicon and, to a lesser extent, its morphological inventory.[2] Similarly, early Armenian literature, history, and society have been in the focus of academic discussion, yielding exemplary pieces of interdisciplinary work like Nina Garsoïan's translation of and commentary on the *Epic Histories* attributed to Pʻawstos Buzand.[3]

Almost inevitably, however, not all Classical Armenian resources have been used to their fullest yet; the study of Armenian comparative and diachronic syntax, for instance, and the socio-linguistics of the language have thus far not received the attention they deserve.

This paper sets out to exemplify what information can be gleaned from syntactic analysis, and how it can be used to obtain a clearer picture of the socio-linguistic situation in preliterary and fifth-century Armenia. It uses as its basis the example of contact-induced alignment change in the Classical Armenian periphrastic perfect, and will make use of the material gathered in a corpus study of fifth-century CE historiographical texts. The diachronic development of the syntax of the perfect suggested here proposes two particular diachronic analyses:

---

1 HÜBSCHMANN 1875.
2 For overviews, cf. MEYER (fthc.), SCHMITT 1983. Key contributions to the field include BENVENISTE 1957; 1964, BOLOGNESI 1960, HÜBSCHMANN 1897, MEILLET 1911.
3 GARSOÏAN 1989.

© ROBIN MEYER, 2022 | DOI:10.1163/9789004508828_010

1.) The tripartite alignment of the perfect is an extension of an ERG–ABS pattern borrowed from Parthian;

2.) This alignment pattern is in a state of change already in the fifth century CE under system pressure from NOM–ACC alignment in the other tenses.

On the socio-linguistic side—based on considerations of the documentary evidence of Parthian, the historical interactions of Armenians and Parthians, and the Armenian literary evidence—the paper further proposes the following:

3.) The Parthian ruling class adopted Armenian as its main language of communication, leading to the eventual (near) death of Parthian and explaining the documentary gap between Inscriptional and Manichaean Parthian.

Following this introduction, section 2 will give a brief overview of the contact between Armenian and the Iranian languages, focusing on the linguistic data in general. Section 3, in turn, will outline the construction of the perfect tense, and present a contact-based explanation thereof. The diachronic development of the morphosyntactic alignment of the perfect is delineated in section 4 on the basis of statistical trends gleaned from the abovementioned corpus study. Turning from linguistics to (language) history, section 5 explores the contact between Armenian and Parthian from a socio-historical perspective, leading to the discussion of the 'death' of Parthian at the hand of Armenian in section 6. Finally, section 7 synthesises the linguistic and historical accounts.

2   Iranian–Armenian Contact in General

While the modern concept of Iranian–Armenian contact goes back to the work of Hübschmann in the late nineteenth century, earlier scholars had already come to the realisation that Armenian was replete with Iranian loanwords.[4] The study of such loanwords, and based on which the discovery of regular phonological correspondences, accounts for a large amount of twentieth-century scholarship in this field. The exploration of morphological, phraseological, and syntactic elements borrowed from Iranian languages has played a lesser role to date.[5] What follows is a very concise summary of the key findings in Iranian–Armenian contact.

---

4   Based on lexical material from Classical and contemporary Persian, Johann Joachim Schröder distinguishes words introduced by the language of the Arsacids into Armenian from those native to that language more than 150 years before Hübschmann; cf. Bolognesi (1988: 563), Schröder (1711: 46).

5   One of the few questions discussed previously with regard to Iranian syntactic borrowings

ALIGNMENT CHANGE AND CHANGING ALIGNMENTS

The Iranian loan lexicon of Armenian is vast and extends beyond the common array of technical and cultural vocabulary well into the realm of basic vocabulary items and closed classes like prepositions and numerals.[6] Exemplarily, consider items like Arm. *pʻaṙkʻ* '(royal) glory' < WMIr. *frḥ* /farrah/ 'id.', next to basic terms like Arm. *seaw* 'black' < Pth. *sy'w* /syāw/, Arm. *hazar* '1,000' < WMIr. *hz'r* /hazār/, or Arm. *vasn* 'on account of, because of' ~ Pth. *wsn'd* /wasnāδ/, MP *wšn* /wašn/.[7]

As regards lexis and phonological correspondences in loan words, two observations can be made which will inform the discussion in later sections. First, it is evident that Parthian is the dominant model or donor language.[8] Middle Persian, the other Iranian language with which Armenian is in contact, provides exclusively cultural, political, and administrative items, not infrequently as a *Doppelentlehnung* ('double loan'), e.g. in the case of Arm. *spayapet* and *sparapet* 'general-in-chief', the former of which is a Middle Persian loan, the latter a Parthian one.[9] Secondly, within the Parthian loans, two distinct layers of loan words can be identified on the basis of phonological divergences. Pth. *w* /ō/, *y* /ē/, and *r-* /r-/ are reflected in early Armenian loans as *oý/u*, *é/i*, and *er-* respectively,[10] but in later loans as *o*, *e*, and *ṙ*.[11]

---

in Armenian is the potential Iranian origin of certain types of Armenian relative clauses (AJELLO 1973; 1997: 251; BENVENISTE 1964: 35); as it turns out, the evidence for borrowing is slim.

6   Based on the data collected by Hübschmann, Belardi (2003: 98–102) calculated that more than a third of the lexical items therein is of Middle Iranian origin, whereas less than a quarter is etymologically Armenian. Given the more recent corrections to Hübschmann's work, these figures may be imprecise, but still indicate the general composition of the Armenian lexicon.

7   The Armenian form does not correspond perfectly to either its Parthian or Middle Persian counterpart, nor to the Old Persian form OP *vašnā* 'by grace of'. Szemerényi (1966) suggests an origin in Pth. **wsn* /wasn/, which later underwent univerbation and phonological reduction with Pth. *r'd* /rāδ/ 'for, owing to'.

8   Certain phonological and morphological correspondences hint at the existence of third West Middle Iranian language, which is not attested in writing; cf. OLSEN 2005, GIPPERT 2005; 2009, KORN—OLSEN 2012, KORN 2016: 409–411.

9   Such double forms can be differentiated on a phonological basis, since Parthian and Middle Persian differ in their treatment of certain Old Iranian sounds. In the case of Arm. *spayapet* (< MP) and *sparapet* (< Pth.), the this difference is expressed in the different treatment of Old Iranian intervocalic /d/ (cp. Av. *spāda-* 'army'), where OIr. **-d-* > MP *-y-*, Pth. *-δ-*. The latter, in turn, is regularly expressed in Armenian loans as Arm. *-r-*.

10   The alternative forms given refer to stressed and unstressed variants.

11   Examples of the earlier layer: Arm. *boyž* 'cure, remedy', *bužem* 'to cure, heal' < Pth. *bwj-* /bōž-/ 'to save, redeem'; Arm. *dēmkʻ* (GEN *dimacʻ*) 'face' < WMIr. *dym* /dēm/; and Arm. *eram* 'troop, flock' < WMIr. *rm* /ram/ 'flock; Manichaean community'. Examples of the

As compared to the lexicon, Armenian morphology has undergone relatively speaking little influence from Parthian or other Iranian languages; only derivation and compounding seem to be affected. Apart from the borrowing of a few common derivative suffixes such as *-akan* (cp. CIr. **-ākana-*) or *-ik* (cp. CIr. **-ika-*) as seen in Arm. *sovorakan* 'usual' or Arm. *spasik* 'servant', the main element of note is the compounding strategy Armenian has adopted, which allows for the complete borrowing of Parthian compounds, semi-calques (in which Armenian and Parthian items are compounded), or straightforward calques (in which the structure of a Parthian compound is imitated with Armenian lexical material).[12]

The two most understudied aspects of the influence of Parthian on Armenian concern phraseology and syntax. The former largely consist of light verb constructions, prevalent also in many modern Iranian languages.[13] Syntactical loans have thus far been found in the use of the intensifier and anaphoric pronoun Arm. *inkʻn* '-self', which is used analogically to Pth. *wxd* /wxad/, as well as in the use of the Armenian complementiser *(e)tʻē* 'that' to introduce direct and indirect questions (unusually including *wh*-questions) paralleled by the Parthian use of *kw* /kū/.[14] The most complex way in which Parthian has influenced Armenian, however, lies in the construction of the periphrastic perfect tense, which is discussed in more detail below.

Even this cursory summary of the most salient interactions between the two languages in question shows that they must have been in contact for an extended period of time, and that the contact itself was pervasive. Its impact on Armenian and Parthian society, as will be argued below, cannot be underestimated.

---

later layer: Arm. *tohm* 'family, seed', cp. Pth. *twxm* /tōxm/; Arm. *den* (GEN *deni*) 'religion, faith' < Pth. *dyn* /dēn/; and Arm. *ṙazm* 'fight, battle' < WMIr. *rzm* /razm/.

12 Note the following examples: for borrowing, Arm. *vattohmak* 'of low birth' < MP *wttwhm* /wattōhm/ (with an optional suffix *-ak*); for semi-calques, Arm. *čʻarabaxt* 'unfortunate', cp. MP *wtbʾht* / watbāxt/; for calques proper, Arm. *jerbakal* 'prisoner (lit. taken by the hand)', cp. Pth. *dstgrb* /dastgraβ/, with an exact correspondence of *jerb-* (cp. *jeṙn* 'hand') and *dst* as well as *-kal* (cp. *kalay*, suppletive aorist of *unim* 'to have, hold') and *-grb* (cp. Pth. *gyrw-* /gīrw/ 'to take, seize').

13 Examples of such constructions are Arm. *heṙi aṙnel* 'to make remote, remove', cp. Pth. *dwr kr* /dūr kar-/, NP *dūr kardan*, or Arm. *pʻoł harkanel* 'to sound the trumpet', cp. MP *nʾy pzd* /nāy pazd-/.

14 For a detailed discussion, cf. MEYER 2013; 2017: 219–252.

ALIGNMENT CHANGE AND CHANGING ALIGNMENTS

215

3 Iranian–Armenian Contact in Particular: The Perfect

In order to understand how Parthian has influenced the syntax of the Armenian perfect, a set of comparanda need to be established first.

To begin with, the syntax of synthetic tenses in classical Armenian (PRS, IPF, AOR) shows, like that of many other early Indo-European languages, NOM–ACC syntax; that is to say, intransitive subjects and transitive agents are both morphosyntactically marked in the same manner (NOM), while the direct object of transitive verbs is marked differently (ACC).[15] In all instances, the verb agrees in number and person with the subject or agent. Examples (1–2) illustrate this behaviour.

(1) Non-perfect, intransitive (subject: NOM; subject agreement)
ew   *duk'*   *darjayk'*   *i*   *molorut'iwn*
CONJ 2.NOM.PL return.2.PL.AOR.IND.MID to error.NOM/ACC.SG
k'rapastut'ean   *naxneac'=n*   *jeroc'*
idolatry.GEN.SG ancestor.GEN.PL=DET 2.PL.POSS.GEN.PL
'And you have returned to the errors of idolatry of your ancestors' (PB I.14)

(2) Non-perfect, transitive (agent: NOM; direct object: ACC; subject agreement)
ew   *duk'*   *z=ordis*   *ew*   *z=žarangs*   *ew*
CONJ 2.NOM.PL OBJ=son.ACC.PL and OBJ=heir.ACC.PL and
z=gorcakic's   *ew*   *z=nmanots*   *noc'in*
OBJ=associate.ACC.PL and OBJ=follower.ACC.PL 3.DEM.EMPH.GEN.PL
spanēk'
kill.2.PL.AOR.IND.ACT
'And you killed their sons and heirs and associates and followers' (PB I.14)

In the perfect—a periphrastic tense composed of the participle in -*eal* and, optionally, a copula—the same behaviour can be observed in intransitive verbs, at least with regard to the use of NOM, as example (3) shows.

(3) Perfect, intransitive (subject: NOM; subject agreement)
ew   *duk'*   *mtealk'*   *ew*   *hatordealk'*
CONJ 2.NOM.PL enter.PTCP.NOM.PL and participate.PTCP.NOM.PL

---

15   Passives also operate along these lines. The logical object is promoted to subject and takes NOM; the logical agent is demoted to an optional adjunct prepositional phrase, Arm. *i* + ABL.

216   MEYER

TABLE 8.1   Summary of the Classical Armenian alignment pattern

	Subject	Agent	Object	Agreement
Synthetic tenses	NOM	NOM	ACC	S_{ITR}, A_{TR}
Analytic tenses	NOM	GEN	ACC	$S_{ITR}, \emptyset_{TR}$

> *ic'ēk'*   *i*   *harsanis*   *Astuacut'ean*
> be.2.PL.PRS.SBJV.ACT into union.ACC.PL god-head.GEN.SG
> '... and that you may enter into and share in the union of the God-head'
> (Ag. §719)

Transitive verbs in the perfect behave differently, however. While the object is still expressed as ACC, the agent of the verb is marked by GEN; if a copula occurs, it shows neither object nor subject agreement, but appears in an invariant 3.SG form. (4) provides an example of this pattern.

(4)   Perfect, transitive (agent: GEN; object: ACC; Ø-agreement)
> *ew*   *du*   *ink'nin*   *isk*   *k'ezēn*
> CONJ 2.NOM.SG self.NOM.SG indeed 2.ABL.SG
> *vkayes*   *inj*   *t'ē*   *oč'*   *erbek'* **asac'eal**
> witness.2.SG.PRS.IND.ACT 1.DAT.SG COMP NEG ever **mention.PTCP**
> *ē*   *noc'a*   *c'=k'ez*   *z=ayd*
> be.3.SG.PRS.IND.ACT 3.GEN.PL to=2.ACC.SG OBJ=DEM.NOM/ACC.SG
> *vasn*   *imoy*   *tanǰeloy=s*   *i*
> concerning 1.SG.POSS.GEN.SG torture.PRS.INF.GEN.SG=DET by
> *k'ēn*
> 2.ABL.SG
> 'And you yourself are indeed witness to me that they [the gods] have never mentioned this to you, about my being tortured at your hands' (Ag. §71)

As a result, Classical Armenian is best analysed as showing a tense-sensitive split-alignment pattern, with a NOM–ACC alignment in all synthetic tenses, and tripartite alignment—in which intransitive subject, transitive agent, and direct object are all marked differently—in analytical tenses like the perfect. Table 8.1 summarises this situation.

Three further observations need to be made. First, Armenian does not consistently distinguish NOM and ACC forms across all paradigms; in all nominal and most pronominal singular paradigms, NOM and ACC are identical. The

ALIGNMENT CHANGE AND CHANGING ALIGNMENTS 217

1./2.SG pronouns are the exception in differentiating Arm. *es, du* 'I, you (NOM)' from *is, k'ez* 'me, you (ACC)'. The formal ambiguity is lessened in a large number of cases owing to the existence of a proclitic definite object marker Arm. *z=*. Nonetheless, at least on the surface, the alignment of the perfect can on occasion appear to be ERG–ABS. Examples (5–6) illustrate this surface ERG–ABS pattern and the use of the *z=* for differential object marking.

(5) Perfect, transitive (agent: GEN; object: NOM=ACC; no copula)
ew   nora   tueal   hraman   ark'ayagund
CONJ 3.GEN.SG give.PTCP order.NOM/ACC.SG royal-guard
banakac'=n
army.DAT.SG=DET
'And he gave an order to the royal army ...' (Ag. § 829)

(6) Perfect, transitive (agent: GEN; object: OBJ + ACC; Ø-agreement)
ew   tesin   zi   zawrut'ean=n Astucoy
CONJ see.3.PL.AOR.IND.ACT COMP power.GEN.SG God.GEN.SG
paheal   ēr   z=marmins   noc'a
preserve.PTCP be.3.SG.PST OBJ=body.ACC.PL 3.GEN.PL
'And they saw that the power of God had preserved their bodies' (Ag. § 223)

The second observation concerns the usage of GEN subjects and NOM agents in the perfect. Although the basic pattern stands as laid out above, there are occasional instances of unexpected intransitive subjects marked as GEN and transitive agents marked as NOM, as indicated by (7–8).

(7) Perfect, intransitive (subject: GEN)
manawand oroc'   nayec'eal i mxit'arut'iwn   aṙak'elakan
moreover   REL.GEN.PL look.PTCP to consolation.ACC.SG apostolic
banic'n   t'ē
word.GEN.PL COMP
'Moreover they considered the consolation of the apostolic words, namely that ...' (Kor. 22)

(8) Perfect, transitive (agent: NOM; object: ACC; no copula)
ew   and matuc'eal   t'agawori=n   išxank'=n
CONJ there present.PTCP king.DAT.SG=DET noble.NOM.PL=DET
ekealk'   z=bereal   patasxani=n
come.PTCP.NOM.PL OBJ=bring.PTCP answer.NOM/ACC.SG=DET

> *olǰunaber*   *t'łt'oyn*
> bearing-greetings letter.DAT.SG=DET
> 'And there the nobles, upon arrival, presented to the king the answer they had brought to his letter of greeting' (Ag. § 819)

Third, it has been argued that languages exhibiting tripartite alignment, whether wholesale or split, are in the process of morphosyntactic re-alignment.[16] This is, self-evidently, true of Classical Armenian, whose medieval and modern forms are exclusively NOM–ACC. One expression of this transitional state is the lack of verbal agreement; a number of languages exhibiting tripartite alignment exhibit similar invariant 3.SG forms, likely as the result of a lack of agreement licensing with cases other than NOM.[17]

These two latter points, in particular, corroborate the assumption that the alignment observed in Classical Armenian is a snapshot of an unstable transitional state. The question that arises is that of the point of origin from which the language embarked upon this trajectory.

Traditional explanations[18] have for the most part failed to observe correctly the alignment type of Armenian in the first place, and have accordingly ignored its implications for previous and subsequent developments. Barring one,[19] they also sought to explain the Armenian pattern language-internally, and frequently did not take into account or were unable to explain satisfactorily the whole gamut of data.[20]

Considering all the observations made above in addition to the potential influence of contact languages, an investigation into the morphosyntactic alignment pattern of Parthian suggests itself. The latter also exhibits tense-sensitive split alignment; in Parthian, the past tense—formed similarly with a copula and a participial form of the verb—exhibits ERG–ABS alignment, a pattern that Armenian, too, could be argued to show in certain surface analyses,

---

16   For some general observations on tripartite alignment, cf. DIXON 1994: 40, 55, 70. Some instances of tripartite alignment as a transitional state are discussed by Skalmowski (1974) and Payne (1980: 150).

17   Such languages include Talyši and Hindi; cf. COMRIE 1978: 342, PAYNE 1979: 442, PIREJKO 1966.

18   Amongst these must be counted BENVENISTE 1957, BOLOGNESI 1960, MEILLET 1936.

19   A Kartvelian origin was suggested already by Meillet (1899: 385); in spite of the clear counterarguments made by Deeters (1927), Meillet still includes his original reasoning in later work (1936: 95). For other, unsuccessful attempts at making a Kartvelian connection, cf. Meyer (2017: 122–124) with bibliography.

20   For a concise analysis of the issues with previous approaches, cf. MEYER 2016.

ALIGNMENT CHANGE AND CHANGING ALIGNMENTS

as illustrated in (5) above. Furthermore, Parthian too has optional object markers like Pth. *w* /ō/. Two key differences between the Armenian and Parthian alignment patterns exist, however. In Parthian, verbal agreement in the past tense is with the object; in the case of 3.SG objects, however, the copula is most commonly left unexpressed in the simple past.[21] The second point of difference concerns the nominal and pronominal system: Parthian has arguably lost most case distinctions.[22] The difference between ERG and ABS is only evident in some pronouns and pronominal clitics.

In spite of these differences—ERG–ABS alignment, not tripartite; different agent marking case; different verbal agreement—Parthian–Armenian contact provides the most straightforward explanatory model to account for the alignment pattern of Classical Armenian. The diachronic and interactional mechanisms behind this explanation are laid out in what follows.

4 Alignment Change: ERG–ABS > TRI > NOM–ACC

Broadly speaking, Armenian alignment change is likely to have taken place as follows:

(1) Pattern replication: in contact with Parthian, Armenian creates a periphrastic perfect tense based on the Parthian model; this construction follows the original ERG–ABS pattern and, based on the later advent of an invariant 3.SG copula, does not contain a finite verbal form. The ERG function is fulfilled by GEN, while ABS is expressed as NOM.

(2) Grammaticalisation: the replicated Parthian construction is adapted to the requirements and 'abilities' of Armenian: in parallel to the rest of the verbal system, the original ABS=NOM for the logical object is reanalysed as ACC in the transitive construction, but left unchanged in the intransitive one; an optional copula with Ø-agreement is introduced.

---

21 In other tenses or moods, however, a 3.SG copula is found, so for instance in the pluperfect or subjunctive; cf. DURKIN-MEISTERERNST 2014: 376, 392–400.

22 Manichaean Parthian certainly has lost this distinction. A consequent execution of the DIR–OBL and indeed the SG–PL distinction is found only in inscriptional Parthian (first century BCE until 3rd century CE), and in the psalter fragments (SKJÆRVØ 1983: 49, 176) and even there only in kinship terms, the personal pronouns of the 1.SG; and in the plural for nouns, pronouns and adjectives. Some examples: *br'd* /brād/ (DIR), *br'dr* /brādar/ (OBL); *pyd* /pid/ (DIR), *pydr* /pidar/ (OBL); *'z* /az/ (DIR), *mn* /man/ (OBL). Given the time in which Parthian and Armenian were interacting most actively, however, it is not implausible that a degree of morphological distinction between DIR and OBL could still have been in effect.

(3) Actualisation: the copula becomes more prevalent; the adapted, tripartite pattern begins to destabilise as the incidence of NOM agents rises.

(4) Disappearance: the TRI pattern is ousted in favour of NOM–ACC alignment.

This outline requires some explanations, which are provided below stage-by-stage.

The creation of the periphrastic perfect tense in stage (1) by pattern replication requires that at least some of the constituent parts of the Armenian pattern have something in common with the Parthian model. In this specific case, this common core is the participle, which as a verbal adjective was used attributively as well as predicatively prior to the creation of the perfect.[23] Since this is also true for Parthian, the participle and its adjectival use act as the pivot for the creation of the new Armenian perfect construction; the latter derives its meaning and structure from the Parthian model by two process, pivot matching and polysemy/polyfunctionality copying.[24]

In the resulting ERG-ABS alignment pattern, the Parthian OBL had to be expressed in Armenian. By the same set of processes, that is pivot matching and polysemy copying, the Armenian GEN took on this function. It was best suited to this role since, like the Parthian OBL, it also expresses possession or appurtenance.[25]

The structure of the earliest instances of the perfect indicate that the use of the copula was not part of the pattern replication process in stage (1). In the earliest texts, Koriwn's *Life of Maštocʻ*, the copula is almost completely absent. This is corroborated by the fact that the copula in Armenian never shows object agreement. On this basis, it must be assumed that the Parthian model pattern had a 3.SG object and thus lacked an overt copula.

---

23 The participle on its own, esp. when used attributively, does not have transitive force but reflects the historically intransitive-passive morphology of the participle; cf. MEYER 2014: 391–394.

24 Pivot matching is the process of 'identifying a structure that plays a pivotal role in the model construction, and matching it with a structure in the replica language, to which a similar, pivotal role is assigned in a new, replica construction' (MATRAS—SAKEL 2007: 830); polysemy copying denotes the realization of 'the potential of a structure in the replica language to cover the (lexical or grammatical) semantics represented by the model' (2007: 852). If sufficient semantic aspects are shared, the replica language can replicate those uses from the model language which were not previously part of the replica language's grammar; also cf. HEINE 2012, HEINE—KUTEVA 2005: 100.

25 Cf. DURKIN-MEISTERERNST 2014: 292. Armenian could not simply have adopted the morphologically largely unmarked pattern of Parthian nouns, as Armenian word order is far less constrained than that of Parthian.

In stage (2), the post-contact adaptation of the replicated pattern takes place. The two adaptations—the development of ERG-ABS into TRI and the rise of an optional copula—both result from different expressions of system pressure.

As regards argument marking, this pressure is exerted by the other, non-perfect tenses, all of which exhibit NOM–ACC. Owing to the formal identity of NOM and ACC in the singular of the nominal and most of the pronominal system, a reanalysis of direct objects marked NOM in the periphrastic perfect as ACC is a logical grammaticalization process. It is possible that this process was further aided by the existence of the DOM clitic $z=$ mentioned above.

The gradual advent of the copula in the perfect must be due to the fact that in all other, non-perfect tenses, predicates containing lexical verbs are always finite. Since participles are adjectival in character, the choice of the copula to express this finiteness is analogical to copulas used with predicative adjectives. The use of a copula further allows for the creation of—or could have been prompted by the need for—pluperfect and future perfect constructions, using a past or future tense of the copula, respectively. Where possible, the copula agrees with the subject in number and person. In transitive verbs, however, the copula invariably shows Ø-agreement, occurring only in the 3.SG. Like the rise of the copula itself, the reason for the invariability of this form must find a language-internal explanation, too. Given that the occurrence of invariant copulas finds parallels in other languages with TRI alignment or, more broadly, in transition between ERG-ABS and NOM–ACC, a correlation between such alignment patterns and lack of verbal agreement seems plausible. The most obvious explanation stipulates that, while system pressure results in the creation of a copula for the periphrastic perfect, in the absence of verbal agreement licensing with anything but a subject marked NOM, the newly created copula defaults to the least-marked form, in this case 3.SG.

Statistics concerning the incidence of the copula corroborate that it must have developed gradually post-contact, as indicated in stage (1) above already, since its relative frequency steadily rises over the course of the fifth century (see Figure 8.1).

By stage (3), the copula has become essentially obligatory in the periphrastic perfect.[26] At the same time, however, statistical analysis indicates that the pattern replicated in stage (1) and grammaticalised in stage (2) is not completely stable from the very beginnings of its attestation. Next to the obligatorification

---

26   On obligatorification as a possible, but not universally necessary pathway of grammaticalisation, cf. HOPPER—TRAUGOTT 2003: 32, HEINE—KUTEVA 2007: 34.

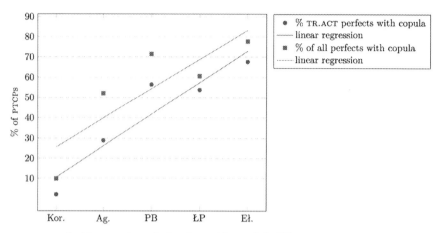

FIGURE 8.1   Incidence and trend of perfects with copula in fifth-century texts
Note: It is difficult to establish specific dates of publication for these texts. Here and in Figure 8.2 below, they are arranged in the most commonly accepted chronological order.

of the copula, other actualisation processes are taking place. Already in some of the earliest sources, analogically extended alignment patterns like in examples (7–8) above can be found; here, either the use of NOM for intransitive subjects is extended to agents of transitive verbs (resulting in apparent NOM–ACC alignment), or the use of GEN for transitive agents extended to subjects of intransitive verbs (creating an apparent ERG-ABS pattern). As Figure 8.2 illustrates, the latter pattern is declining over time whilst the former gains currency; this trend is, once more, in keeping with the pressure exerted by the other, non-perfect tenses, and shows the beginning of the grammaticalization S-curve leading up to stage (4), in which TRI alignment has been ousted in favour of NOM-ABS in all tenses. The rising incidence of the NOM–ACC-type non-standard pattern even in the earliest texts underlines the transitional nature of TRI alignment in Armenian, as its decline begins while the standard construction is still in the process of actualising core elements like the copula.

This delineation addresses all of the key questions regarding the perfect construction when compared to its Parthian model: Why a GEN agent? Why a 3.SG copula? Why an ACC object? It provides a relative chronological order of the development of the perfect, from its replication on the basis of a Parthian model via the grammaticalisation and actualisation of a TRI pattern in Armenian to the decline and eventual loss of this pattern in favour of NOM–ACC alignment.

An absolute chronology is more difficult to arrive at, however. The syntactic patterns found in Koriwn suggest that stage (1) must have taken place and ter-

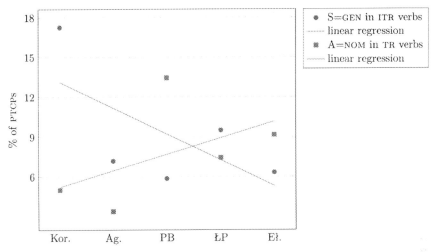

FIGURE 8.2 Incidence of non-standard alignment patterns in fifth-century texts

minated prior to the literary attestation of Armenian. Stage (2) clearly takes place over the course of the 5th century CE, and may be overlapping with stage (3) for a significant period of that time; stage (3) is likely to last longest (fifth to eighth centuries CE), since the complete loss of TRI alignment, and thus stage (4) is not effected until the eighth century. The latter parts of stage (3) are in need of further statistical exploration and evaluation.

5 The Socio-Historical Context

The scenario laid out in §§3–4 above relies on the assumption that contact between Parthians and Armenians in the relevant time period was close enough to facilitate not only lexical and morphological borrowing, but also pattern replication of syntagmata like the Parthian past tense. This and the following section seek to support this assumption first with clear historical evidence of such close contact, and secondly with an outline of the probable socio-linguistic situation obtaining in late pre-literary Armenia.

There are five aspects of particular historical significance that support close ties between Armenians and Parthians in this period:

1) Governance: Parthian rule over Armenia for almost four centuries;
2) Religion: conversion of Armenia to Christianity in the early fourth century;
3) Society: clear evidence of Parthian–Armenian intermarriage and tutelage;

4) Foreign Policy: frequent military conflicts with the neighbouring Sasanians, suggesting Parthian identification with the Armenians;
5) Language: absence of any documentary evidence in the Parthian language from this time and region.

Each of these aspects deserves a few explanatory notes.

The Armenian Kingdom was ruled for almost 400 years by Parthians in particular, and prior to that had been under general Iranian rule since the days of Darius I.[27] Parthian rule over Armenia began in 53 CE, when the Parthian King Vologaeses I installed his younger brother, Trdat I on the Armenian throne;[28] from this point onward, a member of the junior branch of the Arsacid Parthian ruling house would reign over Armenia until the transformation of the kingdom into a Sasanian *marzpanate* in 428 CE. Parthian rule is further cemented by the establishment of a hereditary dynasty in the beginning of the third century CE, just prior to the fall of the Arsacid Empire. Xosrov I (*r.* 198–217 CE), having succeeded his father Vałarš II, passed on the crown to Trdat II and thus established a largely unbroken succession until the end of Armenian autonomy. The existence of a Parthian-speaking ruling family, further compounded by the presence of other noble families of Parthian origin,[29] makes Parthian the overt prestige language at court and for the upper echelons of society, thus motivating the acquisition and imitation of Parthian by Armenian-speakers, or indeed of the Parthians' idiolectal use of Armenian.

Next to the fall of the Arsacid Empire in 224 CE, which resulted in the rise of the Middle Persian-speaking Sasanians and the delegation of the Parthians to second rank in their old domain, the Christianisation of the Armenians by Gregory the Illuminator is the single most important process aligning the Parthian nobility with their Armenian subjects. If the historiographic literature is to be believed, the pivotal moment in this process—the conversion of King Trdat III—is particularly relevant since it involves the conversion of the ethnically Parthian ruler of Armenia adopting Christianity at the hands of another Parthian, Gregory.[30] This change induced a further separation between the Armenians and their Parthian rulers on the one hand, and the neighbouring Sasanian Empire on the other hand, whose Zoroastrian religion the former had

---

27 For an overview of Armenian history prior to Arsacid rule, cf. GARSOÏAN 1997a.

28 This installation was ratified later in the treaty of Rhandeia (61 CE), according to which the rule over Armenia would fall to an Arsacid who was nominated and invested by Rome. Trdat I, although he had reigned since 53 CE, was only crowned by Nero in 66 CE.

29 Overviews of the genealogy of Arsacid and other Armenian families can be found in TOUMANOFF 1969; 1976.

30 This is the version of the Christianisation of Armenia as told by Agat'angełos; for a critical perspective, cf. GARSOÏAN 1997b: 81–84.

ALIGNMENT CHANGE AND CHANGING ALIGNMENTS

shared until this point.[31] Whether Trdat III's decision to adopt Christianity was wholly motivated by religious concerns is unclear, since political calculations may have favoured such a separation from the Sasanians as well.[32] By the beginning of the fifth century, Christianity had succeeded in developing sufficiently strong roots in Armenia to warrant translation of the Bible into Armenian; this required the creation of an alphabet suitable for writing the language and heralded the beginning of the Armenian literary tradition. In the centuries and millennia to come, Christianity and their language would develop into two of the primary pillars of Armenian identity; that the former's foundation was laid and subsequently maintained by Parthians suggests, if perhaps not quite yet an Armenian-Parthian identity, but at least a willingness on part of the ruling class to identify with their subjects.

This willingness also finds expression in certain customs in the higher echelons of Armenian society, particularly among the *naxarar* ('noble') families. Two of these customs are particularly suitable for creating or fostering multilingualism: intermarriage between Armenian and Parthian families, and the *dayeak* ('tutor') system, an 'institution [...] whereby *naxarar* youths were raised by foster-fathers of their own social class'.[33] A prominent and traditional instance of this kind of tutelage can be found in the relationship between the Armenian Arsacid dynasty and the Mamikonean family; the latter's head held the hereditary office of *sparapet* ('commander-in-chief') and would also act as *dayeak* for the heir-apparent to the Arsacid throne. The same two families have also been known to intermarry, so e.g. in the case of Vardanduxt, daughter of Manuēl Mamikonean, and King Aršak III in the late fourth century.[34] While political considerations are more likely to have been the prime reason for establishing such familial ties than linguistic ones, at least one historiographic source suggests that clear communication between powerful married couples and by extension their families was of importance: 'only through intermarriage will they [the Armenians and Iranians] communicate with each other'.[35]

---

31 Conversion is, of course, a process, and not accomplished overnight: Agatʻangełos details Gregory's efforts to spread Christianity in the early third century in some detail; Koriwn, in turn, writes about Mesrop Maštocʻ, who lived a century later and was still engaged in the (re-)Christianisation of the country. For the purposes of the court and the ruling classes, as well as for international politics, however, the principle *cuius regio, eius religio* applies.

32 BOYCE 1979: 84.

33 GARSOÏAN 1989: 521.

34 For a fuller discussion with bibliography of the relevance of intermarriage and tutelage, cf. MEYER 2017: 307–309.

35 ŁP §12.

While many of the contemporaneous historiographic sources touch on all of the above aspects, most of them chiefly deal with politics and warfare. In this context, too, the Parthian rulers of Armenia side with their subjects for the most part and over the centuries try to set themselves apart from their Sasanian neighbours, often in armed conflict. In the third century, the Armenians fought back numerous Sasanian incursions under King Trdat II (*r.* 217–252);[36] Roman losses and Sasanian successes in the middle of the century led to a short period of Sasanian rule over Armenia (*c.* 258–287), which had temporarily lost its importance as a buffer state between East and West.[37] Once Trdat the Great (*r. c.* 298–330), another Arsacid Parthian king, had ascended the Armenian throne, however, he pursued a stringently anti-Sasanian policy, not only by making Christianity the *de facto* state religion, as outlined above, but also by spending 'the whole period of his reign devastating the land of the Persian kingdom'.[38] Across the board, the general depiction of the Sasanians in fifth-century Armenian historiographic literature is negative, whilst the Arsacids are on the whole portrayed not only in a positive light, but indeed as the natural rulers of Armenia.[39]

By considering together these aspects of Parthian–Armenian relations—long-term Parthian ruler over Armenia; a shared religion; ties of marriage and tutelage; and a largely anti-Sasanian foreign policy—the conclusion suggests itself that the Parthian ruling class had integrated well with its Armenian subjects, likely to the extent of identifying with them at the exclusion of their Sasanian cousins. This is fruitful ground for extensive and deep language contact. The final question to consider, namely that of the specifics of this contact situation, will be dealt with in what follows.

6   Changing Alignment: The First 'Death' of Parthian

The socio-historical setting laid out above, when taken together with the large number of Parthian lexical borrowings into Armenian and the Armenian syntactic patterns replicated on the basis of Parthian models, suggests that the

---

36   Ag. § 23.

37   For a concise account of this uncertain and disputed time period, cf. GARSOÏAN 1997b: 73–75.

38   Ag. § 123.

39   For a discussion of the term Arm. *bnak tēr* 'natural lord', cf. GARSOÏAN 1976: 180, 196–197; 1989: 517. This positive depiction is, of course, likely due to the patronage of the writers by the Parthian ruling class.

most plausible contact situation is a superstrate shift, viz. the adoption of a language of the socio-economically less powerful speech community (here: Armenian) by a socio-economically more powerful speech community (here: the Parthian ruling class).[40] This kind of scenario is also applicable to, e.g., Britain in the centuries after the Norman Conquest in 1066, when the French ruling class over time adopted English as their main means of communication, all the while Norman French left its imprint on the English language.[41] In particular, both the Parthian–Armenian and the French–English context have two things in common: the comparatively small number of superstrate language speakers and the loss of a power-base during contact.[42]

Next to the linguistic and socio-historic data presented above, there is one further indication that the Arsacid Parthians adopted Armenian as their language: the lack of any Parthian-language documents from the Armenian Kingdom in the almost four centuries of their rule.[43] After the fall of the Arsacid Empire in 224 CE, Parthian quickly lost its relevance even in its former core territory; the last multilingual Sasanian inscriptions in which Parthian figures are those of Narseh (r. 293–303). Indeed, there is a considerable attestation gap between the last epigraphic attestation of Parthian (late third century CE) and its literary use the as the liturgical language of Manichaeism in the documents from Turfan (ninth–tenth century CE).[44] Judging by the form of the language used in the latter, Parthian was no longer spoken natively at that time; its 'death' must fall somewhere in this time period, viz. between the fourth and ninth centuries.[45]

---

40 For a general overview of language shift in contact situations and associated concepts, cf. THOMASON—KAUFMAN 1988: 37–46, 110–146, THOMASON 2003; 2008, MYERS-SCOTTON 2002: 48–51.

41 For a full discussion, cf. MEYER 2017: 332–336.

42 The percentage of Norman French speakers in Britain is unlikely to have exceeded ten percent of the populace; more conservative estimates suggest closer to one percent (BERNDT 1965: 147); no specific numbers for Parthians in Armenia are available, but since they constituted only a part of the ruling elite, they are unlikely to have made up a significant percentage of the populace. As for the loss of a powerbase, the fall of the Parthian Empire in 224 might be compared to the loss of Normandy in 1204.

43 The Parthian inscriptional evidence in general is very limited. Next to the Nisa ostraka, there are three letters from Avroman and one from Dura Europos, a number of inscriptions of Arsacid kings from the time of the Parthian Empire, and Arsacid coin legends (DURKIN-MEISTERERNST 2014: 4). The inscription of Artašēs I at Zangezur may be Parthian, but is written largely in Aramaic heterograms and belongs to an earlier dynasty, the Orontids (PÉRIKHANIAN 1966).

44 The date of original composition of these texts may, of course, be much earlier (DURKIN-MEISTERERNST 2014: 7–9).

45 There are significant differences of opinion on the subject of the demise of Parthian

The Armenian data suggests that the Arsacid rulers of Armenia were one of the first Parthian speech communities to switch to the locally dominant language as their primary means of communication. This is backed up not only by the linguistic and socio-historical material presented above, but also by the fact that all of the literature about the Arsacid dynasty in Armenia comes from sources in Armenian, not Parthian. While the absence of evidence is not evidence of absence, based on what is known at present it stands to reason that this first localised 'death' of Parthian in Arsacid Armenia is owed to the shift of Parthian-speakers to Armenian and the resulting demise of Parthian over the course of a few generations.

When this shift is likely to have commenced is a difficult question, as the data is insufficient to make such determinations. The establishment of a hereditary Arsacid dynasty in Armenia in the early third century, the Fall of the Arsacid Empire at the hand of the Sasanians in 224, and the Christianisation of Armenia at the end of that century make it a likely candidate for a *terminus a quo*; the invention of the Armenian alphabet and subsequent beginning of a literary tradition entail a plausible *terminus ante quem*. The resulting time period, from the middle of the third to the end of the fourth century, is certainly long enough for a superstrate shift like this to take place.[46]

7   Conclusions

This paper set out to advocate three points: the Iranian origin of the Armenian perfect; the transitory nature of its tripartite alignment pattern; and the super-

---

as a 'living' language, ranging from the end of the fourth century as a *terminus post quem non* (CHRISTENSEN 1930: 4–5; GHILAIN 1939: 28) to the seventh century (DURKIN-MEISTERERNST 2014: 3).

46   The Parthians of the generation in which this shift began were likely unbalanced bilinguals with Parthian as a dominant language. Their social status lent prestige to their idiolectal form of Armenian, sufficiently so to be adopted as the general language of court. The next generation are initially brought up with Parthian as their heritage language, and come into contact with Armenian either in the context of residing with their *dayeak* (tutor), acquiring the Partho-Armenian idiolect of their parents, or both. This, or a subsequent generation, in their lifetime would have shifted to Armenian entirely, speaking either the idiolect of generation 1, or their own Parthian-influenced version of Armenian. Their usage—including the use of Parthian patterns such as the periphrastic perfect—is in time adopted by native Armenian speakers of the ruling classes as well, and crystallises as the Classical Armenian used in fifth-century literature (MEYER 2017: 328–329). This is, by necessity, only a hypothetical and speculative account, but seems to fit the data best.

strate shift of Parthians to Armenian. An attempt has been made to show that the explanations proffered here are a cogent account not only of the development of the periphrastic perfect itself, but also of the Armenian socio-linguistic situation in and before the fifth century CE; one caveat, frequently implied in the above description and analysis, bears repeating here *expressis verbis*: much of the linguistic and extra-linguistic evidence concerning pre-literary Armenian and ancient socio-linguistics in general is based on indirect, circumstantial, or external evidence and inferences; since the linguistic evidence remaining from this time period—synchronic as well as diachronic—is imperfect, so any understanding of the data cannot be more than an approximation of the truth.

That being said, all of the arguments brought forward here have good evidentiary support: the conclusions drawn concerning the contact-based origin of the perfect have contemporary parallels in other constructions gained through pattern replication; the delineation of the development of the perfect itself is backed by statistics; and the explanation of the Parthian superstrate shift has historical parallels in similarly constituted historical linguistic communities. Further corroboration, mitigation, or refutation of these points will have to be found in the course of further research. The study of perfect syntax in sixth- and seventh-century texts will indicate whether the trends evident in the fifth century continue at pace. Comparisons of Armenian and Middle Iranian syntax will unearth whether other structural similarities may be due to language contact between the two languages. Potential archaeological finds of Parthian documents from the first half of the first millennium CE could indicate that Parthian had not died a 'localised death' as mooted here.

Until such time, however, the conclusions presented here may stand, and Iranian–Armenian language contact must be seen in a new light, namely as even closer than thought until a few years ago. The reasoning presented here also emphasises, once more, that only the consideration of both linguistic and extra-linguistic data can yield anything resembling the full picture of historical socio-linguistics, and that, furthermore, extra-linguistic data can have a meaningful impact on the diachronic reconstruction of a syntactic pattern.

Acknowledgements

Versions of this paper were presented at two conferences, *Variation and Contact in the ancient Indo-European Languages* (Oxford, May 2018) and the *8th International Conference on Iranian Linguistics* (Yerevan, October 2018). I am grateful to James Clackson, Theo Maarten van Lint, Wolfgang de Melo, and Elizabeth

Tucker for their constructive comments and suggestions on this topic, and equally to the anonymous reviewers for their constructive criticism; all errors of fact or omission are, of course, mine.

Abbreviations and Transliteration

Abbreviations in glossing follow the Leipzig Glossing Rules; Armenian is transliterated according to the Hübschmann-Meillet-Benveniste system as used by the *Revue des Études Arméniennes*.

Ag. Agat'angełos, History of Armenia THOMSON (1980)
Eł. Ełišē, *The History of Vardan and the Armenian War* THOMSON (1993)
Kor. Koriwn, Life of Maštoc' MAKSOUDIAN (1985)
ŁP Łazar P'arpec'i, *History of the Armenians* KOUYMJIAN (1985)
PB P'awstos Buzand, *The Epic Histories* GARSOÏAN (1984)

References

AJELLO, ROBERTO 1973, *Sulla "frase relativa nominale" e su alcuni procedimenti formali di unione di determinato e determinante in armeno classico*, "Studi e saggi linguistici", 13: 141–184.

AJELLO, ROBERTO 1997, *Armeno*, in A. Giacalone Ramat—P. Ramat (eds.), *Le lingue indoeuropee*, Il Mulino: Bologna: 225–254.

BELARDI, WALTER 2003, *Elementi di armeno aureo*, Rome: Il Calamo.

BENVENISTE, ÉMILE 1957, *Mots d'emprunt iraniens en arménien*, "Bulletin de la Société Linguistique de Paris" 53: 55–71.

BENVENISTE, ÉMILE 1964, *Elements parthes en arménien*, "Revue des Études Arméniennes" 1: 1–39.

BERNDT, ROLF 1965, *The linguistic situation in England from the Norman conquest to the loss of Normandy*, "Philologica Pragensia" 8: 145–163.

BOLOGNESI, GIANCARLO 1960, *Le fonti dialettali degli imprestiti iranici in armeno*, Milan: Società Editrice Vita e Pensiero.

BOLOGNESI, GIANCARLO 1988, *La stratificazione del lessico armeno nell'opera di J.J. Schröder*, in J. Albrecht—H. Thun—J. Lüdtke (eds.), *Energeia und Ergon: sprachliche Variation, Sprachgeschichte, Sprachtypologie. Studia in honorem Eugenio Coseriu*, Narr: Tübingen: 561–571.

BOYCE, MARY 1979, *Zoroastrians: Their Religious Beliefs and Practices*, London/Boston: Routledge/Kegan Paul.

CHRISTENSEN, ARTHUR 1930, *Contributions à la dialectologie iranienne*, Copenhagen: Bianco Lunos.

COMRIE, BERNARD 1978, *Ergativity*, in W.P. Lehmann (ed.), *Syntactic typology: studies in the phenomenology of language*, Austin/London: University of Texas Press: 329–394.

DEETERS, GERHARD 1927, *Armenisch und Südkaukasisch: ein Beitrag zur Frage der Sprachmischung*, Leipzig: Verlag der Asia Major.

DIXON, ROBERT M.W. 1994, *Ergativity*, Cambridge: Cambridge University Press.

DURKIN-MEISTERERNST, DESMOND 2014, *Grammatik des Westmitteliranischen (Parthisch und Mittelpersisch)*, Vienna: Verlag der Österreichischen Akademie der Wissenschaften.

GARSOÏAN, NINA G. 1976, *Prolegomena to a study of the Iranian aspects in Arsacid Armenia*, "Handes Amsorya" 90: 177–234.

GARSOÏAN, NINA G. (ed.) 1984, *Buzandaran patmut'iwnk'= (The epic histories): also known as, Patmut'iwn Hayoc' (History of Armenia)*, Delmar (NY): Caravan Books.

GARSOÏAN, NINA G. 1989, *The Epic Histories (Buzandaran Patmut'iwnk')*, Cambridge (MA): Harvard University Press.

GARSOÏAN, NINA G. 1997a, *The Emergence of Armenia*, in R.G. Hovannisian (ed.), *The Armenian People from Ancient to Modern Times, vol. 1: The Dynastic Periods, from Antiquity to the Fourteenth Century*, New York: St Martin's Press: 37–62.

GARSOÏAN, NINA G. 1997b, *The Aršakuni Dynasty (A.D. 12–[180?]–428)*, in R.G. Hovannisian (ed.), *The Armenian People from Ancient to Modern Times, vol. 1: The Dynastic Periods, from Antiquity to the Fourteenth Century*, New York: St Martin's Press: 63–94.

GHILAIN, ANTOINE 1939, *Essai sur la langue Parthe, son systeme verbal d'après les textes manichéens du Turkestan Oriental*, Leuven: Bureaux du Muséon.

GIPPERT, JOST 2005, *Armeno-albanica*, in G. Schweiger (ed.), *Indogermanica: Festschrift Gert Klingenschmitt. Indische, iranische und indogermanische Studien. Dem verehrten Jubilar dargebracht zu seinem fünfundsechzigsten Geburtstag*, Taimering: VWT-Verlag: 155–165.

GIPPERT, JOST 2009, *An etymological trifle*, in W. Sundermann—A. Hintze—F. de Blois (eds.), *Exegisti monumenta. Festschrift in Honour of Nicholas Sims-Williams*, Wiesbaden: Harrassowitz: 127–140.

HEINE, BERNDT 2012, *On polysemy copying and grammaticalization in language contact*, in C. Chamoreau—I. Léglise (eds.), *Dynamics of Contact-Induced Language Change*, Berlin: De Gruyter Mouton: 125–166.

HEINE, BERNDT—KUTEVA, TANIA 2005, *Language Contact and Grammatical Change*, Cambridge: Cambridge University Press.

HEINE, B.—KUTEVA, TANIA 2007, *The genesis of grammar*, Oxford: Oxford University Press.

HOPPER, PAUL J.—TRAUGOTT, ELIZABETH C. 2003, *Grammaticalization*, Cambridge: Cambridge University Press.

HÜBSCHMANN, HEINRICH 1875, *Ueber die stellung des armenischen im kreise der indogermanischen sprachen*, "Zeitschrift für vergleichende Sprachforschung auf dem Gebiete der Indogermanischen Sprachen" 23/1: 5–49.

HÜBSCHMANN, HEINRICH 1897, *Armenische Grammatik. 1. Theil: Armenische Etymologie*, Leipzig: Breitkopf & Härtel.

KORN, AGNES 2016, *A partial tree of Central Iranian*, "Indogermanische Forschungen" 121: 401–434.

KORN, AGNES—OLSEN, BIRGIT A. 2012, *On Armenian -agin: additional evidence for a third West Middle Iranian dialect?*, "Münchener Studien zur Sprachwissenschaft" 66/2: 201–220.

KOUYMJIAN, DICKRAN (ed.) 1985, *History of the Armenians and The Letter to Vahan Mamikonean*, Delmar, NY: Caravan Books.

MAKSOUDIAN, KRIKOR H. (ed.) 1985, *Varkʻ Maštocʻi*, Delmar, NY: Caravan Books.

MATRAS, YARON—SAKEL, JEANETTE 2007, *Investigating the mechanisms of pattern replication in language convergence*, "Studies in Language" 31/4: 829–865.

MEILLET, ANTOINE 1899, *Recherches sur la syntaxe comparée de l'arménien I*, "Mémoires de la Société Linguistique de Paris" 11/6: 369–388.

MEILLET, ANTOINE 1911, *Sur les mots iraniens empruntés par l'arménien*, "Melanges de la Sociéte Linguistique de Paris" 17: 250–252.

MEILLET, ANTOINE 1936, *Esquisse d'une grammaire comparée de l'arménien classique*, 2. éd, Vienna: Impr. des Pp. Mékhitharistes.

MEYER, ROBIN 2013, *Armeno-Iranian Structural Interaction: The Case of Parthian wxd, Armenian inkʻnʻ*, "Iran and the Caucasus" 17/4: 401–425.

MEYER, ROBIN 2014, *Remodelling the Historical Morphology of the Classical Armenian -eal participle*, "Banber Matenadarani" 21: 385–398.

MEYER, ROBIN 2016, *Morphosyntactic Alignment and the Classical Armenian Periphrastic Perfect*, in S.W. Jamison—H.C. Melchert—B. Vine (eds.), *Proceedings of the 26th Annual UCLA Indo-European Conference: Los Angeles, October 24th and 25th, 2014*, Bremen: Hempen: 117–133.

MEYER, ROBIN 2017, *Iranian-Armenian language contact in and before the 5th century CE. An investigation into pattern replication and societal multilingualism*, DPhil Thesis, University of Oxford.

MEYER, ROBIN (n.d.), *Languages in Contact: Armenian and Iranian*, in A. Orengo—I. Tinti (eds.), *Armenian Linguistics*, Handbuch der Orientalistik, Vol. 23, Leiden: Brill.

MYERS-SCOTTON, CAROL 2002, *Contact Linguistics: Bilingual Encounters and Grammatical Outcomes*, Oxford: Oxford University Press.

OLSEN, BIRGIT A. 2005, *On Iranian dialectal diversity in Armenian*, in O. Hackstein—

G. Meiser (eds.), *Sprachkontakt und Sprachwandel: Akten der XI. Fachtagung der Indogermanischen Gesellschaft, 17.–23. September 2000, Halle an der Saale*, Wiesbaden: Reichert: 473–481.

PAYNE, JOHN R. 1979, *Transitivity and Intransitivity in the Iranian Languages of the U.S.S.R.*, in P.R. Clyne—W.F. Hanks—C.L. Hofbauer (eds.), *The Elements: A Parasession on Linguistic Units and Levels, April 20–21, 1979, including Papers from the Conference on Non-Slavic Languages of the USSR, April 18, 1979*, Chicago: Linguistic Society: 436–447.

PAYNE, JOHN R. 1980, *The Decay of Ergativity in Pamir Languages*, "Lingua" 51: 147–186.

PÉRIKHANIAN, ANAHIT 1966, *Une inscription araméenne du roi Artašēs trouvée à Zanguézour (Siwnikʿ)*, "Revue des Études Arméniennes" 3: 17–29.

PIREJKO, LILJA A. 1966, *Талышский Язык*, in V.V. Vinogradov (ed.), *Языки Народов СССР. Индоевропейские языки*, Москва: Институт Языкознания / Академия Наук СССР: 302–322.

SCHMITT, RÜDIGER 1983, *Iranisches Lehngut im Armenischen*, "Revue des Études Arméniennes" 17: 73–112.

SCHRÖDER, JOHANN J. 1711, *Aramean lezuin gandzi, Hoc est: Joh. Joachimi Schröderi Thesaurus Linguae Armenicae, Antiquae Et Hodiernae: Cum varia Praxios materia, cujus elenchum sequens pagella exhibet*, Amsterdam.

SKALMOWSKI, WOJCIECH 1974, *Transitive verb constructions in the Pamir and Dardic languages*, in J. Kuryłowicz—J. Safarewicz—W. Smoczyński (eds.), *Studia Indoeuropejskie*, Krakow: Polska Akademia Nauk, Zakład Narodowy im. Ossolińskich: 205–212.

SKJÆRVØ, PRODS O. 1983, *Case in inscriptional Middle Persian, inscriptional Parthian and the Pahlavi Psalter*, "Studia Iranica" 12/1: 69–94, 151–181.

SZEMERÉNYI, OSWALD 1966, *Iranica II*, "Die Sprache" 12: 190–226.

THOMASON, SARAH G. 2003, *Contact as a Source of Language Change*, in B.D. Joseph—R.D. Janda (eds.), *Handbook of Historical Linguistics*, Malden, MA: Blackwell: 687–712.

THOMASON, SARAH G. 2008, *Social and Linguistic Factors as Predictors of Contact-Induced Change*, "Journal of Language Contact" 2: 42–56.

THOMASON, SARAH G.,—KAUFMAN, TERENCE 1988, *Language Contact, Creolization, and Genetic Linguistics*, Berkeley/Los Angeles/Oxford: University of California Press.

THOMSON, ROBERT W. (ed.) 1980, *Patmutʿiwn Hayotsʿ*, Delmar, NY: Caravan Books.

THOMSON, ROBERT W. (ed.) 1993, *The history of Vardan and the Armenian war*, Delmar, NY: Caravan Books.

TOUMANOFF, CYRILLE 1969, *The Third-Century Armenian Arsacids: a Chronological and Genealogical Commentary*, "Revue des Études Arméniennes" 6: 233–281.

TOUMANOFF, CYRILLE 1976, *Manuel de généalogie et de chronologie pour l'histoire de la Caucasie chrétienne*, Rome: Edizioni Aquila.

CHAPTER 9

Rewriting the Law: Diachronic Variation and Register in Greek and Hittite Legal Language

Katharine Shields

1   Introduction*

Ancient Greek legal inscriptions and the Hittite Laws are both texts that were repeatedly modified and rewritten. Amendments and additions are often explicitly signposted and the texts situate themselves as part of a legal tradition: even the earliest versions of the Hittite Laws state that the punishment was formerly (*kāru*) something else, but has now been changed and—often—reduced. A late version of the text, KBo 6.4, also known as the 'Parallel Text' contains additional provisions not present in the earlier versions. Greek legal inscriptions also have amendments and additional provisions added after the initial composition, including the Gortyn Code, itself already a compilation and re-inscription of earlier laws.[1] Elsewhere, legal texts are republished by decree, such Drakon's law on homicide (IG I³ 104), originating from the late C7th,[2] which was reinscribed in 409/8.

The (re)writing and amendment of these texts provides useful material for investigating the diachronic development of register, i.e. "situationally defined varieties"[3] of a language. The language used in legal texts is generally considered to be hyper-conservative: it has repeatedly been shown that in English legal language changes advance slowly, and there is little variation among the texts.[4] Since later Hittite scribes sometimes modernised the language of Old Hittite (OH) texts they copied,[5] and "*as a rule* the Greeks took no care to repro-

---

*   I would like to thank Michele Bianconi, Stephen Colvin, Mark Weeden and the anonymous reviewers for their helpful comments.

1   GAGARIN 1982: 130; GAGARIN—PERLMAN 2016: 336.

2   STROUD 1968: 65–70.

3   BIBER 1995: 1.

4   "Some registers (e.g. legal documents) have well defined norms so that there is relatively little variation among the texts within the register" BIBER 1995: 31; "Changes in legal language are slow to take effect, the genre being one of the most conservative of all varieties of language use." HILTUNEN 1990: 60.

5   On the Laws, Hoffner notes: "Some post-OS manuscripts appear to have closely emulated the

REWRITING THE LAW 235

duce the precise form of an original document"[6] the 'updated' orthography, morphology and syntax in these copies can provide valuable evidence for language change, and the selective preservation of more archaic features can be interrogated for indications of what the ancient copyists might have thought was language belonging to a particular genre.

Although both the Greek and Hittite texts discussed in this chapter can be described as 'legal', they come from very different contexts, and consequently there are some significant differences in the characteristics which are usually used to define registers,[7] such as the relationship between addressor and addressee, and the setting and the purpose of the text: the Greek texts are public inscriptions, and even if the entire population would not have been able to read them, they were available and visible in public places to a much larger number of people than the Hittite texts, which were written on clay tablets and stored in official archives. While these inscribed laws were a part of the legal system in Ancient Greece, there is no evidence that the Hittite Laws were used in the same way—perhaps they rather belong to a genre of scholarly texts belonging to the Mesopotamian intellectual tradition of collecting information in lists, along with omens, oracles and astronomical observations.[8] Nonetheless, they share many similarities in content, as well as both being written texts.

In this paper I will discuss two features associated with the revision and replication of legal texts: the use of clause connecting enclitic particles with the conjunctions *takku* and *mān* in the Hittite Laws, and asyndeton in Greek inscriptions.

2 *takku*, *mān* and Clause Connecting Enclitic Particles in the 'Parallel Text' of the Hittite Laws

The *Hittite Laws* (henceforth Laws) is a text which appears in copies on tablets from the whole period of attested Hittite (approximately C16th–C13th BCE). The original author of the text is not known, although modern scholars have attributed it to various early Hittite kings.[9] The copies were written by trained

---

spelling habits of their (hyp)archetypes. while others seem to have been more ready to replace older spellings with those current in their time." 1997: 230.

6　ROBERTSON 1976: 9, emphasis mine. Inscriptions survive "in rival versions which are plainly indifferent to verbal accuracy". ibid.

7　See for example BIBER 1994: 40–41.

8　GUINAN 2014; ZORMAN 2017.

9　Hattušili I, or Muršili I: CARRUBA 1962. Telipinu: ARCHI 1968, GOETZE 1928, GÜTERBOCK 1954.

scribes, and the tablets were found in the context of official archives. There are two 'series' of the Laws, 'If a man' and 'If a vine'.[10] Fragments of at least twenty copies of each series survive, the majority from the New Hittite (NH) period. A handful of Old Script (OS) copies (most importantly KBo 6.2++ for the first series, KUB 29.25++ for the second) show that the content of the text largely remained stable, with the exception of the 'Parallel Text' (henceforth PT) version (KBo 6.4). This NH version of the text has been significantly rewritten: new conditions have been added and others have been modified or removed, the order of the paragraphs has been changed, and the formulas *karū ... kinun=a ...* ('formerly ... but now ...') and *karū kiššan ēššer* ('formerly they used to act in this way'), frequent in the main version of the Laws, never appears in the PT. The PT is also the only copy of the Laws where the name of the scribe (*ᵐḪanikkuili*) survives in the colophon. This scribe is known from the colophons of three other tablets, all ritual compositions.

Although the content of the Laws largely remains stable, there are nonetheless differences between the earlier and later copies reflecting several hundred years of linguistic change. Many features showing an 'updated' form of the language are found in the PT, including the replacement of $\langle iC \rangle$ with $\langle eC \rangle$ such as in the verb *ēšša-/išša-*,[11] and the replacement of transitive medio-passive forms with active ones.[12] But alongside these 'modernised' forms, many archaic features no longer found in original NH compositions are still present in later copies of Old Hittite compositions. One of the most noticeably archaic features of the Laws is the use of the conditional conjunction *takku*, which appears at the start of most paragraphs. The majority of the laws follow an 'if ... then ...' arrangement: the most common structure has the present tense in both the protasis and the apodosis, and the apodosis is usually asyndetic, with the typical structure being something like *takku ... (kuiški)* 3sg. pres., Ø ... 3sg pres., as in the following example:[13]

---

10   The titles are known from the colophons of KBo 6.6 and KUB 13.11 (*ták-ku* LÚ-*aš*) and KBo 6.13 (*ták-ku* ᴳᴵˢGEŠTIN-*aš*).

11   §XXX iii.18 *e-eš-ša-i*, but *i-iš-ša-i* in the OS version (KBo 6.2 ii.20), and *iš-š[a-i* in a NH copy (KBo 6.3 ii.39). Again in PT §XXXI iii.26 *e-eš-ša-[i, i-iš-ša-i* in the OS version (KBo 6.2 ii.25), and *iš-ša-i* and *e-eš-ša-i* in NH copies (KBo 6.3 ii.46, KBo 6.5 iv.4). See HOFFNER 1997: 239 ff. for a list of differences in orthography between the OS and post-OS manuscripts.

12   KBo 6.3 i.37 and KBo 6.5 i.16 *iš-kal-la-a-ri* (NH copies, no OS version survives), but *iš-gal-la-i* in §XIV i.37.

13   Hittite text and paragraph numbers follow HOFFNER 1997.

REWRITING THE LAW 237

⸢ták⸣-ku LÚ.U₁₉.LU-an EL-LAM ⸢KIR₁₄⸣-še-et ku-iš-ki wa-a-ki 1 MA.NA
KÙ.BABBAR pa-a-i

'If anyone bites off a free person's nose, (s)he will pay 1 mina of silver'
> KBo 6.3 i.33, NS

3   *takku* and *mān*

Two conditional conjunctions (meaning 'if') are found in the Laws, *takku*, and
mān. *takku* is the older form, elsewhere found almost exclusively in OH texts,
and it is always clause initial. *mān* in Old Hittite has a temporal meaning,
'when',[14] but it also develops a conditional function. As *takku* drops out of use
in post-Old Hittite, *mān* becomes the primary conditional conjunction, while
maḫḫan takes over the temporal function.[15] It is remarkable that even in the
latest versions of the Laws, *takku* continues to be used at the start of each
paragraph almost without exception, and this has already been highlighted
as a feature of the language of the laws by Sternemann: "Die Einleitung der
Gesetzparagraphen durch *takku*... war anscheinend so typisch, daß es bis in
die jüngste Fassung (KBo VI 4) hinein tradiert wurde."[16] *takku* is overall about
ten times more frequent than *mān* across all copies of the text.

The most obvious difference between the use of *takku* and *mān* is that—
with one possible exception—*mān* is used only to add additional conditions,
not at the start of a law paragraph: this is true even in the PT. The one apparent
exception occurs in § 64:[17]

> 1. *ma-a-an* ANŠE.KUR.RA *tu-u-ri-ia-u-wa⟨-aš⟩ ku-iš-ki*
> 2. *ta-a-i-ia-zi ut-tar-še-et QA-TAM-MA-[pát]*

'If anyone steals a harnessed horse, the matter is the same.'
> KBo 6.8 ii.1–2, NS

---

14   For other functions of OH *mān* when not clause-initial, CHD s. v. *mān* 1–4.

15   HOFFNER—MELCHERT 2008: 416–417. *maḫḫan* found in NS copies only always has the
meaning 'like, as'.

16   "Die Einleitung der Gesetzesparagraphen durch *takku* wurde als stilistisch wichtig
empfunden, so daß sich *takku* hier bis in die jüngsten Abschriften halten konnte, während
im Paragraphinneren bereits in alter Sprache ein teilweiser Ersatz durch *mān* zu beo-
bachten ist." STERNEMANN 1965a: 262. See also TISCHLER 1991 *takku* s. v.

17   Two other copies of this law, where it does not begin a new column, use *takku*: KBo 6.2
iii.43 (OS), KBo 6.3 iii.48 (NS).

238 SHIELDS

This law refers back to the compensation set out for stealing a plow ox in the previous paragraph (§ 63), and begins a new column of the tablet. The apparently exceptional use of *mān* rather than *takku* here is at least partly explainable if we imagine that the scribe might have considered it to be an additional condition to the previous law, running over onto a new column but not beginning a new paragraph.[18]

takku is also used to introduce additional conditions within the main body of a law in all manuscripts. These additional conditions may provide further information about the crime or situation that is the subject of the law, or further consequences for not abiding by the penalty set out, as in the following examples:

> 27. *ták-ku* LÚ.U₁₉.LU-*an ku-iš-ki ku-uš-ša-ni-ez-zi na-aš la-⌈aḫ-ḫa pa-iz-zi⌉ n[a-aš a-ki]*
> 28. **ták-ku** *ku-uš-ša-an pí-ia-a-an šar-ni-ik-zi-il* [NU.GÁL]
> 29. **ták-ku** *ku-uš-ša-na na-at-ta pí-ia-a-an* 1 SAG.DU [*pa-a-i*]

'If anyone hires a person, and he (the person) goes on a military campaign and he dies, **if** the hire has been paid, there will be no compensation, **but if** the hire has not been paid, he (the hirer) will give one slave.'[19]

> KBo 6.2 ii.27–29, OS

> 19. *ták-ku* ŠAḪ *še-e-li-ia na-aš-ma* A.ŠÀ-*ni* ᴳᴵˢKIRI₆-*ni pa-i*[*z-zi ta še*]-⌈*e-li*⌉-*ia-aš*
> 20. *iš-ḫa-a-aš* A.ŠÀ-*na-aš* ᴳᴵˢKIRI₆-*aš wa-al-aḫ-zi na-aš a-ki na-an iš-ḫi-iš-ši*
> 21. EGIR-*pa pa-a-i* **ták-ku**-*an* Ú-UL-**ma** *pa-a-i na-aš* ᴸᵁNÍ.ZU-*aš ki-i-ša*

---

18 § 27 KBo 6.3 i.75–ii.1 and § 28 KBo 6.5 ii.1–iii.5 begin a new column without starting a new law paragraph. There are also several other examples of the paragraph divisions varying between manuscripts, e.g. § 126, § 182. On the photographs of KBo 6.8, it seems that there is no space for a gap to be left at the end of the last line—*šu-wa-a-ez-zi* (or *šu-ú-wa-a-iz-zi*, etc.)—would take up all the space left in the break—to suggest that the scribe definitely intended a new paragraph at the start of the next column. KITAZUMI 2019 argues that the use of paragraph dividers is pragmatic and dependent on choices of individual scribes, with further examples of variation in the use of divisions across copies of the same text.

19 *takku* is also used for additional conditions in the NS versions of this law in KBo 6.3+ and KBo 6.5, which both also add financial compensation.

REWRITING THE LAW

'If a pig enters a grain heap,[20] a field or a garden, (and) the owner of the grain heap, field or garden strikes it, and it dies, he will give it back to its owner. **But if** he does not give it (back), he will be considered a thief.'

KBo 6.3 iv.19–21, NS

Less commonly, *mān* is also used for additional conditions providing additional information about the situation or the penalty. The following table shows conditional uses of *mān* in post-OH copies of the first series of the Laws, excluding the Parallel Text.

In place of *takku* in OS version	§ 40 KBo 6.3 ii.41
	§ 41 KBo 6.3 ii.46, KBo 6.5 iv.5
	§ 64 KBo 6.8+ ii.1[21]
In place of *našma* 'or if' in OS version	§ 5 KBo 6.3 i.12
mān already in OS version	§ 53 KBo 6.6+ i.13, KBo 6.6+ i.17, KBo 6.8+ obv.2, KBo 6.8+ obv.6
	§ 71 KBo 6.3 iii.65
No OS version survives	§ 27 KUB 26.56 ii.9
	§ 171 KBo 6.13 i.14, KBo 6.26 ii.4
	§ 193[22] KBo 6.26 iii.42, KUB 29.34 iv.20

mān replaces *takku* from the OS version relatively rarely, and not consistently— in § 40 and 41, *takku* is retained in one New Script (NS) copy,[23] even though the other NS copies use *mān*. This is also true for the PT, although *mān* is much more common in the PT than the previous versions (about half of the examples are in this copy alone).[24] *mān* in the OS version is never replaced by *takku* in a NS copy. The following table shows *takku* and *mān* introducing additional conditions in the Parallel Text.

---

20 Or 'harvest, harvested goods'. CHD Š3.

21 See discussion in the previous section.

22 HOFFNER 1997: 152 restores *ma-a-an* in the OH version (KUB 29.25+) presumably on the basis of the NH copies.

23 KUB 29.14+ iii.11/8, iii.14.

24 14× in the PT, as opposed to 4× in KBo 6.2 (OS), 4× in KBo 6.3+, 3× in KBo 6.8+, 2× KBo 6.6+ and KBo 6.26, 1× KBo 6.5, KUB 26.56, KBo 6.13, KUB 29.34 (all NS).

	takku	*mān*[25]
takku in main version (OS or NS)	3	1
	§ XXXVIII iv.21, iv.22, iv.25	§ XXX iii.20
	§ XXXIX iv.33	
mān in main version (OS or NS)	-	1
		§ XLI iv.43[26]
New condition not found in main version	9	11
	§ III i.7	§ VII i.18
	§ IV i.9, i.10, i.13	§ X i.28, i.29
	§ V i.15	§ XI i.31
	§ VI i.17	§ XXXIV iv.1
	§ VII i.19	§ XXXV iv.6, iv.9[27]
	§ IX i.26	§ XXXVI iv.13
	§ XI i.32	§ XXXVII iv.18, iv.20
		§ XXXIX iv.29
Incorporating two separate laws (introduced by *takku*) in main version	2	-
	§ II i.3	
	§ XXXIX iv.30	

mān is in fact slightly more common than *takku* for introducing conditions for which there is no precedent (9 examples vs 11), and both can even be found in the same law paragraph (§ XI); but where there is a previous version with *takku*, PT is more likely to continue to use the older form, with *mān* only replacing *takku* once. It is not surprising that the older form is used when the text is clearly based on the main version, but it is remarkable that it is also used frequently when there is no precedent in the main version.[28] That *takku* continues to be used relatively frequently even where the content is original might suggest some sort of "conscious archaizing"[29] on the part of the NH author, who

---

25   There is one more probable attestation of conditional *mān*—KBo 6.4 iii.29—but the context is too broken to include it here.

26   KBo 6.2 ii.54 (OH) *ma-a-am*[-*ma-an*], KBo 6.4 iv.43 (NS) ⌜*ma*⌝-*a*[*m-ma-an*...], *mān=man*, conditional conjunction and potential particle. PT breaks away here.

27   The content of this appears to be derived from both § 45 and § 71, although none of the conditions occur exactly as they do in either of the source laws.

28   CARRUBA—SOUČEK—STERNEMANN 1965: 5; STERNEMANN 1965a: 262, *contra* HOFFNER 1997: 19 n. 16.

29   HOFFNER—MELCHERT 2008: 404.

REWRITING THE LAW   241

is not only imitating the structure and content of the model text, but also its most unusual linguistic features.

4   Clause-Linking Enclitics

The enclitics *-a/-ma* and *-a/-ya* unsurprisingly never occur with *takku* when it is law initial, since they indicate either contrast/change of topic (*-a/-ma*) or parallel (*-a/-ya*) with the previous clause or a constituent in the previous clause, and each law begins a new separate discourse unit.[30] The distribution of these enclitics in clauses expressing additional conditions should nonetheless be investigated, since their position following subordinating conjunctions changes over time: in OH they are attached not to *mān* or *takku* but to the second accented word in a clause, although enclitic pronouns and local particles can be attached directly.[31] In NH, when *takku* has fallen out of use, *mān=ma* instead becomes the regular word order,[32] with the exception of *mān ŪL=ma*, 'but if not', "a fixed idiom" regularly used instead of spelling out a negative condition.[33] The following table shows all the examples of *takku* or *mān* followed by *-a/-ma* or *-a/-ya* or with the particle *nu-* in the PT.

	takku
§II i.3	[*ta*]*kku* MUNUS-*za=ma*
§III i.7	*takku kešširaš=ma*
§IV i.10	*takku* MUNUS-*za=ma*
§IV i.11	*takku ŪL=ma*
§IX i.26	*takku* ARAD-*iš=ma*
§XI i.32	*takku=aš ŪL=ma*

---

30   STERNEMANN 1965b: 399. For the topicalising function of *-a/-ma*, see RIEKEN 2000 and MELCHERT 2009. In the following examples with *mān* in the PT, the scope of *-a/-ma* and *-a/-ya* is the whole clause. In i.10 and i.26 with *takku* it is likely that *=ma* only has scope over the word it is attached to (the contrast is between MUNUS or ARAD-*iš* and LÚ(-*aš*) in i.9 and i.22), but no fronting is possible since *takku* must be in clause initial position.

31   CHD L-N 97 s. v. *-ma* f 2′ a′ 1″; STERNEMANN 1965b: 398; HOFFNER—MELCHERT 2008: 395–396, 400.

32   HOFFNER—MELCHERT 2008: 396. KLOEKHORST 2011, following MELCHERT 1998, argues that *-ma* must be attached to the first stressed word in a clause and *takku* and *mān* were originally unstressed, although in NH *mān* gains stress.

33   CHD L-N 97 s. v. *mān* 7 h.

	mān[34]
§ X i.28	_n=aš mān_
§ X i.29	_mān=aš_ ŪL=_ma_
§ XI i.31	_n=aš mān_
§ XXXIV iv.1	_mān_ É-_ri=ia_
§ XXXV iv.6	_mān_ EN-⟪_iš_⟫=_šin=ma_
§ XXXV iv.9	_mān=za_ ŪL=_ma_
§ XXXVI iv.13	_mān=an=kan_ LUGAL-_uš=ma_
§ XXXVII iv.18	_mān_ EN A.ŠÀ A.GÀR=_ma_

In the PT, the enclitic conjunction continues to be postponed without exception, although by NH the word order _mān⹈ma_ is preferred. In other NS texts from OH models, where this word order would not have been permitted in the original, the enclitic conjunctions, if they are postponed, are not postponed with any consistency, whether _mān_ is used with a conditional or temporal meaning. An example is found in the Palace Building ritual (CTH 414.1): ***ma-a-an-ma*** LUGAL _an-da-an pár-na ú-iz-zi_.[35] Elsewhere this text contains a number of archaic features, including the use of _takku_ rather than _mān_ as a conditional conjunction. _mān⹈ma_ can also be found in texts belonging to genres that— much like the Laws—are considered to be linguistically conservative, and are heavily influenced by Akkadian models, such as oracles: ***ma-a-an-ma*** _ka-a-aš Ù-TUM Ú-UL_ ḪUL-_lu-uš_.[36]

Despite this, the enclitic is always postponed with both _mān_ and _takku_ in the PT—the NH order of constituents is never found with _takku_, and although _n=aš mān_ (which never occurs in the main version of the text) appears twice, the enclitic is never attached to _mān_, both in clauses expressing the 'new' additional conditions and those which already occur in previous versions. Perhaps the postponement of enclitic clause-coordinating conjunctions is a particular feature of Hittite legal language, the continued use of _takku_ influencing the constituent order used with _mān_, which elsewhere in the language has changed.

---

34 [_mān_] _āššu=ma_ i.6 § III not included. See also n. 25.

35 KUB 29.1 i.50 MOUTON 2016: 98. Here _mān_ has a temporal function.

36 CTH 570 Liver Oracle KUB 49.90.9 "Si ce rêve n'(était) pas mauvais" MOUTON 2007: 179.

REWRITING THE LAW 243

However, some examples of *mān* with a postponed enclitic conjunction can be found in NS copies of Middle Hittite (MH) instruction texts, such as the Instructions for Priests and Temple Personnel (CTH 264).[37] But even within the same paragraph this is extremely inconsistent: in §6 we find *mān=at ÚL=ma* (KUB 13.5 ii.7), *mān* LÚ*Ú-BA-RÙ=ma* (KUB 13.5 ii.11), and *mān=ma=aš* (KUB 13.5 ii.14, KUB 13.4 ii.1). The first example is an unsurprising example of the fixed idiom mentioned above, the second preserves the old word order, while in the third *-ma* is attached directly onto *mān* as expected in NH. Parts of this text have been compared to the Laws in both content and structure,[38] and it is possible that the scribe preserves more instances of this feature because it is appropriate to the content, although the variation throughout the text suggests that the association was not as nearly as strong as for the scribe of the PT.

Since the PT text can be ascribed to a particular scribe, ᵐ*Ḫanikkuili*, there is one additional question, the answer to which might suggest that he is deliberately choosing an archaic construction because it belongs to this genre: in other types of texts, which word order does he use? Three other texts naming him as the scribe in the colophon also survive, all rituals (VBoT 24, KBo 10.34, KBo 12.105++). Unfortunately, none of them contain any examples of a comparable construction with *mān* and a clause-linking enclitic.

What does not seem to be unusual for this particular scribe, moreover, is that he has written a significantly revised version of a traditional text: Gordin calls his work "uniquely creative".[39] But unlike all other versions of the Laws, the fact that it is a revised version is never made explicit within the text itself. The *karū ... kinun=a ...* and *karū kiššan ēššer* formulas, common in all other OS and NS versions of the Laws, never occur in the PT. If one takes the view that ᵐ*Ḫanikkuili* is aiming at originality and creativity, one might suggest that historical exemplars show conventionality, not creativity, and that the scribe here is simply not interested in the sort of traditional authority which is created by invoking an existing or previous legal tradition. It is extremely unlikely that this law collection was ever one that was used in practice:[40] one might take the rewritten version as an intellectual or scholarly exercise—by imitating well the

---

37   These instruction texts, however, are probably direct copies of older texts, so the patterns of archaisms vs innovations are likely to be different to texts based on older models but composed by NH scribes.

38   ALAURA 2016: 1.

39   GORDIN 2015: 182.

40   Although this does not necessarily mean that it did not reflect some of the real practices surrounding or was inconsistent with the principles of law enforcement.

244 SHIELDS

key features of the language of the previous versions of the text, ᵐḪanikkuili is demonstrating his thorough mastery of the genre.[41]

5 Asyndeton in Greek legal Inscriptions

Legal inscriptions in Greek begin in the late C7th BCE on Crete: by the end of the C5th they number in the hundreds across a huge geographical area and in many dialects. In this section, I will focus on two particular types of legal inscriptions: firstly, the laws from Crete, in particular Gortyn, until the end of the 5th century, and, secondly, legal texts republished by decree in the 5th and 4th centuries in Athens and Cyrene, which claim to be based on older material. The use of asyndeton shows that these republished laws did indeed contain older material.

Connective particles are extremely common in Greek and sentence-level asyndeton is unusual. Reference grammars usually say that asyndeton occurs when the connection is made clear by the context, or through use of an anaphoric pronoun or demonstrative adverb, or repetition of a significant word or phrase.[42] Denniston describes 'full asyndeton' ("at the colon or full stop, *between sentences*", as opposed to 'half asyndeton', "between words and clauses"),[43] and gives examples of its use with anaphoric or cataphoric pronouns, with repetition, "when a writer forecasts the nature of a statement which he is about to make", when describing circumstances and results, and as part of general rhetorical or narrative style, with examples mainly from orators.[44] Sicking's discussion of particles in Lysias 1 includes asyndeton and lists situations where asyndeton is found in this text: when resuming speech following an interruption and after quoting direct speech, following the introduction of a character with a demonstrative, and with οὕτως.[45]

---

41 "Imitation of archaic characteristics appears to be common in some compositions whose long-standing scholarly tradition was acknowledged by the scribes." GORDIN 2015: 336.

42 Some grammars also suggest a distinction between 'formal' and 'stylistic' asyndeton. The former is used to describe situations where the connection between sentences is indicated by other means, such as a demonstrative adverb or repetition of a word or phrase, the latter where asyndeton is used for emotional or rhetorical effect, such as in rapid speech. DENNISTON—DOVER 1954: xliii; SMYTH 1956: 484, although "grammatical asyndeton cannot always be separated from rhetorical asyndeton," and this distinction is not relevant for the arguments presented here. The CGCG is almost silent on asyndeton.

43 DENNISTON 1960: 99.

44 DENNISTON 1960: 99 ff.

45 OPHUIJSEN 1993: 41.

6 Crete

The Gortyn Code is the longest early Greek inscription, collecting together laws on a range of subjects. Gagarin argues that asyndeton in this inscription marks the beginning of a new provision, where what was previously inscribed as a separate law has been included in a larger text, and that asyndeton with a similar function can be found in other inscriptions from Gortyn.[46] Asyndeton is used as a structuring device to indicate a change of theme (e.g. VI.46, VII.15), specifying a different type of offence or different status of people involved (e.g. III.37 or VIII.30), or, once, to specify that a law does not apply retroactively (a switch from substantive to procedural law, V.1). It is also used to indicate where each amendment begins, often with a gap at the end of the previous line.[47]

In other early Cretan legal inscriptions, asyndeton can also have all these functions. In the 7th and 6th centuries, asyndeton is used to separate different provisions or a change in content within a law: the increase in the uses of asyndeton in the later period is a result of the increasing length and complexity of the laws, which requires more variation—the use of asyndeton for a new provision extends to the change between procedural and substantive law. The following table shows instances of asyndeton in legal inscriptions from Crete prior to 400 BCE.

	c. 650–600	c. 600–500	c. 500–450	c. 450–400
At the start of an inscription or after an enactment formula	SEG 27.631 A.1	IC IV 22.1	IC IV 43 Ba.1	IC IV 76 B.1
	SEG 27.620 1	IC IV 64	IC IV 43 Bb.1	IC IV 78.1
	SEG 23.530 1	IC II xii.16 Ab1	IC IV 43 Aa.1	IC IV 80.1
	BCH 70 600,4 1	IC II xii.16 Ac1	IC IV 43 Ab.1	
	BCH 70 590,2 1	IC I X.2 2	IC IV 47 A.1	
		SEG 41.739 1	SEG 35.991 A.1	
			SEG 35.991 B.1	
Indicating a change of content, including procedural to substantive, or vice versa	SEG 27.631 B.11	IC IV 14 g-p.1	IC IV 41 II.16	IC IV 46 6
		IC IV 21.2	IC IV 41 III.7	IC IV 75 C.3
		IC IV 21.3	IC IV 42.9	IC IV 76 B.8?
		IC IV 21.4	IC IV 53 B.3	IC IV 77 B.4
		IC II xii.11		IC IV 77 B.10
				IC IV 80.12

---

46 GAGARIN 1982.

47 The 'amendments' begin at X.33. GAGARIN—PERLMAN 2016: 413. It seems that each new amendment was started on a new line (with the exception of the amendment at XI.31, since only one letter from the previous amendment appears on that line), although this does not happen in the main body of the laws.

(*cont.*)

	c. 650–600	c. 600–500	c. 500–450	c. 450–400
Connection expressed through adverb, demonstrative etc.			IC IV 43 Ba.3 IC II v.9 11	
Connection expressed through repetition of significant word or phrase			IC IV 42.3	

In the rest of the laws from Crete, asyndeton is common at the start of an inscription, but also including after an enactment formula, and where several separate laws are inscribed on one stone. There is an example of asyndeton with a demonstrative in one of the later inscriptions:

> IC IV 43 Ba.1–7
> θιοί. τὰν ἐ[ν] Κησκόραι καὶ
> τὰν ἐμ Πάλαι πυταλιὰν ἔ⟦ε⟧-
> δοκαν ἁ πόλις πυτεῦσαι. α-
> ἴ τις ταύταν πρίαιτο ἢ κα-
> ταθε[ῖ]το, μὴ κατέκεθαι τô -
> ι πριαμένοι τὰ[ν ὀ]νάν...

> Gods. The polis have given the farmland at Keskora and Pala for growing. If someone buys or gives a mortgage on **it**, the purchase is not to be valid for the purchaser ...[48]

The connection with the previous section of text, which states that the polis has made certain areas of land available for growing, is made explicit through the use of the demonstrative pronoun, referring back to the area of land defined in the previous sentence. Similarly, IC II v.9 11 uses κατὰ τὰ αὐτὰ, 'in the same way', to create a link between the previous regulations about irregularities with payment for sacrifices and a different festival or group of priests (τοῖς Κυδαντεί-οις) who are also to be given payment for sacrifices.[49] As in the Gortyn Code, asyndeton can also be used to indicate a change of content in the law, including a change from substantive to procedural matters.[50] These examples cover

---

48   Trans. GAGARIN—PERLMAN 2016.

49   "The asyndeton in line 11 does suggest a new provision, but the expression *kata ta auta* 'in the same way' (11) ties the two together." GAGARIN—PERLMAN 2016: 171.

50   A switch between procedural and substantive content also occasionally happens without

REWRITING THE LAW

largely the same range of contexts where grammars generally say asyndeton is used, and consequently the use of asyndeton is not an aspect of a special legal register in inscriptions from Crete.

7   Athens and Cyrene

Elsewhere, legal documents are republished the 5th and 4th centuries to restate or reinforce their authority: either because, as in the case of the foundation document of Cyrene, such a long time has passed from the original enactment, or because a proliferation of inscriptions means it is no longer clear which laws are in force,[51] or because of political upheaval. This latter reason is particularly important for the Athenian documents reinscribed after the restoration of the democracy after the originals were undermined or even physically erased under two periods of oligarchic rule.[52] The authenticity of the sections of such inscriptions claiming to be older has often been doubted, and some of the language is probably not original.[53] The use of asyndeton suggests that the revised laws are indeed based on older texts.

The three inscriptions which will be discussed here are Drakon's law on homicide, the original supposedly 7th century, republished by decree in 409/8, the laws about the Council of 500 (IG I^3 105), republished in 409 and probably originating from the very late 6th or early 5th century, and the foundation document of Cyrene (*SEG* IX.3), republished in the 4th century, also supposedly originating from the 7th century.

	Drakon's homicide law, IG I^3 104, original C7th, republished 409/8.	Foundation document of Cyrene, *SEG* IX.3, original C7th?, republished C4th.	Laws about the Council of 500, IG I^3 105, republished 409.
At the start of an inscription or after an enactment formula	1, 2, 3, 3, 3, 4, 4	1, 2, 2, 11, 11, 23, 24	34
Indicating a change of content		20, 44, 46	42, 44
Connection expressed through adverb, demonstrative etc.		40	

---

asyndeton in the Gortyn Code, such as at 1.56. Asyndeton is only one of the strategies used to introduce a change in content in these inscriptions.

51   VOLONAKI 2001: 139.

52   WALBANK 1978: 8; VOLONAKI 2001: 138–141.

53   This has been argued especially for the foundation document of Cyrene. GRAHAM 1960; MEIGGS—LEWIS 1969: 7–9.

248 SHIELDS

Like the Cretan laws, asyndeton is used in and after an enactment formula, even when the enactment formula occurs part way through the inscription. Enactment formulas in Athens in the late 5th and early 4th century are generally much more extensive than those from Crete,[54] and do not contain clause-level connectives:

IG I³ 104, 1–4, Athens 409/8
Διόγν[ε]τος Φρεάρριος ἐγραμμάτε[υε]·
Διοκλῆς ἐρχε·
ἔδοχσεν τῆι βουλῆι καὶ τῶι δέμοι· Ἀκα[μ]αντὶς ἐπ[ρ]υτάνευε, [Δ]ιό[γ]-
νετος ἐγραμμάτευε, Εὐθύδικος [ἐ]πεστάτε, . . Ε . . . ΑΝΕΣ εἶπε·

Diogenes of Phrearrhii was the secretary; Diocles was the archon. Resolved by the council and the people. Acamantis was the prytany; Diognetus was the secretary; Euthydicus was the chairman; ... phanes proposed:[55]

IC IV 78, 1, Gortyn c. 450–400
θιοί. τάδ' ἔϝαδε τοῖς Γορτυνίοις πσαπίδονσ[ι]·

Gods. These things pleased the Gortynians voting.[56]

A comparison could be made between the asyndeton following an enactment formula and the asyndeton that Sicking identifies in Lysias marking the transition between narrative and reported direct speech and vice versa: the verb εἶπε is commonly the last word of the enactment formula at the start of the inscription. The form of the substantive part of a law or decree is often accusative + infinitive or nominative + imperative, and the choice of infinitive or imperative structure is influenced by semantic and pragmatic factors.[57] The accusative + infinitive construction is the usual form of indirect statements following verbs of speaking, including λέγω.[58] In both inscriptions and legal speeches, asyndeton functions to mark the shift between two different levels of text, that

---

54 Here I am including under 'enactment formula' what is sometimes otherwise called the 'prescript' (RHODES—LEWIS 1997: 5), e.g. information about the date and the name of the proposer.

55 Trans. OSBORNE—RHODES 2017.

56 Trans. GAGARIN—PERLMAN 2016.

57 RHODES—LEWIS 1997: 5; ELVIRA ASTORECA 2016.

58 Not all enactment formulas use εἶπε or indeed any verb of speaking.

REWRITING THE LAW 249

existing in the immediate situation of the speech or the inscription, and that repeating or reporting speech which existed in a prior (or hypothetical) setting.[59]

The further instances of asyndeton in the Cyrene foundation inscription can be explained similarly. In line 20, asyndeton marks a shift in types of procedural content from what should be engraved on the stone to who should pay for it. In line 44, the text moves from describing the content and implementation of the original agreement to the performance of the curse mentioned in the agreement, which took place prior to the original agreement being written into a decree.[60] In line 46, the oath itself begins: although it is not introduced by a form of λέγω etc., it seems to be reproducing the form of the oath spoken by those performing it. Here the asyndeton marks a shift in the temporal frame of the of the text, and from narrative to reproduced speech.

In IG I³ 105, the same sequence as in 42, ἄνευ τὸ δέμο τὸ Ἀθεναίον πλεθύοντος 'without the Athenian people assembled en masse', can also almost certainly be restored with asyndeton in 34–35, 36, 37, and 40–41.[61] Ryan claims "that [these] were copied verbatim from another document cannot be doubted",[62] since in line 43 damage from the original seems to have been copied, rather than τοι being reinserted where it is clearly required.[63] Although these regulations concern one general topic, restrictions on the powers of the Council of 500, there is only the repeated sequence ἄνευ τὸ δέμο τὸ Ἀθεναίον πλεθύοντος making the connection between the individual regulations explicit.[64] If in the C6th–5th Athenian laws—from which the material for the re-inscription

---

59   JONES 1975: 112–114 on the text of Athenian decrees being proposed in speech.
60   Whether the text of this section is original or authentic or not does not particularly matter for the chronology of events referred to within it. Edition of this inscription from DOBIAS-LALOU 2017. The shifts between different types of content here have long been noted: "… such an abrupt transition … no indication of a change of type of content within the one general heading." MEIGGS—LEWIS 1969: 8.
61   It is possible that the same sequence also appears in 45–46 without the preposition.
62   RYAN 1994: 122.
63   The use of other archaic features such as the letter *h* and the enactment formula in line 32 show that this text was not entirely updated. See similarly the use of *h* in only the rein-scribed section of IG I³ 104.
64   Similar sequences are found occasionally in other Attic inscriptions as part of individual provisions within inscriptions:
      IG I³ 14 28–29
      [ο]ὐδὲ τὸν μενόντον ἐχσελõ [ἄ]ν[ευ] τῆς β[ο]-
      [λῆς] τῆς Ἀθεναίον καὶ [τõ] δέμο·
      … nor will I exile those who remain **without the Athenian council and the people.**
      However, in these inscriptions the sequence is never repeated more than twice, and never introduces a new sentence with asyndeton. Rather, it usually appears following the

250   SHIELDS

must originate—asyndeton is used at the start of an inscription or in or after an enactment formula,[65] then this supports the suggestion that these were all originally separately enacted provisions,[66] similar to some of the examples of laws collected in inscriptions from Crete.

8   Conclusion

The constituent order patterns used with *takku* and *mān* in the Hittite Laws should be considered a register feature. The position of the clause-connecting enclitic particles is preserved consistently in the Laws (both in copies of the main text and in the Parallel Text), but elsewhere in the language has changed: it is kept only sporadically in copies of a related text (the Instruction Texts), and not at all in versions of other types of texts such as rituals or oracles. That the scribe of the Parallel Text chose to preserve this feature in a text which was not merely a straightforward copy but involved some level of inventiveness suggests that the position of the enclitics -*a*/-*ma* and -*a*/-*ya* was a significant feature of the legal register and the tradition in which he was writing.

While the use of asyndeton does not belong to a special legal register in Greek, it does nonetheless provide evidence for republication based on older material. Asyndeton creates gaps between different levels of the texts, and the shift between the enactment formula and the content of the law is mirrored in the shift between the oath and the narrative description in the Cyrene foundation inscription. Comparisons between the texts at Gortyn and the laws about the Council of the 500 in Athens show that they seem to use asyndeton in the same way when collecting previously separately enacted laws or regulations together. That a higher frequency of asyndeton is a feature of inscriptions which collect previously published laws together, already familiar for Cretan inscriptions, explains why asyndeton in IG I³ 105 is more common than in other legal inscriptions which contain a number of separate provisions on the same topic or are of a similar length.

---

description of the action one must not carry out without the assembly of the people, as in the example from IG I³ 14. See also IG I³ 40 9–10, IG I³ 65 21–22, IG I³ 70 5–6, IG I³ 157 9–10.

65   Examples of this can be found in inscriptions from the late 6th and early 5th century such as IG I³ 1, 5, 34, and 36.

66   "These laws need not have all been originally enacted at the same time," but no particular explanation for this is provided. OSBORNE—RHODES 2017: 512.

References

ALAURA, SILVIA 2016, *Proverbs and Rhetorical Strategies in § 7' of the Hittite Instructions for Priests and Temple Personnel (CTH 264)*, in Š. Velhartická (ed.), *Audias fabulas veteres. Anatolian Studies in Honor of Jana Součková-Siegelová*, Leiden: Brill: 1–15. DOI: https://doi.org/10.1163/9789004312616_002

ARCHI, ALFONSO 1968, *Sulla formazione del testo delle leggi ittite*, "Studi Micenei ed Egeo-Anatolici" 6: 54–89.

BIBER, DOUGLAS 1994, *An Analytical Framework for Register Studies*, in E. Finegan—D. Biber (eds.), *Sociolinguistic perspectives on register*, Oxford: Oxford University Press: 31–56.

BIBER, DOUGLAS 1995, *Dimensions of register variation: a cross-linguistic comparison*, Cambridge: Cambridge University Press.

CARRUBA, ONOFRIO 1962, Review of J. Friedrich 1959, *Die hethitischen Gesetze*, "Kratylos" 7: 155–160.

CHD = GÜTERBOCK, HANS G.—HOFFNER, HARRY A. (eds.), 1980—, *The Hittite dictionary of the Oriental Institute of the University of Chicago*, Chicago: Oriental Institute of the University of Chicago.

DENNISTON, JOHN D. 1960, *Greek prose style*, Oxford: Clarendon Press.

DENNISTON, JOHN D.—DOVER, KENNETH J. 1954², *The Greek particles*, Oxford: Clarendon Press.

DOBIAS-LALOU, CATHERINE 2017, *Inscriptions of Greek Cyrenaica: Greek Verse Inscriptions of Cyrenaica*, DOI: https://doi.org/10.6092/UNIBO/IGCYRGVCYR

ELVIRA ASTORECA, NATALIA 2016, *The use of the imperative in Athenian decrees*, Leiden University dissertation. Retrieved from https://openaccess.leidenuniv.nl/handle/1887/42889

GAGARIN, MICHAEL 1982, *The Organization of the Gortyn Law Code*, "Greek, Roman and Byzantine Studies" 23/2: 129–146.

GAGARIN, MICHAEL—PERLMAN, PAULA 2016, *The laws of Ancient Crete c. 650–400 BCE*, Oxford: Oxford University Press.

GOETZE, ALBRECHT 1928, *Das Hethiter-Reich: Seine Stellung zwischen Ost und West*, Leipzig: J.C. Hinrichs.

GORDIN, SHAI 2015, *Hittite scribal circles: scholarly tradition and writing habits*, Wiesbaden: Harrassowitz Verlag.

GRAHAM, ALEXANDER J. 1960, *The Authenticity of the Opkion ΤΩΝ ΟΙΚΙΣΤΗΡΩΝ of Cyrene*, "The Journal of Hellenic Studies" 80: 94–111. https://doi.org/10.2307/628379

GUINAN, ANN K. 2014, *Laws and Omens: Obverse and Inverse*, in J. Fincke (ed.), *Divination in the Ancient Near East*, Winona Lake, Indiana: Eisenbrauns: 105–122.

GÜTERBOCK, HANS G. 1954, *Authority and Law in the Hittite Kingdom*, "Journal of the American Oriental Society" 16–24.

HILTUNEN, RISTO 1990, *Chapters on legal English: aspects past and present of the language of the law*, Helsinki: Suomalainen Tiedeakatemia, Academic Bookstore.

HOFFNER, HARRY A. 1997, *The laws of the Hittites: a critical edition*, Leiden: Brill.

HOFFNER, HARRY A.—MELCHERT, H. CRAIG 2008, *A grammar of the Hittite language*, Winona Lake, Indiana: Eisenbrauns.

IC = GUARDUCCI, MARGHERITA 1935–1950, *Inscriptiones Creticae*, 4 vols, Rome: Libreria dello Stato.

IG I³ = LEWIS, DAVID M.—JEFFERY, LILIAN H.—ERXLEBEN, EBERHARD—HALLOF, KLAUS (eds.) 1967, *Inscriptiones Graecae, Vol. I. Inscriptiones Atticae Euclidis anno anteriores*, Editio tertia, Berlin: De Gruyter.

JONES, A. HUGO M. 1975, *Athenian democracy*, Oxford: Blackwell.

KITAZUMI, TOMOKI 2019, *Typologies of setting paragraph dividers in the Hittite texts*, in Y. Hazırlayan—A. Süel (eds.), *Acts of the IXth International Congress of Hittitology, Çorum, September 08–14, 2014*, Ankara: Uyum Ajans: Vol. I, 417–458.

KLOEKHORST, ALWIN 2011, *Accentuation and Poetic Meter in Hittite*, in M. Hutter—S. Hutter-Braunsar (eds.), *Hethitische Literatur: Überlieferungsprozesse, Textstrukturen, Ausdrucksformen und Nachwirken; Akten des Symposiums vom 18. bis 20. Februar 2010 in Bonn*, Münster: Ugarit-Verlag: 157–176.

MEIGGS, RUSSELL—LEWIS, DAVID M. 1969, *A selection of Greek historical inscriptions to the end of the fifth century B.C.*, Oxford: Clarendon.

MELCHERT, H. CRAIG 1998, *Poetic Meter and Phrasal Stress in Hittite*, in L. Oliver—H.C. Melchert—J.H. Jasanoff (eds.), *Mír curad: studies in honor of Calvert Watkins*, Innsbruck: Institut für Sprachwissenschaft der Universität Innsbruck: 483–494.

MELCHERT, H. CRAIG 2009, *Discourse Conditioned Use of Hittite -ma*, in E. Rieken—P. Widmer (eds.), *Pragmatische Kategorien: Form, Funktion und Diachronie: Akten der Arbeitstagung der Indogermanischen Gesellschaft vom 24. bis 26. September 2007 in Marburg*, Wiesbaden: Reichert: 187–195.

MOUTON, ALICE 2007, *Rêves hittites: contribution à une histoire et une anthropologie du rêve en Anatolie ancienne*, Leiden: Brill.

MOUTON, ALICE 2016, *Rituels, mythes et prières Hittites*, Paris: Les Éditions du Cerf.

van OPHUIJSEN, JOHANNES M. 1993, *οὖν, ἀρά, δή, τοίνυν: The linguistic articulation of arguments in Plato's Phaedo*, in C.M.J. Sicking,—J.M. van Ophuijsen (eds.), *Two studies in Attic particle usage: Lysias and Plato*, Leiden: Brill: 67–164.

OSBORNE, ROBIN—RHODES, PETER J. (eds.) 2017, *Greek Historical Inscriptions 478–404 BC*, Oxford: Oxford University Press.

RHODES, PETER J.—LEWIS, DAVID M. 1997, *The decrees of the Greek states*, Oxford: Oxford University Press.

RIEKEN, ELISABETH 2000. *Die partikeln -a, -ia, -ma im Althethitischen und das Akkadogramm Ú*, in M. Ofitsch—C. Zinko (eds.), *125 Jahre Indo-Germanistik in Graz: Festband anlässlich des 125jährigen Bestehens der Forschungseinrichtung 'Indogermanistik' an der Karl-Franzens-Universität Graz*, Graz: Leykam: 411–420.

ROBERTSON, NOEL 1976, *False Documents at Athens: Fifth-Century History and Fourth-Century Publicists*, "Historical Reflections / Réflexions Historiques" 3/1: 3–25.

RYAN, FRANCIS X. 1994, *The Original Date of the δῆμος πληϑύων Provisions of IG I³ 105*, "The Journal of Hellenic Studies" 114: 120–134. https://doi.org/10.2307/632737

SEG = *Supplementum Epigraphicum Graecum*.

SMYTH, HERBERT W. 1956, *Greek Grammar*, Cambridge (MA): Harvard University Press.

STERNEMANN, REINHARD 1965a, *Temporale und konditionale Nebensätze des Hethitischen (1. Teil)*, "Mitteilungen Des Instituts Für Orientforschung" 11: 231–274.

STERNEMANN, REINHARD 1965b, *Temporale und konditionale Nebensätze des Hethitischen (2. Teil)*, "Mitteilungen Des Instituts Für Orientforschung" 11: 377–415.

STROUD, RONALD S. 1968, *Drakon's Law on homicide*, Berkeley: University of California Press.

TISCHLER, JOHANN 1991, *Hethitisches etymologisches Glossar, Teil III Lieferung 8*, Innsbruck: Institut für Sprachen und Literaturen der Universität Innsbruck.

VOLONAKI, ELENI 2001, *The Republication of the Athenian Laws in the Last Decade of the Fifth Century B.C.*, "Dike" 4: 137–168.

WALBANK, MICHAEL B. 1978, *Athenian proxenies of the fifth century, B.C.*, Toronto: Samuel Stevens.

ZORMAN, MARINA 2017, *Areal features of Hittite conditionals*, "Diachronica" 34/2: 253–277.

CHAPTER 10

Lexical Variation in Young Avestan: the Problem of the 'Ahuric' and 'Daevic' Vocabularies Revisited

Elizabeth Tucker

The Young Avestan language exhibits a striking example of lexical variation, which has been noted and debated by scholars for more than a century and a half.* To put it simply, some areas of the Young Avestan core vocabulary consist of double terms, for instance two sets of nouns for parts of the body or two sets of verbs for moving and speaking.

The names for these lexical variants 'Ahuric' and 'Daevic' derive on the one hand from the name of Zarathushtra's god Ahura Mazdā (cf. Avestan common noun *ahura-* 'lord', Vedic *ásura-* 'lord'[1]), on the other from Avestan *daēuua-* 'false god', (cf. Old Persian *daiva-* 'false god',[2] but Vedic *devá-*, Latin *deus*, etc. 'god'). These labels go back at least to Ferdinand Justi's *Handbuch der Zendsprache* of 1864, and they are enshrined in the individual lemmata of Bartholomae's 1904 *Altiranisches Wörterbuch*. The terminology arose from the prevailing 19th century opinion that the sacred language of the Avesta has a linguistic reflection of Zoroastrian dualism.[3] This was succinctly stated as follows by James Darmester (1892–1893, I: 93–94, note 74):

---

* I am grateful to all the organisers of the 2018 Pisa and Oxford conferences entitled 'Variation and Contact in the Ancient Indo-European languages: between Linguistics and Philology' for their invitation to participate. My contribution in Oxford represented a much revised version of papers delivered at the 225th Meeting of the American Oriental Society in New Orleans in March 2015 and at an Ancient India and Iran Trust workshop, Cambridge, in April 2015. Members of the audience in Oxford, Cambridge and New Orleans made valuable comments from which this written version has greatly benefitted. In addition I acknowledge the contributions and corrections of two anonymous reviewers.

1 In the *Ṛgveda ásura-* is a title of some individual gods such as Varuṇa and Agni; only in later Vedic texts are *ásuras* (in the plural) supernatural beings who are hostile to the gods.

2 In all Middle and New Iranian languages the inherited Indo-European word means 'demon'. The first element of some Proper Names such as Sogdian *Dēwāštīč* (δyw'štyc) is more plausibly interpreted as an Indo-Aryan loan with the sense 'god' rather than a survival of the prehistoric Indo-Iranian meaning in Iranian.

3 The older literature on Zoroastrian dualism, and more recent opinions, is reviewed by Ahmadi (2015). Cf. also the collection of papers in Swennen (ed., 2015).

© ELIZABETH TUCKER, 2022 | DOI:10.1163/9789004508828_012

LEXICAL VARIATION IN YOUNG AVESTAN

"L'Avesta, reflétant le dualisme du système religieux dans le détail du lexique, a deux mots différents pour le même acte ou le même objet, suivant qu'il s'agit d'un être ohrmazdéen ou d'un être ahrimanien."

In other words, Young Avestan employs a different lexeme according to whether something belongs—in the dualistic system of early Zoroastrianism—to the good creation of Ohrmazd (Av *Ahura Mazdā-*) or to the opposing evil creation represented by the demons (Av *daēuua-* 'false god') led by Ahriman (YAv *aŋra mainiiu-*). Some of the oppositions that were regularly cited by 19th century scholars (e.g. JUSTI 1864, DARMESTETER 1892–1893, JACKSON 1898: 627–628) are shown in the table below:

	'head'	'eye'	'ear'	'mouth'	'hand'	'foot'
ahuric	*vayδana-*	*dōiϑra-*	*uši-*	*āh-, staman-*	*zasta-*	*pād-/pad-*
daevic	*kamərəδa-*	*aši-*	*karəna-*	*zafar-/zafan-*	*gauu(a)-*	*zbaraϑa-*

	'man'	'woman'	'son'	'house'	'army'	'smell'
ahuric	*nar-*	*nāirī-/nāirikā-*	*puϑra-*	*nmāna-*	*spāδa-*	*baoδi-*
daevic	*mairiia-*	*jahī- / jahikā-*	*hūnu-*	*gərəδa-*	*haēnā-*	*ganti-*

	'go'	'run'	'fly'	'speak'	'eat'	'cut'	'die'	'be born'
ahuric	*i-, gam-*	*tak-*	*vaz-*	*mrauu-vaš-*	*xᵛar-*	*ϑβarəs-*	*raēϑ-*	*zan-*
daevic	*zbar-*	*duuar-drauu-*	*pat-*	*dauu-*	*gah-*	*karət-*	*mar-*	*hū-*

From a linguistic point of view, it is a limited type of diglossia that does not make much sense in terms of semantic fields: there are variants for several parts of the body and for humans and their activities, but why in addition are there two nouns for 'house' or 'army' or 'smell' (with no other traces of diglossia in these semantic areas)?

However, such lexical contrasts are used to striking effect in some Young Avestan passages where repetition in the narrative is built up around the variants. For instance, in Haδōxt Nask 2 the account of the fate of the truth-follower's soul immediately after death is followed by a parallel account employing daevic terms for what happens to the soul of the lie-follower:

ahuric *para. iriϑiieiti* vs. daevic *auua.miriieite* 'dies'
vayδana- vs. *kamərəδa-* 'head'
nišhiδaiti vs. *handuuaraiti* 'approaches'
mraoṯ vs. *adauuata* 'spoke', etc.

256   TUCKER

The Zamyād Yašt description (Yt 19.47–50) of the contest for the Xᵛarənah
'the (Kingly) Glory' between Ahura Mazdā's fire and the daevic dragon Aži
Dahāka contains an even more elaborate example. Here the moves and threats
of the two opponents are described in identical sequence save for the differences in the lexicon:[4]

(1)   Yt 19.47 *aδāṯ frašá* **hąm.rāzaiiata** *ātarš mazdå̄ ahurahe uiti auuaϑa
      maṇhānō: aētaṯ xᵛarənō haṇgərəfšāne yaṯ axᵛarətəm. āaṯ hē paskāṯ* **fradu-
      uaraṯ** *ažiš* **ϑrizafå̄** *duždaēnō uiti* **zaxšaϑrəm daomnō:**

      'Then the fire of Ahura Mazdā **went straight ahead** thinking thus as fol-
      lows: "I will take possession of this unseizable Glory." And behind him
      ran the **three-mouthed** dragon of the evil religion **speaking a threat** as
      follows:'

      19.48 *inja auuaṯ haṇdaēsaiiaŋᵛha ātarš mazdå̄ ahurahe: yezi aētaṯ niiās-
      å̄ŋhe yaṯ axᵛarətəm frā ϑβąm paiti apāϑa⟨iieni⟩ nōiṯ apaiia uzraocaiiāi
      ząm paiti ahuraδātąm ϑrāϑāi ašahe gaēϑanąm. aδa ātarš* **zasta** *paiti apa
      .gəuruuaiiaṯ.*

      '"**Inja**, you take note of that you Fire of Ahura Mazdā. If you reach out for
      this which is unseizable I shall make you ?? forth, afterwards you will not
      be able to blaze up on the Ahura-created earth to protect the creatures of
      Truth." Then Fire drew away his **hands** again.'

      19.49 *aδāṯ frašá* **hąm. duuaraṯ** *ažiš ϑrizafå̄ duždaēnō uiti auuaϑa maṇhānō:
      aētaṯ xᵛarənō haṇgərəfšāne yaṯ axᵛarətəm. āaṯ hē paskāṯ* **hąm.rāzaiiata**
      ātarš mazdå̄ ahurahe uiti **vacəbiš aojanō:**

      'Then the three-mouthed dragon of the evil religion **ran forward**, thinking
      as follows: "I will take possession of this unseizable Glory." Then behind
      him the Fire of Ahura Mazdā **went straight ahead, speaking in words** as
      follows:'

      19.50 *tinja auuaṯ haṇdaēsaiiaŋᵛa aže ϑrizafəm dahāka: yezi aētaṯ niiāså̄ŋ-
      hě yaṯ axᵛarətəm frā ϑβąm* **zadaŋha** *paiti uzuxšāne zafarə paiti uzrao-*

---

4   There is even the interesting hint from the different exclamations *inja/tinja* that the two myth-
    ological characters speak variant forms of the same language.

LEXICAL VARIATION IN YOUNG AVESTAN   257

*caiieni. nōiṯ apaiia **afrapatāi** ząm paiti ahuraδātąm mahrkāi aṣahe
gaēϑanąm. aδa ažiš **gauua** paiti apa.gəuruuaiiaṯ ...*

'"*Tinja*, take note of that, three-**mouthed** Aži Dahāka. If you reach out
for this which is unseizable, I will rise forth towards you towards your
buttocks, I will blaze up towards your **mouth**, afterwards you will not
be able to **fly** forth to the Ahura-created earth to destroy the creatures
of Truth." Then the dragon drew away his **hands** again ...,' (Text and translation based on HINTZE 1994: 249–268, HUMBACH 1998: 128–130)

The notion of far-reaching Avestan lexical diglossia was bolstered in scholarly
opinion for a long time by some Young Avestan passages from the Vidēvdād
which were considered to show awareness of this linguistic variation. Here
double names, one of which meets with approval, the other of which is condemned, are given to animals such as hedgehogs, tortoises and cocks:

Vidēvdād 13.1–2 *kaṯ taṯ dąma spəntō.mainiiə̄uš... vīspəm paiti ušā̊ŋhəm
ā hū.vaxšāṯ hazaŋraja aŋrō.mainiiə̄uš paiti.jasaiti. āaṯ mraoṯ ahurō
mazdå spānəm sīždrəm uruuīsarəm yim vaŋhāparəm yim maṣiiāka **auui
.dužuuacaŋhō dužakəm** nąma aojaite*

'Which is that creature of the Holy Spirit ... comes every morning up until
the rising of the sun killing thousands of the creatures of the Evil Spirit?
And Ahura Mazda said "the timid dog with wide spines, the Vaŋhāpara,
which people **of very bad speech** call (verb *aog-*) **the Dužaka**".'

Vidēvdād 13.5–6 *kaṯ taṯ dąma aŋrō.mainiiə̄uš... vīspəm paiti ušā̊ŋhəm
ā hū.vaxšāṯ hazaŋraja spəntō.mainiiə̄uš paiti.jasaiti. āaṯ mraoṯ ahurō
mazdå **daēum yim zairimiiaŋurəm** spitama zaraϑuštra yim maṣiiāka **auui
.dužuuacaŋhō zairimiiākəm** nąma aojaite*

'Which creature of the Evil Spirit ... comes every morning up until the
rising of the sun killing thousands of creatures of the Holy Sprit? And
Ahura Mazdā said "**the demon Zairimyaŋhura**, o Spitamid Zarathushtra,
which people **of very bad speech** call (verb *aog-*) **Zairimyāka**".'

Vidēvdād 18.14–15 *kō asti sraošahe ... sraošāuuarəzō āaṯ mraoṯ ahurō mazdå mərəyō yō parō.darš nąma spitama zaraϑuštra yim maṣiiāka **auui
.dužuuacaŋhō kahrkatās** nąma aojaite. āaṯ hō mərəyō vācim baraiti upa
ušā̊ŋhəm yąm sūrąm*

'Who is the priest of Sraoša… then Ahura Mazdā said "It is the bird called Parō.darš which people **of very bad speech** (*auui.dužuuacaŋhō*) call (verb *aog-*) **Kahrkatāt**, o Spitamid Zarathuštra; and this bird raises its voice towards the strong dawn (3rd part of the night)".' (texts and translations based on BENVENISTE 1931 and ANDRÉS-TOLEDO 2016: 282–285)

The animals themselves are firmly assigned to either the good creation of the Holy Spirit (*spəṇta mainiiu-*) or the bad creation of the Evil Spirit (*aŋra mainiiu-*), and so the pairs of names are not distinguishing a good hedgehog from an evil hedgehog, or a good tortoise from an evil tortoise! Rather they have been taken to show that there were two speech communities which had differences in their lexicon and one group was condemned by the other as having 'bad speech'. It is the speech of the latter which has been supposed to be the source of all the daevic words in the Avestan lexicon. However, it was pointed out already by Benveniste (1931) that these passages are more likely to refer to learned priestly speech versus common speech,[5] not to ahuric versus daevic terms.[6] In the one case where a Younger Avestan Yašt gives a double name, one of the two appears to be a euphemistic/ apotropaic name for a witch:

(5)   Tištrya Yašt (Yt 8.51) *auuaŋhāi pairikaiiāi… yā **dužiiāiriiā** yąm maṣiiāka **auui.dužuuacaŋhō huiiāiriiąm** nąma aojaite*

'(To withstand) that witch … **Bad Harvest** which people **of very bad speech** call by the name **Good Harvest**.'

Since the publication of Bartholomae's *Altiranisches Wörterbuch* in 1904, with its carefully constructed lemmata, there has been evidence that the conception of the two opposing vocabularies does not adequately cover all the facts of the Avesta. In addition to the synonyms that are involved in contrasts there are other words of similar meaning which appear neutral, and, even worse, a number that are capable of changing sides. Hence some 20th century publications

---

5   For instance, *kahrkatāt-* (Vd 18.14) appears onomatopoeic like 'cockadoodledoo', whereas *parō.darəs-* literally 'before-seer' refers to the cock's apparently divinely inspired foresight that dawn is about to break. The verb of speaking, *aog-*, which is used for the people 'of very bad speech' is ahuric or neutral, not *dauu-* which is normally used for daevic speech.

6   Kellens (1977: 56, n. 3) attempted to revive the notion that the Young Avesta refers to daevic speech by distinguishing passages where *auui.dužuuacaŋhō* should be read from those with simply *dužuuacaŋhō*. His claim was that only *dužuuacaŋhō* refers to daevic speech.

LEXICAL VARIATION IN YOUNG AVESTAN

(e.g. GÜNTERT 1914: 11–12; TOPOROV 1981: 209–214) replace diglossia by triglossia, postulating a third set of synonyms that could be used for either:

	'head'	'eye'	'ear'	'mouth'	'go'	'say'
ahuric	vaγδana-	dōiϑra-	uši-	staman-	tak-, car-	vaš-
neutral	sarah-	cašman-	gaoša-	āh-	i-, gam-	aog-, mrauu-
daevic	kamərəδa-	aši-		karəna- zafar- / zafan-	duuar-	dauu-

In some respects this picture is more accurate, but the hypothesis of triglossia has masked inconsistencies in the Avestan evidence that have never been fully investigated.

Most of the scholarly effort during the 20th century was directed towards finding a historical linguistic explanation for the contrasting functions. There was a diachronic problem because in both the daevic and ahuric categories there were words that are clearly inherited from Indo-Iranian, and in many cases also from Indo-European; while others, spread over both categories, are peculiar to Iranian or Avestan alone. No clear diachronic pattern emerges:

Ahuric
e.g. Avestan *zasta-* 'hand': OP *dasta-*, Vedic *hásta-*, Hittite *keššar*, Grk. χείρ
puϑra- 'son': OP *puça-*, Vedic *putrá-*, Oscan *puklum*
vaz- (middle) 'to fly': Vedic *vah-*, *váhati*, Latin *vehor*, Grk. ϝεχέτω
zan- 'to be born': Vedic *jan-*, *jáyate*, Grk. γίγνομαι, Latin *gigno*

But Avestan ahuric *vaγδana-* 'head', *staman-* 'mouth', *vaš-* 'to speak' are without cognates,[7] and *dōiϑra-* 'eye' is an Avestan neologism built with the inherited suffix *-tra-* on the Indo-Iranian root *dhī-* 'to see, to envisage'.

Daevic
e.g. Avestan *aš(i)-* 'eye': Vedic *akṣī́* (dual), Grk. ὄσσε, OCS *oči*, Latin *oculus*
hūnu- 'son': Ved. *sūnú-*, Gothic *sunus*, OCS *synъ*, Lithuanian *sūnùs*
pat- 'to fly': Ved. *pat-*, *pátati*, OP (*ud*)*apatatā*, Grk. πέτομαι, Hitt. *pattai-/patti-*
mar- 'to die': Ved. *mr̥-*, *mriyáte*, OP *amariyatā* 'died', Latin *morior*

---

7   It is difficult to compare *staman-* m. 'mouth' with Greek στόμα as *stāman-* would be expected via Brugmann's Law. *vaš-* 'to speak' has been linked with verbs of speaking in Balochi and Ormuri, but these are more likely to continue the more frequent Old Iranian root *vac-* (cf. CHEUNG 2007: 404), and in footnote 30 below an origin via an inner Avestan innovation will be suggested.

But Avestan *kamərəδa-* 'head', *dauu-* 'to speak' only have cognates in later Iranian languages, while *zbaraθa-* 'leg', *duuarəθra-* 'foot/leg' are Avestan neologisms derived from Indo-Iranian roots.

In spite of the unclear nature of the Young Avestan evidence and the available comparisons, a number of diachronic hypotheses for the genesis of the ahuric/ daevic variants have been proposed, which in most cases envisage a remote prehistoric background to the synchronically attested distribution of lexemes.

Frachtenberg (1908) proposed an origin in double vocabularies referring to humans and animals, with variants similar to French *mourir / crever*, German *sterben / krepieren* for 'to die'. But in the Avesta the divide ahuric/daevic extends to the animal kingdom: a dog is an animal of the Good Creation and when it dies the verb is the same as for humans (*raēθ-* Vd 5.39, 8.1, 4, versus *mar-* for evil beings); *vayδana-* is attested for the head of a camel (Yt 14.13), an ahuric animal, in addition to an ahuric human head.

A suggestion first put forward by Gray (1927: 438–440), and then developed by Burrow (1973), identified the daevic terms as loanwords from Indo-Aryan, e.g. *karəna-* 'ear' and 'deaf' (Sanskrit *kárṇa-/ karṇá-*), *aš(i)-* 'eye' (Sanskrit *akṣí* dual), *hūnu-* 'son' (Sanskrit *sūnú-*), *gərəδa-* 'house' (Sanskrit *grhá-*), *gah-* 'to eat' (Sanskrit *ghas-*). They were explained as lexemes used by **daiva*-worshipping Indo-Aryans which contrasted with those used by the *ahura*-worshipping Iranians. This is a very interesting hypothesis in view of the evidence for Indo-Aryans, the Mitanni, in the Ancient Near East during the 2nd part of the second millennium BCE. However, the supposed 'loanwords' do not show any phonological features which set them apart from words that were inherited by Avestan from Indo-Iranian. Nor are they exclusively Indo-Aryan lexemes as some have cognates in other Iranian languages e.g. Avestan daevic *karəna-*, Sogdian *krn*, New Persian *karr* 'deaf';·Avestan daevic, *kamərəδa-* 'head', Zoroastrian Middle Persian *kamāl*, Khotanese *kamala* 'head, person', Yidγa *kyɛmalγo* 'skull'; Avestan daevic *gərəδa-* 'house', Old Persian **grda-*(or **grdya-*) 'household', reconstructed from loanwords in Elamite (*kurtaš*, very frequently attested) and Aramaic (*grd*).

Toporov (1981: 209–214), updating Güntert (1914), argued that daevic words, which have cognates in Sanskrit but not in other Indo-European languages, continue the colloquial Indo-Iranian language. On the other hand, ahuric words continue the Indo-European inherited poetic language. Obviously there is a temptation to see a development similar to the Homeric 'language of the gods and language of men' (see WATKINS 1970). But this is extremely difficult to work out in detail as the cognates of the ahuric words do not always appear more elevated or poetic, and very few daevic words only have cog-

LEXICAL VARIATION IN YOUNG AVESTAN

nates in Sanskrit and not in the rest of Indo-European. Moreover, the Vedic cognates of the daevic words are not noticeably more frequent in the 'popular registers' of the Atharvaveda and RV 10. On the other hand, it will be argued below that in some cases Vedic usage may provide indications of a pejorative sense which could have existed in the Indo-Iranian parent language.

However, none of the theories outlined above are capable of providing a full account of all the known Young Avestan evidence. The most apposite comment is that of Watkins (1995: 316, ftn. 7) "the question is complex and still not settled."

Younger Avestan passages such as those illustrated above, from the Zamyād Yašt (ex. (1).) and Haδōxt Nask 2, which show contrasting words in parallel contexts, are very rare. Throughout the Young Avesta the daevic vocabulary is easy to recognize as it refers to the villains and, as Toporov emphasised, it is the marked member of any lexical oppositions. But in identifying the opposing ahuric terms scholars have often combined contexts from different Young Avestan texts. Sometimes opposing terms can be identified with certainty from different passages, e.g. daevic *bizəŋgra-* 'two-legged' (of *ašəmaoγa-* 'confuser of Truth, heretic', Y 9.18, Vd 5.35) and *caϑβarə.zəŋgra-* 'four-legged' (of wolves, Y 9.18, Vd 18.38) versus *bipaitištāna-* 'two-legged' (of righteous men and women, Y 19.8, Vd 15.19) and *caϑβarə.paitištāna-* 'four-legged' (of the goddess Anāhitā's horses Yt 5.131, the cow Y 19.8), but favourable cases such as this are also very rare and even here there can be complications.[8]

Thus the conventional lists of ahuric versus daevic vocabulary are to a large extent the concoctions of modern scholars, culled from an assortment of Young Avestan texts.

What was missed in the early published collections of vocabulary which have then been used as the basis for historical linguistic reconstructions is the variability of the vocabulary oppositions from text to text, especially in the case of the older Young Avestan Yašts. If the different texts which make up the Young Avesta are considered individually, a series of different contrasts emerge:

---

8 There are at least two other words for a daevic leg, or part thereof, which occur outside compounds: the apparent neologisms *zbaraϑa-* from *zbar-* 'to move crookedly' (Y 9.29), and *duuaraϑra-* from *duuar-* 'to run' (Yt 11.2): see exx. (7). and (8). In addition there is the problem that *-zəŋgra-/ -zaŋgra-* has usually been interpreted as a daevic noun created within Avestan on the basis of ahuric *zəŋga-/ zaŋga-* 'ankle' (cf. Vedic *jáṅghā-* f. 'lower part of leg, shin'), although the model for such a creation is unclear.

Nouns

(i) 'head'

Hōm Yašt	daevic	*kamərəδa-*	: ahuric	*-sāra-*
Yašt 10		*kamərəδa-*	:	*sarah-*
Hadōxt 2		*kamərəδa-*	:	*vayδana-*

(ii) 'woman'

Yašt 17	daevic	*jahikā-*	: ahuric	*vantā-* 'woman'
Hadōxt 2		*jahikā-*	:	*nāirikā-*
Yašt 5		*strī-*	:	*xšaϑrī-*
Vidēvdād 18		*kū.nāirī-*	:	*nāirikā-*

(iii) Verbs of movement

Hōm Yašt	daevic	*pat-*	: ahuric	*fra-car-* or *fra-stā-*
Yašt 8		*pat-*	:	*ā-i-*
Yašt 19.56–64		*us-pat-*	:	*zgad-*
Yašt 8		*nižduuar-*	:	*auua-i-*
Yašt 5.17		*duuar-*	:	*tak-*
Yašt 19.47–50		*hạm-duuar-*	:	*hạm-raz-*
Yašt 19.40–42		*zbar-*	:	*tak-*

(iv) Verbs of speaking

Hōm Yašt, Yašt 19	daevic	*dauu-*	: ahuric	*aog-, mrauu-*
Yašt 17, Vidēvdād 19		*dauu-*	:	*fra-vaš-*

It cannot be claimed that all these oppositions are equally valid: when the text itself lacks parallel passages that employ variant lexemes there is an element of subjectivity in deciding what contrasts with what. But such text by text pairs do show why the lists in different modern studies are not exactly the same: it all depends on which Young Avestan texts the author based his findings. They also show why there have been such problems explaining the origins of the supposed 'two vocabularies', as there are not two or even three sets of lexical contrasts but multiple sets. A global explanation which accounts linguistically for all the oppositions in the same way is simply impossible.[9]

Although it is the marked member of the lexical oppositions and shows slightly more consistency across the Young Avesta, the daevic vocabulary itself

---

9 Previous treatments of the subject have all attempted some sort of overarching linguistic explanation, but the two most detailed, by Güntert (1914) and Gray (1927), acknowledge that not every lexical opposition can be accounted for in the same fashion.

LEXICAL VARIATION IN YOUNG AVESTAN   263

varies from text to text. This fact is particularly apparent from the words
employed for body parts in what might be called in broad terms Young Avestan
'curses', where a 'divine being worthy of worship', a *yazata* such as Haoma or
Mithra or Sraoša, is asked to hinder the proper functioning of the limbs of evil-
doers. For instance:

(6)   Hōm Yašt (Y 9.28) *gəuruuaiia hē **pāδauue** zāuuarə pairi šē **uši** vərənūiδi
      skəṇdəm šē manō kərənūiδi*

      'Seize the strength from his **feet**, cover around his **ears**, cause destruction
      to his mind.'

(7)   Hōm Yašt (Y 9.29) *mā **zbaraϑaēibiia** fratuiiā̊, mā **gauuaēibiia** aiβitūtuiiā̊,
      mā ząm vaēnōiṯ **ašibiia**, mā gąm vaēnōiṯ **ašibiia***

      'Let him not be able to advance with his **legs**, let him not have strength
      for his **hands**, let him not see the earth with his **eyes**, let him not see the
      cow with his **eyes**.'

(8)   Srōš Yašt (Yt 11.2) (*Sraošəm yazamaide*)... *druuatō druuatiiā̊sca...**aši** ⟨**uši**⟩
      karəna **gauua** duuarəϑra zafarə ... pairi.uruuaēštəm.*

      '(Sraoša we worship) ... best at crushing the **eyes**, ⟨**ears**⟩, **ears**, **hands**, **feet**
      (**legs?**), **mouth** ... of the male and female lie-follower.'

(9)   Mihr Yašt (Yt 10.48) *aϑra narąm miϑrō.drująm apąš **gauuō** darəzaiieiti
      pairi **daēma** vāraiieiti, apa **gaoša** taošaiieiti*

      'There he (Mithra) binds the **hands** of the men who break the contract
      behind them, he turns off their **sight**, he deafens their **ears**.'

In this last 'curse' *gauua-* 'hand'[10] is consistently daevic in other Young Avestan
contexts (see exx. (1)., (7)., (8).). *daēman-* is daevic in the Yašt to Vərəϑrayna (Yt
14.56), but later in the Mihr Yašt (Yt 10.107) it is ahuric. *gaoša-* 'ear' is normally
ahuric but it is also used in another Mihr Yašt 'curse', which is even more out of
step in its vocabulary:

---

10   Kellens (1974: 331–332) explains the form *gauuō* as a thematic acc. pl. (transmitted in place
      of **gauuā*) because of clearly thematic **gauuaēibiia** at Y 9.29.

264 TUCKER

(10) Yt 10.23=10.63 *apa aēšąm **bāzuuå** aojō tūm grantō xšaiiamnō barahi apa pāδaiiå zāuuarə apa **cašmaṇå** sūkəm apa **gaošaiiå** sraoma*

'When angered you (Mithra) are able to carry away the force of their (the contract-breakers') **arms**, the strength of their **feet**, the clearness of their **eyes**, the hearing of their **ears**.'

pad-/ pād- (pāδaiiå thematic genitive dual) is very occasionally daevic elsewhere (cf. Y 9.28, ex. (6). above), but *uʸra.bāzu-* 'strong **armed**', *baēuuarə .cašman-* 'having ten thousand **eyes**', *hazaŋra.gaoša-* 'having a thousand **ears**', *sruṯ.gaoša-* 'having hearing **ears**' are epithets of Mithra himself in this same long Yašt! It appears that in ex. (10). the daevic vocabulary convention is simply ignored.[11]

Much attention has been paid to Young Avestan passages where there are accumulations of daevic vocabulary: for example, the description of the three-mouthed, three-headed, six-eyed dragon killed by Thraētaona in the Hōm Yašt (Yasna 9.8). However, less attention has been paid to passages where it is strangely absent: for example, in the Zamyād Yašt (Yt 19.41) the Gandarəβa (Skt. Gandharva) is characterised by daevic lexemes (*apataṯ vīzaǰārō* 'flew with his mouth open'), but in the Ardvisur Yašt (Yt 5.38) his home is not daevic (ahuric *nmāna-*, not *gərəδa-!*).

In a real diglossic situation one would expect the use of daevic vocabulary to be more or less mandatory when the forces of evil are mentioned, but this is often not the case. The Zamyād Yašt (Yašt 19) makes great use of daevic vocabulary (see, for instance, the extended passage Yt 19.47–50, ex. (1).), but abruptly in its last section about the Saviour, the Saošiiaṇt Astvaṯ.ərəta, the daevic vocabulary stops and the most evil powers in Zoroastrianism are characterised by a series of epithets with prefix *duš-* (cognate with Sanskrit *duṣ-* and Greek δυσ-):

(11) Yt 19.95–96 *frānamāite aēšmō xruuidruš **dušxʸarəṇå**.* "Wrath of the bloody club, **of bad glory** will flee."

---

11 The internal contradictions within the Mihr Yašt itself with regard to the ahuric/daevic lexicon raise interesting questions about the composition of this 143-stanza poem. Do they provide additional evidence for the work of different composers or at least different oral traditions that have been amalgamated? (See SKJÆRVØ 1994 for a general discussion about the creation of such Yašts).

*vanąṯ aṣa akąm drujim yąm **dušciϑrəm** təmaŋhaēnīm.* "He (the Saošiiaṇt-) will defeat through Truth the Evil Lie, who (is) **of bad lineage**, (is) made of darkness."

*frānamāite **dužuuarštāuuarəš** aŋrō mańiiuš axšaiiamnō* "Aŋra Mainyu **the doer of bad deeds** will flee, being without power."

A striking literary effect is achieved through these repetitions of *duš-/ duž-* at the close of the Zamyād Yašt. There are no inhibitions in other Young Avestan compositions about attaching this prefix to ahuric or neutral terms: in the late Ardabehesht Yašt (Yt 3) the normally ahuric neologism *dōiϑra-* 'eye', literally 'instrument of seeing' (root *dī-* 'to see'), becomes 'the Evil Eye' when prefixed with *duž*—(*duždōiϑra-* Yt 3.8, 11; *duždōiϑra. duždōiϑrō.təma-* 'the most evil-eyed one of the evil-eyed' Yt 3.15. Contrast *aγaši-* 'the Evil Eye' Vd 20.3, 7 with the daevic word for 'eye').

A further example where the lack of daevic vocabulary merits comment involves one of the most picturesque conflicts between good and evil in the ancient Yašts, the battle between the rain-bringing star Tištrya and the Demon of Drought Apaoša. The two antagonists take the form of horses, and the contrasts in the appearance of the two horses are beautifully conveyed by linguistic means, but without, apart from the initial verbs of movement (ahuric *auuāiti*, daevic *nižduuaraiti* 'goes down'), ahuric/daevic lexical contrasts. This Tištrya Yašt passage starts:

(12) Yt 8.20 *āaṯ paiti **auuāiti**, spitama zaraϑuštra, tištriia raēuuå xᵛarənaŋᵛå auui zraiiō vourukaṣəm aspahe kəhrpa aurušahe srīrahe zairi.gaošahe zaraniiō.aiβiδānahe.*
Yt 8.21 *ā.dim paiti.yąš **nižduuaraiti** daēvō yō apaošō aspahe kəhrpa sāma-he kauruuahe kauruuō.gaošahe kauruuahe kauruuō.barəšahe kauruuahe kauruuō.dūmahe daγahe aiβiδātō.tarštōiš.*

Then Tištrya the rich the glorious **goes down**, O Spitamid Zarathuštra, to the Vourukaṣa Sea in the form of a beautiful white horse with golden ears and a golden bridle.
Opposing him the Demon Apaoša **runs down** in the form of a mangy black horse, with mangy ears, mangy, with mangy back, mangy, with mangy tail, bald, shying at its bridle'.

The cases outlined above where there is a failure to employ daevic vocabu-lary and the evil creation is characterised (if at all) by other linguistic devices all point in the same direction: daevic vocabulary and daevic/ahuric lexical oppositions are a matter of stylistic choice by individual oral composers. Rather than any sort of linguistic diglossia or triglossia, the wider Young Avestan evidence reveals a literary convention of differentiating the good and evil creations by linguistic means, and the use of lexical oppositions is just one (albeit the most frequent) of these means. The exact choice of lexemes, and the vocabulary oppositions thus created must, at least in so far as the ancient Yašts are concerned, have been worked out by individual composers or built up in the various strands of oral transmission.

In Young Avestan texts which are generally regarded as late compositions, that is the shorter Yašts which are often concocted from other Yašt material, and especially in the Vidēvdād 'the Law which Sets the Demons Apart', the daevic/ahuric lexical contrasts have become more stable, and the same set of lexemes occur from text to text. The following table shows the restricted set of vocabulary oppositions which are used consistently:

Ahuric	*vayδana-*	*nmāna-*	*nar-*	*nāiri(kā-)*	*raēϑ-*	*vaz-*
Daevic	*kamərəδa-*	*gərəδa-*	*mairiia-*	*jahi(kā-)*	*mar-*	*pat-*
Meaning	'head'	'house'	'man'	'woman'	'to die'	'to run, fly'

It is above all the Vidēvdād that has created the impression that there is a rigid system of oppositions between two vocabularies, but its daevic vocabulary is in fact quite limited and it involves some stereotyped pairings with verbs and their subjects:

> *haṃ.duuar-* 'to run together' of daēvas
> *duuar-* 'to run' of *druj-* 'the Lie' (preverbs *apa-, upa-, pairi-*; but *apa-duuar-* is used of other evil beings in imprecations)
> present *dvąsa-* from *dvan-* 'to fly' (preverbs *apa-, upa-, fra-*) of *druj-nasu-* 'the corpse witch'
> *pat-* 'to fly, to move rapidly' of animals and adolescent humans.

I suggest that here we are seeing the end product of a convention of the Avestan compositional tradition which earlier was quite fluid and could be realised in different ways. Or if the Vidēvdād is not a relatively late Avestan text but merely a poorly preserved Avestan text,[12] the greater rigidity in the use of lexical oppositions may be conditioned by its different literary genre. Its very title 'The Law

---

12   See Skjærvø (2007: 112–116) for arguments in favour of this view. The often repeated one

LEXICAL VARIATION IN YOUNG AVESTAN 267

which Sets the Demons Apart' shows that here differentiation between good and evil is intrinsically important to understanding the meaning.

However, even in this part of the Young Avesta, a number of lexemes which are normally cited as daevic also occur in what appears to be their old inherited value without any pejorative connotation.

(13) Vidēvdād 3.33 *vīspō aŋhuš xᵛāše juuaiti axᵛāše **framiriieite***

'All life lives by eating, **dies** through not eating'.

(14) Vidēvdād 5.12 *aētaδa hē uzbaoδąm tanūm nidaiϑiiąn... vīspəm ā ahmāṯ yaṯ frā vaiiō **patąn***

'Here they should deposit his lifeless body ... for all the time until birds **fly forth** (at the coming of spring)'

These two Vidēvdād examples involving the inherited verb 'to die' and *pat-* 'to fly' of birds perhaps contain old gnomic expressions, which were passed down in the oral tradition before the establishment of rigid lexical conventions.

Occasional non-daevic employment of words that are usually daevic is also encountered in the more ancient long Yašts. For instance, *haēnā-* which normally means 'enemy army, army of Lie-followers' is used in the inherited sense 'missile' in a passage of the Ardvīsūr Yašt. This is the most frequent meaning of its Vedic cognate *sénā-* in the Ṛgveda (RV 2.33.11, 5.30.9, 7.3.4, etc.), in addition to 'army' which is continued in Classical Sanskrit:

(15) Yt 5.120 *yeŋhe caϑβārō aršāna hąm.tašaṯ ahurō mazdā̊ vātəmca vārəmca maēyəmca fiiaŋhumca ... yeŋhe auuauuaṯ **haēnanąm** nauua satāiš hazaŋrəmca*

'... whose (the goddess Anāhitā's) four stallions Ahura Mazdā fashioned, the wind, the rain, the mist and the hail ... of whom there are as many **missiles** as one thousand and nine hundred'.[13]

_____

that Avestan was already a dead language when the Vidēvdād was assembled is clearly untenable.

13   Two further examples from the Vidēvdād vis à vis the old Yašts may be added. *karəna-* is normally considered a daevic noun, or rather two nouns meaning respectively 'daevic ear' (Yt 11.2) and 'deaf' (Yt 5.93), corresponding to Vedic *kárṇa-* and *karṇá-* (cf. BARTHOLOMAE 1904: 455). But, as pointed out already by Gray (1927: 429), *karəna-* also occurs in composi-

268 TUCKER

If *hapax legomena* are excluded only a small strangely assorted group of lexemes are applied exclusively to daevic beings across the whole Young Avesta. These consistent words are:

aš(i)- 'eye'
kamərəδa- 'head'
jahi(kā)- 'harlot, evil woman'
mairiia- 'villain, evil man'
hūnu- 'son' and *hū*- 'give birth'
gah- 'to eat'
dauu- 'to speak'
duuar- / *drauu*- 'to run'

To these may be added four lexemes which are frequent as daevic terms, and are only used in a non-daevic sense once or twice:

haēnā- 'army'
mar- 'to die'
pat- 'to fly, to move quickly'
zbar- 'to move crookedly, to zig zag'

If my argument is correct and the words which have been considered to represent daevic vocabulary are to some extent the result of lexical choices made by individual composers, which then helped to build a more fixed set of daevic lexemes in the later Avesta, we may wonder what guided the earlier Avestan composers in their choices?

Avestan inherited an extensive lexicon from Indo-Iranian, and this must have contained many synonyms or near synonyms just as the Vedic lexicon does. There are pieces of evidence to suggest that the early Young Avestan composers may have done no more than select lexemes with a less favourable/slightly pejorative meaning to characterise daevic beings. At least four Rgvedic words which have a mildly pejorative flavour correspond to invariably daevic lexemes in Avestan:

---

tion as the second element in the name of a sacred tree, *gaokarəna*- 'ox-eared' (Yt 1.30, Vd 20.4).

    zbar- is a daevic verb of movement (Yt 15.50, Yt 19.42), and *zbaraθa*- the leg of an evil being, but *zbarah*- n. appears to refer to a geographical feature at Vd 19.4, 11, perhaps a 'hill' (Bartholomae 1904: 1699) or a bend in a river (Redard 2021: 40).

LEXICAL VARIATION IN YOUNG AVESTAN

márya- 'young blood, young man' (RV 7.56.16, 10.30.5, etc.): YAv *mairiia-*
'villain, daevic man'

hasrā́- 'harlot' (RV 1.124.7 of *Uṣas* in simile!) ~ YAv *jahi(kā-)* 'harlot,
daevic woman'

ghas- 'to feed' (sometimes of wild animals feeding, e.g. RV 10.95.15 of
wolves, ŚS 11.2.2 *vighasá-* 'gnawing apart' of flies and birds feeding on
corpses): YAv *gah-* 'to feed' (daevic)

vṛ́kadvaras- 'having the gait of a wolf' (RV 2.30.4): YAv *duuar-* 'to run'
(daevic).[14]

hvṛ- hvárate 'go crookedly, to zig zag' (RV 1.141.1, 10.16.80): YAv *zbar-* 'to
move crookedly' (daevic)

sū- 'to give birth' is used in the RV of human females and animals,[15] and
belongs to a lower register than *jan-* (Avestan ahuric *zan-*): Avestan
hū-, hūnu-.[16]

The derogatory use by Darius of some Old Persian words may be indicative of
a shift in their meaning in prehistoric Iranian vis à vis the Indo-Iranian parent
language, or it could be a case of parallel drift in both Avestan and Old Persian.

OP *hainā-* 'enemy army': YAv *haēnā-* 'enemy army, daevic army'
OP *ud-pat-* (middle) 'rebel, rise up': YAv *us-pat-* 'rise up' (daevic)
OP *zurah-* 'evil', *zurakara-* 'evil-doer': YAv. *zbar-* 'move crookedly'
(daevic)[17]

Güntert's detailed study dating from 1914 of the cognates within Iranian needs
to be repeated taking account of the wealth of Middle Iranian evidence that has
become known and interpreted since then. In one or two cases the cognates of
daevic words have a pejorative meaning in later Iranian languages:

---

14 Young Avestan neologisms such as *duuarəθra* lit. 'two instruments of running, daevic
legs/feet' appear to have been created on the basis of such inherited roots with pejorative
sense. Likewise *zbaraθa-*.

15 Except at RV 3.38.5 where *ásūta* is used to indicate the paradox of an androgynous creator
bull.

16 Because of its derivation inherited *hūnu-* may have appeared to be 'son, Mummy's boy'
versus *puθra*.

17 OP *marīka-* (DNb 50, 55, 59) appears simply to mean 'young man' (SCHMITT 1999: 129–131),
but its morphology differs from that of Avestan *mairiia-*, Vedic *márya-*.

270 TUCKER

Sogdian *krn*, Khotanese *kārra*, New Persian *karr* 'deaf': YAv *karəna-* 'daevic ear', and 'deaf', or 'with deformed ears'(?)[18]

Awromani Kurdish *duǎy* /*du-* 'to talk nonsense, prattle', Khufi *war-δaw-* / *war-δawt* , Sariqoli *war-δεw-*/*war-δεwd* 'to mumble, babble', Shughni (dialect of Bajui) *warδawax̌* 'babbling, prattle' (see CHEUNG 2007: 65): YAv *dauu-* 'to speak' (daevic).

But in at least one case, *kamərəδa-* 'head', Middle Iranian evidence has made the Avestan daevic meaning more difficult to understand. Whereas Zoroastrian Middle Persian *kamāl* continues the Avestan daevic sense, there is no indication of a pejorative meaning from Khotanese *kamala* 'head, person', even less so from the Bactrian divine name καμιρδο.[19] The long-standing etymology of Avestan *kamərəδa-* analyses it as *-mərəδa-* cognate with Sanskrit *mūrdhan-* 'head', Old English *molda* 'top of head', with a pejorative prefix *ka-* (BARTHOLOMAE 1904: 440).[20] Since the inherited Indo-Iranian pejorative prefix *ka-* was infrequent[21] possibly the noun's original morphology quickly became opaque in Iranian languages which were not influenced by the Avestan usage, and so it became a normal word for 'head' without evil connotations.

Obviously I am applying similar or, in some cases, exactly the same reasoning to the selection of these lexemes to describe daevic beings as has been proposed by previous scholars, particularly by Güntert (1914) and by Toporov

---

18 The two Young Avestan occurrences of *karəna-* appear to correspond respectively to Vedic *kárṇa-* 'ear' and *karṇá-* 'long-eared'. The meaning 'deaf' is suggested for the latter by its later Iranian cognates (Sogdian *krn*, Khotanese *kārra*, New Persian *karr* 'deaf'). But since *karṇá-* means 'long-eared' in the Ṛgveda and Atharvaveda (RV 2.34.3, ŚŚ 5.13.9 = PS 8.2.8, PS 15.23.1), and in Yt 5.93 *karəna-* occurs in a list of people who are forbidden to participate in the offerings to Anāhita because of bodily defects, a meaning 'with prominent/deformed ears' is equally likely.

19 I am grateful to Nicholas Sims-Williams for pointing out to me the particular problem of this Bactrian divine name. Yidγa *kyεmalyo* 'skull' could also have developed from a noun 'head' of neutral meaning.

20 See MAYRHOFER 1986–2000: 368 on the loss of the laryngeal in composition from Indo-Iranian * *mṛHdhan-*.

21 Some demon names in the Vidēvdād, *kaxuži-*, *kaxᵛarəδa-*/*kaxᵛaraiδi-* may also show this pejorative prefix *ka-*, but the second element is unclear in both cases. In Vedic only *kapūya-* 'stinking awfully' from the *Chandogya Upaniṣad* seems quotable for *ka-* (WACKERNAGEL-DEBRUNNER II,1: 82–84), but this could be because *ka-* was early on replaced by *kat-* or *kim-* in the Indic branch (e.g. RV 5.32.6 *katpayá-* 'swelling horribly'). Only one example of the pejorative prefix *ku-* is attested in Avestan (*kūnāirī-* Vd 8.31,32), but there are more in early Vedic, e.g. *kúyava-* 'bringing bad harvest' (RV 2.19.6, 7.19.2, etc.), *kunakhín-* 'having bad nails' (ŚŚ 7.65.3), *kúmanas-* 'ill-humoured' (MS 4.2.13). This pejorative prefix may have also been more widespread in some Eastern Old Iranian dialects, eclipsing inherited *ka-*.

LEXICAL VARIATION IN YOUNG AVESTAN

(1981). But since I view it as a gradual development reflecting the tastes of different composers, and their literary styles, it does not seem necessary to take a 'one size fits all approach' and propose the same linguistic history for every daevic lexeme. The synchronic picture in the Young Avesta is complex and unstable, with the exception of the Vidēvdād and the later Yašts, and so the diachronic background likewise has to be reconstructed word by word.

I will conclude with an additional tentative hypothesis about the origin of this literary convention in the Young Avesta. It is conceivable that the use made by Zarathushtra[22] in the Gāthās of a number of words may have sowed the seeds for the Younger Avestan composers' practice of characterising the Good and Evil Creations by different lexical items. There are numerous passages in the Gāthās where the actions of *daēuuas* and their followers are described in unfavourable terms (e.g. Y 30.6, Y 32.3, Y 49.4), but in so far as we can tell from the very small Gāthic corpus[23] there are no regularly occurring lexical characterisations for the forces of evil.[24] However, in the highly crafted poetry of the Gāthās every word is chosen very carefully, and the contrast between synonyms must be significant.[25] Three lexemes employed for evil people contrast with those employed for the truthful or for Ahura Mazda himself.

> *hunu-* (= *hūnu-*) 'son' (Y 51.10) "he is the son of the Lie's creation"; but *puϑra-* (Y 44.7) is a father's good son.
>
> *ašibiiā* 'with his eyes' (dual, Y 32.10) are the eyes of someone who says the worst thing; but *cašman-* (Y 31.8, 13; 45.8; 50.10) is the 'eye' or 'vision' of Ahura Mazdā and Zarathuštra.
>
> *hān-duuar-* 'to run together' (Y 30.6) of the daēvas who ran together towards Fury.

These three words which occur only once in the Gāthās but refer to evil beings are used consistently in a daevic sense throughout the whole Young Avesta. The compound verb *hān-duuar* - is particularly interesting since this is the same compound *hą̄m-duuar-* which is regularly used with the daēvas as subject in the

---

22 I use the traditional name Zarathushtra for the poet of the Gāthās because of the demonstration by Jamison (2007: 30–49) that an individual poetic persona is created via stylistic devices within the poems themselves, and has not merely been retro-projected from later Zoroastrian tradition. See also Hintze (2002).

23 The other Old Avestan text, the Yasna Haptaŋhāiti, never mentions the forces of evil and so cannot provide any evidence.

24 One word, *ašibiiā* (Y 32.10), was interpreted by Gershevitch (1975) as daevic, and in this he has been followed by Schwartz (2006a, 2006b). See further below on Schwartz's views.

25 This point was emphasized by Stanley Insler when I presented an earlier version of this paper at the American Oriental Society Meeting in 2015 in New Orleans.

Vidēvdād. The Hōm Yašt curse *mā ząm vaēnōiṯ ašibiia, mā gąm vaēnōiṯ ašibiia* (Y 9.29, ex. (6).) has usually been regarded[26] as a verbal reminiscence of Y 32.10 *yə̄ acištəm vaēnaŋhē aogədā gąm ašibiiā huuarəcā* 'the one who has professed the worst in order to see the cow and the sun with his eyes' (Insler 1975: 42).

Conversely, *āh-* 'mouth', *zasta-* 'hand' and *gōuša-/gaoša-* 'ear' never refer to the evil creation in the Gāthās, and belong to the ahuric vocabulary in the Young Avesta. The same applies to *cašman-* 'eye' and *puϑra-* 'son' which are the 'good' synonyms for 'evil' *aš(i)-* and *hunu-* in the Gāthās.[27] In the cases where Zarathustra uses the same lexemes for both good and evil beings, for instance, *aog-* 'to speak' or *spāda-* 'army' (which occurs only in the dual for the two opposing armies of good and evil at Y 44.15), this appears to have given licence for Young Avestan composers to use such lexemes for both or neutrally.[28] Even if it is not possible to reconstruct from the restricted Gāthic corpus the exact reasons for the choice of words in 'daevic' and 'ahuric' contexts found in these poems there is no doubt that their lexical usage could have influenced later Avestan composers[29] because of the reverence with which the Gāthās were preserved and sometimes directly quoted.[30]

---

26 Schwartz (2006a, 2006b) has argued at length that both the *Gāthās* and the Young Avestan Hōm Yašt draw on a much more ancient pre-Zarathushtrian composition in praise of Haoma. Although the details about the use the *Gāthās* may have made of this hypothetical proto-type Hōm Yašt are interesting, Schwartz's theory fails to convince me in the face of the simpler explanation for the similarities between some passages of the attested Young Avestan Hōm Yašt (Y 9–11) and the Gāthās: namely that the younger composition was influenced by the older, which had been canonized in the Zoroastrian tradition at an early date.

27 The exception, as noted above, is the use of *cašman-* and *gaoša-* in a 'curse' of the Mihr Yašt (Yt 10.23=10.63), which is aberrant in respect of the whole Young Avesta, and contradicts the use of these words in epithets of Mithra himself.

28 One case presents a difficulty for this generalisation as in Young Avestan *raod-* 'to howl' is a daevic verb (Y 9.24, Vd 3.32, Vd 19.45), but the soul of the cow is the subject of Gāthic *raostā* (Y29.9). On the other hand, an evil Kavi is the subject of *urūdōiiatā* (Y 44.20) which Humbach (1991, II: 162) tentatively connected with *raod-*.

29 There may even be a case where a new wholly ahuric verb of speaking was created in Young Avestan on the basis of a Gāthic passage. *vaš-/vaš̌-* (*medium tantum*, *fra-vaš-* Yt 14.54, Yt 17.18, 21, *vaš-* Vd 5.17, 22, Vd 19.6 ff., Vd 22.6), whose etymology is problematic, could have been extrapolated from *vašiietē / vašiietē* at Y 44.11. Humbach (1991, II: 155) proposed that the Old Avestan form is cognate with RV *vacyáte* 'issues forth, wells forth' from *vañc-* 'to twist' (used of poems, RV 1.142.4, 3.39.1, etc.). This may be correct, but as the Young Avestan composers were without the benefit of Vedic comparisons they may have understood the line *yaēibiiō mazdā ϑβōi vašiietē daēnā* as 'for whom your religion speaks/is spoken/ is taught, O Mazdā'. The Pahlavi version, Bartholomae (1904: 1330), Insler (1975: 247), etc., all translated it in this way! Gray (1927: 431) suggested a comparison between YAv *vaš—* 'say' and Balochi *gvašag*, Ormuri *ɣwacī*, but these could continue the more frequent Old Iranian verb of speaking *vac-* (cf. CHEUNG 2007: 404).

30 The quotations were noted in the lemmata of Bartholomae (1904). Recent studies about

LEXICAL VARIATION IN YOUNG AVESTAN

My suggestion is that the mere fact that such words were used in a certain way in the Gāthās had influence on the Young Avestan tradition, as they provided a kernel of opposing lexemes. The two groups were enlarged piece by piece in accordance with the choices of indiviual composers in the separate traditions of the Yašts, but in the Vidēvdād a more rigid dualistic lexical convention was established.

This study has focussed on the language in the transmitted Avestan texts and their literary conventions. It has deliberately avoided any speculation about the religious background to these conventions as this is still, and will continue to be, an area of controversy. The literary explanation proposed here for a phenomenon which has often been regarded as an interesting example of lexical variation in a language of the 1st millennium BCE underlines the principle in historical linguistics that a detailed philological analysis of what is actually found in the texts should precede attempts at a diachronic linguistic interpretation.

Abbreviations

Avestan

YAv	Young Avestan
Y	Yasna
Yt	Yašt
Vd	Vidēvdād

Vedic

RV	Ṛgveda
AV	Atharvaveda
ŚS	Śaunakasaṃhitā of the Atharvaveda
PS	Paippalādasaṃhitā of the Atharvaveda
MS	Maitrāyaṇīsaṃhitā of the Black Yajurveda

Old Avesta / Young Avesta intertextuality include the contributions by Cantera, Kellens and Skjærvø in Pirart (ed., 2013). Whatever view is taken about controversial topics such as the date and authorship of the Gāthās, their influence upon the Young Avesta is indicated by solid textual facts.

274 TUCKER

References

AHMADI, AMIR 2015, *The Daēva Cult in the Gāthās An ideological archaeology of Zoroastrianism*, London/New York: Routledge.

ANDRÉS-TOLEDO, MIGUEL ÁNGEL 2016, *The Zoroastrian Law to Expel the Demons: Wīdēwdād 10–15*, Wiesbaden: Harrassowitz.

BARTHOLOMAE, CHRISTIAN 1904, *Altiranisches Wörterbuch*, Strassburg: Trübner.

BENVENISTE, ÉMILE 1931, *Une différenciation de vocabulaire dans l'Avesta*, in W. Wüst (ed.), *Studia Indo-Iranica: Ehrengabe für Wilhelm Geiger*, Leipzig: Harrassowitz: 219–226.

BURROW, THOMAS 1973, *The Proto-Indoaryans*, "Journal of the Royal Asiatic Society" 105: 123–140.

CHEUNG, JOHNNY 2007, *Etymological Dictionary of the Iranian Verb*, Leiden: Brill.

DARMESTETER, JAMES 1892–1893, *Le Zend-Avesta*, 3 vols, (*Annales du Musée Guimet*), Paris: Adrien-Maisonneuve.

FRACHTENBERG, LEO J. 1908, *Etymological Studies in Ormazdian and Ahrimanian Words in Avestan*, in J.J. Modi (ed.), *Spiegel Memorial Volume*, Bombay: British India Press: 269–289.

GRAY, LOUIS H. 1927, *The 'Ahurian' and 'Daevian' vocabularies in the Avesta*, "Journal of the Royal Asiatic Society" 59: 427–441.

GÜNTERT, HERMANN 1914, *Über die ahurischen und daevischen Ausdrücke im Avesta* (Sitzungsberichte der Heidelberger Akademie der Wissenschaften (phil.-hist. Klasse), Band 5, No. 11), Heidelberg: Carl Winters Universitätsbuchhandlung: 1–34.

HINTZE, ALMUT 1994, *Der Zamyād-Yašt*, Wiesbaden: Ludwig Reichert.

HINTZE, ALMUT 2002, *On the Literary Structure of the Older Avesta*, "BSOAS" 65: 31–51.

HUMBACH, HELMUT 1991, *The Gāthās of Zarathushtra and Other Old Avestan Texts*, 2 vols, Heidelberg: Carl Winter.

HUMBACH, HELMUT—ICHAPORIA, PALLAN 1998, *Zamyād Yašt*, Wiesbaden: Harrassowitz.

INSLER, STANLEY 1975, *The Gāthās of Zarathustra* (Acta Iranica 8), Tehran/Liège: Brill.

JACKSON, ABRAHAM V.W. 1896–1904, *Die Iranische Religion*, in W. Geiger—E. Kuhn (edd.), *Grundriss der Iranischen Philologie*, Band 2, Strassburg: Trübner: 612–708.

JAMISON, STEPHANIE W. 2007, *The Rig Veda Between Two Worlds* (Collège de France, Publications de l'Institut de Civilisation Indienne, Fascicle 74), Paris: De Boccard.

JUSTI, FERDINAND 1864, *Handbuch der Zendsprache*, Leipzig: F.C.W. Vogel.

KELLENS, JEAN 1974, *Les noms-racines de l'Avesta*, Wiesbaden: Ludwig Reichert.

KELLENS, JEAN 1977, *Une représentation trifonctionelle de l'adolescence*, "MSS" 36: 53–57.

MAYRHOFER, MANFRED 1986–2001, *Etymologisches Wörterbuch des Altindoarischen*, 3 vols., Heidelberg: Carl Winter.

PIRART, ERIC 2013, *Le sort des Gāthās et autres études iraniennes in memoriam Jacques Duchesne-Guillemin* (Acta Iranica 54), Leuven: Peeters.

REDARD, CÉLINE 2021, *Études avestiques et mazdéennes* vol. 8. *Vidēvdād 19*, Leuven: Peeters.

SCHMITT, RÜDIGER 1999, *Bemerkungen zum Schlussabschnitt von Dareios' Grabinschrift DNb*, "Altorientalische Forschungen" 26: 127–139.

SCHWARTZ, MARTIN 2006a, *The Hymn to Haoma in Gathic Transformation: Traces of Iranian Poetry before Zarathushtra*, in A. Panaino (ed.), *The Scholarly Contribution of Ilya Gershevitch to the Development of Iranian Studies (Seminar held in Ravenna on 11th April, 2003)*, Milan: Associazione Culturale Mimesis: 85–106.

SCHWARTZ, MARTIN 2006b, *The Gāthās and other Old Avestan Poetry*, in G.-J. Pinault (ed.), *La Langue Poetique Indo-Européenne: Actes du colloque de travail de la Société des Études Indo-Européennes, Paris 22–23 octobre 2003*, Leuven: Peeters: 459–498.

SKJÆRVØ, PRODS O. 1994, *Hymnic Composition in the Avesta*, "Die Sprache" 36: 199–243.

SKJÆRVØ, PRODS O. 2007, *The Vidēvdād: its Ritual-Mythical Significance*, in V.S. Curtis—S. Stewart (edd.), *The Age of the Parthians*, London: I.B. Tauris: 105–142.

SWENNEN, PHILIPPE (ed.) 2015, *Démons iraniens: actes du colloque international organisé à la Université de Liège les 5 et 6 février 2009 à l'occasion des 65 ans de Jean Kellens*, Liège: Presses Universitaires de Liège.

TOPOROV, VLADIMIR L. 1981, *Die Ursprünge der indoeuropaischen Poetik*, "Poetica" 13: 189–251.

WACKERNAGEL—DEBRUNNER II,1 = WACKERNAGEL, JACOB 1905, *Altindische Grammatik* Vol. II, part 1, *Einleitung zur Wortlehre. Nominalkomposition*, Göttingen: Vandenhoeck & Ruprecht.

WATKINS, CALVERT 1970, *Language of gods and language of men: remarks on some Indo-European metalinguistic traditions*, in J. Puhvel (ed.), *Myth and Law Among the Indo-Europeans*, Berkeley: University of California Press: 1–17.

WATKINS, CALVERT 1995, *How to Kill a Dragon in Indo-European*, Oxford: Oxford University Press.

CHAPTER 11

Greek ἄγυρις 'gathering' between Dialectology and Indo-European Reconstruction

Roberto Batisti

1   Background: Cowgill's Law and irregular *o* ~ *u* variation in Ancient Greek[*]

In a number of cases, Ancient Greek shows a *u* vowel as a reflex of PIE **o*. Most instances have been explained by Warren Cowgill (1965: 156 f.) with the sound law that now bears his name.[1] In its broadest formulation (cf. SIHLER 1995: 42), Cowgill's Law states that PIE **o* became Gk. *u* between a resonant and a labial, in either order. The exact scope of the law, however, has subsequently been questioned. In an important article, Brent Vine (1999) formulated a restricted version of Cowgill's Law proper, which he subdivided into two rules:

1) $o > u / K^w\_N, N\_K^w$ (e.g. $*nok^wt$- > νυκτ- 'night', $*nog^wnó$- > γυμνός 'naked'[2])
2)   -*nom*- > -*num*- (e.g. $*h_3nh_3$-*men*- > $*onomn̥$ > ὄνυμα 'name')

He then added two new, separate rules describing the shift **o > u* in other environments:

3) $*$-*oli̯*- > -υλλ- (e.g. $*b^holi̯om$ > φύλλον 'leaf': Lat. *folium* 'id.')
4) $*$-*Tu̯oR*- > $*$-*Tu̯uR*- (e.g. $*k^wetu̯ores$ > Lesb. πέσσυρες 'four'), perhaps more generally $*$-*Cu̯oC*- > $*$-*Cu̯uC*- ($*su̯opnos$ > ὕπνος 'sleep')

As Vine himself (1999: 582 f.) pointed out, these "analyses [...] have the highly desirable morphological consequence of eliminating altogether the problem-

---

[*]   I am grateful to the audience in Oxford for their comments, and to the organizers of the Colloquium for making this splendid *gathering* of scholars possible. My thanks also go to Nicola Serafini for sharing with me a pre-publication version of his paper on the ἀγύρται that originally sparked my interest in that word's vocalism back in 2014. I am also indebted to Federico Alpi for discussion of Armenian matters, and to Nicole Edmea Pollan for polishing up my English. This paper has benefited greatly from the comments of the two anonymous referees. It goes without saying that I alone take full responsibilities for the views presented here.
[1]   Less precise are approaches like that of Joseph (1979), who admits a "sporadic" change *o > u* "in the context /C_C, where one of the consonants is a labial or a velar, and the other consonant is a sonorant [...] or both are labial or velar".
[2]   With the additional changes $*$-g^wn- > -μν- and $*n$- > $*ŋ$- (by assimilation?) > γ-.

© ROBERTO BATISTI, 2022 | DOI:10.1163/9789004508828_013

GREEK ΑΓΥΡΙΣ 'GATHERING'

atic notion of an unconstrained 'alternate Schwundstufe', or irregular *u*-colored prop vowel treatments". Nevertheless, these notions have not disappeared completely from the literature, possibly because several words with *u* for expected *o* fall outside of the law's scope. While in many cases substrate origin might be the source of irregular variation,[3] the phenomenon is more disturbing in words with a good inner-Greek or PIE etymology. The aim of this paper is to offer a new analysis for one of the most problematic forms (apparently) showing an 'irregular υ' that still resists explanation.

2 The Data

The feminine *i*-stem noun ἄγυρις means 'gathering, assembly, multitude, crowd' (Hom.+), with later, more specialized meanings such as 'army formation, corps' (Them. *Or.* 11.149c), 'collection' (Orph. *L.* 416).[4] In the Homeric poems, ἄγυρις is a near-synonym of ἀγορή, but not its perfect equivalent; while in the epics the latter only refers to gatherings of humans, the former may be used for collections of any kind of things and beings:[5]

Il. 16.661   ... ἐπεὶ βασιλῆα ἴδον βεβλαμμένον ἦτορ
              κείμενον ἐν νεκύων ἀγύρει ...
              ... as they saw the king struck to the heart,
              lying in a **pile** of corpses ...[6]

Il. 10.464 πέμψον ἐπὶ Θρῃκῶν ἀνδρῶν ἵππους (*v.l.* ἄγυρίν) τε καὶ εὐνάς
              lead us to the horses (*v.l.* **assembly-place**) and the tents of the
              Thracian men[7]

Il. 24.141 ὣς οἵ γ' ἐν νηῶν ἀγύρει μήτηρ τε καὶ υἱὸς
              πολλὰ πρὸς ἀλλήλους ἔπεα πτερόεντ' ἀγόρευον
              thus among the **gathering** of ships mother and son
              exchanged many winged words

---

3 Cf. BEEKES, *EDG*: xxxi.
4 LSJ[9]: 16, *Suppl.* 5.
5 *LfgrE* I: 101. All translations are mine unless otherwise indicated.
6 West (2000: 129), following Paley, considers vv. 661f. to be interpolated.
7 Here ἄγυριν, which would be supported by the parallel of *Od.* 3.31, is transmitted by Z and reported as a variant reading in A, but most other manuscripts have ἵππους: see the apparatus by West (1998: 307), who prints ἵππους.

Od. 3.31 ἷξον δ' ἐς Πυλίων ἀνδρῶν ἄγυρίν τε καὶ ἕδρας
they came to the **gathering** and the companies of the men of Pylos

More common than the simplex (which, after these Homeric passages, only occurs once in Classical literature at Eur. *IA* 753) are the compounds ὁμήγυρις, -ᾱγ- (Hom.+, mainly poetic) 'assembly, meeting (esp. of gods)' (→ ὁμηγυρίζομαι 'assemble, call together', *Od.* 16.376) and πανήγυρις, -ᾱγ- (Aesch.+, also in prose) 'general assembly, festival'. The stem ἀγυρ° forms several nominal derivatives, e.g. ἀγυρμός (Dion. Hal.+) 'gathering', ἄγυρμα (*AB* 327) 'collection', and the agent noun ἀγύρτης (Eur.+), -τήρ (Manetho) 'collector; beggar', which developed a specialized meaning 'begging priest', with pejorative connotation 'charlatan, swindler'.[8] From the former meaning derives ἀγυρτάζω (Str.+) 'collect (by begging), gather' (already in *Od.* 19.284 χρήματ' ἀγυρτάζειν πολλὴν ἐπὶ γαῖαν ἰόντι "to gather wealth by roaming over the wide earth"); from the latter, ἀγυρτικά (Str.+) 'vulgar lies', ἀγυρτώδης (Eudem. Rhet.) 'plebeian, vulgar', etc.[9] The lexica preserve a denominative verb ἀγυρίζειν· συνάγειν, ἀγυρτάζειν (Hesych. α 864 C.) and its derivative ἀγυρισμός 'collection' (*Sud.* α 386 A.).[10]

The relationship of this word-family to the verb ἀγείρω < *ager-ie/o-* 'gather'[11] and its *nomen actionis* ἀγορά 'assembly (place)' is usually taken for granted, but the vocalism has long been considered problematic.[12] Explanations proposed so far (most recently by HAWKINS 2013, on which see § 2.2.1 below) focus on the phonological side of the problem, assuming either a dialectal or a pan-Hellenic sound change to account for the υ. Less attention has been paid to the morphological derivation. A typical point of view is expressed by Nikolaev (2015: 262), who analyses ἄγυρις as a deverbative *nomen actionis* from the root of ἀγείρω, with either *o*- or zero grade. After evaluating previous solutions, and pointing out their weaknesses (§ 2), I am going to propose a different path of derivation that does not call for any special phonetic development (§ 3); subsequently, I will discuss the implications of my new proposal for the etymological relationship to ἀγείρω (§ 4).

---

8   On the ἀγύρται in Ancient Greece, see GIAMMELLARO 2006, 2012 and SERAFINI 2016.

9   See Bonsignore (2013: 78–82) on the insulting nature of the epithet Μητρὸς ἀγύρτης for a priest of Cybele in *AP* 6.218 (Alcaeus of Messene) and in other literary sources, sometimes in the compound form μητραγύρτης.

10 On this word-family see also HAWKINS 2013: 76.

11 See § 4 for a more in-depth analysis.

12 E.g. BUCK 1955: 45, HAMP 1981a: 84. Most recently, an assessment of the unsolved difficulties inherent to this form can be found in a lengthy footnote by Sowa (2019: 193 n. 12).

GREEK ΑΓΥΡΙΣ 'GATHERING'

3 Phonological Solutions

Two possibilities have generally been considered: ἀγυρ- could reflect zero-grade *agr̥- with a peculiar vocalization of the syllabic liquid, or o-grade *agor̥- with vowel raising.

3.1 *r̥ > υρ?

Most authorities[13] treat ἀγυρ- as a legitimate outcome of *agr̥-,[14] following in the lead of Schwyzer (1939: 351), who stated that "ρυ (λυ) bzw. υρ υλ stehen in einer Anzahl von Fällen für idg. r̥ l̥". Most of Schwyzer's examples, however, are now explainable as o-grades via Cowgill's Law (e.g. μύλη 'mill', μύλλω 'have sexual intercourse' lit. 'grind': Lat. *mola* 'millstone'); others are of dubious etymology and do not inspire much confidence (e.g. κύρτος 'weel, cage': κάρταλλος 'basket', Lat. *crātis* 'wickerwork, hurdle'?).

It is well known that the vocalization of PIE syllabic liquids took place in the individual Greek dialects, with different outcomes for both the timbre and the place of the vowel. The regular Aeolic reflex is -ρο-/-ορ-; o-coloring is also found in Arcado-Cypriot, possibly already in Mycenean, and as a conditioned reflex after a labial in Cretan; but *r̥ > υρ does not appear to be the regular treatment in any given dialect, not even as a conditioned change (except, perhaps, after *Kʷ-: see VAN BEEK 2022: 21–27). It would be methodologically unsound, then, to assume that this outcome just appeared sporadically in a handful of forms, with no identifiable phonological or geographical distribution.

To my knowledge, only Szemerényi (1964: 86 n. 4) has taken issue with a zero-grade *agr̥-i- from the *morphological* point of view, observing that in an i-stem an o-grade of the root would be more at home and comparing "κόπις, στρόφις, τρόφις, φρόνις, etc.";[15] but apart from the validity of this point, his own solution is unlikely (see § 2.2.1 below).

3.2 o > u?

Starting from an o-grade of the root, one can either think of a change *o* > *u* of Proto-Greek date, comparable to Cowgill's Law if not strictly part of it, or of a

---

13 E.g. H. Seiler in *LfgrE* I s.v., LEJEUNE 1972: 197 n. 1; *DGE s.v.*

14 At any rate, since forms like ἀγύρτης, ἀγυρμός and the like "can readily be derived within Greek from ἄγυρις" (HAMP 1981: 84), they are not necessarily independent testimonia for a phonological development *agr̥- > ἀγυρ-. In fact, most forms with υ are late and built from ἀγύρτης (HAWKINS 2013: 76).

15 On these formations, which included both *nomina agentis* and *nomina actionis*, see now NIKOLAEV 2015.

280   BATISTI

later, dialectal phenomenon, if one wishes to explain the ἀγυρ- forms as inter-dialectal borrowings.

3.2.1   Proto-Greek *o* > *u*

The change *o* > *u* in ἀγυρ- cannot be explained via Cowgill's Law as we know it, since *g_r is not a valid environment for any version of the law, and *g^w_r, which could conceivably be one, is ruled out by the velar in ἀγερ-, ἀγορ-, Myc. *a-ke-re*, *a-ko-ra*: a labiovelar would have produced alphabetic Gk. **ἄδερ-, **ἄβορ-, and would still be attested in Mycenean.[16] On the other hand, it is possible that we are dealing with a hitherto unrecognized sound change, distinct from, but typologically similar to, the ones codified by Cowgill and Vine.

This is the solution recently explored by Hawkins (2013: 28–45, 76–97) in his discussion of words with irregular *o > u. After a convincing rejection of most alleged examples, he narrows down his analysis to a small group of words (including ἄγυρις) where the conditions for the raising can allegedly be captured by the context /_ri̯. The raising would have been followed either by eventual loss of /j/ with compensatory lengthening, or by resyllabification to [i].

3.2.1.1   *Phonetic Motivation*

Hawkins' proposal is at first quite attractive, since it operates with a regular sound change in a well-defined context—Hawkins follows Vine in refusing to work with an "unconstrained 'alternate *Schwundstufe*'"—and it is based on the apparently very close parallel of *-oli̯- > -υλλ-. On further analysis, however, this proposal shows some problematic sides, starting with the typological plaus-ibility of its phonetic mechanism. It is generally agreed that in Greek *-li̯- was phonetically palatalized to a stronger degree than other *-Ri̯- clusters, probably yielding a long palatal lateral [ʎː], as suggested by its almost universal geminate reflex in most dialects regardless of the preceding vowel.[17] This reconstruction is supported by the typological observation that laterals and nasals are cross-linguistically much more likely to undergo palatalization than rhotics, which are, in fact, among the sounds more likely to *block* this process.[18] It is plaus-

---

16   Similarly, Rasmussen's (1985: 39 ff.) root *$h_2g u̯er$- with zero-grade *h_2gur- > ἀγυρ- needs the problematic assumption of a development *$h_2g u̯e/or$- > *h_2ge/or-.

17   See Hellemans (2005: 217–225), with literature.

18   For the universal resistance of rhotics to palatal coarticulation, see the surveys by HALL 2000 and BHAT 1978: 66. On the cross-linguistic avoidance of [rj] sequences see HALL—HAMANN 2010.

GREEK ΑΓΥΡΙΣ 'GATHERING' 281

ible that a strongly palatalized lateral affected the articulation of a preceding vowel; according to Bruce Hayes (*ap.* VINE 1999: 588 n. 68) the change *-*oli̯-* > *-*oľľ-* > -*ull-* had a 'compensatory' nature: "/o/ before palatalized /ľ/ may have developed into a segment with a final raised portion [...] when /ľľ/ depalatalized to /ll/, this preceding segment [...] could have developed toward /u/ as a way of maintaining contrast".[19]

As Vine himself pointed out (1999: 569), it should not be considered problematic that /r/ behaved differently. It should also be noted that *-*ni̯-* clusters, which were probably palatalized to a lesser degree than *-*li̯-*, but still more than *-*ri̯-*, had generally the same outcome as the latter, i.e. the apparent 'metathesis'[20] *-*Ri̯-* > -*i̯R-* after /a, o/, but *-*Ri̯-* > -:*R-* by compensatory lengthening after /e, i, u/: *φάν-jω > φαίνω, but *κρίν-jω > κρῑ́νω. Thus, given that *-*ri̯-* patterns with *-*ni̯-* against *-*li̯-* for the sake of 'metathesis', it would be strange if for the sake of *o*-raising it patterned with *-*li̯-* against *-*ni̯-* (as there are no Cowgill's Law-like effects from the latter).

3.2.1.2 Evidence and Counter-Evidence

Another weakness of Hawkins' proposal is the scarce attention paid to potential counterexamples. Hawkins (2013: 97) only briefly deals with μοῖρα 'part, portion, destiny' < *(*s*)*mor-i̯a*, assuming restoration after the transparently related μόρος 'fate'. This is in itself perfectly possible, but other counterexamples do not lend themselves so easily to this kind of analogical solution. To be sure, the sequence *-*ori̯-* is not very common in reconstructable Proto-Greek, but at least some forms have reliable IE etymologies:

1) κοίρανος[21] 'ruler, leader, commander' is an old derivative of PIE *kor-i̯o- 'Männerbund' (← *koro- 'army, war'[22]); the formation is paralleled by Old Norse *herjann* and British *Coriono-tōtae*. While the base κοιρ(ο)- itself is not unknown in Greek onomastics (Κοίρων, Κοιρωνίδαι, Κοιρόμαχος, Κοιρατάδας), and possibly produced other derivatives in Mycenaean (*ko-re-te* =

---

19 There are parallels for a conditioned raising even when the palatal feature is *not* lost; cf. the Florentine (and Standard Italian) 'anaphonesis' *e* > *i* /_*ʎ*: (Lat. *consĭlium, famĭlia* > Flor./It. *consiglio, famiglia* for expected *conséglio, faméglia*).

20 Hawkins refers to Kiparsky (1967), who assumed abrupt metathesis with no intermediate steps. More realistic, in my opinion, is the approach of Hock (2004), who treats the different outcomes of *-*Ri̯-* as part of the across-the-board palatalization of consonants before *yod* in prehistoric Greek, explaining the *i*-infection of a previous [-high, -front] vowel by gradual phonetic anticipation of the consonant's palatal quality.

21 Frisk, *GEW* I: 894; Chantraine, *DELG*: 553; Beekes, *EDG*: 732.

22 *NIL*: 440 ff.

κοιρητήρ?),[23] there is almost no trace in Greek of a simple *κορ(ο)- that could propel analogical restoration of -οιρ-.[24]

2) χοῖρος 'pig(let)', has less certain connections, but on the strength of Albanian *derr* 'swine' a PIE *$\hat{g}^h$orio- can be reconstructed;[25] in this case, too, no related root *χορ- was available in Greek to serve as a starting point for analogy.

3) Lesb. ὄνοιρος 'dream'[26] may represent zero-grade *$h_3n\underset{\circ}{r}$-io- (cf. Cret. ἄναιρος, with unexplained—assimilated?—initial) as opposed to full grade *h_3ner-io- of other dialects (Att. ὄνειρος).[27] Since the outcome of secondary, dialectal *-ori̯- < *-r̯i̯- was not necessarily the same of Common Greek *-ori̯-, this form is less relevant for our purposes. It is also conceivable, however, that ὄνοιρος goes back to the same lengthened-grade form *$h_3n\bar{o}r$-io- as Arm. *anurǰ*, with the resulting long diphthong shortened by Osthoff's Law (but see VAN BEEK 2022: 419).

4) Even less can be made of μάγοιρος 'cook' (: Att. μάγειρος, Dor. μάγῑρος), labelled as 'Aeolic' in Greg. Cor. p. 606 (cf. LSJ⁹: 1071). The word has no reliable etymology, making an interpretation of the different vocalisms difficult.[28]

5) οἰρών 'furrow, limit' presupposes a noun *οἶρος < *soHiro- (cf. Skt. *sīra*- 'plough'?), thus with a diphthong of different origin.[29]

On the other hand, the solution via Cowgill's Law-style raising is not too compelling for Hawkins' few examples other than ἄγυρις:

1) μορμύρω 'roar and boil' (of water) and πορφύρω 'heave, surge, swirl' (of the sea), 'grow red', may show the same kind of dissimilating reduplication as γογγύζω 'murmur, mumble' and ποππύζω 'smack the lips, cluck', as Hawkins himself admits; moreover, such words can easily be onomato-

---

23 But see GARCÍA RAMÓN 2010 against this connection.

24 Kaczyńska (2007) rightly calls attention to Hesych. κ 3655 L. κόρος· †πλῆθος ἀνθρώπων, which probably represents PIE *koro-; still, it would be the only attestation of this word in Greek, and moreover it is not clear that a synchronic connection with κοίρανος would have been felt.

25 A rival etymology from PIE *g^hoiro-, based on Arm. *gēr* and Russ. *žir* 'fat', is mentioned by Frisk (*GEW* II: 1107 f.) but judged less favourably by Chantraine (*DELG*: 1266 f.) and Beekes (*EDG*: 1640 f.). Hyllested's (2017: 189) suggestion that Finnic *karja* 'wild boar' is a loan from Proto-Germ. *garjaz would strengthen the reconstruction of PIE *$\hat{g}^h$orio-.

26 HAMM 1957: 16 and 28.

27 Frisk, *GEW* II: 393; Chantraine, *DELG*: 802; Beekes, *EDG*: 1082.

28 Frisk, *GEW* II: 156; Chantraine, *DELG*: 656; Beekes, *EDG*: 888 f.

29 Frisk, *GEW* II: 368; Chantraine, *DELG*: 786; Beekes, *EDG*: 1060.

GREEK ΑΓΥΡΙΣ 'GATHERING' 283

poeic, or at least phonosymbolically deformed, which reduces their usefulness in the establishment of a *regular* sound change.[30]

2) πτύρομαι 'be scared, frightened' is less likely to be strictly speaking onomatopoeic, but it is hard to see how it could be related to πτοέω 'terrify' < *p_ioh_2-$éie/o$-. Frisk (*GEW* II: 616) suggested a contamination between the root of πτοέω, πτήσσω and the ending of ὀδύρομαι, μύρομαι, but this solution is rightly rejected by Hawkins (2013: 92 n. 305).[31] One wishes—with ORESHKO (2013: 175)—that Hawkins had elaborated this point further.

3) σφυρίς (σπ-) 'basket', is mentioned on p. 96 as "discussed above", but I could not find any explicit discussion of this word in the foregoing pages.[32] Frisk (*GEW* II: 773) and Chantraine (*DELG*: 1041), both operating unproblematically with *u*-coloured zero-grade reflexes, derived it—either directly or via a noun *σπυρός—from the root *$sper$- of σπεῖρα, σπάρτον, while Beekes (*EDG*: 1387) rejects this derivation and assigns it to Pre-Greek on account of the variation σπ-/σφ-. Hawkins presumably wishes to derive the word from *$sp(^h)or$-id-, but does not specify its etymological connections; does he assume it contains the *o*-grade of *$sper$-?

All in all, then, the combined weight of the examples supporting Hawkins' rule cannot be deemed much higher—either quantitatively or qualitatively—than the weight of the counterexamples discussed above.

3.2.1.3 *Phonological Environment*
The law's phonological environment also calls for comment. Hawkins needs to assume that in ἄγυρις and σφυρίς "syllabic ι was restorable", i.e. that the law operated on oblique stems *$agor$-i-, *sp^hor-i- with zero-grade of the suffix before a vowel, and then spread analogically to the rest of the paradigm. This raises

---

30 On the onomatopoeic value of such forms see Skoda (1982: 92–95) and Tichy (1983: 277–288), assuming dissimilation *mur-mur- > μορμυρ- and *p^hur-p^hur- > πορφυρ-. According to Tichy (1983: 285), these two verbs were "erhaltene Vertreter eines umfangreicheren onomatopoetischen Teilsystems [...], das durch den Vokalismus ŏ-u und den Bezug zum Wasser charakterisiert war". Perpillou (1996: 25–31) points out that vocalism o...u is especially common in Greek words denoting strong noises, and that such a sequence need not be etymological, but is sometimes obtained through formal readjustments: "ces formes sont en fait englobées et *au besoin réorientées* dans un système expressif où la valeur affective des timbres est déterminante" (emphasis mine). At least μορμύρω has IE comparanda (Lat. *murmurō*, Arm. *mṙmṙim/-am* < *$murmur$-) showing that the u was ancient, and the o a likely product of dissimilation. On presents with full root reduplication plus suffix *-ie/o-, and their propensity for irregular dissimilatory changes in the reduplication syllable, see now Willi (2018: 163–165). On πορφύρω see now RODRÍGUEZ-PIEDRABUENA—JIMÉNEZ DELGADO 2021: 257.

31 Cf. already Chantraine (*DELG*: 950); Beekes (*EDG*: 1251).

32 The word appears only on p. 77, where Hamp's pre-Hellenic solution is rejected.

some problems for σφυρίς, which contains the suffix -ίδ- and shows no traces of having been previously inflected as an *i*-stem. Were the law extended to syllabic /i/, it would incur the same problems as Szemerényi's (1964: 85–87) rule of height assimilation *o ... i > u ... i, which is even less acceptable and would be easy to disprove.[33]

3.2.2 Dialectal $o > u$

The idea that the vocalism in ἄγυρις is dialectal, specifically Aeolic, harks back to ancient scholarship. A typical explanation is given by Eustath. *ad Od.* 2.7:

> γίνεται ἡ λέξις ἐκ τοῦ ἀγείρω. ἐξ αὐτῆς δέ, οὐ μόνον ἀγύρτης κατὰ τοὺς παλαιούς, ὁ ἀγείρων ὄχλον καὶ ἀπατεὼν καὶ ἀλαζών, καὶ ὄνομα δὲ βόλου κυβευτικοῦ, ἀλλὰ καὶ ἄγυρις. αἰολίζουσα οὐ μόνον τῇ τροπῇ τοῦ ο εἰς υ, ἀλλὰ καὶ τῷ τόνῳ. ὡς γὰρ ἑορτὴ ἔροτις Αἰολικῶς, οὕτω καὶ ἀγορὰ ἄγυρις.

> The word (*scil.* ἀγορά) comes from ἀγείρω. From it are derived not only ἀγύρτης, which according to the ancients (means) the gatherer of crowds, a cheat and a charlatan, and the name of a throw at dice, but also ἄγυρις. This form is **Aeolic** not only **in the change of** *o* **to** *u*, but also in the accent. For just as ἑορτή (is) ἔροτις in Aeolic, so ἀγορά (is) ἄγυρις.

Similar remarks are often found in the lexicographical tradition,[34] and are even repeated by LSJ[9] s.v. ἄγυρις "Aeol. for ἀγορά" (*sic*). A closer look at the data afforded by modern dialectology makes this simple explanation untenable. Several instances of $o > u$ are indeed attested in East Aeolic[35] (which is the dialect normally meant by 'Aeolic' in ancient scholarship), but none suits the case under consideration:

1) A sporadic change is attested in literary Lesbian before /m/ (e.g. ὕμος : ὁμός, ὕμφαλος : ὀμφαλός) and possibly before /p/ (ὑπίσσω : ὀπίσ(σ)ω).[36] In the inscriptions, it is assured for a single lexical root (ὕμο-, alternating with ὄμο-), but the development seems to be genuine.[37] This condi-

---

33 Szemerényi resorted to this "well-known" rule in order to derive πυκινός from *$poki$-$nó$-. It was partly based on isolated dialect forms (Hom. ἄλλυδις, ἄμυρις, Epidaur. ὑπωρυφία), and partly on cases now explained via Cowgill's Law (φύλλον, μύλλω), but contradicted by his own parallels for *ἄγορις (see § 2.1 above).

34 E.g. *An. Ox.* II 399.5 ἄγυρις· τὸ γ' υ ψιλὸν Αἰολικῶς, *Et. Gud.* 7.9 ἄγυρις Αἰολικόν, *Et. Or.* 27.6 κατ' Αἰολέας ἄγυρις καὶ πανήγυρις.

35 BECHTEL 1921: 27 f., BUCK 1955: 27, HAMM 1958: 27.

36 Hoffmann (1893: 400 f.) restricted the change to originally unaccented syllables.

37 BLÜMEL 1982: 44–46, HODOT 1990: 57–59.

GREEK ΑΓΥΡΙΣ 'GATHERING' 285

tioned raising before /m/ was shared by Arcadian (υμειος : ὅμοιος, στυμεον : στόμιον) and Mycenean (*tu-ma-ko /Stumargos/* besides *to-ma-ko /Stomargos/* 'White-Mouthed').[38] The phonetic environment, however, does not match that of ἄγυρις.

2) γίνυμαι, ὄνυμα are products of 'classic' Cowgill's Law in the context /n_m, while the vocalism of Att. γίγνομαι, ὄνομα is secondary.[39]

3) ἀπύ for ἀπό, also found in Mycenean and Arcado-Cyprian, is probably an old inherited variant.

4) ὕσδος (ὕσδων Sapph. 2.5 V., ὄσδω Sapph. 105a.1codd.: ὕσδῳ L.-P., V.) for ὄζος 'branch' is probably a hyper-Aeolism influenced by grammatical doctrine, if not a mere scribal error (NICKAU 1974).

Apart from the lack of precise parallels, the fundamental problem with any theory explaining the ἀγυρ-forms as Aeolic lies in their dialectal distribution, which has been studied by ADRADOS 1957 and WATHELET 1970. To be sure, ἄγυρις itself is not at home in Classical Attic; it is only attested once in a lyric passage in tragedy (Eur. *IA* 753 ἄγυρις Ἑλλάνων στρατιᾶς "the gathering of the Greek army"), where it can be a Homerism given the Iliadic theme. On the other hand, ἀγύρτης and πανήγυρις (-ἄγ-) are Panhellenic words, and at least ἀγυρμός seems old even in Attic, as it denoted the first day of the Eleusinian Mysteries. This evidence led Adrados (1957: 86) to conclude that "no es de creer que la solución υρ [...] sea específicamente eolia". Wathelet reviewed a dozen putative examples of 'Aeolic' *o > u* in the Homeric language, but concluded that most of them are unreliable. Regarding ἄγυρις, he too observed that in light of Att. πανήγυρις and Dor. παναγυριος (Schwyzer *Del.*[3] 74, l. 103; Messenian: Andane, 1st century BC), παναγυρ[ιε]ς (Schwyzer *Del.*[3] 253, l. 78; Coan: Halasarna, 3rd/2nd c. BC), "une origine uniquement éolienne est [...] fort douteuse" (1970: 166).[40]

4 A Morphological Solution

To sum up, it seems impossible to derive ἄγυρις from either a zero- or an *o*-grade preform by regular sound change at any stage of the history of Greek. It may seem unavoidable to admit that "in some cases a rather free variation

---

38 GARCÍA RAMÓN 2018: 37.

39 BLÜMEL 1982: 49 f.

40 Cf. already Lambert (1903: 49): "ἄγυρις ne peut être revendiqué comme création éolienne". Hawkins (2013: 77) adds that, conversely, ἀγορ-forms *are* attested in the Aeolic domain. See now also Sowa (2019: 194 n. 12) on the difficulty of attributing ἄγυρις "to either epigraphical or literary Lesbian".

between υ- and o-form was possible" (ORESHKO 2013: 175). However, before giving up the possibility of principled explanation, I would like to tackle the problem from a different angle by assuming that the phonology is regular, while the derivational history of the word is somehow different from how it is usually reconstructed.

4.1 The *tʰamu- Cluster

A key to understanding the formation of ἄγυρις may come from a word extremely close in both form and meaning, namely the *i*-stem feminine noun θάμυρις 'assembly'. As a common noun, it is only preserved by Hesychius (θ 90 L.), with the gloss πανήγυρις, σύνοδος ἢ πυκνότης τινῶν. καὶ ὁδοὺς θαμυρὰς τὰς λεωφόρους. ἔστι δὲ καὶ κύριον ὄνομα "assembly, meeting, or thick concentration of something. And highways (are called) *hodoi thamurai*. It is also a personal name". And indeed, Θάμυρις (Att. Θαμύρας) was the name of a mythical Thracian bard known for trying to compete with the Muses, who by way of punishment blinded him and took away his singing and playing ability.[41] As a negative example of punished hybris, he was well-known enough to become proverbial.[42] His story, first told in the *Iliad* (2.591–600), was later taken up by Attic drama: Thamyras was the hero of a lost Sophoclean tragedy and of a play by Antiphanes Comicus (3rd c. BC); he also features in the pseudo-Euripidean *Rhesus* (vv. 915–925). It is precisely the wordplay in Soph. fr. 245 that suggests that his was a 'speaking name', still fully understood by the audiences of 5th century Athens:

> μουσομανεῖ δ' ἐλήφθην
> ἀνάγκαι, ποτὶ δ' εἴραν
> ἔρχομαι, ἔκ τε λύρας
> ἔκ τε νόμων, οὓς Θαμύρας
> περίαλλα μουσοποιεῖ.

> And I was seized by a compulsion
> to be mad for music, and **went**
> **to the place of assembly**, under the force of the lyre
> and the force of the measures, with which Thamyras
> makes music supremely.
>> transl. WILSON 2009

---

41   On the figure of Thamyris in Greek culture, see WILSON 2009 and KÁRPÁTI 2016.

42   Cf. Hesych. θ 92 L. Θάμυρις μαίνεται· παροιμία, ἐπὶ τῶν κατὰ σύνεσιν παράλογόν τι πραττόντων ≈ *Sud.* θ 42 Α.

GREEK ΑΓΥΡΙΣ 'GATHERING'   287

Wilson, following Lloyd-Jones, accepts at v. 2 Campbell's conjecture δ' εἴραν
(: ποτὶ δειράν, ποτίδειραν codd.), which brings into the text a rare Ionic word
for '(place of) assembly' (εἴρη, meaning ἀγορά, or τὴν ἐκκλησίαν καὶ τὴν μαντείαν
according to Eustath. *ad Il.* 18.531). He observes that "this 'place of assembly'—
and perhaps of prophecy—will be where Thamyras played his lyre", invoking
"the linguistic and epigraphic evidence for the meaning of the name Θάμυρις
itself" (WILSON 2009: 69). There has been some debate on the derivational
relationship between the PN and the noun θάμυρις: was Θάμυρις extracted *a
posteriori* from the name of a corporation of *Θαμυρίδαι 'singers at public gatherings', like Homer from the Homeridai (← *ὅμαρος or *ὅμαρις 'public gathering'?) according to the hypothesis of DURANTE 1976 and WEST 1999,[43] or was
it a *Kurzform* of *Θαμυρικλῆς *uel sim.*?[44] The existence of the Thamyridai could
be supported by the θαμυρίδδοντες* mentioned in a Boeotian inscription (gen.
pl. -όντων: SEG XXIII 53.2; Thespiae, c. 400–350 BC) and variously interpreted
as 'Thamyris-worshippers' or simply 'gatherers' ~ 'presidents of the assembly'
(CHANIOTIS 2009: 221f., cf. Hesych. θ 91 L. θαμυρίζει· ἀθροίζει, συνάγει).[45] More
likely, the name Thamyris is simply identical to the noun θάμυρις,[46] characteriz-
ing the bard as a personification of the "centripetal force of song, the gathering
into union and collectivity" (WILSON 2009: 50f.).[47]

Now, θάμυρις is part of a word-family centred on the *u*-stem adjective θαμύς
'thick, packed, crowded',[48] attested in the singular only by Ap. Dysc. *Adv.* 153.4,

---

43   On the importance of assemblies—featuring poetic contests—among Indo-European
      peoples, see WEST 2007: 72–74.

44   Cf. Ἄριστις, Δᾶμις, Κάλλις as diminutives of compound names in Ἀριστο°, Δημο°, Καλλι°
      (MASSON 1987).

45   ROESCH (1982: 140) does not rule out that "le choix du verbe θαμυρίζειν, qui ne semble
      pas attesté ailleurs, ait été dicté par le double sens de θάμυρις"; similarly CLAY 2004: 153,
      WILSON 2009: 51.

46   There is no reason to think, with B. Mader (*LfgrE* 11: 969) and De Lamberterie (1990: 670),
      that the *name* itself is Thracian. But even if it were, it seems clear that it underwent folk-
      etymological identification with the noun θάμυρις.

47   Wilson (2009: 68 n. 91) even speculates that "Sophocles may have [...] punned, with ety-
      mological force, on the name of Thamyras at some point in the play, associating the idea
      of 'populous gathering' with him *via* terms such as θαμά, θαμέες, θαμίζω". Wilson's explan-
      ation of the name is accepted by KÁRPÁTI 2016: 188.

48   See DE LAMBERTERIE 1990: 664–675. Root unknown: not *dʰehₗ- (τίθημι 'put', θωμός θημῶν
      'heap'), which has a zero-grade θε- (*pace* SZEMERÉNYI 1964: 88). Nikolaev (2009: 476)
      draws up an interesting comparison with Lat. *femur*, gen. *feminis/femoris* 'thigh', also
      without a good etymology, which would go back to a heteroclite *dʰemuṛ/-n- 'thick muscle'
      built on the loc. *dʰm̥-u-én 'in thickness' of a *u*-stem noun *dʰo/emu- 'thickness', which
      also acted as derivational basis of the adj. *dʰém-u-, *dʰm̥-éu̯-s seen in Gk. θαμύς. As a
      formal and semantic parallel, Nikolaev cites Gk. αὐχήν, Aeol. ἄμφην (Theocr. 30.28) 'neck'

but normally found in the plural m. θαμέες (Hom.), f. θαμειαί. Other traces of a *u*-stem surface in the comparative θαμύντεραι· πυκνότεραι (Hesych. θ 89 L., *metri causa* for *θαμύτεραι) and in the PN Θαμυκλῆς 'he who acquires lasting glory'. Hesychian "ὁδοὺς θαμυράς" attests an adjective θαμυρός*, with a 'complex Caland suffix' *-*u-ró*- besides the simple *-*u*- of θαμύς (cf. pairs like λιγύς : λιγυρός 'clear-toned, shrill'). Further related forms include an adverb θαμά 'thickly, frequently' (→ θαμίζω 'frequent, haunt'), the adjective θαμ(ε)ινός 'crowded', and perhaps the noun θάμνος 'bush'.

4.2 The *agu- Cluster

The striking accentuation of θαμειαί is shared by, among others, the noun ἄγυια pl. ἀγυιαί 'street(s)' (Hom+, mainly but not exclusively poetic; see CHRISTOL 1979, DU BOUCHET 2004: 62–90). According to a recent analysis by LUNDQUIST (2021: 279–285), ἀγυιαί implies an old adjective *ἀγύς. Building on work by DE LAMBERTERIE (1990: 644–646), Lundquist argues that the oxytonesis in forms such as θαμειαί and ἀγυιαί is an archaism, reflecting the alleged PIE accentuation of feminine *u*-stem adjectives (cf. Ved. -*ví* < PIE *-*u̯-íh₂*), in contrast to Classical -εῖα(ι) remade after the masculine/neuter stem. The same archaism is also preserved in a few other fossilized forms: the placename Πλαταιαί (vs. paradigmatic πλατεῖαι 'broad'), ταρφειαί 'thick, close', ὀργυιαί 'length of the outstretched arms' (cf. ὀρέγω 'stretch' < *$h_3$reǵ-). These forms differ in the ablaut of the suffix: -υιαί would preserve the inherited zero grade, while -ειαί adopted the ablaut (but not the accent) of the masc./neut. oblique stem -έ(ϝ)-.[49] Forms frozen in the singular (θάλεια, λάχεια, λίγεια) or backformed from the plural (ἄγυια, ὄργυια) shifted instead to default recessive accentuation;[50] but even in the singular ἄγυια and ὄργυια remained finally accented in the oblique cases (ἀγυιᾶς, -υιᾷ, ὀργυιᾶς, -υιᾷ, cf. Ved. gen.-abl. sg. *pr̥thivyā́s*, dat. *pr̥thvyái*).

< *h_2mǵʰ-u̯-én-, Arm. *awjik'* 'collar' < *h_2mǵʰ-u̯-ii̯ā, from PIE *$h_2$emǵʰ-u̯-* 'narrow' (Ved. *aṁhú°*, Goth. *aggwu*-). For the designation of the thigh as 'thick (muscle)', one could add the Homeric formula παχέος παρὰ μηροῦ (*Il.* 16.473 = *Od.* 10.439, 11.231), and compare *Il.* 16.314 f. πρυμνὸν σκέλος, ἔνθα **πάχιστος** | μυῶν ἀνθρώπου πέλεται.

49 The variant -αιαί is ambiguous in this respect, as it could reflect either e-grade *$pl̥th_2$-eu̯íh₂ or zero-grade *$pl̥th_2$-u̯íh₂.

50 DIEU (2016: 323–357) also argues for old suffixal accent, although he suspects that ἄγυια owes its accentuation to the analogical influence of ὄργυια (343–346). According to other analyses, these nouns reflect instead an old mobile paradigm: cf. SIHLER 1995: 349 f. (Pre-PIE **-éu̯-ih₂/**-u̯iéh₂-, differently levelled in Gk. and Indo-Ir.); JASANOFF 2018: 15 (PIE *R(é)-u-ih₂/*R(z)-u-i̯éh₂-, preserved in Gk. relic forms but lost in Vedic). The question of ablaut in the root is immaterial in our case, since both zero-grade *h_2ǵ- and full-grade *h_2eǵ- would yield Gk. ἀγ-.

GREEK ΑΓΥΙΣ 'GATHERING' 289

Outside Greek, a possible cognate of ἄγυια is found in Armenian *acu* 'garden bed' (MARTIROSYAN, *EDAIL*: 18; 2013: 109).[51] Martirosyan reconstructs an *us*-stem *$*aǵ-us-ih_2$*, which is a definite morphological possibility,[52] but the outcome of *$*aǵ-u-ih_2$* would arguably be the same, in Armenian[53] as well as in Greek. If this word-equation is correct, the adjective *$*aǵ-ú-$* could be of at least 'Greco-Armenian' date, possibly a common innovation.[54] In view of "ὁδοὺς θαμυράς", the meaning of *$*ἀγυιαί$* (*scil.* ὁδοί) could have been 'crowded (streets)', rather than 'the leading ones' *uel sim.*, usually—but quite problematically—assumed by those analysing it as a perfect participle of ἄγω (see further § 4 below).[55]

The striking formal and semantic parallelism between the families θαμύς : θαμειαί : θάμυρις and *$*ἀγύς$* : ἀγυιαί : ἄγυρις[56] suggests that the last form, just like θάμυρις, may owe its -υ- to derivation from an old *u*-stem adjective. As for the derivational path leading from this adjective to an *i*-stem noun, the intermediate step was probably an adjective in -*ro*-. In fact, it seems likely that θάμυρις 'gathering' was derived from θαμυρός* 'frequented'[57] according to the well-known pattern forming *i*-stem abstract nouns from *o*-stem adjectives, first recognized by Schindler (1980):

1) *$*h_2aḱro-$* 'high' (Gk. ἄκρος 'topmost')
    → *$*h_2e/oḱri-$* 'height, top' (Ved. °*áśri-* 'edge', Gk. ὄκρις 'point'; Gk. ἄκρις, Lat. *ocris* 'peak');

2) *$*n̥bʰró-$* 'wet' (Ved. *abhrá-* 'rain-cloud', Gk. ἀφρός 'foam')
    → *$*n̥bʰri-$* 'wetness' (Lat. *imber* 'rain');

---

51 For the semantic shift 'road, path' > 'garden bed', Martirosyan adduces the parallel of Arm. *marg* 'meadow', dial. 'garden bed', from an Iranian source (Parth. *marγ* 'wood, meadow') cognate with Skt. *mārga-* '(wild) path, road'.

52 For an analysis of Greek nouns in -υια as reflexes of PIE *us*-stems, with Vedic and Germanic comparanda, see e.g. MALZAHN 2014 and SCHAFFNER 2019.

53 Cf. Arm. (*y*)*artʿu* 'wide, broad; mighty, victorious' < *$*pl̥th_2uih_2$* (: Ved. *pr̥thvī́-*, Gk. πλατεῖα).

54 Middle Irish *ág* 'battle' was probably inflected as a *u*-stem, but its original stem-class and ablaut grade are doubtful (REPANŠEK 2013: 76 f.).

55 Lat. *agēa* 'gangway in a ship' (Enn. *fr.* 512 S.) is suspected of being a loan from Gk. ἄγυια or, rather, a West-Gk. byform *$*ἀγεια$* 'street'. Du Bouchet (2004: 89) observes that it is unlikely that the suffix was remade after dialectal pf. ptc. in -εῖα, since the word probably was never a participle and it did not look like one. On the other hand, if it was still perceived as a *u*-stem adjective, it could have participated in the general remodeling of -υῖα to -εῖα.

56 Interestingly, the parallelism partly extends to the family of ταρφύς*, f. pl. ταρφειαί 'thick', another near-synonym of θαμύς, and like it confined to epic and poetic language. In the sense 'close, compact, crowded' these words were replaced in later Greek by the family of πυκνός.

57 In view of θαμυρός, it seems unlikely that θάμυρις was formed after πανήγυρις, as suggested by the etymological dictionaries and by De Lamberterie (1990: 669), who briefly hints at the solution presented here, only to reject it.

3) $*d^heg^{wh}ro$- 'hot, burning' (Gk. τέφρα 'ashes')

   → $*d^heg^{wh}ri$- 'heat' (Lat. *febris* 'fever').

By the same token, ἄγυρις could conceivably be an abstract noun built to an adjective $*aguró$- 'collected', 'crowded'.[58] Such an adjective is admittedly unattested; however, it might lie behind the denominative verb ἀγυρέω virtually attested in Hesychius. The gloss, transmitted by the manuscript as ἀγυρεῖ· ἀθροισματεῖ συγκροτεῖ and printed by Latte as α 863 ἀγύρει· [ἀθροίσματι. ἢ] συγκροτεῖ, is now separated by Cunningham, no doubt correctly, into 862a ἀγύρει· ἀθροίσματι "in a gathering" and 862b ⟨ἀγυρεῖ·⟩ συγκροτεῖ "collects".[59]

The connection between ἀγυιαί and ἄγυρις may be reinforced by semantic considerations. In his lexical study of ἄγυια, Du Bouchet (2004: 67–90) has shown that, while in certain dialects (Elean, Delphic) it apparently became the unmarked word for 'street', its oldest attestations show connotations that are quite compatible with the hypothesis just proposed. In Homeric usage, ἄγυια is specifically the *urban* street, characterized as a "lieu de circulation et de rencontre" (68). In later poetry, it is typically employed "pour désigner le lieu où les *rejouissances publiques* ont lieu, [...] *souvent lié à l'agora* [...], lieu de la vie judiciaire [...] ou commerciale" (72, my emphasis). Even Attic, where the word was otherwise obsolete, preserved the archaic religious formula κνισᾶν ἀγυιάς 'to fill the streets with the smoke (of sacrifices)', which describes "des célébrations auxquelles participe la ville tout entière" (73). In other words, one may say that, not unlike the ἀγορά, the ἀγυιαί were a place apt for (παν)αγύρεις— an association that would be easily explainable if these terms were ultimately related.[60]

5   Back to ἀγείρω: Deeper Etymological Connections

A new account of ἄγυρις must still explain the closeness in form and meaning to ἀγείρω, which can hardly be accidental. The present ἀγείρω, Lesb. ἀγέρρω can be traced back to Proto-Gk. $*ager\text{-}ie/o$-.[61] According to Kümmel (LIV^2: 276),

---

58   The shift from an abstract meaning 'multitude, gathering' to more concrete or individualizing ones 'crowd, pile, collection' is trivial and paralleled by other formations in -*i*-, as shown by the examples above.

59   The reading ἀγυρεῖ was already in Schmidt's edition, and is quoted by LSJ⁹: 16.

60   It is suggestive that all three words occur together in Luc. *Prom.* 14, quoting Arat. *Phaen.* 1.2 f.: ἀπανταχοῦ δὲ βωμοὺς καὶ θυσίας καὶ ναοὺς καὶ **πανηγύρεις**· 'μεσταὶ δὲ Διὸς πᾶσαι μὲν ἀγυιαί, / πᾶσαι δ' ἀνθρώπων ἀγοραί' "everywhere there are altars, sacrifices, temples, and **festivals**: 'all the **streets** are full of Zeus, / and all the **market-places** of men'".

61   Compare the similar-sounding $*h_1ger\text{-}ie/o$- > ἐγείρω 'awaken, rouse, stir up', some of whose forms were in fact confused with those of ἀγείρω.

GREEK ΑΓΥΡΙΣ 'GATHERING' 291

the Homeric thematic aorist ἀγέροντο, ἀγρόμενοι is the most archaic form;[62] the -ι̯e/o- present is analogical to the s-aor. ἤγειρα, itself a *Neubildung*. Both creations are already Mycenean: PY Cc 660 *a-ke-re* (= Att. ἀγείρει), PY Vn 493.1 *a-ke-ra₂-te* (= Att. ἀγείραντες).[63] The *nomen actionis* ἀγορά 'assembly (place)', Myc. *a-ko-ra* (KN, PY; cf. adj. *a-ko-ra-jo* [KN]) was created after the common and productive pattern φέρω : φορά, φθείρω : φθορά, etc.

The root is apparently confined to Greek, but allows reconstruction as PIE *h_2ger-,[64] and a possible Tocharian cognate is now mentioned by Adams (2013: 162; cf. *LIV Addenda s.v.*): Toch. B *kār*- 'gather' could represent an *o*-grade present *h_2gor-. Other potential traces of *h_2ger- augmented with further root extensions or suffixes have been detected in other IE branches:[65]

1) *$h_2g\acute{r}$-em- in Ved. *grā́ma*- 'troop; inhabitants of a place; village, hamlet' (*EWAia* I: 508), Lat. *gremium* 'lap', PSl *$gramada$, *$gr\partial mada$ 'heap, pile', Lith. *grùmulas* 'lump'? (*EDLIL*: 272, *EDSIL*: 190, *EDBIL*: 191);

2) *$h_2g\acute{r}$-tro- in Proto-Germ. *$kurpra$ ~ *$kurdra$ 'flock'? (*EDPG*: 312);

3) *$h_2g\acute{r}$-nó- in Ved. *gaṇá*- 'flock, troop, multitude' < *$gṛṇá$-? (*EWAia* I: 459).

It is often assumed that *h_2ger- was not a primitive root in PIE, but somehow derived from *h_2eg- 'drive, lead' (: Gk. ἄγω, Lat. *agō*, Skt. *ajati* etc.; *IEW* I: 4–6, *LIV²*: 255 f.) via a root extension *-(e)r- (BORGHINI 1980), or as a denominative verb from an -r-stem neuter noun *h_2eg-r- (ANTTILA 2000) or a thematic derivative *h_2eg-er(-o)- (BAMMESBERGER 1982). More speculatively, Cowgill (1978) suggested that ἀγείρω was built on the strong stem of a heteroclitic noun *h_2eg-r/n-, with the weak stem preserved in ἀγών 'gathering' > 'games'; but he unnecessarily doubted the connection to ἄγω on semantic grounds. The same *r*-extension that underlies *h_2ger- was possibly the basis for thematized *h_2egro- 'field' (Gk. ἀγρός, Lat. *ager*, Ved. *ájra*-, Goth. *akrs*, etc.), but an assessment of the

---

62 According to Willi (2018: 339 n. 72), ἀγέροντο, ἀγέρεσθαι may be substitutes for older *ἄγροντο, *ἀγρέσθαι.

63 These forms are of course much discussed in the context of the Mycenean treatment of *-Rs- and *-Ri̯-clusters. The *vexata quaestio* whether these spellings represent /agēr-/ with compensatory lengthening, /agerr-/ with gemination, or an intermediate stage /ageri̯-/, /agerʰ-/ or /ageʰr-/, though of great import for the historical phonology of Greek, is not immediately relevant here, and will be left open.

64 *LIV²*: 276; BEEKES, *EDG*: 10. Implausible Semitic etymologies in SEMERANO 1994: 6 and VERNET PONS 2012. HAMP 1981a, 1981b, 1991 resorts to 'Pelasgian', i.e. a hypothetical Pre-Greek IE substrate language. At any rate, ἀ- is hardly the zero grade of ἐν, as per *IEW* II: 382 f. s.v. I. *ger, gere*. The very existence of a zero-grade variant *ṇ of the PIE local particle *en 'in' has most recently been doubted by VAN BEEK 2018.

65 On the other hand, it remains very dubious that Gk. γάργαρα ~ γέργερα 'heaps, lot, plenty', γαργαίρω 'swarm with' or Lat. *grex* 'herd, flock' belong here.

exact relationship between these forms (and ἀγρέω 'take, seize', ἀγρετός* 'taken', ἄγρα 'hunting') is notoriously complicated, and cannot be pursued here; see the discussion and the bibliography in *NIL*: 267–277 s.v. *h₂eĝ-.[66]

According to Lundquist (2017: 53), the root *h₂eĝ- is also the most likely candidate for the etymology of *ἀγύς, ἄγυια. The idea of a relationship between ἄγω and ἄγυια is not a new one, and in fact it dates back to antiquity. It was rejected as folk-etymology by Szemerényi (1964: 206–208) and Christol (1979: 69–71),[67] but, as Lundquist (2021: 285) remarks, these authors object "mainly to the semantics of ἄγυια if taken from a perfect participle". More recently, Malzahn (2014: 168f.) defended the connection, though reconstructing an *us*-stem *h₂ĝ-us-ih₂.[68] The case for a genuine etymological relationship is further strengthened, in Martirosyan's view (*EDAIL*: 18), by the parallelism between Gk. ἄγω 'lead': ἄγυια 'street' and Arm. *acem* 'lead, move, bring': *acu* 'garden bed'. It remains to be seen what semantic development could lead from a root meaning 'to drive' to an adjective meaning 'compact, thick'. In fact, *u*-stem adjectives are typical members of the Caland system. The root *h₂eĝ- does build a good number of Caland-like formations in the IE languages,[69] but unlike typical Caland roots do it does not express a basic, non-verbal and non-relational adjectival meaning.[70] This advises caution in deriving *ἀγύς and related forms from this root, even though it is not impossible that this kind of derivation was extended to roots that did not originally take part in the Caland system: *u*-stem adjectives were a closed class in historical Greek, but may have enjoyed some degree of productivity at a prehistorical stage.[71]

If the above reconstruction is correct, ἄγυρις—derived from *ἀγύς via *ἀγυρός—*would* be related to ἀγείρω after all, but only inasmuch as both would be distant derivatives of the very productive root *h₂eĝ-. Even if ἀγυρ° forms were not originally derived from *h₂ĝer-, in historical times they were doubtless attracted to the system of ἀγείρω.[72] This connection, strongly supported

---

66 Cf. also VINE 1998: 50; ANTTILA 2000: 133–155 and *passim*.

67 Beekes (1998: 25f.) took the extreme view that this and all nouns in -υια are Pre-Greek.

68 More generally, Malzahn (2014) prefers to see Greek isolated words in -υια as derivatives of *us*-stems rather than *u*-stems, while leaving open the possibility that at least in some cases the former may presuppose the latter. The analysis as *us*-stems is most recently endorsed by Schaffner (2019).

69 Cf. HÖFLER 2016: 2, with a list of nominal formations.

70 Cf. RAU 2009: 77–109.

71 Cf. DE LAMBERTERIE 1990: 960.

72 The equivalence was already fully in place in the Homeric language, where ὁμηγερέες 'assembled' (*v.l.* -ηγυρ-!) coexists with ὁμήγυρις 'assembly'; cf. the *figura etymologica* ὁμηγυρίσασθαι ... εἰς ἀγορήν 'summon to assembly' (*Od.* 16.376). This also answers to the question,

GREEK ΑΓΥΡΙΣ 'GATHERING'   293

by the closeness in form and meaning, was fated to become unavoidable after
*ἀγύς was lost and ἄγυια acquired a specialized meaning. In other words, ἀγυρ-
was felt by now as a possible stem variant of ἀγείρω besides ἀγερ- and ἀγορ-.
Evidence in this direction comes from the dialectal variants ἄγερσις, °ἄγορσις,
ἄγορρις, ἄγαρρις discussed by Van Beek (2022: 134 f). These look like parallel,
more transparent formations built from the 'neo-root' ἀγερ-/ἀγορ-/ἀγr̥-[73] with
the common abstract-forming suffix -σις < *-ti-. It should be noted that ἄγῠρις
did *not* contain -σις, as it was an *i*-stem, not a *-ti*-stem. Blass (1890: xiii–xiv)
found it difficult to reconcile all these forms precisely because he started from
the false premise that all of them contained -σις: "man muss […] wie hier [i.e.
in ἄγορρις, ἄγαρρις] das doppelte ρ, so in πανήγυρις und ἄγυρις das einfache auf
ρσ zurückführen. Nach welchem Lautgesetze?" There was in fact no sound law
involved, just a different suffix.

6   Conclusions

I have proposed that ἄγυρις 'gathering' is an *i*-stem nominalization of a thematic adjective *ἀγυρός 'tightly packed, crowded', in turn derived from a *u*-stem
adjective *ἀγύς of similar meaning, whose feminine plural survived substant-
ivized as ἀγυιαί 'streets'. It is possible that this adjective belonged to the root
*$h_2e\acute{g}$- 'drive', which is also the probable ultimate origin of the verb ἀγείρω
'gather'. If this was the case, ἄγυρις was indeed related to ἀγείρω, but not as a
direct derivative.

If the above is correct, ἄγυρις and its family can be explained with recourse to
well-attested processes of morphological derivation, and with no need to postulate a special dialectal development, or an irregular Proto-Greek *u*-coloured

---

raised by an anonymous referee, of why the agent noun ἀγύρτης, -τήρ and the action/result
nouns ἀγυρμός, ἄγυρμα show an athematic stem ἀγυρ- if the ultimate origin of the family
was an *o*-stem adj. *ἀγυρός. In fact, one would not expect such forms to be derived from
an adjective at all, but rather from a verbal stem. In my opinion, these nouns show that
ἀγυρ- was already felt as a possible stem variant of ἀγερ-/ἀγορ-, probably after ἄγυρις was
interpreted as an abstract of ἀγείρω.

73   Arcad. °ἄγορσις (*IG* V 2,3.26), ἄγορρις (Hesych.; of uncertain dialectal appurtenance, cf.
     SOWA 2019: 193f.), W. Ion. ἄγαρρις (*IG* XIV 759, Naples) can all reflect zero-grade *agr̥-ti-
     (the first two, in principle, also an *o*-grade). E. Ion. ἄγερσις (Hdt. 7.5.48; *SIG* 2660.3, Mile-
     tus) copies the full grade of ἀγείρω similarly to other *ti*-stem nouns with secondary full
     grade after the present, e.g. ἔγερσις ← ἐγείρω, φεῦξις (besides older φύξις) ← φεύγω (VINE
     2004: 358). The recourse to all possible ablaut grades also speaks against the antiquity of
     these formations. Cf. also ἀγερμός besides ἀγυρμός.

reduced grade. Moreover, the proposed etymology brings additional evidence for a prehistorical *u*-stem adjective *ἀγύς, already suggested on independent grounds by Lundquist (2021) and potentially supported by Armenian data.

Methodologically, while it is true that when facing irregular variation an "explanation [...] in terms of Greek dialectology or areal linguistics" is often preferable to one in terms of IE reconstruction (ORESHKO 2013: 175), I argue that in the present case the dialectological explanations pursued so far may prove inferior to one grounded in Greek and PIE derivational morphology.

Appendix: The PN Ἄγυρις and the Place-Name Ἀγύριον

In onomastics, Ἄγυρις is mentioned by Diodorus Siculus (14.9.2, 78.7, 95.4–96.1) as a tyrant of Agyrion in Sicily (5th/4th century BC).[74] The PN could be a diminutive of a compound with a first member Ἀγυρι° or Ἀγυρο° (see § 3.1. on Θάμυρις), which perhaps not coincidentally echoed the name of the town. The place-name Ἀγύριον is transmitted with variants (Ἀγούριον Ptol. 3.4.7, Ἀγύρινα Steph. Byz. α 52 B.) which could suggest foreign origin. I think, however, that it could well mean 'place of (festive) gathering', either as a Greek formation (← ἄγυρις) or as folk-etymological reinterpretation of a native name. The town was renowned for its ancient cult of Heracles, who was honored—jointly with Iolaos and Geryon—with splendid gatherings (ἀπαντήσεις, πανηγύρεις!). These festivals had the important function of bringing together Greeks and Sicels, free men and slaves, and Agyrion was "un *lieu de rencontre* particulièrement adapté" for such "rituels intégrateurs proposés par les colons grecs, un moyen d'attirer les Sicules en voie d'hellénisation" (JOURDAIN-ANNEQUIN 1992: 132, emphasis mine). In particular, Agyrion laid claim to having been the first *polis* to bestow divine honours on Heracles.[75] The first, spontaneous *gathering* of the inhabitants to greet the hero on his arrival was a key moment in the foundation myth of the local cult,[76] and could well have been remembered in the name of the town itself.[77]

---

74 Diodorus (98.2.7) also mentions once a king Agyris of Cyprus; the name could be a mistake for Anaxagoras.

75 This tradition was in competition with a Delphic and an Athenian one; see GIANGIULIO 1983: 833–845.

76 The myth is told at length by Diodorus (4.24.1), himself a native of Agyrion.

77 "Gli abitanti chiamavano porta Eraclea quella, davanti alla quale *radunatisi* essi avrebbero accolto solennemente al suo arrivo il dio [...] e fatti i sacrifici in suo onore. Il termine impiegato da Diodoro, ἀπαντήσεις, evoca gli *assembramenti* e le festose accoglienze che sarebbero state tributate al dio al suo arrivo dalla popolazione di Agyrion" (MANGANARO 1991: 218, emphasis mine).

References

DELG = CHANTRAINE, PIERRE 1969–1980, *Dictionnaire Étymologique de la Langue Grecque. Histoire des mots*, Paris: Klincksieck.

DGE = ADRADOS, FRANCISCO R. et al. (edd.) 1980-, *Diccionario griego-español*, Madrid: CSIC.

EDAIL = MARTIROSYAN, HRACH K. 2009, *Etymological Dictionary of the Armenian Inherited Lexicon*, Leiden/Boston: Brill.

EDBIL= DERKSEN, RICK 2015, *Etymological Dictionary of the Baltic Inherited Lexicon*, Leiden/Boston: Brill.

EDG = BEEKES, ROBERT S.P. 2010, *Etymological Dictionary of Greek*, Leiden/Boston: Brill.

EDLIL = DE VAAN, MICHIEL 2008, *Etymological Dictionary of Latin and the other Italic Languages*, Leiden/Boston: Brill.

EDPG = KROONEN, GUUS 2013, *Etymological Dictionary of Proto-Germanic*, Leiden/Boston: Brill.

EDSIL = DERKSEN, RICK 2008, *Etymological Dictionary of the Slavic Inherited Lexicon*, Leiden/Boston: Brill.

EWAia = MAYRHOFER, MANFRED 1992–2001, *Etymologisches Wörterbuch des Altindoarischen*, Heidelberg: Winter.

GEW = FRISK, HJALMAR 1954–1961, *Griechisches etymologisches Wörterbuch*, Heidelberg: Winter.

IEW= POKORNY, JULIUS 1957–1969, *Indogermanisches etymologisches Wörterbuch*, Tübingen/Bern/München: Francke.

LfgrE = SNELL, BRUNO et al. (edd.) 1955–2010, *Lexikon des frühgriechischen Epos*, Göttingen: Vandenhoeck & Ruprecht.

LIV^2 = RIX, HELMUT—KÜMMEL, MARTIN J. et al. (edd.) 2001, *Lexikon der Indogermanischen Verben*, Wiesbaden: Reichert.

LIV Addenda = KÜMMEL, MARTIN J., *Addenda et corrigenda zu LIV*^{2}, http://www.oriindufa.uni-jena.de/iskvomedia/indogermanistik/liv2add.html
(last updated 17/04/2019).

LSJ^9 = LIDDELL, HENRY G.—SCOTT, ROBERT—JONES, HENRY S., 1940. *A Greek-English Lexicon*, rev. H. Stuart-Jones et al., Oxford: Oxford University Press.

NIL = WODTKO, DAGMAR S.—IRSLINGER, BRITTA S.—SCHNEIDER, CAROLIN 2008, *Nomina im indogermanischen Lexikon*, Heidelberg: Winter.

ADAMS, DOUGLAS Q. 2013, *A Dictionary of Tocharian B. Revised and greatly enlarged*, Amsterdam/New York: Benjamins.

ADRADOS, FRANCISCO R. 1957, *Sobre los orígenes del vocabulario ático, II*, "Emerita" 25: 81–121.

ANTTILA, RAIMO 2000, *Greek and Indo-European Etymology in Action. Proto-Indo-European *aǵ*, Amsterdam/Philadelphia: Benjamins.

BAMMESBERGER, ALFRED 1982, Ἀγών *und* ἀγείρω, "Die Sprache" 28: 27–30.

BECHTEL, FRIEDRICH B. 1921–1924, *Die griechischen Dialekte*, Berlin: Weidmann.

VAN BEEK, LUCIEN 2018, Ἄτλας ἀστεμφής: *Traces of local particles in Greek compounds and the origins of intensive alpha*, "Glotta" 94: 38–81.

VAN BEEK, LUCIEN 2022, *The Reflexes of Syllabic Liquids in Ancient Greek. Linguistic Prehistory of the Greek Dialects and Homeric* Kunstsprache, Leiden/Boston: Brill.

BEEKES, ROBERT S.P. 1969, *The Development of Proto-Indo-European Laryngeals in Greek*, The Hague/Paris: Mouton.

BEEKES, ROBERT S.P. 1998, *Hades and Elysion*, in J. Jasanoff—H.C. Melchert—L. Oliver (edd.), *Mír curad. Studies in Honor of Calvert Watkins*, Innsbruck: Institut für Sprachwissenschaft: 17–28.

BHAT, DARBHE N.S. 1978, *A general study of palatalization*, in J.H. Greenberg (ed.), *Universals of Human Language, 2. Phonology*, Stanford: Stanford University Press: 47–92.

BLÜMEL, WOLFGANG 1982, *Die aiolischen Dialekte. Phonologie und Morphologie der inschriftlichen Texte aus generativer Sicht*, Göttingen: Vandenhoeck & Ruprecht.

BONSIGNORE, CHIARA 2013, Μητρὸς ἀγύρτης: *sguardo greco e realtà orientale in un epigramma di Alceo di Messene* (A.P. 6.128 = 21 G-P), "ARF" 15: 67–90.

BORGHINI, D. 1980, *Homérique* ἄγω, ἄγρει, ἀγείρω *et les dérivés grecs de la racine i.-e.* *ə₂eg, "LAMA" 6: 1–26.

DU BOUCHET, JULIEN 2004, *Recherches sur les noms de la rue en grec ancien*, PhD Diss. Paris X—Nanterre.

BUCK, CARL D. 1955, *The Greek Dialects*, Chicago/London: Chicago University Press.

CHANIOTIS, ANGELOS 2009, *Epigraphic Bulletin for Greek Religion 2006*, "Kernos" 22: 209–243.

CHANTRAINE, PIERRE 1933, *La formation des noms en grec ancien*, Paris: Champion.

CHRISTOL, ALAIN 1979, Ἄγυια. *Étude synchronique et diachronique d'un champ sémantique*, "RPh" 53: 59–79.

CLAY, DISKIN 2004, *Archilochos Heros. The Cult of the Poets in the Greek Polis*, Cambridge, MA: Harvard University Press.

COWGILL, WARREN 1965, *Evidence in Greek*, in W. Winter (ed.), *Evidence for Laryngeals*, The Hague: Mouton: 142–180.

COWGILL, WARREN 1978, *Agṓn : ageírō. A new r/n-alternation*, in M.A. Jazayery et al. (edd.), *Linguistic and Literary Studies in Honor of A.A. Hill*, vol. III, The Hague/Paris/New York: Mouton: 29–31.

DIEU, ERIC 2016, *L'accentuation des noms en *-ā (*-eh₂) en grec ancien et dans les langues indo-européennes. Étude morphologique et sémantique*, Innsbruck: Institut für Sprachen und Literaturen.

DURANTE, MARCELLO 1976, *Sulla preistoria della tradizione poetica greca. Parte seconda: Risultanze della comparazione indoeuropea*, Roma: Edizioni dell'Ateneo.

GARCÍA RAMÓN, JOSÉ LUIS 2010, *Reconstructing IE lexicon and phraseology: inherited patterns and lexical renewal*, in S.W. Jamison—H.C. Melchert—B. Vine (eds.), *Proceedings of the 21st Annual UCLA Indo-European Conference*, Bremen: Hempen: 69–106.

GARCÍA RAMÓN, JOSÉ LUIS 2018, *Ancient Greek dialectology: old and new questions, recent developments*, in G.K. Giannakis—E. Crespo—P. Filos (edd.), *Studies in Ancient Greek Dialects: From Central Greece to the Black Sea*, Berlin: De Gruyter: 29–106.

GIAMMELLARO, PIETRO 2006, *Fuori e dentro la città. Saperi marginali e religione istituzionale nella Grecia antica*, in G. Regalzi (ed.), *Mutuare, interpretare, tradurre: storie di culture a confronto. Atti del 2° incontro 'Orientalisti' (Roma, 11–12 dicembre 2002)*, Roma: La Sapienza: 169–214.

GIAMMELLARO, PIETRO 2012, *Agyrtai. Pratiche magiche, itineranza e marginalità religiosa nella Grecia antica*, in M. Piranomonte—F.M. Simón (edd.), *Contesti Magici— Contextos Mágicos (Atti del Convegno Internazionale Contextos Mágicos—Contesti Magici, Roma, 4–6 Novembre 2009)*, Roma: De Luca: 279–282.

GIANGIULIO, MAURIZIO 1983, *Greci e non-Greci in Sicilia alla luce dei culti e delle leggende di Eracle*, in AA.VV., *Forme di contatto e processi di trasformazione delle società antiche. Atti del convegno di Cortona (24–30 maggio 1981)*, Pisa/Roma: Scuola Normale Superiore: 785–846.

HALL, TRACY A. 2000, *Typological generalizations concerning secondary palatalization*, "Lingua" 110: 1–25.

HALL, TRACY A.—HAMANN, SILKE 2010, *On the cross-linguistic avoidance of rhotic plus high front vocoid sequences*, "Lingua" 120: 1821–1844.

HAMM, EVA-MARIA 1957, *Grammatik zu Sappho und Alkaios*, Berlin: Akademie-Verlag.

HAMP, ERIC P. 1981a, ἀγοστός, ἀγείρω, "Živa Antika" 31: 83–84.

HAMP, ERIC P. 1981b, *Some Greek forms in σ*, "Živa Antika" 31: 95–96.

HAMP, ERIC P. 1991, *Prehellenic μύλη, σπυρίς, ἄγυρις*, "Lingua Posnaniensis" 32/33: 87.

HAWKINS, SHANE 2013, *Studies in the Language of Hipponax*, Bremen: Hempen.

HELLEMANS, GEERT 2005, *Étude phonétique et graphique du [j] (jod) en grec mycénien*, PhD diss. Leuven.

HOCK, HANS H. 2004, *Fish, push, and Greek R+y clusters: a return to Danielson 1903*, in K. Jones-Bley et al. (edd.), *Proceedings of the 15th UCLA Indo-European Conference*, Washington DC: Institute for the Study of Man: 155–167.

HODOT, RENÉ 1990, *Le dialecte éolien d'Asie. La langue des inscriptions, VIIe s. a.C.–IVe s. p.C.*, Paris: Éd. Recherche sur les Civilisations.

HOFFMANN, OTTO 1891–1898, *Die griechischen Dialekte in ihren historischen Zusammenhange mit den wichtigsten ihren Quellen*, Göttingen: Vandenhoeck & Ruprecht.

HÖFLER, STEFAN (*in press*), *Ein Potpourri aus 'süß' und 'schleimig': Caland-Wurzeln, Wortbildung, Etymologie und Co.*, in M. Malzahn (ed.), *Proceedings of the 15th Fachtagung der Indogermanischen Gesellschaft, September 13–16, 2016, Vienna.*

HYLLESTED, ADAM 2017, *Again on pigs in ancient Europe: the Fennic connection*, in B.S.S. Hansen et al. (edd.), *Etymology and the Indo-European Lexicon. Proceedings of the 14th Fachtagung der Indogermanischen Gesellschaft, 17–22 September 2012, Copenhagen*, Wiesbaden: Reichert: 183–196.

JASANOFF, JAY H. 2018, *The Prehistory of the Balto-Slavic Accent*, Leiden/Boston: Brill.

JOSEPH, BRIAN D. 1979, *Irregular [u] in Greek*, "Die Sprache" 25: 46–48.

JOURDAIN-ANNEQUIN, COLETTE 1992, *À propos d'un rituel pour Iolaos à Agyrion: Héraclès et l'initiation des jeunes gens*, in A. Moreau (ed.), *L'initiation. Actes du colloque international de Montpellier, 11–14 avril 1991, I. Les rites d'adolescence et les mystères*, Montpellier: Université Paul Valéry: 121–141.

KACZYŃSKA, ELWIRA 2007, *Greek (Hesychian) κόρος 'great number of men' and related words*, "Emerita" 75: 273–278.

KÁRPÁTI, ANDRÁS 2016, *Thamyras' song contest and the Muse figures*, in L. Bravi et al. (edd.), *Tra lyra e aulos. Tradizioni musicali e generi poetici*, Pisa/Roma: Fabrizio Serra: 167–198.

KÜHNER, RAPHAEL—BLASS, FRIEDRICH 1890, *Ausführliche Grammatik der griechischen Sprache, Erster Teil: Elementar und Formenlehre*, Hannover: Hahn.

LAMBERT, CHARLES 1903, *Étude sur le dialecte éolien; sa place dans l'ensemble des dialectes grecs*, Dijon: Damidot frères.

DE LAMBERTERIE, CHARLES 1990, *Les adjectifs grecs en -υς. Sémantique et comparaison*, 2 vols., Louvain-la-Neuve: Peeters.

LEJEUNE, MICHEL 1972, *Phonétique historique du mycénien et du grec ancien*, Paris: Klincksieck.

LUNDQUIST, JESSE 2021, *παλίντονος. Reconstructing the prehistory of accents (Homeric -ειαί, -εια, -υιαί)*, "Indogermanische Forschungen" 126: 261–304.

MALZAHN, MELANIE 2014, *Pūṣan, Pan, and Neuter Stems in *-us(-)*, in C. Melchert—E. Rieken—T. Steer (edd.), *Munus amicitiae: Norbert Oettinger a collegis et amicis dicatum*, Ann Arbor: Beech Stave Press: 160–180.

MANGANARO, GIACOMO 1991, *Note diodoree*, in E. Galvagno—C. Molè Ventura (edd.), *Mito storia tradizione. Diodoro Siculo e la storiografia classica. Atti del Convegno Internazionale Catania-Agira 7–8 dicembre 1984*, Catania: Edizioni del Prisma: 201–226.

MARTIROSYAN, HRACH K. 2013, *The place of Armenian in the Indo-European language family. The relationship with Greek and Indo-Iranian*, "Journal of Language Relationship/Вопросы языкового родства" 10: 85–138.

MASSON, OLIVIER 1987, *Remarques d'onomastique cyrénéenne: quelques noms masculins en -ις*, "QAL" 12: 245–248 (= 1990, *Onomastica Graeca Selecta*, vol. 2, Paris: Université de Paris-X: 613–616).

GREEK ΑΓΥΡΙΣ 'GATHERING' 299

NICKAU, KLAUS 1974, *Planudes und Moschopulos als Zeugen für Sappho*, "ZPE" 14: 15–17.

NIKOLAEV, ALEXANDER 2009, *The Germanic word for 'sword' and delocatival derivation in Proto-Indo-European*, "JIES" 37: 461–488.

NIKOLAEV, ALEXANDER 2015, *Hittite wattaēš 'birds'*, "MSS" 69: 257–267.

ORESHKO, ROSTISLAV 2013, Review of Hawkins 2013, "Hephaistos" 30: 173–178.

RASMUSSEN, JENS E. 1985, *Miscellaneous morphological problems in Indo-European languages, I–II*, "Lingua Posnaniensis" 28: 27–62 (= *Selected Papers on Indo-European Linguistics. With a Section on Comparative Eskimo Linguistics*, vol. 1, Copenhagen: Museum Tusculanum: 100–145).

RAU, JEREMY 2009, *Indo-European Nominal Morphology: The Decads and the Caland System*, Innsbruck: Institut für Sprachen und Literaturen.

REPANŠEK, LUKA 2013, *The historical morphology of primary u-stems in Celtic*, MA diss. Aberystwyth.

RODRÍGUEZ-PIEDRABUENA, SANDRA—JIMÉNEZ DELGADO, JOSÉ M. 2021, *On the etymology of* πορφύρα *'purple'*, "Glotta" 97: 246–261.

ROESCH, PAUL 1982, *Études béotiennes*, Paris: De Boccard.

SCHAFFNER, STEFAN 2019, *Zur Wortbildung von griechisch ἄγυια, Ἅρπυια, ὄργυια und Verwandtem*, "MSS" 73: 157–183.

SCHINDLER, JOACHIM 1980, *Zur Herkunft der altindischen cvi-Bildungen*, in M. Mayrhofer et al. (edd.), *Lautgeschichte und Etymologie. Akten der VI. Fachtagung der Indogermanischen Gesellschaft*, Wiesbaden: Reichert: 386–393.

SCHWYZER, EDUARD 1939, *Griechische Grammatik. Bd. 1: Allgemeiner Teil, Lautlehre, Wortbildung, Flexion*, München: Beck.

SEMERANO, GIOVANNI 1994, *Le origini della cultura europea. Vol. II: Basi semitiche delle lingue indoeuropee. Dizionario della lingua greca*, Firenze: Olschki.

SERAFINI, NICOLA 2016, *Sacerdoti mendicanti e itineranti: gli agyrtai nell'antica Grecia*, "MH" 73: 24–41.

SIHLER, ANDREW L. 1995, *New Comparative Grammar of Greek and Latin*, New York/Oxford: Oxford University Press.

SKODA, FRANÇOISE 1982, *Le redoublement expressif: un universal linguistique. Analyse du procédé en grec ancien et en d'autres langues*, Paris: Peeters.

SOWA, WOJCIECH 2019, *Macedonian βίῤῥοξ (Hsch. B 627)*, in G.K. Giannakis et al. (edd.), *Studies in Greek Lexicography. In Honor of John N. Kazazis*, Berlin/Boston: De Gruyter: 187–203.

SZEMERÉNYI, OSWALD 1964, *Syncope in Greek and Indo-European and the Nature of Indo-European Accent*, Napoli: Istituto Universitario Orientale.

TICHY, EVA 1983, *Onomatopoetische Verbalbildungen des Griechischen*, Wien: Verlag des Österreichischen Akademie der Wissenschaften.

VERNET PONS, EULALIA 2012, *Sumerio É.KUR, acadio ekurru, arameo ʾeg/kūrā, griego ἀγορά: una nueva aportación etimológica*, in A. Agud et al. (edd.), *Séptimo centenario de los estudios orientales en Salamanca*, Salamanca: Ediciones Universidad de Salamanca: 159–169.

VINE, BRENT 1998, *Aeolic ὄρπετον and Deverbative *-eto- in Greek and Indo-European*, Innsbruck: Institut für Sprachwissenschaft.

VINE, BRENT 1999, *On 'Cowgill's law' in Greek*, in C. Luschützky—H. Eichner (edd.), *Compositiones Indogermanicae in memoriam Jochem Schindler*, Prague/Vienna: Enigma Corporation: 555–600.

VINE, BRENT 2004, *On PIE full grades in some zero-grade contexts: *-tí-, *-tó-*, in J. Clackson—B.A. Olsen (edd.), *Indo-European Word Formation. Proceedings of the Conference Held at the University of Copenhagen, October 20th–22nd 2000*, Copenhagen: Museum Tusculanum: 357–379.

WATHELET, PAUL 1970, *Les traits éoliens dans la langue de l'épopée grecque*, Roma: Edizioni dell'Ateneo.

WEST, MARTIN L. 1998–2000, *Homeri Ilias*, 2 vols., Stuttgart/Leipzig: Teubner; Munich/Leipzig: Saur.

WEST, MARTIN L. 1999, *The invention of Homer*, "CQ" 49: 364–382.

WEST, MARTIN L. 2007, *Indo-European Poetry and Myth*, Oxford: Oxford University Press.

WILLI, ANDREAS 2018, *Origins of the Greek verb*, Cambridge: Cambridge University Press.

WILSON, PETER 2009, *Thamyris the Thracian: the archetypal wandering poet?*, in R. Hunter—I. Rutherford (edd.), *Wandering Poets in Ancient Greek Culture. Travel, Locality and Pan-Hellenism*, Cambridge: Cambridge University Press: 46–79.

CHAPTER 12

Here's to a Long Life! Albanian Reflections of Proto-Indo-European Semantics

Brian D. Joseph

1 Introduction

The study of diachronic semantics, taking in both semantic reconstruction and semantic change, has long been one of the less systematic enterprises in historical linguistics. While some advances have been made in the area of shifts in grammatical meaning, diachronic lexical semantics is perhaps less well understood. Metaphor appears to be a powerful force in semantic change, and both the linguistic context and the pragmatic/social milieu (CHRISTIANSEN— JOSEPH 2016) can play a key role as well. These observations have meant that some seemingly unusual changes have to be recognized that would be inexplicable without an understanding of the cultural milieu in which the change takes place; the shift of earlier English *bede* (later *bead*) from 'prayer' to 'small round glass or ceramic object with a hole through it' is a classic case of this sort. Nonetheless, a confounding aspect in the study of semantic change is the fact that proper attention to the cultural and pragmatic milieu can also reveal instances of semantic persistence (see immediately below), sometimes over long stretches of time. In what follows, I examine a far-reaching example of such persistence in the Balkans, with particular attention to Albanian. First, though, by way of providing some background, I present some known instances of such lexical reflections of earlier semantics, and then zero in on the details of usage for various present-day Albanian and Balkan words and phrases that reveal aspects of what can plausibly be reconstructed as Proto-Indo-European cultural semantics having to do with an interest in longevity, as reflected in continuations of the language more than six millennia later.

The semantic "reflections"—"echoes", to use another metaphor—referred to here can be defined as traces in later usage of earlier semantics (whether directly attested or reconstructed). Such reflections are seen in change leading to new grammatical semantics, as with Albanian nonactive (medio-passive) *-h-* (e.g. *la-h-em* 'I wash myself / I am washed') from the Proto-Indo-European (PIE) stem-forming suffix *-sḱ-*, which seems to have had a presential orientation in PIE, based on its inchoative/iterative sense in, for instance, Latin, Hittite, and

© BRIAN D. JOSEPH, 2022 | DOI:10.1163/9789004508828_014

Ionic Greek, but also on its function as a simple marker of present tense, as (ultimately) in Sanskrit and Avestan. In Albanian, despite the clear shift in the value of this *-h-* morpheme, from presential marker to nonactive marker, nonetheless it betrays its original present-oriented semantics in that it is restricted to non-past forms.[1] There thus has been persistence of the presential orientation despite the shift in the primary function of *-sḱ-*.

The occurrence of such semantic reflections—traces in a certain sense—is akin to what HOPPER 1991 calls the "principle of persistence", whereby original lexical semantics "persist" after an item enters the grammatical arena. But we can also see semantic persistence in the purely lexical domain. For instance, as discussed in Joseph—Karnitis (1999, 2006) there is an Indo-Iranian root *muč-* with the meanings 'losbinden/untie; abstreifen/strip off' (*LIV* 443; *IEW* 744), that gives rise to a wide range of meanings in Indic:

- Vedic Sanskrit: 'untie, loosen, unfasten, loosen, set free; release (streams); undo, dissolve; cause to disappear, strip off'
- Classical Sanskrit: 'loosen, set free, release, let go, let loose, deliver; relax (the throat); slacken (reins); let live, spare; leave, quit, give up; die; set apart; dismiss; cast, throw, hurl, discharge; emit, drop, shed, let fall; utter, give forth; give away, grant, bestow; put on (middle voice); void (excrement); sacrifice; deceive, cheat' ...

But, Proto-Indo-Iranian (PIIr) *muč-* is highly restricted in Iranian, occurring in only two forms in Avestan, both, significantly, it is argued, with shoe-/foot-related meanings:

> *framuxti-* 'taking off of footwear' (1×: *Fragments* 6.27)
> *paitišmuxta-* 'having shoes' (3×: *Yashts* 5.64, 5.78, 10.125)

And, there is some shoe-/foot-related meanings for derivatives of this root in Sanskrit, e.g. Classical Sanskrit *vi-ava-√muc-* 'take off shoes', but also in late Vedic, with *upa-√muc-*

> *kārṣṇī upānahau upa muñcate*   (TS 5.4.4, repeated 5.6.6)
> '(two) black-antelope leather-sandals he-puts on'

> *vārāhī upānahau upamuñcate*   (TB 1.7.9)
> '(two) pig's leather-sandals he-puts-on'

---

1 The past nonactive is marked rather by a particle *u* (see footnote 10) occurring together with the active forms, e.g. *u la* 'I washed myself / I was washed'.

HERE'S TO A LONG LIFE!

> *vārāhyā upānahā upamuñcate* (ŚB 5.4.3.19)
> '(two) sow's leather-sandals he-puts-on'

Based on these facts, Joseph and Karnitis make the suggestion that PIIr **muč*-had the range of meaning seen in Sanskrit, but among those was meanings was a use referring specifically to shoes/feet, as with *upa-√muc-* and *vi-ava-√muc-*; echoes of that original shoe-/foot-related meaning then carried over into Iranian, giving the Avestan distribution of derivatives of this root. In this account, there is thus "persistence" of earlier lexical semantics, and a distributional "echo" of that original meaning.[2]

2   An Extended Case Study from Albanian: Etymological Details

Albanian has a negative prefix *as-*, with the meaning 'no-, not (in compounds)', as in *asnjë* 'none' (cf. *një* 'one'), *asgjë* 'nothing' (cf. *gjë* 'thing'), *askund* 'nowhere' (cf. *kund* 'somewhere'). It can be equated etymologically with Ancient Greek οὐ 'not', as argued explicitly in JOSEPH 2002 and 2005,[3] fleshing out a suggestion for the Albanian free word *as* 'and not; neither' made in PEDERSEN 1900 and in COWGILL 1960, though with no details. Now, Greek οὐ, especially in its extended prevocalic form οὐκ, is argued by Cowgill to derive from a PIE emphatic negative phrase **(ne) ... H_2oyu k^wid* 'not ever; not on your (long) life', consisting of the negative marker **ne*, the noun **H_2oyu* meaning 'long life; vital energy' (cf. Vedic Sanskrit *āyu-* 'long life', Greek ἀεί/αἰεί 'always'), and **k^wid* (as in the Sanskrit particle *cid* 'even'), serving as an emphatic; he argues also for connecting Armenian *oč'* 'not' with οὐκ as well, so that he derives it from this same PIE collocation.[4]

All of the elements needed to make this etymological connection work for Albanian *as-* are available. For instance, the several phonological developments

---

2   In §5 below, some further thoughts are offered on the nature of semantic persistence.

3   Many of the etymological and derivational details from these earlier works concerning *as-* and **ne ... H_2oyu k^wid* are repeated here for the sake of completeness in the exposition, but some new material is added here including the overall thrust of viewing these developments through the lens of semantic persistence.

4   Pedersen (1900: 321) mentions Latin *haud* 'not' in the context of a discussion of the etymology of Albanian negation, including *as*, but he claims to be uncertain about whether it belongs, and in any case does not develop the idea at all. See now GARNIER 2014 for a fully developed account of *haud* as belonging to the family of Greek οὐκ, etc. Adding Latin into the equation gives a solid basis for viewing **(ne) ... H_2oyu k^wid* as being an element in PIE and not just a dialectally created collocation within the family.

304 JOSEPH

needed to go from PIE $*H_2oyu\ k^wid$ to Albanian *as-* all have solid parallels else-where in Albanian historical phonology:

– loss of initial $*H_2$, e.g. *ag* 'dawn' < $*H_2eug$- (cf. Grk αὐγή 'sunlight; dawn')
– assibilation of $*k^w$ before front vowels; e.g.:

   si 'how' from $*k^wiV$- (cf. Latin *quia* 'why')
   sjell 'bring' from $*k^wel$- 'turn'
   sorrë 'blackbird' from $*k^wērsnā$- (cf. Sanskrit *kṛṣṇa-* 'black')

– final syllable reduction, instantiated as full truncation for at least (some) high vowel syllables, e.g. *kam* 'I have' < $*kap-mi$, *elb* 'barley' < $*albhit$ (cf. Grk ἄλφι 'type of grain', ἄλφιτον 'pearl barley')
– loss of intervocalic $*-y-$, e.g. *tre* 'three' < $*treyes$ (with final syllable truncation too)
– $*o > a$, e.g.

   natë 'night' < $*nok^wt-i$-
   asht 'bone' < $*Hosteyo$-
   darkë 'evening meal' < $*dork^wom$ (cf. Greek δόρπον 'evening meal')

– $*ou > a$, with loss of labial glide in diphthong, e.g.:

   hedh 'throw' < $*sḱeud$- (cf. OEng *sceotan* 'shoot')
   ag 'dawn' < $*H_2eug$- (cf. Grk αὐγή 'sunlight; dawn')
   ar 'gold' (borrowing from Latin *aurum* 'gold')

Putting these developments together, we get:

$*H_2$	o	y	u	k^w	id
⇓	⇓	⇓	⇓	⇓	⇓
Ø	a	Ø	Ø	s	øø

The loss of *ne in this collocation can be likened to the loss of *ne* in colloquial French, as in *J'aime pas ce restaurant* 'I do not like this restaurant', with only *pas* marking negation, from an earlier bipartite negation marking *ne ... pas*. Moreover, even this loss has a parallel within Albanian, based on the etymology of the Albanian verbal negation marker *s'* 'not' as being from $*ne ... k^wid$ (or possibly $*ne ... k^we$) with truncation of *ne.[5]

An important detail here is that the function of prefixal/compound *as-* is to mark a simple negation within a compound.[6] In this way, this usage is consistent with the use posited for $*ne ... H_2oyu\ k^wid$. Furthermore, there is

---

5 This account would mean that *s'* is not derived from the present-day negative word *as* 'and not' (even if it might show some connection to it); see also footnotes 7 and 8.

6 By "simple negation", I mean negation serving simply as a logical operator, i.e. giving from X the reading 'not X' (in logical notation, ¬ X).

evidence for such a neutral sentential negation usage in Albanian from the question tag *aspo*, 'n'est-ce pas; nicht wahr; eh?', arguably from *as-* in an original (highly elliptical) neutral sentence negation use plus *po* 'yes', thus literally "no—yes?". Thus, under the analyses offered here, the simple negative function of *as-* matches Greek οὐκ and Armenian *oč'*, and so the source of these three forms, PIE *(ne)* ... *H₂oyu kʷid*, is very likely to have been (or, better, to have become) a neutral (non-emphatic/non-temporal) sentential negator even in PIE.

It can thus be concluded there very likely was a free word *as** in pre-Albanian for simple negation, and that it is the source of the prefixal/compound *as-*, an element that has that same function of signaling simple negation (as seen with *gjë* 'thing' ~ *asgjë* 'nothing'), albeit restricted now to certain compounds. This early free word negator *as** should be kept distinct from the currently existing free word *as*, which, although a marker of negation, nonetheless functions quite differently, inasmuch as it has a different meaning, namely 'and not; neither; not even', and shows semantics that go beyond simple negation due to its coordinative sense.[7] This modern free word *as* may thus well have an entirely different etymological source from prefixal/compound *as-*, and in fact can be seen as a univerbation of *a* 'but' (a borrowing from Latin *aut*) with *s'* 'not'. Such an derivation offers a better account of the semantics of *as*.[8]

Thus on a phraseological level, prefixal/compound *as-* shows that both Albanian and Greek share an ancient metaphor involving 'long life' in negation. What is relevant for the issue of persistence of original meaning is that there are traces of Indo-European 'long life' phraseology to be found in the present-day Balkans, centering on Albanian. In particular, there are numerous indications—reflections, i.e. echoes or persistences—of an interest in longevity on the part of early Balkan Indo-European speakers, as revealed through various lexical items and phrases. I turn now to these echoes.

---

7 HACKSTEIN 2020: §1b also details several specialized uses of the free word *as*, such as the doubled use (*as* ... *as*) for 'neither ... nor' and what he calls the "inchoative negative focus particle" meaning 'not even'. All of these uses go beyond the simple negation function of *s'*, and thus suggest separating it from the compound negator *as-*.

8 As an aside, I note that the need to distinguish compound prefixal negator *as-* from the present-day free word *as* is a reason for being cautious in claiming evidence of "grammaticalization" based just on existing forms; in this account, the *re*-creation of a free word *as* (from *a* 'or' + *s'* 'not') gives the impression of a connection (ultimately an ahistorical one) between the present-day free word *as* and the (present-day) compound/prefixal *as-*.

3 Albanian and Balkan Reflections Concerning Longevity

3.1 *Reflection 1: Albanian* jetë *'life'*

The first reflection is the Albanian word itself for 'life', namely *jetë* 'life'. While it may reflect an internal Albanian etymology from *jes-/jet-* 'exist', HAMP 1968 argues that it shows some influence from, with reanalysis triggered by, Latin *aetas* 'age'; thus, via those contact effects, *jetë* belongs to the lexical family of *H_2oyu, inasmuch as *aetas* is related to *aevus* 'period of time'. Interestingly, and perhaps importantly, *jetë* offers a further reflection, or perhaps even a renewal, of the ancient "long life" semantics in the Albanian composite form *përjetë* 'forever' (literally "for life") and the derivative *përjetësi* 'eternity'. Admittedly, there is surely a degree of some "naturalness" of semantic extension involved here, as there are independent instances with similar composition and similar semantics, such as German *fürs Leben* 'for life; forever', but still this expression shows the possibility of longevity semantics being associated with *jetë* in Albanian.

3.2 *Reflection 2: Albanian 'for eternity'*

A second and perhaps more overt reflection is the Albanian phrase *për (në) jetë të jetëve* 'for eternity'. This phrase is literally "for (a) life(time) of lifetimes", with the lexeme *jetë* repeated in different cases, first accusative (singular) and then genitive (plural). Structurally, this expression is reminiscent of Old Persian "king of kings" phraseology, though it may well be independent of it (note that it is a Biblical usage; cf. *Revelations* 17:14). Even more telling, however, this structure with an accusative and genitive of the same word repeated and having a meaning suggestive of the endurance of an entity, or in the case of negation, of the absence of an entity, over a long stretch of time, provides a link to the use of "long life" in negation (*(ne) ... $H_2oyu\ k^wid$). The connection comes via a colloquial expression in Albanian, *kurrën e kurrës* 'never at all; not in a million years', an emphatic 'ever'-based negative phrase which is literally the adverb *kurrë* 'never', treated as a noun and occurring as accusative and then repeated as a genitive, i.e. 'never.ACC of a-never.GEN'. Thus one sees here both parallel structure to *për (në) jetë të jetëve* and parallel "eternal" semantics.

Interestingly, this Albanian phrase *kurrën e kurrës* is matched semantically by the Modern Greek expression ποτέ των ποτών (*poté ton potón*) 'never at all', which is literally "never of-the nevers.GEN.PL". The Greek phrase itself actually matches *për (në) jetë të jetëve* structurally, through its repetition of the 'ever' word—here 'never' (ποτέ)—and also through its use of the genitive plural, and through the order of the words, with the genitive form occurring second.[9]

---

9 There is no way to tell directly what case the first word, ποτέ ([poté]) 'never' is in, as there is

HERE'S TO A LONG LIFE!

Moreover, the synchronically odd nominalization of the adverbs Albanian *kurrë* and Greek ποτέ in these apparently linked phrases ties in with 'ever' and **H₂oyu* in another way besides the parallel accusative-genitive(plural) structure. In particular, HAMP 1983 draws attention to the grammatical oddity in English of *for ever*—it is significant that *ever* is based ultimately on PIE **H₂oyu*—with *for* apparently as a preposition and *ever* as a noun. The *Oxford English Dictionary* (s.v.) talks about a "quasi-substantive" *ever* and there is some evidence that it was somewhat noun-like, via the reanalysis of *for ever and ay*— where *ay* originally meant 'always' and is ultimately connected to the **H₂oyu* complex of forms—as *for ever and a day*, where both *ever* and *day* would be nouns if one follows the usual assumption in syntactic studies that coordination is possible only between like categories. It can be speculated, therefore, that the Balkan nominalization process is picking up on an old property of **H₂oyu*, as seen in English (quasi-substantive) *ever*, even if these Albanian and Greek phrases are just the result of a playful nonce formation; the effect of these phrases, after all, is stylistically like English expressive *never in a million years!*.

In this regard, an important detail is that there are adverbials from case forms of **H₂oyu-*, e.g. Aeolic Greek αἰέν 'always' (from an endingless locative) and from case forms of derivatives of ***H₂oyu-*, e.g. αἰεί 'always' (from a locative of an *s*-stem form, **H₂e/oy-w-es-i*), but no clear evidence of an adverbial use of **H₂oyu* directly, e.g. in Vedic. Still, the hypothesis can be put forward, admittedly quite speculatively, that some instances of Greek αὖ, an adverb of 'repeated action', could possibly be from **H₂oyu* or **H₂eyu* where the meaning 'again, anew, further' might be construed as deriving from 'continued/sustained activity' (of the sort associated with longevity); this would contrast with the more 'standard' etymology (e.g. as in BEEKES 2010: s.v.) connecting it with Sanskrit preverb *ava-*.

One can wonder too about the Sanskrit *jātu* (1× in Rigveda, more frequent in later texts) as a parallel for a bare *u*-stem (admittedly a *-tu*-stem) neuter used adverbially; in its one Rigvedic occurrence (10.27.11) it seems to mean 'from birth' (so JAMISON – BRERETON 2014, given below), but that in a sense is a way of saying "forever" or at least for an individual's "forever"; GRIFFITH 1896 translates it as 'ever', and Monier-Williams (1899: s.v.) gives the translation for Classical usage as 'ever'):

---

no indication of case (unlike the overt accusative case marker *-n* in the Albanian *kurrën*), but many adverbs in Greek have the same form as accusative plurals, so it is not unreasonable to think of ποτέ as an accusative here, like its Albanian counterpart.

yasyānakṣā duhitā **jātu** āsa
kastāṃ vidvānabhimanyāte andhām |
kataro meniṃ prati taṃ mucāte
ya īṃ vahāte ya īṃ vā vareyāt

'(A father) who has a daughter blind **from birth**—who, knowing her (as) blind will have designs on her. (On the other hand, not knowing her state), which of the two will unleash (the power of) violated exchange against him—the one who marries her or the one who woos her (on the bridegroom's behalf)' (cf. Griffith: 'When a man's daughter hath been **ever** eyeless ...')

A speculative interpretation here is that *jātu*, from √*jan-* (thus **ǵṇH₁-*, zerograde to **ǵenH₁*) could point to an (unattested) adverbial *āyu**, based on the shared neuter -*u*-stem morphology and the shared meaning 'ever'; possibly relevant here is the fact of meanings for the two forms that are in the same semantic sphere—'life' for **H₂oyu* and 'birth' for *jātu*—coupled with the fact that forms with parallel meanings in PIE often have parallel morphology, as with shared **-u*-stem inflection for words for 'sweet', from different roots, seen in Sanskrit *madh-u-* and Greek ἡδ-ύ-.

3.3 *Reflection 3: A Greek greeting*

A third reflection of the original 'long life' semantics of **H₂oyu* can be seen in the Modern Greek greeting γεια σου ([ja su]), literally, "health to-you" (or "(to) your health"). The first part, γεια, is from Ancient Greek ὑγιεῖαν 'health.ACC', and thus is connected (ultimately) to ὑ–γιής 'long-lived; healthy' and therefore, in the analysis of WEISS 1994, indirectly to the 'long life' nexus. Moreover, this greeting is also used as a drinking toast in Greek, in fact the most common toast, a detail which becomes important once some additional considerations are discussed.

3.4 *Reflection 4: An Albanian greeting*

A fourth reflection is evident in the Albanian greeting *tungjatjeta* 'hello'. This expression is literally *"të u ngjattë jeta"* "for-you may be-lengthened life-the", with a 2SG dative of interest *të*, the past nonactive marker *u*,[10] the 3SG form of the optative of a causative/factitive verb *ngjat-* 'lengthen' derived from *gjatë*

---

10   The nonactive *u* derives from old reflexive marker (**we*, the regular Albanian form of the PIE reflexive **swe*) contracted with the augment; see HAMP 2019 for details.

'long, broad', and definite form of *jetë* 'life'. This greeting shows, by overt jux-taposition of 'long' and 'life', a union of the semantics of the pieces in the metaphor underlying *as-* in the account given above (*$^*ne...H_2oyu\ k^wid$*). There is more, however, since *tungjatjeta* has also been used dialectally as a toast in drinking,[11] so that functionally it has the exact same range as Greek γεια σου. This suggests a persistent, perhaps millennia-old, Balkan interest in 'long life', expressed through everyday exchanges among acquaintances and friends, and in the sharing of drink.

Admittedly a wish for long life is a likely universal of humanity, though it is not always expressed in exactly this way in Indo-European circles. In Vedic, for instance, a similar wish is expressed via reference to *śatam śarádas* 'hundred autumns', thus with a different trope. Possibly relevant here is the suggestion by SOUTHERN 2004 that the Vedic interjected call *śam yoḥ* 'health (and) blessing' might have been a drinking toast; if correct, this phrase would be of interest here since *yoḥ* is relatable to the base of *āyu*, from *$^*H_2y$-ew-*, and thus to Greek οὐκ and ὑγιείαν, as well as Albanian *as-*.

It can be noted here, with regard to both γεια σου and *tungjatjeta* as toasts, that archaisms are found in toasts in Slavic; Friedman (2012: 33) observes:

> At some late stage in Common Slavic ... what was the *l*-participle developed an optative usage in the third person singular to replace the third singular imperative which ... was lost. ... The popular Bosnian/Croatian/Serbian/Montenegrin toast *živ(j)eli* ['may we/you live!'] as well as the use of invariant *bilo* in the meaning of 'any' ... are examples of such [archaic] optative usage.

This typological parallel means that finding an archaic semantic reflection in these Greek and Albanian toasts should not be considered unexpected.

4   One Further Closing Example: (From drinking to ...) Eating

With all the discussion of drinking, it is perhaps appropriate to turn to reflections of earlier semantics in the Albanian verb for 'eat', present tense *ha* with suppletive participle *ngrënë* 'eaten' and suppletive past tense *hëngra* '(I) ate'. The present stem derives from a preverb *$^*Ho$-* with the root *$^*H_1ed$-* (as in Eng-

---

11   I have this on the authority of Eric P. Hamp (p.c.), who witnessed this use of *tungjatjeta* during fieldwork in northwest Geg territory.

lish *eat*, Latin *edō*, etc.) and the participle *ngrënë* derives from a preverb **en-* with the root **gʷrō-* (as in Latin *vor-ō* 'swallow', Greek βι-βρώ-σκω 'devour'), a formation also seen in the past tense (HAMP 1971). Suppletion here may reflect a different aspect or other nuance of what eating involves; given the meanings associated in Greek and Latin with **gʷrō-*, *ngrënë* (and *hëngra*) may reflect some sort of completed aspect, swallowing to complete the act of eating or taking in a large quantity or mass as a whole, leaving *ha* to some other dimension of the act.

A suggestion here is that originally *ha* was something like 'take a bite', either as a momentary aspectual sort of thing or referring to the biting part of eating. This meaning can be motivated by the connection between **H₁ed-* and the word for 'tooth' as a present participle (cf. Greek variant ἐδοντ- for 'tooth') with 'tooth' as "the biting (thing par excellence)", and other connections between **H₁ed-* and 'pain' words, as argued by Schindler (1975: 62), shown in derivatives such as Greek ὀδύνη, ὠδίν- for 'pain', 'birth pangs'; the German metaphorical *es beisst* (literally "it bites") for 'it stings' or 'it is painful' points to the same linkage of pain with biting.

In this case, then, even though *ha* and *ngrënë* do not preserve the original semantics, since both mean simply 'eat', the suppletion would be a reflection of an original semantic distinction between the roots involved, a distributional fact of present-day Albanian that has an explanation in ancient semantics.

5 Conclusion

By way of concluding, it is perhaps sufficient to turn to DUNKEL 1993, who discusses various ways in which the Hittite lexicon reveals its Indo-European heritage. He points to several instances of what he calls (p. 105) "new forms but old meanings" in which we see "the preservation of the structure of old phraseology despite the formal renewal of its surface expression". He goes on to suggest (p. 115) that "semantic structure is at times more stable than form, i.e. meaning may survive while its morphic realisation shifts". That sums up succinctly what is shown here by the several examples from the Balkans that began with a PIE semantic structure of 'long life' and underwent various shifts in their realization while nonetheless retaining echoes, traces, reflections—what have you—of their original semantics, and thus showing a certain stability—persistence—over long stretches of time.[12]

---

12 JOSEPH 2019 is a companion piece to this paper, with other instances of persistence in Albanian of PIE semantic features.

References

BEEKES, ROBERT S.P. 2010, *Etymological Dictionary of Greek*, Leiden: Brill.

CHRISTIANSEN, BETHANY J.—JOSEPH, BRIAN D. 2016, *On the Relationship between Argument Structure Change and Semantic Change*, "Proceedings of the Annual Meeting of the Linguistic Society of America" Vol. 1, 26: 1–11 (URL: http://journals.linguistic society.org/proceedings/index.php/PLSA/article/view/3726; DOI: http://dx.doi.org/ 10.3765/plsa.v1i0.3726).

COWGILL, WARREN 1960, *Greek* ou *and Armenian* oč', "Language" 36: 347–350.

DUNKEL, GEORGE 1993, *Periphrastica homerohittitovedica*, in B. Brogyanyi—R. Lipp (edd.), *Comparative-Historical Linguistics. Indo-European and Finno-Ugric. Papers in honor of Oswald Szemerényi III*, Amsterdam: John Benjamins: 103–118.

FRIEDMAN, VICTOR A. 2012, *Conjunction Calquing—A Heartland Balkanism*, in T. Kahl—M. Metzelin—H. Schaller (edd.), *Balkanismen heute—Balkanisms Today —Balkanizmy segodnja*, Vienna: Lit Verlag: 31–37.

GARNIER, ROMAIN 2014, *Italique commun *né=χe=ái̯ud "jamais de la vie"*, "Wékwos" 1: 95–110.

GRIFFITH, RALPH 1896, *The Hymns of the Rigveda Translated with a Popular Commentary*, Kotagiri (Nilgiri).

HACKSTEIN, OLAV 2020, *The System of Negation in Albanian: Synchronic Constraints and Diachronic Explanations*, in B. Demiraj (ed.), *Altalbanische Schriftkultur—aus der Perspektive der historischen Lexikographie und der Philologie der Gegenwart. Akten der 6. Deutsch-Albanischen Kulturwissenschaftlichen Tagung (27. September 2019, Buçimas bei Pogradec, Albanien)* [*Albanische Forschungen* Bd. 44], Wiesbaden: Harrassowitz: 13–32.

HAMP, ERIC 1968, *Albanian* jetë *'life'*, in J. Corominas (ed.), *Essays in Romance Philology from the University of Chicago in honor of the XII International Congress of Romance Linguistics and Philology, București, 15–20 April 1968*, Chicago: Departments of Romance Languages and Literatures and of Linguistics, University of Chicago: 41–47.

HAMP, ERIC 1971, *I.* ha = *Indo-European* *ed-; *II.* 'viscum album', "Studia Albanica" 8: 153–155.

HAMP, ERIC 1983, *for()ever and ever*, "American Speech" 58: 374–376.

HAMP, ERIC 2019, *Albanian and the Proto-Indo-European Augment*, in B. Joseph—D. Dyer—M. Johnson (edd.), *The Current State of Balkan Linguistics: Celebrating Twenty Years of the Kenneth E. Naylor Lectures* (= *Balkanistica* 32.1), Oxford (MS): University Printing Services: 223–232.

HOPPER, PAUL 1991, *On some principles of grammaticalization*, in E. Traugott—B. Heine (edd.), *Approaches to Grammaticalization*, Volume I, Amsterdam: John Benjamins Publishing Company: 17–35.

IEW = POKORNY 1959.

JAMISON, STEPHANIE W.—BRERETON 2014, *The Rigveda. The earliest religious poetry of India*, Oxford: Oxford University Press.

JOSEPH, BRIAN D. 2002, *More on the PIE and post-PIE dimensions to Albanian-Greek negation parallels*, paper presented at 21st Annual East Coast Indo-European Conference (ECIEC), University of Pennsylvania 13 June 2002.

JOSEPH, BRIAN D. 2005, *Some ancient shared metaphors in the Balkans*, "Studia Albanica" 42: 45–48.

JOSEPH, BRIAN D. 2019, *Echoes of Indo-European Cultural Semantics in Albanian*, in A. Balas—S. Giannopoulou—A. Zagoura (edd.), *Proceedings of the 5th Patras International Conference of Graduate students in Linguistics (PICGL5), Patras, May 27–29, 2018*, Patras: Department of Linguistics, University of Patras: 23–33.

JOSEPH, BRIAN D.—KARNITIS, CATHERINE S. 1999, *Evaluating Semantic Shifts: The case of Indo-European* *(s)meuk—*and Indo-Iranian* *muc-, "Ohio State University Working Papers in Linguistics" 52: 151–158.

JOSEPH, BRIAN D.—KARNITIS, CATHERINE S. 2006, *The Specialized Semantics of* *(s)meuk—*in Iranian*, "Indogermanische Forschungen" 111: 355–364.

LIV = RIX 2001.

MONIER-WILLIAMS, MONIER 1899, *Sanskrit-English Dictionary, etymologically and philologically arranged with special reference to cognate Indo-European languages*, Oxford: Clarendon Press.

PEDERSEN, HOLGER 1900, *Die gutturale im Albanesischen*, "Zeitschrift für vergleichende Sprachforschung" 36: 277–340.

POKORNY, JULIUS 1959, *Indogermanisches etymologisches Wörterbuch*, Bern: Francke.

RIX, HELMUT 2001, *Lexikon der indogermanischen Verben* (2nd edn.), Wiesbaden: Dr. Ludwig Reichert Verlag.

SCHINDLER, JOACHIM 1975, *Armenisch* erkn, *griechisch* ὀδύνη, *irisch* idu, "Zeitschrift für vergleichende Sprachforschung" 85: 53–65.

SOUTHERN, MARK R.V. 2002 [2006], *Grain, the staff of life: Indo-European* *(h2)yew-os, "Münchener Studien zur Sprachwissenschaft" 62: 173–217.

WEISS, MICHAEL 1994, *Life Everlasting: Latin* iūgis *"everflowing", Greek* ὑγιής *"healthy", Gothic* ajukdūþ *"eternity" and Avestan* yauuaē̆jī- *"living forever"*, "Münchener Studien zur Sprachwissenschaft" 55: 131–156.

Index

agreement
  nominal agreement 7, 215
  verbal agreement 219
alignment
  ergative-absolutive 7
archives
  Anatolian archives 235
  Egyptian archives 174
  Persian archives 77n100
assimilation (cultural) 28
assimilation (phonetic) 6, 100, 103, 107, 155, 159, 284

bilingual letters 175, 184
bilingualism 104, 115, 117, 117n4, 122, 155, 184
borrowing 134, 144, 170, 170n1, 280
  borrowability of numerals 108
  lexical borrowings 226
  syntactic borrowings 212n5
borrowing (cultural) 7
  borrowings of literary motifs 13, 32
  borrowing of religious features 207

clitics 64, 74, 74n85, 217, 241–243, 250
  pronominal clitics 219
codeswitching 110
collocation 175
compensatory lengthenings 64, 280, 281
compounds 52, 62, 67, 67n56, 214, 261n8, 271, 278n9, 287n44, 294, 304
conjunctions 7, 69n67, 235, 237, 241, 243
contact
  substrate 145, 153–157, 162
  superstrate 227–229
  theory of language contact 2, 13, 137, 143
copula 7, 215, 216, 218–221
Cowgill's Law 276, 282

deities 21, 24, 28, 196, 204
  Anatolian deities 23–28, 203–208
  Greek deities 15, 196
  Iranian deities 23, 23n20, 254–255, 261, 267
  Near-Eastern deities 28, 33

diachrony 219, 301
  diachronic changes 7, 22, 78, 211
  diachronic variation 234, 260
diglossia 255, 257, 266

formula xiii, 7, 15, 31, 69, 167, 175, 180, 243, 248, 250, 290

genitive
  genitive agents 7
grammaticalisation 68, 69n67, 221, 221n26, 222

idiolects 166, 184, 224
idiom 69, 73n78, 167, 243
interference 108, 166, 168, 180, 183, 185, 186
  lexical interference 223
  morphological interference 110
  phonetic interference 2, 101, 110
  shift-induced transfer 137
  syntactic interference 184

L1 116, 118, 121, 122, 139, 142, 143, 145, 156, 158, 162, 167, 184, 185
L2 6, 118–125, 133, 137, 139, 142, 145, 156
language death 212, 227, 229
lexical oppositions 261, 262
loanwords 105, 108, 110, 115, 122, 137, 140, 170, 212, 260

multilingualism 116, 119, 225

negation 49, 51, 53, 58, 60, 65, 75, 76, 304, 306
nominalisation 293, 307
non-active → *Vedi* passive 7, 179, 301
non-linguistic causes for language contact
  religious causes 208, 223
  socio-political causes 170, 223, 224, 227
numerals 54, 73–75, 75n88, 77, 104, 106, 108, 138, 213

perfect 212, 216, 221, 229, 289
  periphrastic perfect x, 211, 214, 219, 221, 229

PIE IX, X, 1, 20, 52, 67, 71, 75n88, 276–277, 279, 281–282, 288–289, 291, 294, 301–305, 307–8, 310
pragmatics 173, 175, 183, 248, 301
prefixation 60, 145
pronouns 69, 241
    anaphoric pronouns 244
    demonstrative pronouns 246
    indefinite pronouns 49, 58, 64, 65, 70, 72, 73
    interrogative pronouns 59, 67
    reflexive pronouns 140
    relative pronouns 64, 72
    resumptive pronouns 77

reconstruction (cultural) ix, 11–13, 33
reconstruction (linguistic) ix, 2, 12, 162, 261, 301
reduplication patterns 60, 62n39, 66n53, 67n56, 140
register 7, 48, 171, 180, 234, 235, 247, 250, 261
relative clauses 57, 66, 67, 70
ritual 7, 15, 68, 203

sociolinguistics 3, 142
synonyms 258, 277
TAM
    aspect 141, 310
    tense 215, 216, 236, 309

textual genres 235, 243
    legal 22, 242, 248
    legal documents 116, 234, 235, 244, 247
    literary 90, 143, 180, 266
    liturgic 227
    narrative 244

poetic 260
private letters 118, 167
typology 13, 33, 57, 88, 92, 124, 137, 142, 280, 309

variation 22, 97, 107
    allophonic variation 91, 120
    morphological variation 117, 125
    morphosyntactic 116
    orthographic variation 115, 183
    phonetic variation 144
    phonological variation 115, 117, 123
    sociolinguistic variation ix
verbal complementation patterns 184, 187
    asyndetic 172, 173
    clausal 172, 173, 176
    dependent 173
    factive 172
    independent 173, 183
    infinitival 167, 184
    nominal 173
    syndetic 172, 173

writing supports
    inscriptions 68, 89, 94, 98, 108, 109, 171, 227, 234, 248, 250
    manuscripts 4, 5, 234n5
    papyri 109, 125, 167, 173
    tablets 55, 66, 75, 77, 235
writing systems
    Armenian alphabet 228
    Coptic alphabet 170
    cuneiform 48, 48n2, 65
    Greek alphabet 153, 168, 170
    Linear Elamite 48n2

Printed in the United States
by Baker & Taylor Publisher Services